Cradle of Freedom

The University of Alabama Press • Tuscaloosa

Frye Gaillard

Cradle of Freedom

ALABAMA AND THE MOVEMENT THAT CHANGED AMERICA

Written with the support of the Auburn University Center for the
Arts and Humanities

Typeface: AGaramond
Designer: Michele Myatt Quinn

∞

The paper on which this book is printed meets the minimum
requirements of American National Standard for Information
Science–Permanence of Paper for Printed Library Materials, ANSI
Z39.48-1984.

Library of Congresss Cataloging-in-Publication Data

Gaillard, Frye, 1946–
    Cradle of freedom: Alabama and the movement that changed
America / Frye Gaillard.
        p.   cm.
    Includes biblographical references (p.) and index.
    ISBN 0-8173-1388-5 (cloth: alk. paper)
    1. African americans—Civil rights—Alabama—History—20th
century. 2. Civil rights movements—Alabama—History—20th century. 3. Alabama—Race relations. I. Title.
E185.93.A3G35 2004
323.1196'0730761—dc22   2003018348

To the thousands of men and women, black and white, who helped make us all a little more free.

Contents

Prologue

Birmingham, Good Friday, 1963. I was barely sixteen when I stumbled on the scene—Martin Luther King on a Birmingham sidewalk, two burly policemen with a hand on his belt, shoving him along. That at least is the way I remember it, as they took him away in a paddy wagon and then to a cell in the Birmingham jail. It was a pivotal moment in the civil rights movement, but I didn't know that. All I noticed was the look in his eyes. He didn't seem afraid, which surprised me at first, for there was something in the scene that I found terrifying—some purity of malice in the faces of the policemen that I had not seen very often in my life. I had grown up southern in a prominent, white Alabama family—for the most part, people of good will who nevertheless supported segregation.

Certainly, they didn't support Martin Luther King, and to the extent that such things crossed my mind, neither did I. But now here he was, a smallish man in a denim work shirt, his dignity a rebuke to the menace of his captors. It was an image for me that never went away, and from that moment on the news reports coming out of Birmingham—the snarling dogs, the fire hoses and bombs—became a reality that I couldn't put aside. I realized later that I was coming of age on hallowed ground, at the geographic heart of the civil rights movement. There seemed to be something in the Alabama soil that produced strong leaders—John Lewis, Ralph Abernathy, Fred Shuttlesworth, all of them born in the hamlets and farmlands of rural Alabama—and Dr. King, who discovered his calling in the city of Montgomery.

As a young reporter in the 1960s, I found myself drawn inexorably to this story, and it was more than a matter of professional curiosity. In the American South, there were many people in my generation—white people and black—for whom the civil rights movement became the defining reality in their lives. There was no other issue that called the moral questions more completely. Who are we and what do we believe? What kind of place is this? What are the political ideals that define us? In the years just before the movement made headlines, the great southern novelist William Faulkner, who wrote from the neighboring state of Mississippi, said the only thing worth writing about was "the human heart in conflict with itself." In Alabama our collective heart was in a state of turmoil, as we wrestled with fundamental contradictions—the gap between the professions of equality that we held to be self-evident, and the way we behaved.

When the civil rights movement won its painful victory in Birmingham, Fred Shuttlesworth, the greatest leader to come out of that city, summarized the achievement this way: "The City of Birmingham has reached an accord with its conscience." For most of our history, white Alabamians, like our counterparts in the rest of the South, struggled to keep our consciences at bay, rationalizing both slavery and segregation, and a level of cruelty that we could not acknowledge.

For me, the fundamental harshness of our place began to take on a face as I became more serious about the work of a journalist. One of my early interviews was with C. Eric Lincoln, a black Alabamian who was a scholar of international renown. He taught at Duke University, among other places, and his field was the sociology of religion. In the course of his career, he did the first serious study of the Black Muslim faith, became a friend and confidant of Malcolm X, and kept up a personal correspondence with the Pope. But in a corner of his heart, he never strayed very far from Alabama. He was born in Athens, a little town in the northern part of the state, and he loved the fishing holes and the creeks and the dusty back roads that felt like velvet to the soles of his feet. There was an easy rhythm in the life of this place— the gatherings every Sunday morning at his church, the smell of fried chicken when he came back home. His grandparents Less and Mattie Lincoln were the anchors of his life, gentle farm people who taught him the world could be a decent place and the final measure of any man's goodness was his ability to "respect everybody respectable." Lincoln learned, however, that not everybody saw it that way.

"When I was thirteen or fourteen," he said, "my grandfather was on his deathbed. This would have been in the 1930s. There was no food in the house, no fire in the house, no money in the house. My grandmother and I went out to the fields where the cotton had already been picked, not only our fields but those nearby, and we pulled the only bolls that were left."

That night, he said, they picked the cotton from the bolls and put it in a bag, and the first thing the next morning, Eric took it to the gin. It was barely seven o'clock when he arrived, and the owner, Mr. Beasley, was sitting on the porch. "Whatcha got there, boy?" he said.

"Cotton, sir."

"Well, dump it out."

So they put it on the scales, and the weight came to forty pounds and young Eric made a quick calculation. At nine cents a pound, that would mean $3.60 for food, firewood, and all the other things that his family didn't have. He was startled, therefore, when the white man casually flipped him a quarter.

"Mr. Beasley," he said, after a long hesitation, "I think you made a mistake."

Beasley's face turned red and he got up abruptly and bolted the door. The boy was puzzled, but then he found himself gasping for air, his lungs suddenly empty from a blow to the midsection, as the white man hit him again and again, then kicked him in the head. "He was in a frenzy," Lincoln remembered, "and I'll never forget his words: 'Nigger, as long as you live, don't you never count behind no white man again.'"

Forty years later, when he told the story, Eric Lincoln wept. His tears, he said, were not only from the pain of personal recollection but from the knowledge that the world could have ever been as mean. He knew, of course, that his own situation could have been much worse. In addition to the random humiliation, the casual cruelties of the segregation years, there were also people who were tortured and killed. In a fifty-year period beginning in 1889, blacks in America were lynched at a rate of more than one a week, and most of those killings occurred in the South. Around the turn of the century, nineteen lynchings took place in Dallas County, Alabama, and more in Lowndes, one county to the east. Many of these murders were grisly affairs, and the stories reverberated through the state.

Through the occasional newspaper accounts, which were sketchy and horrifying all at once, and a grapevine of face-to-face conversation that connected the black communities of Alabama, a person like Lincoln knew what could happen if he stepped out of line. In 1931, for example, there was the story of a black teenager in Lowndes, a young man of sixteen, murdered for allegedly accosting a white girl. They found his body chained tightly to a tree, riddled essentially to the point of mutilation by thirty-two bullet holes.

Many of the lynchings that occurred in the South were tied to allegations of sexual aggression, a threat to the purity of white womanhood, but not all of them were. When black sharecroppers began to organize in the 1930s, threatening the shape of the Alabama economy, the official repression was immediate and fierce—county sheriffs hunting down the organizers and doing whatever was needed to make their point. In Lowndes County, that simply meant death, a half dozen organizers shot and killed and others beaten until they begged for their lives. Not everyone approved of such tactics. The daily newspapers in Montgomery and Mobile might run editorials condemning the excessive use of force, but the truth of it was, white supremacy in Alabama was a matter of law, a concept essentially unchallenged in the state, except by a handful of brave human beings.

In the Constitution of 1901, the state's white leaders set out explicitly to disenfranchise blacks, and thus to subjugate them politically. They saw no need to be subtle about it, no need to deny or disguise their intent. The state's all-white Democratic Party, the driving force behind the new document, adopted a resolution declaring that blacks, based on the state's experience with Reconstruction, were "incapable of self-government."

One newspaper, the *Wilcox Progressive,* declared that the time had come for "white supremacy and purer politics," and that the two, in fact, could not be separated. All over the state, politicians echoed that sentiment, and those who opposed it, or even expressed some minor reservation, found themselves overwhelmed.

Former Alabama governor William Oates was one of the supporters of the new constitution and was expected to chair the constitutional convention, until he wrote a letter to the *Montgomery Advertiser.* "The disfranchisement of the whole Negro race would be unwise and unjust," he declared, and the delegates immediately passed him over, choosing as their chairman a man who harbored no such hesitations. John B. Knox was an Anniston lawyer, a political leader of "distinguished ability," according to the *Mobile Register,* who believed essentially that every black Alabamian should be stripped of the vote "by law—not by force or fraud." In his speech to the convention, he defined the issue this way: "The negro is not being discriminated against on account of his race, but on account of his intellectual and moral condition."

Such was the prevailing opinion in the state, and for more than sixty years, it became the defining reality of life in Alabama. There were always people who spoke out against it. At the constitutional convention, Napoleon Bonaparte Spears, a Populist-Republican from St. Clair County, denounced the fundamental purpose of the gathering and declared that many of his fellow delegates had cast themselves as the enemies of democracy. Thirty years later, Aubrey Williams, a New Deal liberal, not only supported Franklin Roosevelt but also argued in the trenches of his own native state that all men really were created equal.

Williams was a white man, the drawling, soft-spoken son of a blacksmith who grew up poor outside of Birmingham. During the Depression, he went to work for the Roosevelt administration, where he championed the concept of work relief—federal job programs for the poor and unemployed to give them dignity, as well as a paycheck. He became director of the National Youth Administration, which provided jobs and training to needy young people, black as well as white, and even among his Washington colleagues, he developed a reputation as a radical idealist who believed in the doctrine of racial equality. He returned to Alabama, and with his fellow white liberal Gould Beech, he began to publish the *Southern Farmer,* a monthly tabloid where, among other things, he spoke out strongly against segregation. There was a core of such people in the state of Alabama—a group that included U.S. senator Hugo Black, Montgomery lawyer Clifford Durr and his wife, Virginia, and a handful of other hardy souls who seemed to revel in their boat-rocker status. These were not outsiders by birth; they were, instead, a stubborn cadre of high-minded people who rejected the prevailing assumptions of their place. With the birth of the civil rights movement in the 1950s, they endured their share of intense ostracism, but they understood clearly that the price they paid was far more benign than the one exacted from their black counterparts.

From the very beginning, of course, more blacks than whites were moved to take a stand. There were the educators such as Booker T. Washington, who at the turn of the century, spoke out against the new constitution. In the 1930s Charles Gomillion, a professor at Washington's Tuskegee Institute, began a thirty-year crusade for the ballot, and there were lawyers and civil rights professionals—people such as W. C. Patton and Arthur Shores—who pushed for the notion of political equality long before there was a movement to sustain them. There were also the people whose names are forgotten, black sharecroppers and union organizers in the steel mills of Birmingham, who demanded an end to the exploitation that had been so rampant in the Alabama economy.

And by the 1950s there were also the preachers. Not many at first. But in the city of Montgomery an eloquent maverick named Vernon Johns, the pastor at Dexter Avenue Baptist, spoke from his pulpit against police brutality and the other indignities that went with segregation. He was a farmer's son from rural Virginia, a square-jawed, barrel-chested bear of a man who wore disheveled suits and wire-rimmed glasses, and who was fluent in Greek and Hebrew and Latin. He loved the poetry of Byron and Keats almost as much as he did the old Negro spirituals, and his gift for metaphor was at the heart of his national reputation as a preacher. In 1926, when he was thirty-four, one of his sermons, "Transfigured Moments," was included in an anthology of the greatest pulpit orations in America. Citing passages from both the Old and New Testaments, he spoke of the symbolism of the mountains, the places where Jesus Christ and the prophets were struck by the vision of new possibilities—not only for themselves but also for those in the world who had been left behind.

"It is a heart strangely un-Christian," he wrote, "that cannot thrill with joy when the least of men begin to pull in the direction of the stars."

Twenty-five years later at Dexter Avenue Baptist, his congregation was inspired by his words, but frightened sometimes by his fearless personality. There were the maddening moments in a segregated world when Vernon Johns had simply had enough, when he would defy the laws and customs of the South, not as the leader of a great social movement but as a lone eccentric—a prophet, some said—who had decided that he would not take it anymore. Once as he boarded a Montgomery bus, the driver ordered him to pay his fare and then get off and reboard from the back. It was a common practice on the city bus lines, not a matter of law, but a custom intended to protect white riders from the indignity of a black man passing by their seats. Johns refused to be a part of it. He paid his money and took his seat at the front of the bus, and when the driver refused to continue his route, Johns rose and urged the other black passengers to walk off the bus together in protest.

The passengers did not follow that day. But the time would come just a few years later when they followed his successor, Dr. Martin Luther King, in a great boycott of the Montgomery buses—the opening battle in a civil rights movement that would transform the segregated face of the South. It was, I believe, a time as critical as any in our history, ranking in the company of the American Revolution, when we defined our hopes and dreams as a nation, or the Civil War, when the valiant pigheadedness of Abraham Lincoln prevented the country from dividing in two. In the civil rights era, we averted racial war—not by much, but we kept it at bay—thanks to the ability of the civil rights leaders to appeal somehow to the best that was in us. It was a radical movement, rooted in the most conservative assumptions—the idea of equality in the eyes of the law and of brotherhood in the eyes of God—and it was part of the genius of Martin Luther King that he kept those assumptions from getting lost in the noise.

But the epic story of the civil rights movement is not primarily the story of King, or any of the others in a leadership role. It is true enough that John Lewis and Fred Shuttlesworth, Rosa Parks and Ralph Abernathy have carved their indelible places in history. In the face of the incredible pressures of the times, they mustered a level of bravery and wisdom that most of us can only marvel at. But as King and many others were quick to acknowledge, the unwelcome burden of leadership was one they could not have carried by themselves. They owed a debt to the people before them—to Vernon Johns and all the other apostles of decency who had made their lonely witness through the years. But the greater debt was to the people who followed, to the masses of people in Montgomery and other places who believed it was possible to build a better world. These were the everyday people of the South, a few of them white, most of them black, who believed despite the evidence around them that the Heart of Dixie was not as hard as it seemed.

I have tried to write the story of these people—not all of them, of course, for there are simply too many, but in the pages that follow, I have written about the foot soldiers as well as the generals. From the bus boycott to the Freedom Rides, the Birmingham movement to the eventual rise of the Black Panther Party, ordinary people were caught in the crush of extraordinary forces, and I have tried to put a human face on their stories. I write, inevitably, as a person who is white, with whatever limitations that may imply. But I also write as an Alabama native who lived through the times, who covered the civil rights movement as a journalist, and who has attempted to bring a storyteller's eye to the powerful recollections of the people in the trenches. I have tried to be fair—even to the people with whom I disagree—but I make no claim to objectivity. I am proud of Alabama's role in the story. A state once known as the Cradle of the Confederacy can now make its case as the cradle of freedom—arguably the most important piece of geography in the most important movement of our times.

Maybe there was something in the Alabama soil, or maybe there was a certain quality of leadership—white as well as black—that made for a powerful clash of ideas, that made us ask who we really want to be. Whatever the realities of unfinished business, the answer we are able to give today is different from the one of fifty years ago.

All of us ought to be happy about that. But none of us should ever forget what it cost.

PART ONE

DAYBREAK

CHAPTER I

We Are Not Wrong

THEY FILLED THE CHURCH by late afternoon, and soon they were lining the sanctuary walls and spilling from the balcony to the stairs and then to the parking lot outside. Bob Graetz had gotten there late. Already he could hear the music and the prayers, the fervent voices coming from a source that he couldn't really see. By the time he arrived, the crowd had spread across the street, maybe four thousand people scattered across the yards in this all-black neighborhood in Montgomery, Alabama.

In a sense they were there to honor Rosa Parks, a respected black woman who had refused to give up her seat on a bus. But as Graetz understood it, there was a lot more at stake. Graetz was a white man, the Lutheran minister to a black congregation, not yet fully plugged into the community. He had called Mrs. Parks, a neighbor and a friend, when he had heard there was some kind of trouble on a bus—an arrest, perhaps, of somebody important.

"Do you know who it was?" he wanted to know.

There was a moment of silence on the other end of the line, and then Mrs. Parks admitted with a sigh, "Well, you see, Pastor Graetz, it was me."

As the word quickly spread, Graetz was astonished at what happened next. On December 5, 1955, the black community of Montgomery seemed to change. It was a day that would live forever in his memory—that would become, for him, a kind of demarcation in time, a dividing line between the days of racial oppression in the South and the dawn of an era a little more just.

There had been a few people who dreamed of such a day, who believed it could happen, but there were not many. What Graetz discovered when he came to Montgomery was a people defeated, devoid of any hope. Even their body language made it clear: the slouch of the shoulders, the aversion of the eyes as they made their way through their daily routines. But this particular day it was different. They came together at Holt Street Baptist, a church that was chosen that night for its size. It was a handsome building of sturdy red brick, with Corinthian columns and stained glass windows and wooden bell towers that made it the tallest building on the street. The people were dressed for a festive occasion, the women in hats, the men wearing ties, but there was a certain solemnity in the moment also.

When Graetz arrived with a deacon from his church, he noticed that the crowd was almost silent. Soon that would change with the singing and the prayers, a release of emotion that was so overwhelming, one white reporter from Montgomery would declare: "That audience was so on fire . . . on fire for freedom."

Graetz was determined to take it all in, and with his deacon, Robert Dandridge, at his side he squeezed through the door and into the vestibule of the church. But the sanctuary was already full, and there was simply no way to make it any farther. Graetz couldn't see the pulpit from where he was standing, and he thought it was strange when the program began that none of the speakers was introduced by name. It was a remnant of fear, he would later understand, an old terror of retribution by the whites.

Soon it would vanish, but in the meantime, Deacon Dandridge knew the sound of every voice. "That's Ralph Abernathy," he would say, and then at the end: "That's Martin Luther King."

Graetz had already met Dr. King, and like most people he was favorably impressed. King was young, still a few weeks short of his twenty-seventh birthday, but he was bright and articulate, a black man who was finishing his Ph.D., and there were not many of those in the state of Alabama. He seemed to be a man who was sure of himself, and for Graetz, it was hard to imagine, when he heard about it later, that on the afternoon of the speech King had been so overwhelmed by his doubts, his sense of inadequacy for the task that lay ahead, that he laid his trembling pen aside and prayed that God would help him find the words.

King had only twenty minutes to prepare, and he knew that his mission that night was double-edged. On the one hand, it was important for blacks in Montgomery to draw the line, to proclaim with unmistakable resolve that the years of mistreatment on the buses had to stop. All over Alabama, it was perhaps the most insulting form of segregation—black people paying their money at the front, then walking around to the rear door of the bus and taking their seats in the rows near the back. The price for defying the system was high. In the city of Mobile a few years earlier, a black man had been killed by a white bus driver, and in Montgomery, Birmingham, and other places, there were stories of black women cursed by the drivers and sometimes arrested and hauled off to jail.

Now, suddenly, the Negro community in Montgomery had a symbol, a woman revered by everybody who knew her. If it could happen to Mrs. Parks, King had heard people say, then of course it could happen to anybody in town. He was determined to channel the new wave of anger, to encourage the awakening they had seen that day, as black people by the thousands stayed off the buses, demanding justice as the price of their return. And yet he knew they were playing with fire, stoking a rage that ran deep in the psyche of virtually every black person in the South. It was a rage that could easily get out of hand, and so he told the people at the church: "In our protest, there will be no cross burnings. No white person will be taken from his home by a hooded Negro mob and brutally murdered. There will be no threats and intimidation. We will be guided by the highest principles of law and order."

But they were not wrong, and they would not stop.

"If we are wrong, the Supreme Court of this nation is wrong. If we are wrong, the Constitution of the United States is wrong. If we are wrong, God Almighty is wrong. . . . If we are wrong, justice is a lie."

In the decades after that December 5 speech, many historians understood clearly that the civil rights movement found a leader that night—a man of such rare and unaccustomed eloquence that black and white people all over America would be struck by the power of his vision for the country. Many would admire him; some would hate him, but he was not a man many people could ignore.

Bob Graetz certainly believed that was true. But as a person who was both a foot soldier in the movement, and later a historian, Graetz also believed that the opening day of the bus boycott had an importance much larger than Martin Luther King. December 5, 1955, was a day for the people. Dr. King may have put their feelings into words, but the feelings, Graetz believed, would have been there without him. For the Negro citizens of Montgomery, Alabama, the time had finally come to take a stand.

It began with Rosa Parks and a private act of defiance, then quickly evolved into something much bigger: a remarkable assemblage of grassroots leaders—preachers, teachers, a Pullman porter on a train—who came together and made common cause in a way that few of them could remember.

One by one, they all heard the story—how she was tired that day, December 1, 1955, a cold winter Thursday, almost dark when she left her downtown job at 5:30. She worked as a seamstress at the Montgomery Fair Department Store, and her chronic bursitis had flared up again, that throbbing pain in her shoulder and her arm that made her long once again for some rest. As was often the case, the bus was crowded when it stopped to pick her up, only one seat available, and it was near the front, a row behind the whites-only section. She took it gratefully and settled in for the ride.

A short time later, the bus made a stop at the Empire Theater, and one of the new passengers, a white man, found himself with no place to sit. The bus driver, James F. Blake, turned to the blacks in Mrs. Parks's row and ordered them to move. When nobody responded, Blake told them sternly, "You better make it light on yourselves and let me have those seats."

Three of the Negro passengers obeyed, but Mrs. Parks did not. She recognized the driver right away. One day in 1943, she had paid her money at the front of his bus and walked straight to her seat, instead of backing down the steps and reentering from the rear. James Blake had ordered her evicted from the bus. She had never forgotten her feeling of embarrassment, but it was not simply that memory, bitter as it was, that triggered her resistance in 1955. Mrs. Parks had long been active in the cause of civil rights, a leader in the NAACP, where one of her duties was to work with young people.

They came every Sunday to her well-kept apartment on the west side of town, listening intently as she talked about citizenship and the right to vote and the crippling reality of racial segregation. Mrs. Parks knew the children often jeered at the rules. Sometimes just for fun, they would sit in the whites-only section of the buses and swap the signs on the public water fountains, giggling as the white people stopped to take a drink. Mrs. Parks did her best to rechannel their rebellion—to prepare them for a day when the game was likely to turn more serious—and the children adored her. Many years later, they remembered her warmth and her radiant smile, and also a certain toughness at her core.

She had gone away in the summer of 1955, spending two weeks at the Highlander Folk School in Monteagle, Tennessee. It was a beautiful spot nestled back in the hills, where a white Tennessean by the name of Myles Horton set out to train a new generation of activists. Horton himself was an even-tempered man known for his wit. Asked one time in the 1950s how he managed to get blacks and whites to eat together at his school, he told his interrogators it was easy. "First, the food is prepared. Second, it's put on the table. Third, we ring the bell."

Mrs. Parks was impressed with the spirit of the place, especially as she studied the details of its history. Beginning in 1932, when the Depression's grip deepened in much of the South, Horton was determined to create a retreat, a sanctuary, where people could gather—Appalachian miners and textile workers and men who made a living cutting timber in the forests. In the early years his constituency was white, but that began to change in the 1950s after the Supreme Court's landmark decision in *Brown vs. Board of Education,* which overturned racial segregation in the schools.

To Horton in the '50s it was suddenly apparent that racial understanding was the issue of the day, and Highlander was a place for the barriers to fall. He invited interracial groups to the school, and together they talked about the tools of rebellion—simple things like picket lines and citizenship schools where people could prepare themselves for the vote.

Rosa Parks took it all in, but in the end the thing that stayed with her most was not so much the content of the classes; it was the simple reality of interracial living. Never, she said, in her forty-two years had she been around a group of white people who were willing to accept a black person as an equal. It was a new and almost startling experience, and it left her with a different understanding of the world. She had always known that segregation was wrong, and now at Highlander she had seen the alternative, a fleeting glimpse of a better way of life.

All of this she remembered on December 1, 1955, when the Montgomery bus driver ordered her to move. She told him no, she couldn't do that, and when the driver threatened to have her arrested, she looked up from where she was sitting and replied: "You may do that."

The police came quickly and took her away, and it was then that she felt her first rush of fear. She had never been to jail, had never imagined that such a thing might occur, and suddenly she noticed that her throat felt dry. She glanced at the water fountain at the station, but there was only one, and the policemen told her it was only for the whites.

They did allow her to make a phone call, and by the time she was able to reach her family, the word of her arrest had already spread. E. D. Nixon was one of the first to get the news, which was no surprise, for if you were black and in trouble in Montgomery, Alabama, Nixon was usually the person you called. He was a Pullman porter, the president of his union, and a protégé of A. Philip Randolph, one of the country's most respected civil rights leaders.

Nixon was tough. He was a handsome, dark-skinned man, ramrod straight with iron-gray hair as he began to age, and as one friend put it, a face that looked like it was carved out of ebony. He was given, on occasion, to fearless confrontations with people in power—governors, mayors, it didn't really matter—and he often got what he wanted. One southern journalist thought he "had the bearing of an African prince—which he might well have been if not for the intervention of slavery."

The journalist, Ray Jenkins, remembered a telling encounter with Nixon in Montgomery. They had stopped to chat on a busy street corner, and Jenkins automatically extended his hand. Nixon, the old warhorse, became suddenly emotional, telling Jenkins with a catch in his voice: "You don't know what this means." Jenkins was puzzled. He thought of

Nixon as one of the most formidable men in the city, physically impos-ing, and mentally as strong as any public figure he had ever met. But this was Alabama, the segregated South, and Nixon explained that never in his life—and he was now pushing sixty—had a white man shaken his hand in public.

For the young reporter, it was a watershed in his understanding of the movement. It was true, of course, that it was partly about overturning old laws, those devastating codes of racial segregation that blacks encountered every day of their lives. But beneath that goal was something more basic, a mission so pure and easy to understand that Jenkins was amazed that many people had missed it. For E. D. Nixon and many others of his gen-eration, the issue at the heart of the movement was respect.

That was the quality that was missing on the buses, and for some time now Nixon had been searching for the perfect test case, the perfect vehi-cle, to bring about a change. A few months earlier, on March 2, 1955, a young black woman named Claudette Colvin had also refused to give up her seat. She was handcuffed and taken to jail, which Nixon, of course, regarded as a travesty. He knew, however, that Claudette Colvin was a teenage girl, not serene or secure in the way of Mrs. Parks. She had cursed her tormentors as they carried her away, and the word quickly spread fol-lowing her arrest that she was pregnant out of wedlock.

Reluctantly, Nixon was compelled to conclude that this was not the symbol he was seeking. Colvin, he knew, would bear the brunt of attacks that no teenager ought to have to endure, and the issues were certain to become muddied in the process. Rosa Parks, however, was a whole differ-ent matter. Nixon was certain that she could be the one, the rallying point for a bus boycott and perhaps for a legal challenge to segregation. But the first order of business was to get her out of jail.

He knew the city's most prominent black lawyer, Fred Gray, was out of town, so he called his friend Clifford Durr, a white man sympathetic to the cause. Durr was a well-known attorney and a liberal on race, known for his gentle and clear-headed views. In his later years, he reminded one reporter of Jimmy Carter. His wife, Virginia, was more outspoken—a firebrand, some people said, less tolerant of people with whom she dis-agreed. Both the Durrs were fond of Rosa Parks, and they agreed to go with Nixon to the jail, where they posted bond and then took her to her home.

There, over coffee, they talked about the future. Nixon made the case with characteristic passion that this was the time—the moment they had dreamed about for many years. Mrs. Parks was not so sure, and her husband, Raymond, was even less so. "The white folks will kill you, Rosa," he said. She knew that his fears were not overstated; black people had been murdered for less in Montgomery. And yet as she listened to E. D. Nixon and thought about the lessons of the last several months—her visit to Highlander, her evening in jail—she knew in her heart what she needed to do.

"I'll go along with you, Mr. Nixon," she said.

With that, it was settled, and soon the grapevine was beginning to work, that intricate web of personal communication that held the black community together. Attorney Fred Gray returned to the city and put in a call to Jo Ann Robinson, who was eager to take advantage of the moment. Mrs. Robinson taught English at Alabama State College and was president of the Women's Political Council, where she had emerged through the years as a sometimes angry and outspoken activist. She had had her own experience with the buses. One day near Christmas in 1949, not long after her arrival in the city, she was on her way to the airport for a trip back home to Cleveland. She boarded the bus, and sat near the front, and soon her holiday reverie was interrupted.

"Get up from there!" the bus driver screamed, and as he rushed toward her seat with his hand drawn back, she thought for a moment he intended to hit her. Startled and frightened, she fled from the bus, and would tell an interviewer years later, "I felt like a dog. I think he wanted to hurt me, and he did. . . . I cried all the way to Cleveland."

In the years since then, she had often complained about the treatment black people endured on the buses, but local officials had paid no attention. Now, however, she saw a new opportunity. After talking to Gray and some of the leaders of the WPC, she drove to the college, and spent the rest of the night running off flyers. By the time she was finished, she had more than thirty-five thousand copies, which she began to distribute with the help of her students.

"Another Negro woman," the flyers began, "has been arrested and thrown into jail because she refused to get up out of her seat on the bus for a white person to sit down. . . . Negroes have rights too. . . . We are, therefore, asking every Negro to stay off the buses Monday in protest."

On Friday, December 2, E. D. Nixon gave a copy to Joe Azbell, a white reporter for the *Montgomery Advertiser*. "I've got a big story for you," he said. He knew, of course, that Azbell's editors would not be sympathetic to the boycott, but he also knew that any kind of story, no matter what the tone, would help spread the word. In the meantime, he had already taken other steps. Thirty-five thousand handbills was a start, but there was another resource that was even more critical. He had to have the support of black preachers—specifically, a proclamation from the pulpits that Negro citizens should stay off the buses.

At 5 A.M. on December 2 he called his friend Ralph Abernathy, the twenty-nine-year-old pastor at First Baptist Church, one of the largest black congregations in the city. Abernathy was a native Alabamian, a farmer's son from Marengo County, and it was easy to believe he came from the country. He seemed to be a sleepy-eyed, slow-moving man, a down-home preacher who liked to tell funny stories, but as the coming weeks and months would make clear, there was another side to Abernathy as well. "He was tough as iron," said one fellow minister, and he was a man who knew how to work up a crowd. He could stalk back and forth in the pulpit of his church, sweat dripping from his face as he gripped the microphone and proclaimed: "My God is here, and we gon' have a good time."

More than most Montgomery preachers, he was deeply impatient with the racial order of the day, and he quickly agreed when Nixon asked him to support a boycott. As Nixon continued making phone calls, working steadily down the list of other preachers, the pieces seemed to be falling into place—the leaders all sensing that this was the time.

One of those ministers who stepped forward quickly was Robert Graetz, pastor at Trinity Lutheran Church. Nixon was pleased and a little bit surprised, for Graetz was a white man, a young West Virginian who had promised his denominational leaders that when he got to Montgomery he would stay out of trouble. He also had two children to consider, and on the Saturday after the arrest of Mrs. Parks, he and Jeannie, his wife, prayed for guidance about what they should do. They understood the risks—how the color of their skin, which gave them immunity in ordinary times, might make them a target as the city grew tense. None of that was to be taken lightly. On the other hand, the person at the heart of it all was Rosa Parks, their neighbor and friend who had taken her stand for dignity and freedom. How could they justify not standing with her, and with the people of their church?

The more they prayed, the clearer it became. This was a moment so full of possibility they could only explain it as the handiwork of God— and now was not the time to let Him down. On Sunday morning, Graetz rose in the pulpit and pleaded with the members of his black congregation not to ride the buses on Monday. He was heartened by a story in the morning newspaper, Joe Azbell's even-handed account that ran under the headline: NEGRO GROUPS READY BOYCOTT OF CITY LINES. Nobody could say they hadn't gotten out the word.

On Monday morning, Graetz got up early and headed for his car, a '55 Chevy without any frills, no radio, not even a heater. If people, in fact, were staying off the buses, he wanted to be available to help them get to work. Graetz was amazed at what he saw that day. All over Montgomery, the empty buses rumbled through the streets, as Negro citizens crowded into taxis and others simply walked.

He would remember that moment for the rest of his life, the image of the people walking proud and tall, coming together on behalf of what was right. The question was whether they could keep on pushing.

On Monday afternoon, December 5, several dozen black leaders called a meeting to consider what to do. Mrs. Robinson's flyers had simply proclaimed a one-day protest. Now that the day had gone so well, should they declare a victory and begin negotiations with the city? Or should they extend the boycott and the economic pressure and the powerful opportunity to be heard? Certainly, there had to be talks with white leaders, but who would do the talking, and what specific concessions would they seek?

Those were the questions that had to be answered. In the late afternoon, they gathered at Mount Zion AME Church, pastored by the Rev. L. Roy Bennett, and decided they needed a new organization to send a message that these were different times. At Abernathy's suggestion they named the new group the Montgomery Improvement Association and set about the task of selecting a president. One obvious possibility was E. D. Nixon; another was Rufus Lewis, a former football coach at Alabama State College, who had long been a powerful figure in the community. There were prominent ministers like Solomon Seay, and there was Jo Ann

Robinson, who was articulate and strong, but ran the risk of being fired from the state-supported college where she worked.

The choice, quite clearly, was going to be hard, but then Rufus Lewis took them by surprise. He rose to nominate Martin Luther King Jr., the minister at his church, Dexter Avenue Baptist. King was relatively new to Montgomery, but he had made a favorable impression from the start. He had been recruited in the fall of 1953 by a Dexter Avenue deacon named R. D. Nesbitt. On a Friday afternoon at two o'clock, Nesbitt had paid a call to King's father's house at 200 Thompson Street in Atlanta. Martin Luther King Sr. received him gruffly, as was his habit, and led him to the den, where Martin King Jr. was eating pork chops.

As Nesbitt remembers it, the elder King was not an ally. "Martin," he said, "don't you go to that big nigger church. They'll kick you out." Martin, however, simply smiled at his father's bombast and agreed to do a guest sermon on January 17, 1954. The effect of that appearance was electric, and three months later, at a salary of five thousand dollars a year, he became the new pastor at Dexter Avenue Baptist. He liked the feel of this little brick church, almost literally in the shadow of the capitol. A block up the street, Jefferson Davis had taken his oath as the first president of the Confederacy, a troubling and symbolic piece of history, King thought, and the historical marker was a daily reminder that there was still some work to be done in Montgomery.

Ninety years after the fall of the Confederacy, they were not yet free.

And so it was that King came to Alabama, and on December 5, 1955, was chosen officially as the leader of the movement. He was, at first, the compromise candidate, a man who hadn't been in Montgomery long enough to make a lot of enemies. But the people at his church thought the choice was inspired. John Porter, for example, was the pulpit assistant, a college senior at Alabama State who gave the opening prayer at King's installation. He said he had never encountered a preacher like this, so compelling in his bearing that Porter, who was only two years younger, refused to call him anything but "Dr. King."

The odd thing was, King never expected it. True, his pulpit presence was impressive. He was a conservative dresser, not flashy, but neat, as he gazed out across the people in the crowd, and his gift for the language would take you by surprise. But there was something else, Porter thought, about this preacher with the Ph.D. The thing that made him the near-perfect choice when the Montgomery movement was looking for a leader was the quality at the heart of his greatness over time:

"He could undress you," said Porter, "with his humility."

What Porter meant was that King was the calm at the center of the storm. He never seemed tempted or drawn to competition with E. D. Nixon or Rufus Lewis or any of the others who emerged through the years. There were occasions, of course, when the egos swirled, stirred by the tension and the passion of the times, but King somehow seemed to be unaffected, sitting back quietly in the strategy sessions, a slight, self-deprecating smile on his face, never doubting that his own authority would prevail.

That, at least, was how Porter saw it, and it was an impression that only grew stronger over time, as Porter himself achieved a position of leadership in the movement. He knew that King would not have put it that way—certainly not on the night of December 5, when he made his way to Holt Street Baptist and was startled, like the others, by the size of the crowd. King's goal was simply to be worthy of the moment, worthy of the people who had turned out to hear him.

That was the amazing thing about Montgomery. As the coming months would reveal, it was a movement of the masses, a time when black people straightened their backs, and as King was fond of saying in his speeches, "A man can't ride your back unless it's bent."

The change wasn't easy. There were moments of euphoria like the first mass meeting at Holt Street Baptist, when the soaring voice of Dr. King, with the help of Amos, the Old Testament prophet, gave a shape to the spirit that was building in the crowd: "We are not wrong in what we are doing. . . . And we are determined here in Montgomery to work and fight until justice runs down like water, and righteousness like a mighty stream!"

It was easy to have faith in a moment such as that, to believe in the face of the evidence all around—in the face of the power that white people had, and their willingness to use it in defense of segregation—that something fundamental was about to change. But they knew even then, as they left the building and braced themselves against the damp winter's night, that the faith they discovered on December 5 was about to be tested.

Together, they were facing some difficult days, and there was only one thing they could all know for sure. The city of Montgomery was bracing for a fight.

CHAPTER 2

The Resistance

ONE OF THE IRONIES OF THE civil rights movement was that the demands at the start were nearly always modest. A few years earlier in South Carolina, a group of black families in Clarendon County made a simple request. They wanted a school bus for their children. There were buses, after all, provided for whites, and it didn't seem fair that black children had to walk. School officials turned down that request, which led to a lawsuit and an immediate escalation of demands, and before it was over the case of *Briggs vs. Elliott* made its way to the U.S. Supreme Court. There, it was considered with four other lawsuits from Virginia to Kansas, and the result was the watershed ruling of 1954, the *Brown* decision overturning racial segregation in the schools.

Many years later, one black leader in Clarendon County simply shook his head when a reporter asked him about those days, wondering at the turns that history might have taken. "If only they had given us a bus," he said.

There were people in Montgomery who understood what he meant, for in the beginning stages of the bus boycott, the Negro citizens weren't asking for much. On the afternoon of December 5, 1955, E. D. Nixon, Ralph Abernathy, and another young minister named Edgar French sketched out a specific set of demands: Bus drivers would treat all riders with respect. No more name-calling, no more slamming the doors in the face of black passengers. Blacks would fill the buses from the back, whites from the front, but when they met in the middle it was first-come, first-served, and no one would have to give up a seat. And on those routes that were exclusively black, the bus company would begin to hire black drivers.

The heart of the proposal had been around for many years, supported by Jo Ann Robinson and the Women's Political Council, who were buoyed by the fact that something similar was in place in Mobile. If such an arrangement could work in that city, surely it could work just as well in Montgomery.

What Robinson and the others did not mention, if indeed they knew, was that the Mobile model did not come easily. It was the product of long and often bitter negotiations, going back all the way to 1942, when a young army private named Henry Williams was shot and killed by a white bus driver. Newspapers were sketchy about the details, but it was a hot August day; there had been an altercation on the bus; and Henry Williams, at the moment of his death, was wearing the uniform of his country. To the black community, that was the greatest insult of all.

The city's Negro leaders knew Mobile was a difficult place, with acts of racial violence on the rise. With the coming of the war, it had been transformed from a city caught up in the memory of its past—a slow-moving port on the Gulf of Mexico known for its live oak trees and Mardi Gras parades and the fading splendor of its antebellum houses. Then suddenly, in the '40s, Mobile was a boomtown. There was a military base on the shores of the bay, and down at the shipyards thousands of workers poured in seeking jobs. Many were black. The Negro population of the city rose from twenty-nine thousand in 1940 to nearly forty-six thousand a decade later.

In the beginning, many of the new arrivals were disappointed. The Alabama Dry Dock and Shipbuilding Company reserved its high-paying jobs for white workers, but the Mobile chapter of the NAACP pushed hard for equal pay, and slowly but surely the barriers began to fall. In May

1943, twelve black welders—all highly trained—reported for work amid a swirl of rumor that their mission was simply to take away white jobs. A short time later the white workers attacked. For nearly two days, they armed themselves with scrap-iron and pipe and assaulted every black worker they could find. And even when order was restored at the plant, tensions in the city did not go away.

In the black community, the man who tried to deal with all this was a postal carrier named John LeFlore who had devoted his life to the cause of civil rights. It was an obsession going back to the 1920s when he was arrested after a scuffle on a streetcar. He had told the story many times to his family—how he had gotten on the trolley at his usual stop and taken the only seat that was left. A few minutes later, a white man boarded and demanded his seat. If it had been a woman or somebody infirm, he might have complied—might have offered, in fact, to give up his seat even before he was asked. But this was a passenger perfectly able to stand who felt entitled by the color of his skin to the seat that was occupied by LeFlore. They began to argue, and when the argument degenerated into a fight, the policemen came and took him to jail. The white man was allowed to go free.

LeFlore, at the time, was barely seventeen, but he told his mother when she came to pay his bail that things had to change, and he was going to be the one to make it happen. "You're talking crazy," she said, but she knew even then that her son wasn't listening.

In 1925 he founded a chapter of the NAACP, and for the next thirty years he attacked segregation on every front he could find. He investigated lynchings all over the South, and pushed for better jobs, and in 1944, he led a group of a dozen black citizens who attempted to vote in the Democratic primary. They were turned away. Incredibly enough in the hindsight of history, the Democrats declared that in the state of Alabama their party existed for white voters only. LeFlore refused to accept that verdict. Working late at night at his dining room table—two or three in the morning was not uncommon—he typed out a complaint to the U.S. Department of Justice, which threatened to intervene, and within eighteen months the Democratic party was compelled to desegregate its elections.

Over the years, the successes became intermingled with the failures, and for a while, it seemed, there was no issue more exasperating than the buses. Following the murder of Pvt. Henry Williams, LeFlore threatened to call for a boycott unless some fundamental changes were made. Negroes, he said, would "walk to work, walk to church, walk to shop" if bus drivers didn't stop going armed. In addition to that, it was time to address the issue of discourtesy—drivers using slurs or passing black passengers as they waited in the rain—and to come up with a system in which blacks would fill the buses from the rear, and whites from the front, but no one would have to give up a seat.

The bus company agreed to most of those provisions, but the problems didn't stop. The drivers disarmed, but sporadic acts of discourtesy were common, and for more than a decade LeFlore continued to struggle with the issue.

Shortly after World War II, he found himself with an unexpected ally. Joseph Langan was a Mobile native, a white politician who was different from the rest. He was a tallish man with steel-gray hair and steady blue eyes who came home from the fighting in the South Pacific more convinced than ever that there were racial problems that had to be addressed. As a younger man growing up in Mobile, he said he knew little of racial animosity. There were black families living not far from his own, good and sturdy people, he thought, whose well-kept houses near the heart of downtown were a handsome testament to the fundamental character and ambition of his neighbors.

Through all those years, his faith affirmed what he saw with his eyes—that people were people, all children of God, and the color of their skin didn't matter much at all. Langan was a Roman Catholic, a religious man whose faith eventually became intertwined with political ideas that he studied in school. Those notions of Jeffersonian democracy— *we hold these truths to be self-evident, that all men are created equal*— seemed to Langan to be so obvious that for almost as long as he could remember he was troubled by his region's inclination to ignore them. If he had any doubts, they vanished in the war. From Guadalcanal to Papua New Guinea he saw black soldiers fighting for their country, willing to die for the ideal of freedom, even though they themselves did not possess it.

He could only marvel at that kind of courage, and at the end of the war, he came back to Mobile determined to do what he could to be fair. He was soon elected to the state legislature, where he led the push for equal pay for black teachers and filibustered against the Boswell Amendment, which would have made it harder for black citizens to vote.

Once in Montgomery, while the legislature was in session, he boarded a bus on which almost all the passengers were black. The driver was white, a belligerent man who was berating one black rider in particular. Langan was amazed. Without black passengers, the bus company could not have survived, but the hostility of the drivers seemed to be a constant. Finally, Langan couldn't take it anymore. He rose to his full height of six-foot-three and stepped between the driver and the object of his rage.

"Cap'm," he said, "it's none of my business, but you don't seem to understand who is paying your salary."

For Langan, there was a fleeting moment of satisfaction, but he knew it didn't really change anything, for the problem seemed to be so pervasive. In Mobile one day on his way to his law office, he had gotten on a bus at Saint Joseph Street, one of the tree-lined avenues of downtown, and noticed immediately that the bus was nearly full. One stop later, at Concepcion Street, the driver ignored a group of waiting blacks, but he continued, periodically, to pick up whites. That same afternoon, Langan wrote a letter to the bus company, the National City Lines, wondering whether, at the end of the war, he had "come home to Germany instead of Mobile."

He began to talk about the problem with LeFlore, and finally in 1953, when he was elected to the Mobile City Commission, he decided the time had come for a change. With his fellow commissioners Henry Luscher and Charles Hackmeyer, he set up a test case—a carefully orchestrated challenge in which a black man got on a bus and sat in the front. The police were summoned, and the case was heard in a Mobile court, where the judge quickly ruled in the black man's favor.

"That," said Langan, "was the end of bus segregation in Mobile."

He knew there would still be some problems after that, but he also knew they were slowly making progress, slowly chipping away at the old attitudes, and with the help of leaders like John LeFlore, he thought they could do it with civility and grace. He was proud of his city for making the attempt, but more and more as time went by, he was troubled by the stories coming out of Montgomery. In the Christmas season of 1955, the white leaders there seemed to be digging in.

On the watershed night of December 5, the black citizens who gathered at Holt Street Baptist adopted the agenda recommended by their leaders—a seating arrangement for the Montgomery buses based essentially on the Mobile model. The following Thursday a delegation of blacks led by Martin Luther King sat down to negotiate with white leaders. They were optimistic at the start—certain, they said, that a solution as moderate as the one they proposed could be adopted by anyone of good faith.

They were taken by surprise when the bus company's lawyer, Jack Crenshaw, rejected their proposal out of hand. "If it were legal," he said, "I would be the first to go along with it, but it just isn't legal."

King tried to say that Crenshaw was wrong. The city's segregation laws were not at issue, at least not yet. All they were asking was a fairer application, a promise in writing that black bus riders like Rosa Parks would not be humiliated or abused. They continued to talk on December 8, and there were two more sessions before the Christmas holiday. But they were unsuccessful and King berated himself for the failure. Had he pushed too hard? Not hard enough? Or was it simply an impossible situation?

The answer came from Jack Crenshaw. At one of the negotiating sessions in December, which was going nowhere, Montgomery mayor W. A. Gayle ordered a smaller group to reassemble behind closed doors, away from the immediate scrutiny of the media. One of the white leaders, City Commissioner Frank Parks, opened the session with an optimistic assessment: "I don't see why we can't accept this seating proposal," he said, referring to the one being offered by King. "We can work it within our segregation laws."

Crenshaw immediately rose to disagree. "Frank," he warned, "If we granted the Negroes these demands, they would go about boasting of a victory that they had won over the white people, and this we will not allow." And there it was—within earshot of King and the others, an expression of the fear that was gripping white people all over Montgomery, indeed all over Alabama and the South. Even in the modest demands of the moment, they saw intimations of a shredded status quo—a black community no longer compliant, a white community no longer in control. In Mobile under the leadership of Joe Langan, they were beginning to make a certain peace with the change, giving ground slowly in the pursuit of public calm. But in Montgomery, the attitude was different. With the battle lines drawn in such a visible way, it was simply unacceptable for the Negroes to win.

On December 8, Police Commissioner Clyde Sellers decided it was time to turn up the heat. He announced that black taxi drivers who were supporting the boycott with cut-rate fairs—in many cases, only ten cents a ride—would soon be arrested. King understood that the threat was serious, for he regarded Sellers as perhaps the most racist of the leaders who opposed them. He had no doubt that the police commissioner would do what he could to undermine the boycott and put the black people back in their place.

King decided immediately to call an old friend, T. J. Jemison, who, two years earlier, had organized a boycott in Baton Rouge, Louisiana. The authorities there had banned the use of cut-rate taxis, and Jemison had responded with an intricate car pool to keep the protest alive. At a mass meeting on the night of December 8, King asked for volunteers—black people with cars who would agree to drive people to work every morning, and home again at the end of each day. More than 100 drivers stepped forward that night, and in less than a month the number had swelled to 350.

It fell to Rufus Lewis, chairman of the transportation committee, to put a system together, and soon it was working in defiance of the odds. They gathered in the morning at the pickup spots—shopping centers and old vacant lots and the parking areas of black-owned stores. There were cars of every shape and variety, Chevrolets, Plymouths, a Chrysler here and there, lined up waiting for the people to arrive. Many black workers continued to walk, but thousands also rode in the cars, where nobody paid anybody for the rides, at least not directly. At the mass meetings every week at the churches, the Montgomery Improvement Association took up a collection—money for gas, and wear and tear on the tires.

It became the crowning achievement of the boycott, as the movement held steady through the long winter months without any visible traces of progress. The resistance, meanwhile, grew stiffer all the time. The police began harassing the car pool drivers, pulling them over on charges both trivial and contrived, issuing citations or taking them to jail.

Bob Graetz remembered one harrowing moment that began on the morning of December 19. He had stopped at a meter near Dean's Drug Store, which was one of the pickup spots, and waited for his passengers. As soon as they arrived, he pulled out slowly, careful as always to obey the traffic laws, and was proceeding uneventfully toward Dexter Avenue, when he heard the sound of a siren just behind him. He pulled to the curb, and the county sheriff, Mac Sim Butler, walked to the driver's window and demanded: "What are you doing, running a taxi?"

Graetz said no, these were merely his friends, but the sheriff said it looked like a taxi to him, and ordered Graetz to follow him over to the jail. Suddenly, for the first time, the preacher felt afraid. He could imagine the sheriff or one of his deputies taking out his hatred on a young white man from another part of the country who had come to Montgomery to help the colored people break all the rules. Graetz said a quick prayer and braced himself for whatever Mac Sim Butler had in mind.

What he didn't know was that in the black community, the state of alarm was much greater than his own. The people in the movement were not afraid of the sheriff. They were afraid of the prisoners who were locked in his jail. Like everything else in Montgomery County, the jail was segregated, and with black and white prisoners kept carefully apart, Graetz would find himself with the whites. It was hard to imagine a less sympathetic group, and the leaders in the MIA were convinced that unless they were able to post bond in a hurry, Pastor Bob Graetz wouldn't make it through the day.

Fortunately, those fears were never put to the test. Sheriff Butler took Graetz to his office at the jail and told him to sit while he made a call to the judge. "Hello, this is Mac Sim Butler. I've got a man here who was hauling niggers. . . . Yes, but this is a white man!" Clearly frustrated, Butler hung up the phone, entrusting Graetz temporarily to the care of a deputy, a large and somewhat menacing man, "gorilla-like," as Graetz later put it, who issued a personal warning of his own: "We like things the way they are down here."

According to one newspaper account, the sheriff returned a few minutes later, his mood even lower than it was when he left. He had run down the list of possible charges with the judge, who had rejected them all and ordered him simply to let the preacher go. The sheriff wasn't happy, but he did as he was told. "I don't see how you can claim to be a Christian," he said, and then it was over.

For Graetz, in the aftermath of that encounter, the dangers of the movement were immediately more real—not a theoretical possibility, but part of the cost of doing what was right—and he understood that he was not alone. For some of the leaders, there was a slow and steady escalation of the pressure. Jo Ann Robinson, for example, was ticketed seventeen times while driving for the car pool, and on the afternoon of January 26, Martin Luther King was arrested and taken away by police. He was leaving his office at Dexter Avenue Baptist when he pulled over to pick up a load of passengers at one of the car pool stops downtown. Almost immediately, two motorcycle policemen fell in behind him. King drove slowly, hoping the officers would leave him alone, but when he made a stop to let the passengers unload, the policemen told him he was under arrest.

They called for a cruiser and put him in the back, and King noticed to his horror that the police car was heading away from downtown. He tried not to panic, but he knew what could happen to black people in the South. He could imagine himself on a backcountry road, where the policemen could accuse him of trying to escape, maybe shoot him in the head or beat him unconscious and leave him to die, or maybe they would simply turn him over to the Klan. As the possibilities continued to race through his mind, he thought about the pressures of the past several weeks, and the signals that had come from the white leadership that they were ready now to escalate the war.

On January 6 Police Commissioner Clyde Sellers had appeared at a rally of the White Citizens Council, an organization born in Mississippi, which quickly replicated itself in Alabama, first in Selma and then in Montgomery. Some people said it was the gentleman's version of the Ku Klux Klan, advocating not violence but economic pressure. As one leader put it, the Council intended "to make it difficult, if not impossible, for any Negro who advocates desegregation to find and hold a job, get credit, or renew a mortgage." Sellers embraced that strategy, announcing at the meeting on January 6 that he was proud to be the newest member of the group. Before the end of the month Mayor W. A. Gayle and City Commissioner Frank Parks had followed his lead, as the Montgomery membership grew to six thousand. One month later, it was nearly twelve thousand.

King took those numbers as a measure of white rage, and he knew the police were the first line of defense. It fell to officers like the ones with him now to make sure things didn't get out of hand. But exactly how would they interpret that assignment? Was it enough to arrest him and haul him off to jail, or were the authorities planning to do something more? As they crossed the bridge at the Alabama River, he could imagine his body floating face down, and he was trembling badly when the police car finally arrived at the jail.

Embarrassed now by the depth of his fear, he gathered himself and walked inside where he was fingerprinted and taken to a cell. Abernathy, who had gotten word of the arrest, was not at all reassured by the fact that King had made it to the jail. Too many things could happen to him there. He rushed to the scene in a frantic effort to bail out his friend but was told that a property bond would not be accepted. He would have to put up cash. He hurried off again to try to raise the money, only to discover as soon as he returned that King had been released on his own recognizance.

All in all it was a disconcerting event, an assault on the psyche of King and his friends, and the effects of it lingered for the next several days. On Friday night, January 27, King came home late from a meeting of the MIA and found himself unable to sleep. The telephone rang, and it was another white caller threatening his life: "Nigger, we are tired of you and your mess now. If you aren't out of this town in three days—" King hung up the phone and went into the kitchen to make a pot of coffee.

It wasn't just the threats or the evening at the jail. The pressure now seemed to come from every side. A few days earlier, in a maddening digression, three black ministers with no connection to the MIA, and no authority in the movement, had negotiated an agreement with city officials to put an end to the boycott. The *Montgomery Advertiser* played up the story, and King had to scramble to undo the damage. On Saturday night, January 21, he made the rounds of the Montgomery nightspots, the rowdy juke joints that were scattered through the county, and he told the people who were blowing off steam to disregard the newspaper's account. The boycott was not yet over.

A part of him enjoyed his mission that night, rolling up his sleeves and getting out there where the real people were, but the cynicism of the white leadership—negotiating a bogus agreement with three black ministers who represented no one—and the foolishness of the ministers themselves . . . all of that became entangled in the danger and the fear and his failure so far to accomplish anything at all. Sitting alone in his kitchen at midnight and staring at the pot of coffee on the stove, he had to wonder if he was up to the job. He could feel a prayer taking shape in his mind, not really a plea for divine intervention, just some words of resignation that he could not suppress: "Lord, I must confess that I'm weak now. I'm faltering. I'm losing my courage. And I can't let the people see me like this."

He said he heard an inner voice in reply, telling him simply to keep the faith and do what he must, and he would never be alone. It was an experience unlike any other in his life, a moment, he said, when his faith became real. As a college student, he had studied the writings of the great theologians— Paul Tillich, Reinhold Niebuhr—marveling at the wisdom and brilliance they possessed, their understanding of the faith. But now there was more. Now, in addition to the *idea* of God, there was also a personal sense of his presence.

The feeling grew even stronger on Monday, when he was speaking at a meeting at Abernathy's church and an old woman rose from one of the pews to say that the preacher seemed troubled this night. King recognized Mrs. Pollard right away—Mother Pollard, as many people called her, a village elder known for her eloquence and the kind of folk wisdom that set her apart. "My feets is tired, but my soul is rested," she had once declared in support of the boycott. On the night of Monday, January 30, she put her arms around Dr. King and told him there was no need to worry, no need to be afraid. "God's gonna take care of you," she said.

A few minutes later, King glanced down and saw a worried look on Abernathy's face. "What's wrong?" he asked, and Abernathy told him he had some bad news. A few minutes earlier King's house had been bombed. There was no word yet on the fate of his wife, Coretta, or his daughter, Yolanda, barely ten weeks old. King responded calmly to the news, his spirits soothed by the words of Mother Pollard and his midnight reflections from three days before. He told the crowd to stay calm as well, then rushed to his house, where he found Coretta and the baby unhurt.

She said she had heard a noise outside—the sound of footsteps and something landing on the porch—and carried Yolanda to a back room of the house. A few seconds later, the dynamite exploded. The damage was not as bad as she had feared, and the baby was fine; that was the thing that mattered to her most. King listened to her story, and took her in his arms, then returned to the porch where a large group of people, black and white, was beginning to gather. Mayor W. A. Gayle was there, along with Police Commissioner Clyde Sellers, who told King gravely: "I do not agree with you and your beliefs, but I will do everything within my power to defend you against such acts as this."

King nodded his appreciation, but one of his friends, C. T. Smiley, told the commissioner it was not that easy. "Regrets are fine, Mr. Sellers," he said. "But you created the atmosphere for this bombing with your 'get tough' policy. You've got to face that responsibility." Though King himself had been more polite, he had to admire the candor of his friend, for Smiley was principal at a local high school, dependent on the white power structure for his job. Smiley, however, was too angry to worry, and he was not alone. As word of the bombing spread through the black community of Montgomery, the crowd at King's house continued to swell. The people came armed, and several of the white reporters on the scene, along with the police, became increasingly nervous about what would happen next.

Sellers asked King if he would speak to the crowd, and King agreed. "We are not advocating violence," he said, in a voice that was authoritative and steady. "I want you to love our enemies. Be good to them. . . . I did not start this boycott. I was asked by you to serve as your spokesman. I want it known the length and breadth of this land that if I am stopped, this movement will not stop. If I am stopped, our work will not stop. For what we are doing is right. What we are doing is just. And God is with us."

One man who took his measure of King that night was Thomas Gray, a board member of the MIA whose brother Fred Gray would emerge as the principal lawyer for the movement. Thomas was a businessman, tough and unsentimental. He had served in the navy during World War II, where he saw combat in the Marshall Islands, and even before the bus boycott he had led a civil rights demonstration at the courthouse. He first met the Kings when Coretta bought a washing machine from his store. He thought of Martin as a nice young man, though not necessarily as a leader for the movement. Gray preferred the toughness of E. D. Nixon, and yet there was something about King from the start, a political shrewdness with all his talk about nonviolence and meeting hatred with love—those phrases that played so well in the press. Gray once complimented King for being clever.

"I said, 'Martin, that's a nice ploy,'" Gray remembered. "He said, 'No, Tom, that is not a ploy.' I was surprised at first, and then I said to myself, 'This man really means it.'"

After the bombing, there wasn't any doubt. King's plea for nonviolence on the porch of his home became part of his legend, another piece of his mystique. Gray understood that it was not absolute, for less than two days after the attack, King applied for a gun permit in order to protect the members of his family. But it seemed to Gray and many of the others who observed King closely as if some corner had now been turned.

Many years later, Martin Luther King Sr. talked about these events as a defining moment in the life of his son. The bombing of the house, the midnight conversation with God, the battle with terror on the night of his arrest—all of these, he said, came together for Martin Jr. to produce a leader more seasoned, more sure of his moorings, more certain that he was able to do what he must.

In an interview in the 1970s Daddy King told the story this way, making the biblical comparison explicit: "They tried to tempt Jesus to come down from the cross. The devil tried to say, 'If you're the Son of God, come on down.' Well, he didn't come down, and I'm glad about that. And I'm glad that Martin Luther King Jr. didn't come down that night in Montgomery when they put him in the back of a police car and drove around for hours, trying to decide what to do with him. Finally, they told him, 'If you'll go back to Georgia and don't cause no more trouble, we'll let you go.' But he told them, 'Gentlemen, I can't do it.' He said, 'I can't fail these people.' And they said, 'We ain't never heard a nigger talk like that. There's something peculiar about this fellow.'"

There was one inaccuracy in King Sr.'s account. In January 1956, the agent of temptation was not the policeman, but Daddy King himself. On the night of the bombing, Martin King Jr. heard a knock on the door. It was his father, who had driven over from Atlanta, demanding that his son come home for a while, back to where it was safe. If the bombers struck once, there was no reason why they couldn't do it again.

When Martin resisted, his father grew enraged. "It's better to be a live dog than a dead lion," he shouted. But Martin shook his head. He had found the courage he needed to continue, and now it was critically important that he stay. The MIA was about to raise the stakes. In Montgomery, Alabama, the battle of the buses was about to enter a whole new phase.

CHAPTER 3

The Courts and the Klan

On February 1, 1956, attorney Fred Gray went down to the federal building in Montgomery and filed a lawsuit before U.S. district judge Frank Johnson. Gray demanded the total integration of the buses—no more talk of simple things like courtesy, or halfway measures like blacks filling up the buses from the rear and whites from the front, and no one having to give up a seat. This was a frontal assault on the segregated system, and as one civil rights historian later said, it was regarded by the white community of Montgomery as "the social equivalent of atomic warfare." In the eyes of black leaders, there was nothing to lose. After the bombing of King's home, the physical dangers were already apparent, and the negotiations were going nowhere.

"We began with a compromise," said King, "when we didn't ask for complete integration. Now we're asked to compromise on the compromise." King was convinced they had made a mistake, violating a principle that seasoned businessmen took for granted. Never open with your bottom line offer. That was what they had done, leaving them essentially no room to maneuver, and even worse, they had been willing to compromise with segregation, the fundamental evil they were seeking to destroy. By the end of January, King and the MIA had decided it was time to go after what they had wanted all along.

Nobody knew what would happen, of course. Judge Johnson was still an unknown quantity, having been on the bench for fewer than three months. The good news was, he seemed to be a maverick, not a part of that growing majority of Alabama politicians who might sign on with the Citizens Council or issue their pronouncements about the permanence and rectitude of segregation. Johnson clearly was not like that. He came from Winston County near the Tennessee line, an area very different from the rest of the state. For one thing, Republicans in the county outnumbered Democrats, which was an oddity in the South of the 1950s. These were holdovers from the party of Lincoln, fiercely independent and proud of their history of being out of step. Just before the Civil War, when the state of Alabama seceded from the union, the county of Winston seceded from the state, and over the next five years most of its young men fought for the Union.

Frank Johnson was the heir to all that, a tall, stubborn man with a hawk-like nose and piercing eyes, well educated with a law degree from the University of Alabama, but in many ways, a hillbilly to the bone. He liked to fish and chew tobacco (Levi Garrett was his brand), and he was always partial to a good country song. He once declared, with the opinionated certainty that became his trademark, "To me, there are only two kinds of guitar players in the world: those that imitate Chet Atkins and those that ought to."

In 1953 Johnson was named U.S. attorney for the Middle District of Alabama, and was immediately confronted with the most disturbing case of his career. In May of that year, the mangled body of a black farm worker, Herbert Thompson, was delivered to a funeral home in Sumter County, Alabama. The FBI began to investigate and soon concluded that the killers came from a prominent white family, which was using slave labor to run its plantation. According to the evidence, the Dial brothers would pay the fines of black men arrested in a nearby county, then compel them to work to pay off the debt. It was a system enforced by the most insidious pattern of brutality—black workers forced at gunpoint to beat their fellow workers who rebelled.

Finally, Herbert Thompson couldn't take it anymore. After two months of hard labor in exchange for a fine of fifty-five dollars, he tried to run away, but was caught and beaten to death for his troubles.

Frank Johnson was appalled. He prosecuted the case with a cool and efficient sense of outrage, and on May 14, 1954—three days before the Supreme Court's landmark ruling in *Brown*—he secured a conviction from an all-white jury. The black leaders of Montgomery were encouraged by that. In the early winter of 1956 they understood the stakes involved in the suit to desegregate the buses. If they won, the critical precedents established in *Brown* would expand from education to other areas of life, but if they lost, it would be a setback—not only for the Negro population of Montgomery, but for people all over the South who were determined to rid the region of segregation.

Frank Johnson, too, understood the magnitude of the issue, and since he was new to the bench, having just been promoted from U.S. attorney, he didn't want to hear the case by himself. He asked for a three-judge federal panel, and on May 11, 1956, the panel convened at the federal courthouse. Johnson was flanked by two other jurists, both of them men very different from himself. To his immediate right was Judge Richard Rives, the senior member of the group, a round-faced man with gentle eyes and dark-framed glasses, his gray hair thinning and a little bit askew. For most of his life, Rives was regarded as an Old South lawyer, aristocratic, reflective, not a boat-rocker on the issue of race.

In private, however, he had begun to brood about the issue more and more, partly because of his son. Dick Rives Jr. had gone away to the University of Michigan, where he concluded from his studies that something was terribly wrong in the South. He persuaded his father to read Gunnar Myrdal's famous treatise *An American Dilemma,* and the two of them agreed that this was a remarkable piece of scholarship, raising fundamental questions about the nature of race relations in America.

Father and son were unusually close, and it was a devastating moment in 1949 when Dick Rives Jr. was killed in a car wreck. He was a junior in law school, a young man of sensitivity and promise who intended to go into practice with his father. Many people said it was part of the father's tribute to his son to pay attention to issues that mattered to him most. Whatever the case, the racial views of Richard Rives Sr. were in a state of evolution in 1956 when he accepted his place on the three-judge panel.

The third member of the group, Seybourn Lynne, was more conservative than either of his colleagues. As a jurist and a man, he was deeply skeptical of judicial activism—the tendency of federal judges, including a few in the South, to offer new interpretations of the law. Once again, he said, that was what the Negro lawyers seemed to want, and he thought the burden of proof was on the plaintiffs.

At 9 A.M., the judges took their seats behind a hardwood bench that was polished to a shine. For a witness who had never been there before, it was not the kind of setting to put you at ease, but all the plaintiffs said they were ready.

Aurelia Browder went first. Alphabetically, that's the way it fell, as her name became a part of legal history in the landmark case of *Browder vs. Gayle*. On the stand, she made a good witness, telling the court that before the boycott she used to ride the buses every day, sometimes to school, sometimes to her job. She was a widow at the age of thirty-four, a nurse's aide and the mother of four, and a student at Alabama State College. When Fred Gray asked her why she had stopped, why she preferred to walk or use the car pool, she said it was simple: "I wanted better treatment."

Under Gray's gentle prodding, she told the story of the multiple occasions when she was forced to stand in order for somebody white to sit down. What made it worse was that on many of those occasions, two or three Negroes would have to give up their seats for a single white person, thus saving the white passenger the indignity of sitting next to somebody colored. Fred Gray nodded gravely. "And if you were permitted to sit any place you wanted on the bus, would you ride? Would you be willing to ride it again?"

"Yes, I would."

"That is all."

Out in the courtroom, the black spectators began to stir just a little, began to shift uncomfortably in their seats, waiting for the cross-examination of Mrs. Browder. They were dressed for the occasion, the men in dark, conservative suits, the women in dresses they might wear to church. A few of them had seen the courtroom before, the soft green carpeting, the pale yellow drapes, the clock behind the bench that told the time of day in roman numerals. The majesty of the place only added to the tension, as the team of lawyers for the city of Montgomery glanced quickly at their notes. There was John Patterson, the attorney general of Alabama, a dark-haired man with clear, steady eyes, intelligent, aggressive, a popular figure in the state; and there was Truman Hobbs, who two years later would become a federal judge, and Walter Knabe, the city attorney for Montgomery, who began to ask the first set of questions.

Knabe didn't look like a frightening figure. He was short and slim with closely cropped hair and a soft-spoken manner, but from the start he seemed disdainful of Mrs. Browder. He asked if she decided to boycott the buses essentially on the orders of Martin Luther King—a man he insisted on calling "Negro King." No, she said, she decided on her own. But when that happened, Knabe demanded, when she and the others began to boycott the buses, they were not asking for integration, were they? They were asking for courtesy and first-come, first-served seating.

"Yes," she replied.

"So in other words, you did not stop on account of segregation, but you stopped riding before the segregation issue was ever raised. That is correct, isn't it?"

Mrs. Browder didn't hesitate. "It is the segregation laws that cause all of it," she said.

The attorney now grew visibly annoyed. "Just answer the question," he snapped.

It continued that way through three more witnesses, Knabe sparring, badgering, trying to paint the women as the pawns of Dr. King, opposed to segregation only because he told them to be. It was an excruciating scene, and to the Negro citizens in the room that day, Knabe seemed even more of a bully because of the ages of the women on the stand. The second witness, Susie McDonald, was seventy-seven years old, and Mary Louise Smith was only nineteen.

And yet through it all, the women held firm. Mrs. McDonald told of the time when, despite her age, she had to surrender her seat to "some white people," and Smith recounted her arrest for refusing to do the same. And then came the final plaintiff of the day, the youngest of the group, and arguably the star. Claudette Colvin, who was now sixteen, told the story again of her arrest in March, how she refused to surrender her seat on a bus, and how the policemen handcuffed her and took her away. "I was very hurt," she said, "because I didn't know that white people would act like that, and I . . . I was crying."

When Knabe tried to say that her testimony was all part of a plan, "a scheme," by Martin Luther King and a small group of black leaders, Colvin said no. She, like the others, was speaking for herself. But Knabe persisted. There had to be somebody in charge, some organizer behind a movement so elaborate. The whole community, after all, had abandoned the buses on the same Monday morning. "Why," he said, his voice more intense, "did you stop riding on December 5?"

"Because," said Colvin, to scattered murmurs of approval from the crowd, "we were treated wrong, dirty and nasty."

Altogether, the hearing lasted five hours, and it seemed clear enough at the end of the day that all the women had done well. They were not polished, the grammar in some of their answers was flawed, but they spoke from the heart. Out in the audience, Martin Luther King allowed himself a brief moment of hope. He leaned and whispered to Ralph Abernathy, "It looks as if we may get a favorable verdict."

What King didn't know was that the judges already had made up their minds. When they retired to deliberate on the case, Judge Rives, the senior member of the group, turned first to Johnson and asked his opinion.

"Judge," said Johnson, with barely a pause, "as far as I'm concerned, state-imposed segregation on public facilities violates the Constitution. I'm going to rule with the plaintiffs here."

Rives nodded his agreement. "You know I feel the same way as you."

Judge Lynne dissented, arguing that the precedent of *Plessy vs. Ferguson*—the segregationists' doctrine of separate but equal—was still the law of the land, except in the realm of public education, unless the Supreme Court decided otherwise. But Lynne was outvoted, and in less than ten minutes the issue was settled.

On June 5, a cool and cloudy day in Montgomery, the formal opinion of the court, written by Rives, was released to the public: "There is no rational basis upon which the 'separate but equal' doctrine can validly be applied to public transportation in the city of Montgomery. In their private affairs, in the conduct of their private businesses, it is clear that the people themselves have the liberty to select their own associates and the persons with whom they do business, unimpaired by the 14th Amendment. . . . There is, however, a difference, a constitutional difference, between voluntary adherence to custom and the perpetuation and enforcement of that custom by law."

The ruling was immediately appealed by the city, and the tension in Montgomery continued unabated. Indeed, it was building, and for some time now, had been spreading slowly but surely through the state.

On February 1, 1956, the day of the filing, a bomb exploded at the home of E. D. Nixon. The terrorists this time didn't accomplish very much. The dynamite was thrown from a car and exploded in the yard, and except for the ugly crater on the lawn, the damage was minor. But over in the western part of Alabama, the Citizens Council and the Ku Klux Klan were getting ready for a war if that's what it took. On Saturday night, February 4, a cross went up in flames in Tuscaloosa, and it was not the first. The burnings, always a calling card of the Klan, started to occur in January, as word leaked out that the University of Alabama, a bastion of whiteness, was about to admit a Negro student.

In Alabama, the university was not the first institution of higher learning to take that step. Down in Mobile, a little Jesuit school called Spring Hill College had lowered its barriers in the 1940s. Spring Hill had long been a place of innovation. Founded in 1830, it was the oldest college in the state, a place of beauty on the western border of Mobile, where the lanes curved gently through the canopy of oaks, and off in the distance from a vantage point near the chapel, you could see all the way to the waters of the bay.

In May 1948 the president of the school, Patrick Donnelly, delivered a commencement address, criticizing the great universities in the South for their silence on the issue of desegregation. "Let Spring Hill break that silence," he declared, and the following summer a group of black teachers—all of them seeking recertification—enrolled in a course on English literature. The desegregation of evening classes soon followed, and then in 1954, the school's new president, Father Andrew Smith, embarked on the final leg of the journey. In a commencement speech on May 25 he praised the Supreme Court's ruling in *Brown:* "It is clearly the duty of educators, public and private, to hail the decision of May 17, 1954. It goes without saying that this historic college, always the champion of social justice, stands ready to play its part."

What Smith didn't say was that ten days before the Supreme Court decision, Spring Hill had accepted a black coed, Julia Ponquinette, for admission as a full-time student in the fall. When the term began Miss Ponquinette was joined by seven other blacks, who entered the school without any fanfare, and took their places in the student body of one thousand. On September 18 the *Mobile Register* discovered their presence and asked Father Smith if such a thing could be true—if the barriers in higher education had fallen and Negro students were now at Spring Hill.

"I presume there are some in the classes," said Smith. "We have never asked if they were white or Negro."

And with that it was settled, no hysteria or protests, barely a ruffled feather in the town. With luck and leadership in Tuscaloosa, the University of Alabama might have achieved a similar result, but the university, unfortunately, had little of either.

That became clear almost from the start, when two black women, Pollie Anne Myers and Autherine Lucy, applied for admission in 1952. Within a few days, each had received a dormitory assignment and a letter of welcome, the administrators having failed to ascertain that the women were black. On September 20 Myers and Lucy appeared at the admissions office on campus, where the startled dean, Ralph Adams, told them simply, "an error has been made." Pollie Myers asked if there were some kind of problem with the application forms.

Easily the more outspoken of the two, Pollie was a handsome, dark-skinned woman, articulate and confident, a supporter of the NAACP. She had been a reporter at the *Birmingham World,* a distinguished African American newspaper where the editor, Emory Jackson, was a fearless champion of the cause of black freedom. Her friend Autherine was soft-spoken and shy, a farmer's daughter from Marengo County, who wanted to be a teacher. She had spent two years at Selma University, a junior college that would produce its share of leaders for the movement. She was still looking for work when Pollie suggested they apply to the University of Alabama.

From the start, of course, they expected resistance, and it did not surprise them when Dean Adams rescinded their welcome from a few days before. On September 24 they went to Arthur Shores, a prominent black attorney in Birmingham, and asked for his help. Shores was happy to take the case. He had once been an educator himself, a former high school principal who became a lawyer in 1937. He was a proper-looking man with a thin mustache in the style of Errol Flynn, an immaculate dresser known for tenacity in defense of his clients. He believed immediately this was a case he could win, and he was confident and patient in the face of delays—first administratively and then in the courts.

He filed suit in the summer of 1953, and after nearly two years of procedural wrangling, the case came to trial on June 29, 1955. From that point on, everything moved quickly. U.S. district judge Hobart Grooms issued his ruling in forty-eight hours, ordering the university to desegregate. Once again, the university appealed, delaying the inevitable until the winter semester, but the appeals were futile, as the lawyers in the case understood that they would be. On February 1, 1956, Autherine Lucy was admitted as a student.

It was a cold Wednesday morning, the rain falling in sheets, when Lucy arrived on campus. She had recently discovered that she was making this perilous journey on her own, for on the previous afternoon the university had rejected Pollie Myers. Several months earlier, investigators hired by the college set about the task of digging up some dirt. In the case of Autherine, they had failed. But they discovered that Myers had given birth to a baby less than seven months after she was married, and they deduced from that that the baby had been conceived out of wedlock. In the 1950s it was the kind of sin that made her unfit, at least in the eyes of the board of trustees.

Myers was devastated by the news, but she vowed nevertheless to support Autherine. Nobody knew what would happen on campus, but in the city of Tuscaloosa nobody could remember a more tension-filled time. The mood had been different since May 17, 1954, when the Supreme Court handed down its ruling in *Brown*, first raising the prospect of integrated schools. Now in the winter of 1956 the fears and hostility were exponentially worse, inflamed by the news coming out of Montgomery. Everywhere, it seemed, black Alabamians were forgetting their place, their second-class status that the white majority had long taken for granted. In Tuscaloosa the word quickly spread that this new black student, Autherine Lucy, had arrived on the campus with her own entourage—leaders, apparently, from the NAACP—and in a final and provocative gesture of defiance, they had come in a Cadillac.

On Friday night, after an uneventful day of classes—there were, in fact, a handful of students who wished her the best—a crowd assembled at the Union Building on campus, and it wasn't long before the mood turned ugly. They burned a cross, then marched on the mansion of the university's president, Oliver Carmichael. Finding that the president had gone out of town, a remarkable decision under the circumstances, the crowd regrouped and headed downtown, singing "Dixie" and carrying the battle flag of the Confederacy. Along the way, there were spontaneous cheers of a pep rally gone bad: "Hey, hey, ho, ho, Autherine has got to go"—and when a car full of blacks was caught in the way, the students began to rock it back and forth, smashing a window before they were through. In the heart of downtown, at a monument honoring Alabama's war dead, Leonard Wilson, a sophomore from Selma, hoisted himself to the base of the memorial and proclaimed to the crowd of more than five hundred: "The governor will read about this tomorrow."

For the next several days, Wilson reveled in his moment of fame. He was a young white supremacist who, as a high school senior, had introduced a measure in the Youth Legislature to ship Alabama's black people back to Africa. When another mob assembled on Saturday night, marching once again on the president's house, threatening the passengers on a Greyhound bus, stomping on the roof of a black man's car and smashing the windshield before the terrified passengers were able to escape, Wilson once more was in the middle of it. He later insisted that he had done everything he could to keep the peace, but when he addressed the crowd, as he had done on Friday, he told a string of jokes, comparing black people to monkeys and apes, and urged his followers to reassemble on Monday. They would be waiting at 9 A.M., he said, when Autherine Lucy reported to class.

Despite the dangers, she reported on time. Because the university had refused so far to assign her a dorm room, she was forced to commute every day from Birmingham, where she lived. The first couple of times she came with friends, first to register and then to attend the opening day of class. Among the supporters who made the fifty-mile trip, determined to be there in a difficult time, were Fred Shuttlesworth, a leader in the NAACP; Emory Jackson, the great newspaper editor; Mrs. Geneva Lee, a friend of the family; and of course, Pollie Myers. But on Monday morning, February 6, Autherine came alone, except for H. N. Guinn, another of Birmingham's successful businessmen, who had agreed to drive her.

They came in a Cadillac, the Guinn family car, and improbably enough, they didn't attract much attention from the crowd. Lucy got out, walked past the clusters of whites at Smith Hall and waved to Mr. Guinn from the top of the stairs. Soon, however, the surly crowd realized its mistake, and its numbers swelled to more than five hundred. Dr. Carmichael, the president of the school, appeared with a bullhorn and pleaded with the demonstrators to disperse, but his words only seemed to make people angry. The mob this time was a volatile mixture, perhaps even more than on Saturday night. There were students, of course, many in their teens, filled with excitement and surging hormones, and they were goaded by members of the Ku Klux Klan. Robert Chambliss, or "Dynamite Bob," as he was known in the Klan, made the drive from Birmingham, and he was working the crowd with the help of Asa Carter, who, in the next several years, would become the most prominent Klansman in the state.

Soon, there were shouts of "lynch the nigger" and "keep Bama white," as Autherine Lucy tried to listen to the lecture in her nine o'clock class. She wondered what she would do when it ended, and two administrators were wondering the same. Dean Sarah Healy and Jefferson Bennett, a special assistant to the president, were both at Smith Hall, casting anxious glances at the crowd. Under the circumstances, they decided that Lucy should stick to her schedule; otherwise, the mob would have won.

When the first class ended, Healy and Bennett led Autherine to the rear of Smith Hall, where Healy's Oldsmobile was parked. The crowd, however, surged around from the front and began to shower them with gravel and eggs. They ran for the car and jumped inside, Lucy sandwiched between Healy and Bennett, and as Bennett drove away gravel continued to rain down on the car. Now the mob was in a murderous mood, screaming "nigger-lovers" and "hit the nigger whore." But they made it to Lucy's second class of the day, where, behind locked doors, she listened to a lecture that had to seem surreal—a discussion of children's literature and the classics.

Through it all, she showed little fear, praying not for her safety, but simply for courage in the face of being killed. In the end, she survived her terrible ordeal, making her escape from campus that day lying face down in the back of a police car.

It was what happened next that took her by surprise. The university board of trustees, meeting that night, suspended her from school. It was simply too dangerous, they said, for her to stay. Her lawyers made a final plea to the court, charging that in suspending Autherine the university had conspired with the Klan "to defy the injunction order of this court." In response President Carmichael called a press conference to express his dismay, calling the conspiracy charge "untrue, unwarranted, and outrageous," and the board of trustees made the suspension of Autherine permanent. They said she had damaged the university's good name.

At that point, Lucy and her lawyers decided to let it drop. Exhausted now by the whole ordeal, they knew that legally she had made her case. The courts ordered the university to desegregate, and at least theoretically the order still stood. But as a practical matter, the ruling had been overturned by a mob, and for the moment at least, the university remained all white. Jefferson Bennett, the special assistant to the president, told his boss that sadly, there was only one conclusion they could draw: "The mob won."

Certainly, the white supremacists thought so. Meeting in Montgomery on February 10, the White Citizens Council held the largest rally in its history, inflamed by events in Montgomery and Tuscaloosa, which were now interwoven in the psyche of the state. As many as fifteen thousand people showed up, cheering the words of Mississippi senator James Eastland, who urged the people of Alabama to be strong.

Meanwhile, on the other side of the divide, the black people of Montgomery pressed on. They held out hope for a victory in the courts, but they also knew that the Klansmen were out there, emboldened by the victory in the streets of Tuscaloosa. As they waited for a final resolution of the issue, the weary followers of Martin Luther King held fast to the only path that they knew: They stayed off the buses. Week after week through the cold winter months, then into the spring and finally through the broiling heat of the summer, they walked to work or turned to the car pools at the rate of twenty thousand people every day. But it was hard to imagine when the struggle would end.

Finally, in the hottest dog days of August, Rosa Parks decided it was time to get away. She made a pilgrimage again to the Highlander Folk School, the place in the rolling hills of Tennessee that had always been such an inspiration for her. She traveled this time with Bob and Jeannie Graetz, her neighbors and friends, who were quietly emerging in the minds of many blacks as the white people most supportive of the movement. The only others who might make that claim were Clifford Durr and his wife, Virginia. Clifford, a lawyer, had played an important role in the preparation of the lawsuit, and Virginia, the firebrand, reserved the right to speak her mind on any issue she thought was important. But Bob and Jeannie were there every day, driving people to work, doing what they could. Their phone often rang in the middle of the night, and over time they began to grow accustomed to the threats and the scattered acts of petty vandalism—like the time somebody poured sugar in the gas tank of their car.

On their trip to Highlander, they were impressed with the tranquil beauty of the place, and like Mrs. Parks, they were energized by their weeklong stay. They found themselves, after one particular meal, washing dishes with Benjamin Mays, the great black educator from Atlanta who had been a mentor to Martin Luther King. They found it humbling just to be in his presence, and yet at Highlander it seemed so easy, for that was the spirit created by the staff. They were deeply impressed by the founder Myles Horton, who had endured the harassment of the state of Tennessee, and by one of their teachers, Septima Clark, a gracious black woman whose humility and warmth had to remind them a little of Rosa Parks.

More and more as the days went by, they felt a sense of renewal and hope—not that they were ever given to despair. They were optimistic people by nature, and so far at least, their view of the issues in the bus boycott had been sustained by the courts. But the Supreme Court ruling had not yet come, and as the movement slogged its way through the summer, it was good to get away, to be with Mrs. Parks and a group of people who believed in the possibility of progress.

Suddenly, however, on a Saturday morning, they received a telephone call from a reporter, telling them that their home in Montgomery had been bombed. There was no report on the extent of the damage, but it was easy enough to anticipate the worst. They gathered in a circle with their friends from Highlander and sang a few verses of a Negro spiritual that was emerging already as an anthem of the movement: "We Shall Not Be Moved." Then they packed up quickly and in the company of Mrs. Parks started the long drive back to Montgomery.

They arrived to a mixture of horror and relief. There was a crater in the yard, where the dynamite had exploded, and there were broken windows and dishes in the house, but they could see immediately that it could have been worse. As they surveyed the damage, talking softly and wandering in a daze among the yellow police ropes, they noticed that a member of their group had disappeared.

"Where is Mrs. Parks?" said Graetz.

After a brief search, they found her in the kitchen, cleaning up the dishes that had broken in the blast. Graetz had to smile. That, he thought, was typical of Mrs. Parks, who had not announced her intentions or done anything to call attention to the gesture. She was simply a neighbor, trying to do what she could to be of help. He thought of the bonds they had forged since December, and he couldn't help but wonder when the whole thing would end—when this movement triggered by a good woman's courage would accomplish at least a part of what it should.

CHAPTER 4

The Price of Victory

For Graetz and the others, the answer finally came on November 13, 1956, which began, ironically, as a day of gloom for Martin Luther King. There was a hearing on a lawsuit filed by the city, challenging the legality of the car pool system, which had long been a critical ingredient in the boycott. Without it, black people couldn't get to work.

Fred Gray, among others, wondered why the city hadn't done it before. Officials had sanctioned every form of harassment, including arrests and charges against King, but the result most often was to stir the black community's indignation, and thus its resolve. This particular lawsuit was different. If Eugene Carter, a segregationist judge, ruled for the city—and everybody understood that he would—the boycott was doomed, at least until the order could be overturned.

As King was contemplating that possibility, the issue was suddenly rendered irrelevant. A TV reporter appeared at Carter's courtroom with a remarkable and unexpected piece of news. The U.S. Supreme Court had just upheld the three-judge panel, declaring that the segregation of the buses—like the segregation of schools—was unconstitutional.

The city immediately asked the court to reconsider, and the limbo lasted until December 20, when the issue, at last, was officially resolved. By a final order of the highest court in the land, the city buses of Montgomery would have to desegregate.

That same night, people by the thousands gathered at the Holt Street Baptist Church, and it was a scene reminiscent of the cold winter evening when the boycott began. For more than twelve months the people had sustained it, and now once again they were full of song, spilling out to the streets near the church and listening to the amplified voice of Dr. King: "When we go back to the buses," he said, "go back with dignity. Don't push your way. Just sit where there is an open seat. If someone pushes you, don't push back. The universe is on the side of justice."

The following morning they gathered at dawn—King, Rosa Parks, Ralph Abernathy, and a white man by the name of Glenn Smiley, a national advocate of nonviolent protest who had quietly emerged as an adviser to the movement. At 6 A.M., they boarded a bus and sat near the front.

"I believe," said the driver, "that you are Reverend King."

"Yes, I am."

"We are glad to have you this morning."

And with that it was settled, the first mass protest of the civil rights era. There had been some skirmishes in a few other places—Baton Rouge, Tuscaloosa, Mobile—but Montgomery was different. In later years, a few historians would minimize the accomplishment, pointing out that the only tangible achievement—the desegregation of the buses—was the result of a court case, not a movement of the masses. But Dr. King was convinced that the greatest victory in Montgomery was not the right to sit anywhere on the buses. It was a victory that happened in the psyche and the heart.

For the first time anybody could remember, an entire Negro community took a stand and, in the face of bombings and official harassment, remained united for more than a year. By anyone's standards, it was a historic display of tenacity and courage, a victory as sweet as anyone could have hoped, and people all over the South paid attention. Martin Luther

King made sure of that. During the course of the protest, he brought in other leaders from the region for consultation and nonviolent workshops. The Reverend Joseph Lowery came up from Mobile, and Theodore Jemison from Baton Rouge, and more intriguing than any of the others was Fred Shuttlesworth, who came from Birmingham.

Shuttlesworth and King had met in 1954, and though their personalities couldn't have been more different, they liked and respected each other from the start. King had come to Birmingham for a speech, and as Shuttlesworth remembers it, the people were "goo-goo eyed" about his Ph.D. Shuttlesworth was deliberately unimpressed. He was more of a self-made man, a scrapper, who had grown up hard outside of Birmingham, raised by his mother and his bootlegger stepfather in a house with no electricity or indoor plumbing.

During World War II he moved to Mobile and took a job as a truck driver at Brookley Field. It was a time of racial hostility at the base, so intense at one point that black and white soldiers found themselves in a two-hour shootout. Remarkably enough, nobody was killed, but more than thirty black soldiers were arrested, while the whites went free. Shuttlesworth was not surprised. He was already wise in the ways of the South, and by the time he met Martin Luther King he was a young man ready to take on the world.

He was the newly called pastor at the Bethel Baptist Church in Birmingham, a fiery pulpiteer, wiry and lean, almost skinny back in those days, as if he was simply too busy to eat. He talked about the issues important to his community, beginning with the "little things"—getting street lights, covering up ditches that were breeding grounds for disease, urging his people to get out and vote. In the vestibule of his church, he posted the names of those who were registered, giving them a place of visibility and honor.

Then one day, after he had been at the church a little more than a year, he saw a headline in a newspaper downtown, in front of the old federal building on Fifth Avenue: SUPREME COURT OUTLAWS SEGREGATION. "That did something to me," he said. It was May 17, 1954, and as he read the account of the decision in *Brown,* he felt a sense of possibility that had never been there before. He was disappointed later when the Supreme Court failed to enforce its decision, and year after year, southern school districts remained segregated. But flawed as it was, the ruling was a pivotal moment in his life. "It awakened me," he said. "That was God moving in the world."

He and King talked about all of that and took their measure of each other as men. Shuttlesworth was impressed by King's humility, his self-effacement, which seemed to be a ballast for his vision and eloquence. King, meanwhile, was equally impressed by Shuttlesworth's brashness. Later, he would say: "Fred, you always have a ready answer. I wish I could do that."

"That's my gift," Shuttlesworth replied. "We all have our gifts."

By the summer of 1956 Shuttlesworth had declared his personal war on segregation, and nothing was any more galling than the buses. It sometimes seemed as if everyone he knew had some kind of humiliating story. His secretary, Lola Hendricks, for example, remembered the time when she was sixteen, and she and her mother were on a Birmingham bus. There was a wooden sign with the words WHITE on one side and COLORED on the other, a kind of movable line of demarcation that the bus driver adjusted whenever the white people needed more seats. On this particular day, Lola and her mother were sitting near the sign. When the bus driver moved it, her mother got up to surrender her seat, but Lola did not.

"Get up, child," Addie Haynes commanded.

"Why do I have to?" Lola insisted.

"I'll tell you when we get off."

Lola moved to the back of the bus with her mother, and they rode along in silence for a while, reflecting on the evidence that Negroes were lesser people than whites. Their rights and feelings didn't matter as much, and if they engaged in any act of defiance, the consequences struck terror in their hearts. That certainly seemed to be the case with Lola's mother, who sank more deeply into herself, and still said nothing when they disembarked from the bus. Finally, Lola had to ask her again.

"Mama, why?"

"Because it's the law," replied Mrs. Haynes, and her voice sounded tired.

They didn't talk about it anymore, but Lola could never push the memory from her mind, and she was thrilled in the winter of 1956 when Shuttlesworth decided to integrate the buses. He had kept up with King and the Montgomery movement and on December 20, when the Supreme Court's ruling arrived in Montgomery, he thought it should apply to Birmingham as well. He warned the city fathers that on the morning after Christmas, he would ride the buses on an integrated basis.

On Christmas night he was lying in his bed, talking to a deacon, Charlie Robinson, who was sitting across the room. The conversation was casual, just a late-night visit between two friends, when a bomb exploded just beneath the bed. Shuttlesworth felt himself falling through the floor, and he knew immediately that this was not a warning. It was an attempt by the Ku Klux Klan to kill him. But he had the feeling, even as he fell, that he was somehow landing in the arms of God. Shuttlesworth was that kind of man, often earthy and vain, occasionally profane, but with a swashbuckling certainty that was rooted in his faith. As he sat up gingerly and climbed unhurt through the rubble of his house, he had no doubt about the reason he survived. "I understood it was God," he told one reporter. "If I had any fear, I lost it after that."

The following morning, he got up early and did what he promised. He led a nonviolent protest against the buses—a wary, but resolute group of demonstrators who paid their fares and sat in the areas still reserved for whites. Twenty-one Negroes were arrested, as the city of Birmingham served notice: The Supreme Court could order what it wanted, but in this particular part of Alabama the laws of segregation still applied.

Shuttlesworth knew then that it was going to be a long and frustrating struggle. The resistance came on so many levels—the Klan, the city officials, the police—and sometimes it was difficult to tell the difference. Even in Montgomery, where the buses now were officially integrated, the battle raged on. Aurelia Browder, the brave young woman whose name, alphabetically, was first on the lawsuit, began to grow accustomed to threats on her life. When one caller promised to dynamite her house, Mrs. Browder replied: "Blow it up. I need a new house anyway."

For Judge Richard Rives, who wrote the opinion of the three-judge panel, life was also more complicated—much more lonely than it had been in the past. He had always been a popular man, a respected leader in his Presbyterian church, but now when he took his place in the pew, people around him would get up and move. He never complained, but his shrinking circle of friends knew it hurt. Once on a visit to the grave of his son, the judge found the grave site littered with garbage.

Rives understood that it could have been worse. He knew there were snipers who fired on the buses, wounding one black woman in the legs, and already they had fired on the house of Dr. King—a shotgun blast on December 23 that left a hideous gash in his door. Then came the new year, 1957, and the bombs began exploding once again. Early on the morning of January 10, Ralph Abernathy got a call from his wife. He had traveled to Atlanta where he and King and a few other leaders were mapping out plans for a new organization, a civil rights group that would soon become known as the Southern Christian Leadership Conference. Abernathy was excited about the possibilities, and in his rush of anticipation he had left Juanita and the baby home alone. Now she had called to say that a bomb had exploded on the porch, just a few feet from the bedroom window, and she could only assume that divine intervention had protected her life and the life of her child. As the two of them talked, Abernathy berating himself for leaving home, Juanita heard another explosion, and saw a flash of light in the distance.

"What was that?" she gasped, clutching harder at the phone.

The policeman on her front porch overheard the question and looked at her coldly. "That would be your First Baptist Church," he said.

In that terrifying moment Juanita understood that the officer knew there would be other bombs—and knew, in fact, where they had been placed. Before it was over that night, there were six—four at black churches and two at the homes of civil rights leaders.

The other attack that could have been deadly came at the home of Bob and Jeannie Graetz. The explosion occurred at 2 A.M., a terrifying blast that shattered windows and blew in the door and left the roof sitting tilted on the frame. Bob rushed to the room where his children were sleeping and after confirming that nobody was hurt hurried through the wreckage that had once been his door. Outside, he stumbled over something in the driveway, an even bigger bomb that had not gone off—eleven sticks of dynamite and some TNT, rigged together with a handle so the terrorists could throw it. The policemen told him that if it had worked, it could easily have leveled the whole neighborhood.

"It was obviously intended to kill us," said Graetz, and for a moment he was deeply disappointed in God. He had prayed many times that the people of Montgomery would be spared such violence, but God, apparently, had ignored his plea. As the crime wave continued—Dr. King's home was bombed soon after—it was beginning to feel like guerilla warfare, with only one side doing all the shooting. "Somebody may have to die," said King, and all of them knew it was only a matter of time.

But in this embryonic moment in the life of the movement, that was not their only reason for concern. At least as disturbing in the eyes of black leaders were their enemies who stayed within the letter of the law.

John Patterson never intended to be a politician. He was simply a young and ambitious lawyer who decided to go into practice with his father. Everybody knew he was bright. He entered World War II as a private and came out a major, and after graduating from law school at the University of Alabama, he returned to the town of Phenix City and went to work in the family law firm. "I wanted to make money," he said, "have time to travel. Politics was the furthest thing from my mind."

But his father, Albert Patterson, was drawn to that arena, a fact that mildly irritated John, for he thought it interfered with their practice. Still, he admired his father's ambition, ennobled as it was by a sense of public service. The Pattersons were an old, aristocratic family, having farmed successfully for more than a century in the rolling hills of Tallapoosa County, cattle country in the eastern part of the state. During the Depression, they moved to Phenix City, a military town on the Georgia line where the local economy seemed to be more stable. Albert put out a shingle and did well enough in the practice of law, but as the years went by he began to worry about the drift of the town. By the 1950s Phenix City was a rollicking place, "a kind of poor man's Las Vegas," as the Pattersons put it, full of gambling, prostitution, and organized crime. Albert Patterson set out to clean it up. In 1954 he ran for attorney general of the state, promising to make life harder on the criminals, who took him at his word.

Seventeen days after the election, which Patterson won, he was murdered in the alley behind his law office, a gangland shooting that made him a martyr to the cause of law and order. The Democratic Party turned quickly to his son. They urged him to run for the now vacant office, and in his rage and his grief, John Patterson agreed. Nobody dared run against him, of course, given the martyrdom of his father, and the state of Alabama suddenly had a new star—a handsome, charismatic crusader, who pursued his father's killers to the end, and drove the mob from the town of Phenix City. He was quick to say he didn't do it alone, but in the rush of acclaim that followed his victory, his own ambitions began to come into focus. He saw that he had a chance to be governor.

Already, he knew there was another issue more important than crime, or at least more volatile in the minds of white voters. It was not an issue he had thought much about. His father was a moderate on the subject of race, a man who treated black people with respect and insisted that the members of his family do the same. "Growing up," said John, "I never heard a derogatory remark. That was not tolerated in my family." But now they were living in a whole different time—the Supreme Court rulings, the bus boycott, the specter of integration at the University of Alabama . . . all these things had stirred the passions of white Alabamians, and the politicians had to make their adjustments. For the next several years, John Patterson was on the cutting edge of that change.

Early in his tenure as attorney general, he met with some of his counterparts in the South—political leaders from Mississippi, Georgia, Tennessee, and Alabama, who gathered in secret at a Birmingham law office to discuss the legal future of segregation. They decided there was none. The drift of the courts was now unmistakable, and these leaders from the South, all of them learned in the ways of the law, concluded with reluctance that the Constitution was the enemy of segregation, at least in the case of public institutions.

"The consensus of the group," Patterson later explained, "was that we could never win this fight. But we wanted to delay the inevitable as long as we could—to buy time for the public to adjust without violence. I sort of followed that policy the rest of my time."

Though it later became a source of regret, he did it with enthusiasm and resolve, understanding clearly that it was good for his career. If he could establish himself as the state's great champion of racial segregation, he could ride the resulting wave of popularity all the way to the governor's mansion and beyond.

He started with the NAACP, an organization regarded with fear and loathing by a growing majority of white Alabamians. As Patterson remembers it, he was talking to the attorney general of Virginia, an innovative man named Lindsey Almond, who would soon become governor. Almond became a valued confidante, and during the course of one of their discussions he said to Patterson, "It's highly possible that the NAACP has never qualified to do business under the statutes of Alabama." He remembered a case of Ku Klux Klan and the state of New York, a strategic prece-dent delicious in its irony, in which a branch of the Klan was driven out of business for failing to register as an out-of-state corporation. Patterson did some checking and discovered that Almond's guess had been correct. The NAACP had not yet registered as a "foreign corporation," which was technically what the state of Alabama required. Patterson seized that tiny opportunity, attacking the technicality with a vengeance. He filed suit in the court of Judge Walter B. Jones, and insisted as a part of the discovery process that the NAACP produce its records, including a detailed list of its members. Patterson maintained his intentions were benign—simply to demonstrate that the NAACP was doing business in the state. But the black leaders feared a more sinister intent. They were deeply concerned that black Alabamians who were members of the group would be singled out for harassment or worse. So the NAACP held back, refusing to divulge its membership list, and Judge Jones—a segregationist at least as ardent as Patterson—held the organization in contempt, and levied a fine of $100,000.

The NAACP appealed and won, but it took eight years, and during that time, as Patterson put it, "We did effectively run them out of busi-ness."

By the end of 1956 he was clearly on a roll, creating a new identity for himself as a fearless crusader against the forces of darkness—against organized crime in the town of Phenix City, and just as dramatically, against the most powerful civil rights group in the country, which was try-ing to impose its agenda on the South. Flush with victory, he turned his attention to the city of Tuskegee, which was hallowed ground to many black Alabamians. It was there that the legendary Booker T. Washington, president of Tuskegee Institute, had worked out his theories on the advancement of the race. In the years just after the turn of the century, with the forces of white supremacy on the rise, Washington argued that the most critical and realistic goal for black people was to get an educa-tion, then pursue a course of economic independence. He won a measure of favor with whites, turning his back, at least for a time, on the possibil-ity of integration and political power.

By the 1940s a new generation had emerged in Tuskegee—a strong and confident group of leaders who believed they had taken Booker Washington's advice. They had, in fact, educated themselves, many of them at Tuskegee Institute, and now they were ready to take the next step. Having prepared themselves fully for the rights and responsibilities of citizenship, they set out on a quest for political equality. Charles Gomillion was one of their leaders—an outspoken sociologist, born and raised in South Carolina, a slender, well-dressed man with high cheekbones and closely cropped hair—the very portrait, some people said, of a black intellectual.

"He was the epitome of what I wanted to be," remembered Charles Hamilton, a young sociologist in the 1950s, who came to Tuskegee because of Gomillion. "He had all the virtues—civility, intelligence—and he was a scholar." But Hamilton also detected, and others did too, a simmering rage somewhere at his core, as if Gomillion regarded segregation as some kind of deeply personal affront. He chafed at the racist condescension all around him—that pervasive assumption among many whites that they were inherently superior to people who were black. For an educated man like Charles Gomillion, it was an insult that cut all the way to his heart.

And yet as far as Hamilton could tell, Gomillion had no interest in revenge. That was the truly remarkable thing. He understood that blacks were a majority in the city of Tuskegee and in the wooded farmlands of the county just beyond. But his goal was an interracial democracy, not a black oligarchy that ruled like the whites. He urged black people to register and vote, and he battled the resistance of white registrars, who had one standard for blacks and another for whites, and often managed to be away from their desks when the black citizens came to fill out the forms.

As the 1940s drew to a close, only a smattering of blacks had been able to register, but that was about to change. In December 1949 Gomillion wrote a letter to Gov. Jim Folsom, declaring simply that "all law-abiding citizens . . . have the right, and should have the opportunity, to participate in self- government." Gomillion may not have known it at the time, but it was the perfect approach to take with the governor, a populist who believed in the wisdom of the people. Folsom was a character, a kind of raw-boned Jacksonian Democrat, and more amazingly, in the words of one journalist who knew him at the time, "a closet integrationist." He once compared die-hard segregationists to a group of "hound dogs baying at the moon," and when Gomillion told him of the plight of black voters, Folsom decided to do something about it.

He called an old friend, a Macon County farmer by the name of Herman Bentley, a tall, thin, weather-beaten man who worked his own land without the help of sharecroppers or tenants. One day in 1946 Bentley was startled when Big Jim Folsom, who was running for governor, appeared at his hog pen while the farmer was up to his knees in the muck. Folsom, a giant of a man at six-feet-eight, asked for his vote, then took off his shoes and helped clean the pen. Bentley never forgot it, and when Folsom called in 1949 and asked him to serve as a registrar for Macon County, Bentley agreed.

In a two-year period, he registered more than five hundred black voters, which was enough to change the balance of power in the county. Gomillion and the other black leaders were astonished. They had never met a man like this particular farmer—a fearless, plain-spoken, backcountry Methodist who had taken his Sunday school lessons to heart. The Bible made it clear that people were people, and black or white, they were the children of God and therefore the brothers and sisters of one another. "I know I'm right," he once told his son, "because of the way I was raised."

Not everyone saw it that way, of course, and chief among Herman Bentley's opponents was a state legislator named Sam Engelhardt, a farmer, merchant, and cotton gin owner with a curious, multilayered reputation. On the one hand, he was a genial man with a wry sense of humor, a wealthy landowner regarded as fair by the black men and women who worked on his place. But even by the standards of the 1950s, he was one of the most racist politicians in the state. "If you have a nigger tax assessor," he asked one reporter, "what would he do?" That seemed to be one of Engelhardt's worries—the pocketbook implications of losing his grip on political power, and he knew it could happen. By the middle of the decade, there were more than a thousand black voters in the county, and in the city of Tuskegee, they represented 40 percent of the electorate.

From Engelhardt's perspective, the situation was getting worse every year, and in the summer of 1957 he pushed through a bill in the state legislature with a startlingly simple solution to the problem. He removed virtually every black voter from the town. Under Engelhardt's prodding, the legislature redrew the boundaries of the city, intricately excluding the black neighborhoods and transforming Tuskegee from a perfect square into a metropolis that now had twenty-eight sides. For the legislators who flinched, Engelhardt responded with a barrage of white supremacist rhetoric, and in the polarized climate of 1957 the legislators quickly fell into line.

Charles Gomillion could hardly believe it. For more than a decade, he and the members of his organization, the Tuskegee Civic Association (TCA), had been so patient—persistent, yes, in their pursuit of the vote, but civil and dignified and understanding. Now they could see that sterner measures were required. Inspired by the recent success in Montgomery, they decided to try a boycott of their own, a selective buying campaign aimed at the Tuskegee merchants who supported the gerrymander of the city. Gomillion called for a meeting of the masses, and on June 25, 1957, it was a scene reminiscent of the Holt Street Baptist Church, as more than three thousand people gathered at the Butler AME Zion Chapel.

Dressed conservatively in a light-colored suit, Gomillion leaned against the lectern and told the people who were cheering in the pews: "We appealed to the citizens of Alabama not to stand by and allow this injustice to be perpetrated against a people who have sought to live honorably and industriously within the law. Our voices have been as the voices crying in the wilderness."

But now they were not going to take it anymore. Now they would find a way to hit back. "We are going to buy our goods and services," he declared, "from those who help us, from those who make no effort to hinder us, from those who recognize us as first-class citizens. Soon the time will come when they will have to respect us. They may hate our guts, but they will respect us."

Within a few days, John Patterson, the attorney general of Alabama, came to Tuskegee and raided the offices of the TCA, seizing the tape recordings of its meetings. Privately, he had a high opinion of Gomillion, but now was not the time to let it show. Patterson was waging his own guerilla war—a legal crusade in defense of segregation, which was a cause he knew from the beginning he would lose. But in the delicate and complicated psyche of the South, winning or losing wasn't always the point. There was heroism simply in the fight, and Patterson was ready to be a hero. Somewhere he could still hear the whisper of his father, that all men ought to be treated with respect, but he was caught up now in the mood of the voters. *You can be for segregation or you can be a martyr.* That was the way he put it to himself, and Patterson did not want to be a martyr. He wanted to be governor.

In the approaching election of 1958, his most formidable opponent was a young circuit judge by the name of George Wallace, who had an interesting reputation on the issue of race. Black attorneys who practiced in his court were almost always impressed by his courtesy. The civil rights lawyer J. L. Chestnut called Wallace "the most liberal judge I had ever practiced in front of. He was the first judge in Alabama to call me 'Mister' in his courtroom."

Wallace was a longtime supporter of Jim Folsom, and several years earlier, he had asked the governor to appoint him to the board of Tuskegee Institute, where by all accounts he served with distinction. Later, when he was running for governor himself, he stared at the camera during one of his ads, his dark eyes softer than they would seem later on, and he declared with an evident sense of conviction: "I want to tell the good people of this state . . . if I didn't have what it took to treat a man fair regardless of the color of his skin, then I don't have what it takes to be the governor of your great state."

John Patterson made no such pronouncements. Somewhere in his heart, he may have agreed, but in the governor's race of 1958, he was careful not to say so. Instead, he talked about segregation, promising never to compromise on the issue. "Once you let the bar down," he proclaimed, "it's all over." There were no qualifications, no words to soften or moderate his stand, and to the chagrin of the majority of black Alabamians, Patterson won overwhelmingly.

Such was the prevailing mood in the state, and it was Patterson, not Wallace, who could feel it in his bones. There was, however, more to his victory than a cynical calculation, a Faustian compromise with his conscience. Patterson also managed to believe he was right. There was a powerful mythology still at work in the South, a way of thinking and looking at the world that had its roots in the days just before the Civil War. Patterson could hear the echoes of those times—the South under siege, as it had been so often through the bitter years of war, and then through the era of Reconstruction and beyond. Now it was the courts and the NAACP—and the black boycotters in Montgomery and Tuskegee—who stirred those resentments going back into time, and there was something righteous about digging in his heels. Patterson knew it was a feeling that was sweeping through the state, intertwining itself with a fear of change and the prevailing assumptions of white superiority.

It was a powerful tonic to many white Alabamians. There were people who were willing to die for those beliefs, and even more certainly, as the coming years would make clear, there were also people who were willing to kill.

PART TWO

THE BELLY OF THE BEAST

CHAPTER 5

A Ten Dollar Fine

THE CIVIL RIGHTS MOVEMENT LIMPED along for a while. Charles Gomillion and his followers in Tuskegee filed a federal lawsuit to go along with their boycott, and they eventually won, restoring Tuskegee to its original boundaries. Martin Luther King moved back to Atlanta and started a new organization called the Southern Christian Leadership Conference. And over in Birmingham, Fred Shuttlesworth was attacking segregation on every front he could find. But the movement was looking for some kind of spark, another symbol perhaps with the power of Rosa Parks to generate a new wave of energy. The passion was difficult to contrive, and even the eloquence of Martin Luther King, as he toured the country and preached in pulpits all over the world, seemed to have no effect. He could stir the crowds who turned out to hear him, but in the larger sense, as the 1950s drew to a close, what the movement lacked was a feeling of momentum.

There *was* one thing, one tiny pebble that was tossed in the pond, and the ripples were slowly, almost invisibly, beginning to spread. It happened on a cold December night, just before Christmas in 1958. Bruce Boynton, a young law student, was starting to feel homesick, missing his family back in Selma, Alabama. He was a man of great promise, tall and gangly back in those days, barely twenty-one, as he came to the final year in his studies. He had graduated from high school at the age of fourteen, and Fisk University only four years later, and he was now enrolled at Howard University, the most prestigious black law school in the country. The people who knew him expected nothing less. He came from a family of achievers, including his parents, Sam and Amelia, the most courageous civil rights advocates in Selma.

Going back all the way to the 1930s the Boyntons were the original voting rights activists, which, in the majority black counties of central Alabama, was the most radical stand a black person could take. The political power enjoyed by whites was dependent, of course, on the disenfranchisement of the masses of blacks. The Boyntons were determined to resist that pattern, which was a maddening challenge in Dallas County, Alabama. As Mrs. Boynton remembers it, when she registered to vote in 1932, two white people had to vouch for her character, and if she wanted to vote in the Democratic primary—an essential decision in a one-party state—she had to swallow her pride. The symbol of the party was a strutting rooster with a ribbon on its chest, stenciled with the words WHITE SUPREMACY FOR THE RIGHT.

Despite the obstacles, the Boyntons persevered, sustained in part by the story of the family. Their oldest ancestor in the United States was a master carpenter by the name of Bart Hicks, a free black man who had never been a slave. He was born in Ghana and came to America from Liverpool, England, bringing his white indentured servant with him. They settled near Beaufort, South Carolina, and often for the public consumption of their neighbors, they pretended to reverse the master-servant roles—a resourceful charade that seemed to be good for the carpentry business.

A generation later, Amelia's great-uncle, Robert Smalls, emerged dramatically as a Civil War hero. On May 12, 1862, he commandeered a Confederate steamer and turned it over to the Union. As the darkness settled on the Charleston harbor, the white sailors on the *Planter* decided to go ashore for a party, leaving a skeletal crew of black seamen. Like the others, Smalls, the wheelman, had been impressed into service by the Confederate navy, and suddenly he saw the opportunity to escape. For some time now, he and the others had talked in whispers about what they would do—how they would depend on Smalls, who knew the channels, to get them past the guns of Fort Sumter and out to the point of the Union blockade. They knew the dangers they would face at every turn—first from the Confederates, and then from the Union armada also, as a Southern warship steamed from the harbor. But as the Confederate cannons fired on the *Planter*, the Union commanders could see what was happening and accepted the defection of the ship and its crew.

After the war, Robert Smalls took his place in the rough and tumble of Reconstruction politics, first running successfully for the South Carolina legislature, and then in 1875 for the first of five terms in the U.S. Congress. He amassed a record of distinction through the years, but he was also a man caught squarely in the middle of the greatest heartbreak his people ever faced. Certainly, it felt that way at the time, as the nineteenth century drew to a close, and the Democratic Party, in collusion with the Klan, took up the cause of white supremacy and power. As the night riders burned and looted and killed, Democratic leaders in eight southern states pushed for constitutional conventions, which adopted new and intricate provisions designed to strip black people of the vote. In the Alabama constitution of 1901, the primary instrument of disenfranchisement was the U.S. Constitution itself. Prospective voters now had to read, write, or interpret any provision the registrars required—and the registrars were the only judge of their success. The unspoken promise of the Democratic Party was that the registrars would be harder on the blacks.

Robert Smalls saw all this coming. He was a part of the generation of African Americans who lived through the final days of slavery and expected in the moment of emancipation to take their place as full citizens of the country. But the promise was abruptly snatched from their grasp, and Smalls spoke out against that cruelty with all the indignation he could muster. As he saw his own power beginning to fade, he damned with equal fervor the "rifle squads" of the Ku Klux Klan, who set out to intimidate black voters, and the white politicians who did it through the law.

"We do not intend to go anywhere," he warned, "but will remain right here."

Bruce Boynton knew all this about his family, and it came to him naturally to take his own stand. Many times in the 1950s, on the train trips home from Howard University or visits with family members in the North, he had refused to sit in the segregated cars. Then came December 1958. "I was feeling homesick," he remembers, facing a January of law school exams, when he decided he needed a little time with his family. At 8 P.M. on December 18, he boarded a Trailways bus in Washington, D.C., bound eventually for Selma, Alabama. Between 10 and 11, the bus made a stop in Richmond, a scheduled break of forty-five minutes in which the passengers were urged to get something to eat.

Boynton entered the Trailways terminal, and what he saw was "a clinically clean white restaurant and an absolutely filthy black cafe. I was really insulted that someone would expect me to eat in the black restaurant in that kind of condition. I went over and sat in the white restaurant. Even though I didn't expect to be served, I expected something like, 'It's not me. It's the law.' But the white waitress called the manager who put his finger in my face and said, 'Nigger, move.' That crystalized what I was going to do. I did not move."

Boynton said later he felt no fear. He thought for a moment about Rosa Parks and her example of courage on a Montgomery bus, but he thought even more about the members of his family—those still living and those whose stories he knew from the past. "I made the stand I thought my family would expect," he said. "I had internalized all this as a part of who I was."

After a few minutes, the policemen came and took him away, and he spent the weekend in the Richmond jail, studying quietly for his law school exams. On Monday morning, he was taken to the city's Police Justice Court, where he was convicted of misdemeanor trespass and fined ten dollars. He understood that it could have been worse. Under provisions of the Virginia trespass statute, he could have been fined ten times that amount and sentenced to thirty days in jail. Nevertheless, he decided to appeal.

Over the next two years, the case made its way from the state courts of Virginia to the U.S. Supreme Court in Washington, where the justices finally ruled in his favor. The opinion was written by Hugo Black, the former U.S. senator from Alabama, who, deep in his past, had once been a member of the Ku Klux Klan but was now emerging as a liberal on race. Black concluded that the federal Interstate Commerce Act prohibited racial discrimination, not only on buses, trains, and other methods of interstate transportation but also in the terminal facilities, including restaurants, that were "an integral part" of a bus company's service.

It was an argument that Boynton, the law student, had made all along, but one rejected by his Supreme Court attorney, Thurgood Marshall, the director-counsel for the NAACP Legal Defense Fund. Marshall, a gruff and aggressive lawyer who was determined to change the legal face of civil rights, argued for a broader interpretation from the court. He contended that Boynton's arrest in Virginia was a violation not only of the commerce statute, but of the U.S. Constitution itself—especially the Fourteenth Amendment. Marshall's agenda went beyond Bruce Boynton. By the time of the Supreme Court hearing on October 12, 1960, the nation had lived through nine months of sit-ins—direct action protests, mostly by students, at lunch counters scattered throughout the South. If it was *unconstitutional* to arrest Bruce Boynton, and not simply a matter of interstate commerce, it was unconstitutional to arrest the demonstrators as well.

Whatever their personal sympathies might have been, Hugo Black and the members of the court were not quite ready to go that far. Interstate commerce was one thing, an area long subject to federal regulation. But a ruling that would eradicate segregation in virtually every restaurant in the South represented new and uncertain ground. Justice Black and his colleagues were determined for the moment to be more cautious.

Ironically enough, there was no way to know when their ruling was released on December 5 that they were about to trigger a volatile wave of civil rights protests—by anybody's standards, the most dangerous confrontation since Montgomery.

The Freedom Rides sounded simple enough, an integrated bus trip through the South to test the decision in *Boynton vs. Virginia.* John Lewis, a young ministerial student from Alabama, knew from the start that he wanted to be a part of it.

Lewis came from the wiregrass country, a swatch of scrubby farmland tucked away in the southeastern corner of the state. As he came of age in the 1950s, Pike County, Alabama, was a flat and lonesome stretch of peanut fields and stands of pine and kudzu climbing up the sides of old barns, abandoned by people who had left for something better. John was the third of ten children born to Eddie and Willie Mae Lewis. From the very beginning, everybody knew he was different from the rest. He didn't much like hard labor in the fields, particularly not at cotton-picking time, when his fingers turned raw and his muscles were burning at the end of the day. He preferred instead to spend time in the barnyard, looking after the animals, dreaming of the day when he would be a preacher.

"I fell in love with raising chickens," he remembers. "It gave me a sense of caring for living things. When my mother or father wanted to kill one, or sell it, I would protest. I think it was my first nonviolent protest. I grew up with the idea of becoming a minister, and I would practice my sermons on the chickens. When a chicken would die, we would have a chicken funeral."

It wasn't long before a small boy's fancy began to turn more serious. One Sunday morning in 1955, when he was nearly fifteen, he turned on the radio and listened to a sermon coming out of Montgomery. There on station WRMA was the most mesmerizing voice he had ever heard—a rich baritone, rising and falling in that old, familiar style of black preachers. What was different this time was the message—not a promise of rewards in the life everlasting but a call to action right there in Alabama. The minister that morning was Martin Luther King, who would soon become the leader of a great crusade, and John Lewis wanted to be a part of it.

Soon after that, he went down to the library in the small town of Troy and asked the librarian to give him a card. He already knew she would turn him down, for the Pike County Library served only whites. The librarian was polite as he had expected, but she told him simply that the rules were the rules.

Lewis went back to the three-room house he shared with his family—a homey cabin with high wooden ceilings, a rambling porch, and a pecan tree offering its shade outside. He had felt safe there, nurtured by the gentle example of his parents, but he was starting to see that the world outside was not the kind of place he thought it should be. Determined to do his part to make it better, he drafted a petition against the Pike County Library, reminding the various officials who ran it that black people paid their taxes also. Most of his friends were afraid to sign, for they had all heard the stories of Emmett Till, a fourteen-year-old resident of Chicago, murdered in Mississippi in 1955, his body mutilated, merely for the offense of speaking to a white woman.

Lewis was impatient with that kind of thinking. He thought it was time to put aside the fear and the crippling power it had held for so long, and he knew the petition, mild as it was, would not be his final gesture of defiance.

For all those reasons, John Lewis was ready when he went off to college, when he boarded a Greyhound bus in Alabama and headed north to Nashville, Tennessee. His destination was American Baptist Theological Seminary, an unimposing little school on a hill overlooking the Cumberland River. Many years later, there were those who argued that there was not a college anywhere more important to the movement—not Howard University with its venerated law school, not even Morehouse, which would gain its share of international renown as the alma mater of Martin Luther King. For Lewis and others at the Nashville seminary, American Baptist would quietly emerge as the cradle of the southern civil rights movement.

One of the reasons was Kelly Miller Smith, a homiletics professor and a minister at Nashville's First Baptist Church. Smith was a tall and handsome man, full of courtesy and warmth, and as the students at American Baptist quickly learned, a radical understanding of the meaning of his faith. In the fall of 1957, when John Lewis first arrived at the college, Nashville was in the midst of an integration crisis. Nine black students, all first-graders, had broken the color barrier in the all-white schools, and one of the nine was Kelly Smith's daughter. On her first day of class, Joy Smith held tight to her father's hand as they walked past a crowd of hecklers on the corner, and in the next several days the mood of the city turned darker by the hour. One elementary school was bombed, and there were threats periodically on Kelly Smith's life. But he was worried most of all about his daughter.

One night in his study, he was peering out the window with a white Baptist friend, a Mississippi preacher by the name of Will Campbell who had dropped by for a while to help keep watch. After a period of silence Campbell turned and asked the question he couldn't quite suppress:

"Kelly, what if something happens to little Joy?"

As Campbell remembers it, Smith opened his Bible and began to read the story of Abraham and Isaac—how God had demanded the sacrifice of a son, and Abraham had been prepared to obey. But there in the thicket, a ram was caught by the horns, and God in the end had decided to relent, allowing instead the sacrifice of the ram. "Lord," said Smith, quietly closing up his Bible, "make the thicket tight, and the ram's horns long. Amen."

As the weeks went by at American Baptist, John Lewis was in awe of Kelly Miller Smith—not only for his eloquence, which was apparent in his sermons and his lectures in class, but also his deep understanding of the faith. Christianity, said Smith, was full of "hard sayings," sweeping demands about justice, brotherhood, and forgiveness that the conscientious Christian was obliged to obey, regardless of the cost.

Lewis listened carefully, absorbing it all, and as the months went by a curious realization began to dawn on him. His admiration was not a one-way street. Kelly Smith was impressed with the quality of the students at the little seminary, and Lewis was always one of his favorites. He was country to the bone, shy and awkward, with a slight speech impediment, but he was intelligent and serious and respected by his peers, even those more worldly like Bernard Lafayette. Smith watched carefully as that friendship developed, for on the surface it didn't seem likely. Lafayette was everything Lewis was not. He was quick and confident, with a touch of charisma and a touch of the clown—a carpenter's son who came out of Florida with a well-developed academic background.

He arrived at American in 1958, a year after Lewis, and became another of Smith's protégés. On his father's side, Lafayette's family came from the islands—cigar makers, part Cuban, part French. They were regarded as smart and resourceful people, and Bernard himself seemed to have those genes. As a small boy in Tampa he worked at his grandmother's boarding house, taking care of the business when the old woman fell ill and nursing her gradually back to health with the help, he said, of "pot likker and cornbread."

At American Baptist, he found himself immediately in the company of equals. In addition to Lewis, there was C. T. Vivian, a theology student a little bit older who came to Tennessee from Illinois, having already taken his stand for civil rights. In the 1940s in the city of Peoria, Vivian and a group of white friends protested segregation at the local lunch counter—an early act in what would become a lifelong commitment to the cause of nonviolence. In the 1950s, when he was almost thirty, he decided to enter the Baptist seminary after a religious conversion that took him by surprise. He was working in a mail order house, when it suddenly seemed as if the sky opened up and he could hear the voices coming out of heaven. He looked around, dumbfounded to discover that everybody else was going about their business, as if they hadn't noticed a thing. It was a moment when he knew, or started to believe, that his life was a part of some larger purpose.

"It was not an accident that all of us showed up at the same seminary," Vivian said years later. He was impressed by the wisdom of Kelly Miller Smith, the palpable integrity of John Lewis, and the wit and intelligence of Bernard Lafayette. He also knew that as the oldest student, he was able to add his own special fire. He was not a man who suffered fools gladly, and he was particularly impatient with the white segregationists and the insufferable arrogance at the heart of their position.

As Vivian understood it, the whole became larger than the sum of its parts when the American students and some of their elders began attending workshops on the theory of nonviolence. It was Kelly Smith's idea, and the first meeting was held in the basement of his church, led by a man they came to regard as the most remarkable leader in the city. He was a Methodist minister by the name of James Lawson, a young Ohioan who had spent a year in prison for refusing to serve in the Korean War. After his release, he went to India as a Methodist missionary and was there at the time of the Montgomery bus boycott. Reading about it in the city of Nagpur, he remembered the prediction of Mohandas Gandhi that perhaps one day a black man from America would push the cause of nonviolence even further, achieving a level of success that had eluded even the Mahatma himself.

Lawson believed that Martin Luther King might be that man, that embodiment of prophecy, and he told King so when they met in February 1957. Lawson had returned by then to the United States and was working on his masters at Oberlin College in Ohio. When King came to speak, the two of them talked, and their mutual admiration was immediate. Lawson found King surprisingly modest, given the soaring dimensions of his fame, a man who took his cause quite seriously but himself less so. King, meanwhile, saw Lawson as a peer, perhaps even a potential mentor for himself, and certainly for the people who would take up the cause and seek to bring down the walls of segregation. He urged Lawson to move to the South at once and to impart his knowledge—his deep understanding of the philosophy of nonviolence, nurtured in India and steeled by his time in a federal penitentiary.

Lawson agreed and settled in Nashville, a segregated city more moderate perhaps than those in Alabama or Mississippi, but nonetheless a perfect training ground for a group of young people who would one day venture into the belly of the beast. As Lawson ran his workshops in 1959, he knew that Lewis, Lafayette, and Vivian—and others also, like Diane Nash, a pretty coed from Fisk University, and James Bevel, one of the latecomers from American Baptist—all had what it took.

They met every Tuesday and studied nonviolence as a new way of life. They talked about Gandhi, Niebuhr, and Thoreau, about redemptive suffering and the ability to forgive, and John Lewis seemed to understand it right away. "Suffering," he wrote, "puts us and those around us in touch with our consciences. . . . It makes us feel compassion where we need to and guilt if we must." As a matter of theory, Bernard Lafayette understood it also, but when the workshops began to get more specific he knew he was facing a personal test. They began to learn about protecting their bodies—how to curl on the ground to shield their internal organs from the blows, and how they needed to remember, even in the moment of a vicious attack, that this was a fellow human being they were facing.

Lafayette wasn't quite sure he could do it. He was confident enough in his physical courage, for he had spent some time as a boy in Philadelphia, where he ran with the gangs, and learned to intimidate and to fight. But now he was facing a much tougher challenge, for nonviolence in the way that James Lawson understood it was more than a tactic, more than a strategy for confronting segregation.

"We were talking about a whole new relationship," Lafayette remembered, "about winning our opponents over as our friends. We would provide the example of how to behave. But when the time really came to turn the other cheek, I wanted to know if I could do that. Could I turn the other cheek *on the inside?* Could I actually feel love for somebody who was abusing me? Those were the questions that I had to face."

The moment of truth came in February 1960. The students in Nashville had been planning for the day when they would march as a group to the lunch counters uptown and take their seats on the white people's stools. In the meetings with Lawson, they had rehearsed the scenario again and again, talking about how they would dress and what they would say and how they would treat their opponents with respect. They knew they were ready and were eager to begin when they suddenly learned they had been upstaged. On February 1 four college freshmen in the city of Greensboro, North Carolina, acting without any training at all, staged the first sit-in of the 1960s civil rights era. It was a moment so filled with purity and drama that the movement quickly spread to other cities in the South.

Down in Montgomery a group of students from Alabama State College headed for the cafeteria at the capitol. It was a segregated restaurant of the most public kind, and the three dozen students who assembled politely and asked to be served were simply trying to make that point. In many ways, their protest was milder than those in other places. When service was denied, they rose as a group and returned to the campus. But almost as soon as they walked out the door Gov. John Patterson sent for the president of Alabama State, Councill Trenholm, and demanded that he expel the students from his school.

"The citizens of this state," the governor declared, "do not intend to spend their tax money to educate law violators and race agitators, and if you do not put a stop to it, you might well find yourself out of public funds."

President Trenholm's response was sad and to the point. "I have no choice," he said, "but to comply."

On Friday night, more than four thousand Negroes, many of them students from Alabama State, met at the Hutchinson Street Baptist Church. They cheered the words of Martin Luther King, the featured speaker of the evening, but just as dramatically they also cheered for Bernard Lee, the student spokesman at the cafeteria sit-in. The following Tuesday, more than half the student body from Alabama State marched on the capitol, where Lee made another speech and the students sang the "Star-Spangled Banner" before marching peacefully back to the campus. The next day, the State Board of Education expelled Lee from the school.

A few miles away in the town of Tuskegee, there were similar marches and a similar price. Charles Hamilton, a sociology professor who had been a protégé of Charles Gomillion, led a demonstration of several hundred students in support of the sit-ins. In his short time at Tuskegee, Hamilton had grown restless with what he regarded as the plodding style of Gomillion—the maddening patience he seemed to display in his stead-fast battle against segregation. Hamilton was looking for something more dramatic, and he was delighted as the sit-ins spread throughout the South, engaging the imagination of the students. Gomillion, however, was an old school leader, not happy about professors marching in the streets. The following April he decided as head of the social science department not to renew Charles Hamilton's contract.

It was, in a sense, one of the first generational rifts in the movement, made more painful by the fact that Hamilton had always admired Gomillion and, on a certain level, would continue to admire him for the rest of his life. They were fully in agreement about the evil of racism, but Gomillion was wary of the street demonstrations and the increasing volatility of the times. Hamilton thought they were long overdue. He was deeply impressed with the protesters' bearing, that surprising combination of dignity and militance that was present from the start.

As Hamilton knew from everything he had read, the combination was particularly apparent in Nashville, the spiritual center of the sit-in move-ment, where the demonstrations were larger, more effective, and more sustained than they had been in most other cities in the South. The Nashville protests started on a Saturday, February 13—more than a hun-dred students marching through the snow from Kelly Smith's church, the men in suits, the women wearing heels, walking in silence, two abreast, to the lunch counters downtown. Many years later John Lewis would remember the startled words of one white waitress. "Oh my God, here's the niggers," she said. He thought at the time that she didn't seem hostile, just bewildered and a little bit afraid. He said he couldn't help feeling sorry for her.

They targeted three lunch counters that day and kept on coming in the weeks after that—hundreds at a time, disciplined, polite, but always relentless—and gradually the city became more tense. Roving bands of white teenagers began showing up at the student demonstrations, push-ing, taunting, stubbing lit cigarettes into protesters' backs. The violence escalated over time, and the injuries to demonstrators became more seri-ous. It was about this time that James Bevel and John Lewis were sitting in at a Krystal, a little hamburger stand, where the manager, as usual, refused to serve them. He locked the door and turned out the lights, and as Lewis and Bevel waited at the counter, he slipped out the back, turning on a fumigator as he left. The room quickly filled with a poisonous gas, and Lewis and Bevel realized they were trapped. They covered their mouths and pounded in desperation on the door, and Lewis thought for a moment they would die, until some firemen arrived and finally broke through the glass.

Given the level of danger, Kelly Miller Smith and some of the adults decided it was time for a cooling-off period. They called a meeting to explain their position, and Lewis listened quietly to what they were saying, nodding at the clarity and rationality of their points. But he told them softly when they asked his opinion, "We're gonna march."

Smith and the others argued some more, but Lewis merely kept repeating his mantra: "We're gonna march."

Will Campbell, the white Southern Baptist who supported the movement, decided finally that he had heard enough. "John," he said with a bit of an edge, "you keep agreeing with everything everyone is saying, but all you say is, 'We're gonna march.' You know there is apt to be violence, and still you say, 'We're gonna march.' What it comes down to is hubris. What it comes down to is pride. This is about your stubbornness and sin."

There was a startled silence in the face of Campbell's candor, but Lewis only smiled and answered as softly as he had answered every time. "Okay, Will, I'm a sinner. But we're still gonna march."

When he thought about it later, Campbell realized he had been wrong. John Lewis was not simply stubborn or proud, though there was, of course, a touch of those things. He was a young man certain of what he must do—a farmer's son from rural Alabama, still a little raw and awkward at times, but a man more committed than any of his elders to the nonviolent calling they were claiming to embrace. Lewis was saying that his mission was to march. There were others in the world who would do what they had to. They might throw rocks or beat him with clubs or scream racial slurs at the top of their lungs. But his calling was to march and he would continue to do it until the day when justice rolled down like the waters, and violence was never going to turn him around.

It came as no surprise, therefore, when the word reached Campbell that Lewis had decided to join the Freedom Rides. It was a mission more dangerous than any they had seen, a bus ride back to the heart of the

South—to cities like Birmingham and Montgomery, the places that inevitably made them afraid.

In the spring of 1961 Lewis believed this was where they must go, to test the victory Bruce Boynton had achieved, and to serve notice to the nation that there were no safe havens for segregation anymore.

Battle-hardened from a year's worth of sit-ins, he was ready for an escalation of the stakes.

CHAPTER 6

The Burning of the Bus

THERE WERE TIMES ON THE CAMPUS of American Baptist, often late at night, when Lewis and Lafayette talked about the fear. They agreed it was something to be overcome, just as they sang it in the civil rights anthem. "We Shall Overcome" . . . the fear, the doubt, the feeling that nothing was ever going to change. Bernard would laugh sometimes about one of the sit-ins at the Campus Grill, a little greasy spoon diner across the street from Vanderbilt. There was a crowd of young toughs who had gathered to heckle, and one of them screamed in a moment of scorn: "I bet you wouldn't do this in Mississippi."

You got that right, Bernard thought to himself, or Alabama either. But he knew, in fact, that one day soon they would have to go to the deepest, most dangerous regions in the South, and even before the official Freedom Rides, he and John had staged a ride of their own. They were going home for the holidays in 1960, just after the *Boynton* decision in December, and they decided they would abide by the law. The Supreme

Court had been clear in banning segregation in interstate travel, and as they boarded the bus at the Nashville station, Bernard and John took their seats near the front. The driver was furious, particularly with Bernard who was sitting just behind him, and the tension mounted as the bus headed south through the hills of Tennessee.

It became even worse at the Alabama line, for it was nighttime now, and the land was a shadowy, rolling silhouette, empty and vast, and it was easy to see how a man could disappear. At every stop at a small-town station, they imagined the worst—a posse of Klansmen waiting in the dark—particularly when the driver would disembark from the bus and disappear through the doors of the terminal. This was different from the sit-ins, which had been so intricate in their organization, so carefully planned. Now it was just the two of them alone, and they knew this time if they were pulled from the bus, there was no backup. Their friends in the movement wouldn't know where to find them.

The worst moment came near the town of Troy, just a few miles from the Lewis family farm. John left the bus and waved to Bernard from the shoulder of the road, and Bernard thought how small and vulnerable his best friend appeared, standing there in the Alabama darkness. He also felt a new fear for himself, for it was a long way from Troy to the gulf coast of Florida where his own family lived, and he would be making the rest of that journey by himself. It occurred to him then, as it had many times, that fear had become a constant in the South, one of the central realities in the lives of black people, and perhaps as much as anything else it was the issue at the heart of the civil rights movement. They were working for the day when they wouldn't be afraid.

Both of them knew it was certain to be a long and difficult road that would lead them straight through the heartland of terror. But they were young and determined and eager to get started, and after they survived their holiday adventure, they were ready to embark on the real Freedom Ride. Early in 1961 they had seen the flyer from the Congress of Racial Equality (CORE), the sponsor of the ride, a small but committed civil rights group with roots going back to the 1940s. For Bernard Lafayette, there was only one problem. Because of the obvious dangers of the protest, CORE required every rider under the age of twenty-one to produce a letter of consent from his parents, and Lafayette's parents had refused to sign.

His father, Bernard Sr., was a wiry little man, a Florida carpenter who had a gift for working with his hands. All his life he had been a good provider, a devoted parent who had grown fatalistic about his son's involvement in the civil rights movement. "I always told the wife," he remembered, "'his life is in danger. He can get killed for this.' But it was something I had no control over. We had to put him in the hands of the Lord." Then came the Freedom Rides and CORE's requirement for a letter of permission, and for Bernard Sr. it was simply too much. "I felt like it was a death warrant," he said. "This was my son—the only one we had at the time." He refused to sign, exercising a final moment of control over a son determined to make his own way.

For Bernard Jr. it was a bitter disappointment, but there was nothing he could do except wish his friend, John Lewis, the best. Lewis was disappointed also, for it would have been easier in the company of Bernard. But when he arrived in Washington at the end of April he was immediately taken with this odd mix of people. There were thirteen freedom riders in all, including a half dozen whites—pacifists mostly, like Albert Bigelow, a navy captain in World War II who had developed a loathing for the idea of war. Lewis liked Bigelow right away—this strapping white man who looked like a New England whaler from the nineteenth century—and he was also drawn to young Hank Thomas, who had grown up poor and black in the South and was now a student at Howard University.

On May 3, 1961, the day before the trip, they gathered for dinner at a Chinese restaurant, the first time Lewis had ever tasted such food. The mood on the surface was jovial enough. Somebody said this could be their Last Supper, and for many in the group the gallows humor was a mask against the danger that lay just ahead. The following morning, they headed for the station, where six of them boarded a Greyhound bus and the rest of them went to the Trailways counter. Lewis took his seat next to Bigelow, and gazed out the window at the Virginia countryside.

The first several stops were essentially uneventful. They made it through Virginia and North Carolina with nothing more than a few cold stares and an arrest in Charlotte. Then came Rock Hill, South Carolina, a town with racial tensions on the rise. There had been some arrests at a local sit-in, and as the Greyhound bus pulled into the station, the requisite crowd of young toughs was at the door. They looked like all the others, Lewis thought, with their duck-tailed haircuts and cigarettes dangling from the corners of their mouths, and he knew this time there would probably be trouble.

"Other side, nigger," one of them growled, as Lewis headed for the white waiting room. Lewis said he didn't feel any fear, didn't even feel nervous as he looked the young white men in the eye and told them he had a right to be there. He cited the precedent of the *Boynton* decision, and he could tell from their blank and menacing stares that he could have been speaking Greek. "Shit on that," a white boy said, and they began to hit him, first on the side of the head and then the face. When he crumpled to the ground, they kicked him in the ribs until Albert Bigelow stepped in between. Lewis could see it was disconcerting at first, this burly white man now middle-aged who still looked fit enough to take them all. The boys hesitated until they realized Bigelow wasn't hitting back, and then they attacked him, along with Genevieve Hughes, another freedom rider who rushed to the fray.

Finally, a policeman moved in to stop them, and almost as quickly as it started it was over. Lewis was bleeding profusely from the mouth, and he had a feeling they hadn't seen the worst. There were reports of trouble waiting down in Alabama, particularly in Anniston, a hill country town just across the Georgia line. For Lewis this represented a dilemma. Sometime earlier he had applied for an overseas assignment with the American Friends Service Committee, a Quaker organization with projects in Africa. As a sharecropper's son from rural Alabama, he was excited about seeing the motherland, but when a telegram was waiting for him in Rock Hill, inviting him to come for an interview with the Friends, Lewis felt torn. He didn't want to leave the other freedom riders, especially at a moment of escalating danger, but they told him to go. He could rejoin the ride when the interview was over.

The others, meanwhile, headed west to Atlanta, their final overnight stop before Alabama. They gathered for dinner with Martin Luther King, a festive occasion at least on the surface, but King was worried about the safety of the group. After a round of toasts, he leaned over and whispered to Simeon Booker, a black reporter who was traveling with the riders, "You'll never make it through Alabama." Booker tried at first to laugh it off, but he understood it was not an idle warning, and he was far more nervous than he wanted to admit. He had a feeling King was probably right.

Down in Montgomery, Gov. John Patterson was worried also, for the race question now was more than the fodder for his campaign speeches. It was a painful reality they all had to face. He had known all along, he said years later, that they would have to give ground on the issue of segregation, and in that regard he was happy to have John Kennedy in the White House. They had met each other in Birmingham when Patterson was still the attorney general, and Kennedy was an aspiring presidential candidate. They had talked a little about organized crime and the gangland murder of Patterson's father, and Patterson became the first southern governor to endorse Kennedy for president.

The two men liked each other right away. Patterson saw in the Massachusetts senator some of the same qualities he aspired to himself. Kennedy was bright and personable and sure of himself, a man who was able to look you in the eye. He was also a Catholic, which was hard to swallow in certain parts of Alabama, but Patterson understood that it shouldn't really matter. He campaigned for Kennedy in West Virginia and Wisconsin, and helped raise money, and the two of them would visit on occasion in Washington. Patterson knew all along, for it was clear in the things that Kennedy had said, that the new young president was sympathetic to civil rights. To one degree or another, he was almost certain to pursue the changes that Patterson resisted, but Patterson had chosen to support him anyway. Change was coming; that much was clear, and it didn't hurt at all to have a friend in the White House—a man who might be able to see that the whole thing was delicate. "I figured," said Patterson, "that if he had to put his foot on us, it would be lightly."

All this was a part of the governor's strategy—to give ground slowly on the issue of civil rights, choosing the battlefields when he could, while he worked for his own more progressive agenda, including a push for better public schools. Then came the Freedom Rides. This was precisely what he didn't want to see, a public provocation by a group of demonstrators coming from the North, inflaming the passions of the people of Alabama in a way that was almost certain to explode. Things would begin to get messy at this point. The issue would become much harder to control.

Patterson was already worried about the Klan, which was active in Anniston, and was an organization he knew very well. In the election of 1958 he had been endorsed by the faction of the Klan in Tuscaloosa, and when George Wallace tried to make an issue of it, Patterson refused to renounce their support. "I just by God wouldn't do it," he said. Privately, however, he was ambivalent about the Klan and its message of hate, for it all ran counter to the way he was raised. As a boy growing up in Talla- poosa County, he was forbidden to utter a racial epithet, much less be a party to an act of racial violence, but in May 1961, intimations of vio- lence were clearly in the air.

In the heat of the moment, Patterson was inclined to blame the free- dom riders—a group of disgruntled people who he thought should have taken their grievance to the courts, a forum where they had a good chance of winning, but who had chosen instead to take it to the streets. His frus- tration bordered on the edge of fury when he thought about the provoca- tion of the riders and the effect it would have on the people of his state.

It had to be deliberate, he declared many times, the work of "agitators" and "fools," and in fact he was right about the premeditation. It was one of the tenets of the civil rights movement, particularly the activist wing that emerged in the sit-ins, that nonviolent demonstrations would bring the evil of segregation to the surface, for it was there, and only there, that good and decent people could address it. Patterson had never seen it that way, and wouldn't until many years after the fact, for he was caught in a different set of assumptions. He simply knew that a dangerous situation lay ahead, and it would not be good for the state of Alabama.

As the riders were getting ready to leave Atlanta, Patterson's director of public safety, Floyd Mann, sent an undercover officer, E. L. Cowling, to ride along on the bus. Patterson and Mann wanted at least to know what was happening, to keep an eye on this unpredictable group of demonstra- tors and be ready for the worst. They had no way of knowing that their decision would save the freedom riders' lives.

On Mother's Day, May 14, the Greyhound bus pulled into Anniston, arriving on Highway 78. There was a subtle beauty to the countryside there, the rolling hills of the southern Appalachians descending slowly toward the Talladega National Forest, but the scene at the Greyhound sta- tion was ugly. There was a crowd of maybe two hundred people, armed with bats and bricks and pipes, and Hank Thomas, the youngest of the riders, who had faked a permission letter from his mother in order to be included on the trip, thought he was going to die. He had never seen such fury in a mob as they surged toward the bus and tried to force their way inside. E. L. Cowling rushed to the front and braced himself against the lever of the door, keeping the attackers momentarily at bay. Screaming with rage, they turned their assault on the Greyhound itself, beating on the sides, smashing windows, slashing at the tires.

The bus driver tried to pull away from the station, but an armada of Klansmen gave chase down the highway, until the wounded bus finally gave up the ghost. The tires went flat, and as the Greyhound lurched to a stop on the road, the freedom riders once again were surrounded. Somebody threw a firebomb through one of the broken windows in the back, and the bus filled with smoke, acrid, toxic, impossible to breathe. Now the attackers, who had tried to break in, began blocking the door, doing their best to keep the riders inside. It was then that E. L. Cowling drew his gun, and the mob pulled back just enough for the passengers to stumble down the steps, gasping for air.

Then the beatings began, as the attackers knocked Hank Thomas to the ground, their fury tempered only slightly by the presence of Officer Cowling and his gun. Reinforcements soon arrived in the form of Alabama State Troopers, who fired some warning shots in the air, and the freedom riders, bloody and choking, were carried away to the Anniston hospital.

About an hour later, the Trailways bus, the second of the two, pulled into the station, greeted this time by an eerie quiet. With the mob still waiting out on the highway, a group of tough-looking men, flanked by police, boarded the bus and ordered "the niggers" to ride in the back. When one of the freedom riders explained that, under the *Boynton* decision and the well-established laws of interstate commerce, they had a right to sit where they wanted, the white men attacked. Their rage fell hardest on the white freedom riders, including Jim Peck, a member of CORE, and Walter Bergman, a sixty-year-old professor from Michigan. One blow from a fist sent Peck reeling, blood streaming from his face, and Bergman was beaten unconscious on the floor. Two black riders, Charles Person and Herbert Harris, were dragged summarily to the back of the bus, and with that the driver restarted the engine, and headed off down the back roads to Birmingham.

Another mob was waiting for them there, and the riders were filled with resignation and dread. Person and Peck stepped first through the door and into the crowd near the white waiting room. The beatings began once again in earnest, first with fists and then with bicycle chains and clubs. There were no policemen anywhere in sight.

"The riders were being dragged from the bus into the station," remembered television reporter Howard K. Smith, who was there on assignment for CBS. "In a corridor I entered they were being beaten with bicycle chains and blackjacks and steel knucks. When they fell they were kicked mercilessly, the scrotum being the favored target, and pounded with baseball bats. One man made his way to the waiting room still vertical, but his head was a red mass of blood. Another was on all fours and could not get up."

Simeon Booker, the black reporter who was traveling on the bus, somehow made his way through the chaos and flagged down a taxi. He gave the driver the address for the only safe haven any of them knew, Fred Shuttlesworth's house, and one by one over the next several hours other freedom riders made their way there as well. The police had finally moved in at the station, having kept their part of a bargain with the Klan—fifteen minutes to do with the freedom riders as they pleased.

Shuttlesworth grimly surveyed the damage, the broken teeth and swollen faces of the black and white demonstrators at his house. He called an ambulance for Jim Peck, who seemed to be the most seriously injured, and then the telephone rang. It was a call from the freedom riders in Anniston, the survivors of the burning Greyhound bus who had been taken away to the hospital there. They reported that the mob was outside the building, still hungry for blood, and the hospital authorities had ordered them to leave.

Shuttlesworth called the bravest men he knew and sent them to Anniston on a rescue mission. One of the leaders was Colonel Stone Johnson, a union organizer and toughened expatriate of the railroad yards, who had demonstrated his bravery under fire. Ever since the Christmas night bombing of Shuttlesworth's house, Johnson was part of a brotherhood called "the ushers," the ironic name for a group of armed guards who kept watch every night at Shuttlesworth's church and other potential targets of the Klan. Most, like Johnson, were union men—John Hulett, Will Hall—and they would circulate among the Birmingham churches and the homes of leaders in the civil rights movement.

On a summer afternoon in 1958—Johnson remembers it as broad

daylight—he had been pulling guard duty at Bethel Baptist, just as Shuttlesworth was finishing his sermon. His friend Will Hall was there also, and as they glanced up the street they were astonished to discover that J. B. Stoner was walking toward the church. Stoner was a Birmingham lawyer of sorts, known around the city as a white supremacist who believed in violence. Hall confronted him and asked what he wanted, and Stoner insisted with an ironic smile that he wanted Reverend Shuttlesworth to pray for him. Hall and Johnson weren't sure what to do with this pinch-faced man who walked with a limp, but they were certain enough that he was up to no good. They ordered him to leave, and Stoner, still smiling, departed in a cab.

Barely one week later, they were guarding the church, sitting on the porch of a house across the street. It was 1:30 A.M. when Laverne Revis, a young woman who lived nearby, came home from working the late-night shift and reported seeing smoke at the side of the church. Johnson and Hall were skeptical at first. They had been there all evening and had seen nothing wrong, but they rushed to the spot and discovered ten sticks of dynamite in a bucket, attached to a smoldering, half-spent fuse. They grabbed the bucket and ran toward a ditch at the edge of the road. With the fuse nearly gone, they dropped the bomb and were backing away, when the dynamite exploded, slinging shrapnel everywhere. At the time they were less than ten yards away, maybe closer to five, but miraculously they escaped unhurt.

These were the kind of men Fred Shuttlesworth admired, a mirror of the toughness he aspired to himself. He was happy to entrust to Colonel Stone Johnson the mission of mercy to the freedom riders trapped at the Anniston hospital.

They went armed that day, for it was one of the realities of the civil rights movement that however nonviolent it may have been at its heart, there was always a current of "any means necessary," as the black power advocates would say later on. Shuttlesworth's secretary, Lola Hendricks, remembers the anxiety she felt at the time when her husband, Joe, headed off down the highway with a group of black men armed to the teeth, facing a certain confrontation with the Klan.

According to Colonel Johnson, they made the sixty-mile drive in less than an hour, and the marauding Klansmen were taken by surprise. "We walked right between those Ku Klux," he said. "Some of them had clubs.

There were some deputies too. You couldn't tell the deputies from the Ku Klux."

They gathered up the terrified freedom riders, and the convoy immediately rushed back to Birmingham, where the riders were taken to places of safety. Two of them came to stay with Lola Hendricks, who washed their clothes and sent them to bed. "They were white," she remembers. "I never did get their names. They were upset, terrified. They had no idea what was going to happen to them."

Up in Washington, D.C., John Seigenthaler was following the story, and he already knew how bad it had been. There was a photo of the burning Greyhound bus that ran in newspapers all across the country. Seigenthaler worked for the Justice Department; he was a southerner from Nashville who had become a close friend of Robert Kennedy, the new attorney general of the United States. He knew the Kennedys were struggling with the issue of civil rights. From the start their hearts were in the right place, but there were other items at the top of their agenda, and an event as volatile as the Freedom Rides made the race question that much harder to manage. Many years later, Seigenthaler recounted an early conversation between Robert Kennedy and Martin Luther King—a meeting, he said, between two young men with brilliant minds and a totally different understanding of the world. The attorney general, at the time, was a pragmatic man, chilly in the calculations he made about the political self-interests of his brother, the president. He urged Dr. King as the leader of a movement to turn his attentions from street demonstrations to voter registration—a realm, he said, in which the federal government could be of more help.

Seigenthaler remembers the conversation as "warm, friendly, almost affectionate," a meeting in which Robert Kennedy and King each made a favorable impression on the other. King was a listener; that much was clear. He was quiet and attentive as Kennedy made his pitch—how the Justice Department could take the struggle for voting rights to the courts, and how the public overwhelmingly would support that effort. Seigenthaler knew what Kennedy was thinking. If they could register thousands of black voters in the South, it would be, without question, the right thing to do, and could bring about a revolutionary change. It would also be of benefit to the president, for many of the new voters would vote Democratic. In the meantime, they could lower the decibel level of protest and ease the political strain on the country.

Clearly, King understood that logic, and he agreed that voter registration was important. But there in his meeting with the new administration, speaking without any shrillness at all, he made it clear that the demonstrations would continue. "I just have to tell you," he said, "it is my need to confront the corruption of segregation wherever I can." He said he understood that in many southern states, the FBI had close connections to the local police, which often had close connections to the Klan. Nevertheless, he said, "I'd like you to protect us when you can."

With that it was over, one of the first attempts by the Kennedy administration to position itself with the civil rights movement. Seigenthaler thought it had gone pretty well. Kennedy, the pragmatist, and Martin Luther King, "the absolute idealist," seemed to understand what the ground rules were, how they were caught up together in this delicate moment in the history of the country, but how their interests inevitably were not quite the same. They accepted this reality with courtesy and grace, but the Freedom Rides brought the tension to the surface.

After the burning of the bus, Kennedy sent Seigenthaler to Alabama. He came to Birmingham as the riders, embattled and depressed, were trying desperately to find a way out. Their plan initially was to go by bus, but John Patterson was refusing to guarantee their safety, and the Greyhound drivers were refusing to drive any bus they were on. Lacking any choice, they waited at the station while Shuttlesworth talked on the phone to Robert Kennedy, and Kennedy to Patterson. The Birmingham police, whose antipathy was clear, offered only the most tenuous protection against a mob as angry as the one the day before.

They decided then that it was time to give it up. They would fly out of Birmingham to New Orleans, and put this terrible adventure behind them. That was still the plan when Seigenthaler arrived in the city, only to find them stranded once again. Bomb threats had grounded the Delta flight, and the riders were huddled in a corner of the airport, stricken with fear. Another mob had gathered outside, and Seigenthaler could see that time was running out.

"I went to see the people at Delta," he remembered, "and told them,

'This is what we want to do. Look through the baggage, make sure there is no bomb, and then don't take any more phone calls until the plane is in the air.'"

The airline officials did as they were told, and Seigenthaler flew on the plane to New Orleans, where the shell-shocked activists were met by a group of supporters and friends. There were a few hecklers in the crowd also, including some in the ranks of the police, but for the first time since they had arrived in Alabama, the freedom riders were safe.

Seigenthaler went to his motel room, thinking to himself, "Well done, young man," but at 2 A.M. his telephone rang, and Robert Kennedy was on the other end.

"John," he said, "this is not over. Do you know a woman named Diane Nash?"

The attorney general went on to explain that Nash, a veteran of the Nashville sit-ins, had made the decision with some of her friends to continue the Freedom Rides from where they had stopped. Despite the terrible dangers they would face, Nash was sending out a new group of riders to catch a bus from Birmingham to Montgomery and then to Mississippi. If the immediate past was any indication, violence was certain and killings were possible, and for the Kennedy administration in Washington, this was tantamount to disaster. All it needed this early in its life was the perception of chaos, a feeling that the country was coming apart at the seams.

Talk her out of it, Robert Kennedy had said, but Seigenthaler was not optimistic. He knew enough about Diane Nash to believe she would not be easy to dissuade. As a reporter in Nashville in 1960, his job before he went into politics, Seigenthaler was fascinated by the sit-ins. Late at night when the *Nashville Tennessean* went to bed, the reporters would gather in the cluttered newsroom— Seigenthaler, David Halberstam, and others— and they would marvel at the story that was taking shape around them. Despite their toughness and objectivity, they had developed an affection for the people they were covering. John Lewis, even then, was a man of such courage that some people talked about him as a saint. Bernard Lafayette and C. T. Vivian were some of the brightest people they had known, and there was nobody more impressive than Diane Nash.

They remembered the time when she confronted the mayor on the steps of city hall. She was gentle and sure as she looked him in the eyes and demanded to know, as the reporters took notes, if he would use the power and prestige of his office to end the segregation of the lunch counters.

"I appeal to all citizens," responded Mayor Ben West, "to end discrimination, to have no bigotry, no bias, no hatred."

It was a nice enough statement as far as it went, but Diane Nash continued to push. "Then, Mayor, do you recommend that lunch counters be desegregated? Do you?"

The mayor hesitated for a moment, caught by the certainty and force of her question, and then answered with a word that would make headlines in the morning newspaper and launch his city on a whole different course. "Yes," he said, and just like that the first major battle of the sit-ins was won.

Seigenthaler knew the story well enough, knew that Diane Nash had been a hero, but he was deeply frustrated when he called her on the phone and demanded this time that she listen to reason. The country couldn't stand another Freedom Ride.

"Mr. Seigenthaler," she replied, "you are a good man, but we are not going to be moved. This has to end. We will not let violence overcome nonviolence."

For Seigenthaler, the irony of the moment came slowly into focus—how people like himself and the Kennedys, who moved so comfortably in the corridors of power, were caught in the limitations of what they could do. It was the new generation of civil rights leaders, some of whom were barely in their twenties, who were setting the political agenda for the country.

CHAPTER 7

The Message

DIANE NASH DID NOT MAKE the decision by herself. On John Lewis's return from Philadelphia, where he met with the American Friends Service Committee, he stopped in Nashville to visit briefly with his friends from the sit-ins. From there, he planned to drive down to Birmingham to rejoin the Freedom Rides for the trip to Montgomery. His plan was interrupted by the disturbing news that the ride had been abandoned—a decision he saw as a tragic mistake. He could understand the trauma that the riders had experienced, and perhaps they needed another group that was fresh. But to abandon the protest—to admit defeat at the hands of the Ku Klux Klan and their thuggish allies in the ranks of the police—would send the wrong message to the forces of violence. They would understand quite correctly that with enough brutality, they could stop the civil rights movement in its tracks.

That simply wouldn't do, John Lewis believed, and as he and Nash announced their intention to take up the banner, they grew impatient with the warnings that came from every side. Even Fred Shuttlesworth had cautioned them at first, asking whether they really understood that they might be sending demonstrators to their deaths. Of course they understood. That was why they had made out their wills, writing letters to their loved ones before they set out on the road to Birmingham. But in the end their deaths wouldn't make any difference, for if they were killed there were others who would come to take their places, and if they died too, there would be still more. Such was the militancy engendered by the sit-ins.

They were members now of a new organization, the Student Non-violent Coordinating Committee, or SNCC, established in April 1960 at Shaw University in North Carolina. There were institutional jurisdictions to consider, for if the Freedom Rides became a SNCC operation, they would need at least the tacit endorsement of CORE, the original sponsor. The Nashville students called James Farmer, CORE's national director, and asked for his blessing. Farmer gave it, though he was deeply worried about the fate of the group as they set out from Nashville early on the morning of May 17.

John Lewis thought there was poetry in the timing. Seven years earlier on precisely this date, the U.S. Supreme Court had issued its landmark ruling in *Brown,* a moment in history that gave hope to black people throughout the South. Lewis understood, without any sense of his own self-importance, that they were making more history with what they were doing, but he also knew it would come at a price. During the difficult meetings leading up to their departure, he had seen the fear on the face of Kelly Miller Smith, the gentle and eloquent mentor for the group— not a fear for himself, but a feeling of dread for these bright and committed young people, whom he had come to regard almost as his children.

There was, in fact, plenty of reason to be afraid. Late at night just before they left, Bernard Lafayette had walked the campus of American Baptist, strolling past the cluster of buildings near the river, trying to decide what to say to his parents. He wouldn't need their permission this time, no letter of acquiescence in his choice, for this was a decision he would make on his own. In the end, he concluded, it came down to this: At the age of twenty, was he ready to die for the civil rights movement? It was not an overstatement to put it that way, given the level of danger just ahead, and for Bernard the answer did not come easily. But he could see the determination in John, and the courage of Diane, and this was, he decided, the moment he had known in his heart he would face. There was really nothing to do but push ahead.

The plan was to send twenty riders to Birmingham, one group by bus, another by train, and to meet up there with Fred Shuttlesworth. Diane was chosen to stay behind in Nashville, where she would act as coordinator of the effort. Knowing that their telephone lines were tapped, they had worked out a code, and she and Shuttlesworth talked periodically, not about the people he would meet at the station, but about shipments of chickens. "Rhode Island Reds" was the code for white women, while other breeds stood for black women, and still others for the men. It was crude, but momentarily effective, and on May 17, a Wednesday morning, the first "shipment" left the station at 6:30.

The night before, they had written a check for nine hundred dollars to pay for the tickets, but they discovered, according to Bernard Lafayette, that it was too late to cash it. Finally, they tracked down a numbers man, a black racketeer in the Nashville ghetto, and somehow persuaded him to put up the cash.

Those who were riding the Greyhound bus—a group of ten that included John Lewis—were the first to depart. They had agreed in advance that as a matter of strategy they would try not to call any attention to themselves until they were safely in the company of Fred Shuttlesworth. Immediately, however, that plan went awry. One of the white riders, a brave young man by the name of Jim Zwerg, a transfer student at Fisk University, took his seat with Paul Brooks, a black freedom rider, near the front of the bus. To Zwerg and Brooks, segregation was offensive wherever it occurred, and they refused to make any compromise at all, even at the risk of blowing their cover.

The problem was, Bull Connor was waiting. Connor was Birmingham's commissioner of public safety, first elected in 1937 and reelected overwhelmingly to his sixth term in office less than two weeks before the Freedom Rides. Already, he was a legendary figure in the city, a stocky, florid-faced man with dark-rimmed glasses and a swagger in his step, a former minor league baseball announcer who made no secret of his deep and personal hatred of integration. He once told a reporter in a famous malaprop that as long as he was commissioner of police, "The niggers and white folks ain't gon' segregate together in this town."

Alerted to the presence of suspicious bus riders, his police were ready at the Birmingham city line, where they flagged down the bus and stared hard for a moment at Paul Brooks and Jim Zwerg. "Y'all have got to be Freedom Riders," one officer said. They escorted the bus to the Greyhound station, and as the predictable crowd began to gather outside, they taped newspaper over the windows and held the freedom riders on board. As the spokesman for the group, John Lewis asked why. They were ticketed passengers like everyone else, scheduled to continue that day to Montgomery. Lewis was polite as he presented the case, doing his best to humanize the enemy, which was the principle Jim Lawson had taught them, and sometimes it worked. This time, however, a policeman jabbed him roughly in the stomach, using a nightstick to force him to his seat.

For nearly three hours, they waited on the bus with the crowd outside getting louder all the time, until the police finally ordered them into the station. They sang freedom songs and waited some more, and despite the tension that all of them felt, Lewis thought things were going pretty well. There had been no violence, and in less than an hour their next bus was scheduled to leave for Montgomery. But about that time Bull Connor appeared, and announced that they were all under arrest. "For your own protection," he said with a smile. He took them away to the Birmingham jail, where once again the young demonstrators burst into song. Music had long been a cornerstone for them, an acceptable way to rally their resolve, and it had been that way in every phase of the movement.

All the way back to the bus boycott, when the people came together at the Holt Street church, they had rocked the rafters with an old-fashioned hymn—"What a Fellowship, What a Joy Divine"—which contained just a hint of revolution in the words. That was often the case with some of the old songs, and one of the things they learned in the movement was how the music had become intertwined with a history of protest. There was a young folk singer named Guy Carawan who knew that history as well as anyone. At the Highlander Folk School, he taught a whole generation of activists a repertoire of songs that evolved through the labor movement of the 1930s—"We Shall Not Be Moved," "Keep Your Eyes on the Prize"—most of them up-tempo anthems that raised the adrenaline level in the crowd.

Then in 1960, at one particular demonstration in Nashville, Carawan showed up with his guitar, and his choice of songs was a little bit different, quieter this time, as he strummed out the chords and sang along gently in his backcountry voice. He tinkered just a little with the lyrics of a standard, an old church song called "I'll Overcome Someday." Carawan changed the pronoun to "we," and gave the movement another new weapon to chase away the fear.

The music took root among the students of Nashville, and when they carried their protest south to Alabama, the freedom songs became a part of their defiance. They sang all night in the Birmingham jail, and part of the next day too, and later John Seigenthaler was convinced that it was one of the reasons for Bull Connor's sudden appearance at the jail. It was after midnight on Friday morning when the commissioner himself informed the freedom riders that they were going home. He led seven of them out into the Birmingham night, all but Brooks and Zwerg and a young white woman named Selyn McCollum, who had been released already to the custody of her father. Three black station wagons were waiting, all unmarked, and the freedom riders were shoved inside.

Lewis found himself in a car that was driven by Connor, who said he was taking them back to Nashville. Lewis had his doubts, for there was a lot of highway between them and Tennessee, and a lot of bad things could happen on the way. John Seigenthaler knew that was true. He had gotten a call from the FBI, telling him that the freedom riders had disappeared, and for a moment he panicked. He had met Bull Connor, having tried and failed to get the riders released, and he thought the commissioner was capable of anything. Connor, he remembered, had called him "boy" and laughed in his face, telling him finally through an ironic smile: "Yeah, boy, we got those niggers over here. They're an interesting group."

"He was just condescending and mean as hell," Seigenthaler said. "And then I got the call from the FBI. I go crazy. I call Robert Kennedy and tell him, 'Jesus Christ, Bull has kidnapped them. He's going to kill them.'"

In fact, at the start, the ride up Highway 31 was going so smoothly it was nearly surreal. Connor had fallen into pleasant conversation with Katherine Burks, a young black woman respected for her poise. They talked about breakfast, for the freedom riders had been on a hunger strike since their arrest on Wednesday, and hadn't had a full meal since the night before that. "You ought to eat with us," Katherine Burks declared. "You ought to get to know us better."

"Well, you know," said Bull, "I might just do that."

Connor, however, never made it to Nashville. Some time around three or four in the morning, with the land still dark, he pulled to a stop at the Tennessee line. Actually, they were just on the Alabama side in the town of Ardmore, a sleepy-looking place that was even more so at this particular hour. There were some railroad tracks that ran through the town, and Connor announced this was where they were getting out. "You can take the train home from here," he said, "or maybe a bus."

As Connor and the other policemen drove away, the freedom riders huddled together in the dark, trying to get their bearings and decide what to do. This was Klan country; that much they knew, and every shadow seemed to carry the possibility of an ambush. They needed to find some place that was safe, but in a community like Ardmore where would it be? The cluster of houses near the place they were standing all appeared to be owned by whites, just a little too prosperous looking to take a chance. So they started up the tracks and walked for a mile, as John Lewis remembers it, talking only in whispers. The night was dark, oppressive almost, not a light anywhere to show them the way, and they were sure that the Klansmen were out there somewhere—sure that Bull Connor had told them he was coming. People disappeared in a place like this and were never heard from again, and Lewis thought they were running out of time.

Finally, they came to a three-room cabin, a little shotgun shack standing off by itself. This, they thought, had to be the home of somebody black. They walked up quietly and knocked on the door, and after a few minutes an old man appeared, looking frightened and confused. "We're freedom riders," John Lewis said. "We're in trouble. Will you help us?"

At first, the old man told them no. "I'm sorry," he said, but after a moment they heard a woman's voice just behind him.

"Honey," she said, "let them in."

Once inside, the freedom riders tried to get some sleep. A couple of them lay down across the bed, the rest on the floor, and just after sunrise the old man left to get them some food. He was careful to go to two or three different stores so that the size of his purchase wouldn't attract much attention, and he returned to the cabin with an armload of groceries—baloney, cheese, some white bread, and milk. Later in his life, it was a source of painful regret for John Lewis that he never even asked the old couple's name. He was a prisoner of the moment, caught in the hunger, exhaustion, and fear—and in his activists' resolve to get back to Birmingham. Later, when he thought about it, of course, he saw the man and the woman as heroes—people who were willing to risk their lives to save a group of young people in trouble. Did they do it for the movement? Or was it a simple act of human kindness? Lewis never knew, but one thing was clear. Without the courage of this elderly couple, the freedom riders might well have died.

Back in Nashville, Diane Nash heard the telephone ring. She had set up a twenty-four-hour headquarters with one phone line that anyone could use—the media, the Justice Department—whoever needed to be in touch. But there was a second number that was secret, given only to the freedom riders in the field, and that was the phone that was ringing this time. Diane guessed it was 2 A.M., but it might have been later, when she heard the voice of John Lewis on the line. He told her what had happened, and said that despite their harrowing experience, they wanted to return to Birmingham when they could.

Another group of riders was already there, having made it by train, so Nash sent a car for Lewis and the others. The driver was a veteran of the sit-in movement, a young Nashvillian named Leo Lillard, who was happy to be chosen for this particular assignment. He made the ninety-mile drive in less than an hour, and the seven freedom riders piled into his car, heading south again on Highway 31. There were already radio reports that they were coming, and fearing detection again by police, they huddled together on the floor of the car. Finally, they made it to Shuttlesworth's house, and the two groups of riders—those in a contingent with Bernard Lafayette, who had made it to Alabama by train, and those who had survived their adventure in Ardmore—gathered together at the Birmingham station.

This time the police offered grudging protection as a crowd of angry white people grew to three thousand. Lafayette noticed that the Ku Klux Klansmen were wearing robes but no hoods, unafraid of detection, and the leader of the group, Imperial Wizard Robert Shelton, was dressed in black with the image of a serpent on the back of his robe. Lafayette was fascinated by Shelton. He was clearly the man in charge, small and wiry, strutting like a peacock, a sandy-haired man very different physically from the rest of his group. Most of the others, as Lafayette remembered them, were overweight, unkempt, good old boys who seemed ordinary and a little ill at ease.

"They were doing silly antics," Lafayette said later, "stepping on us when we were sitting on the floor, throwing water on us in the presence of police. I kept wondering why they didn't just attack us, and all the while I kept watching Shelton. He was very sharp looking and very comfortable in his black robe. I was caught by that—how black seemed to be the symbol of authority. He just didn't care very much for black *people*."

They waited all night in the Birmingham station, intermittently aware of the tense negotiations that were taking place around them. Robert Kennedy was on the phone with the governor, who had refused a little earlier to take a call from the president, a man he had once regarded as a friend. Patterson had made his public pronouncements that the freedom riders could not be protected. "We can't act as nursemaids to agitators," he said. "You can't guarantee the safety of a fool." Now on Friday, Robert Kennedy was pressing him hard to reconsider—"giving me instructions like I was a private in the army," as Patterson remembered it.

Patterson balked, saying any further discussion would occur face-to-face between himself and a representative of the president. John Seigenthaler, already in Alabama, was picked for the mission, and he rushed from Birmingham to Montgomery, not especially optimistic about how it would go. He had seen the governor on the TV news—"saying the things he said with that carnation in his buttonhole. You think to yourself, 'what an asshole.'" But when the meeting began, Seigenthaler was surprised. There were certainly some moments in the tense negotiations when Patterson grew angry, but generally speaking he was courteous and bright, just as Robert Kennedy had predicted.

Seigenthaler felt certain when the meeting was over that Patterson hadn't known about the attacks in Anniston and Birmingham, had not been a party to the agreement with the Klan. It was true that he was angry about the Freedom Rides, and he had his image in Alabama to consider. But there was a moment in the meeting in the governor's office that stayed forever in Seigenthaler's mind. There had been a sharp exchange on the issue of safety, with Patterson declaring that the stand he had taken against the freedom riders—against "the niggers," as he put it at the time—had made him more popular in the country than John Kennedy.

Seigenthaler wanted to shift the conversation, to reframe the debate, but he knew it would not be easy to do. He was clearly outnumbered in the governor's office, for Patterson was flanked by the members of his cabinet and the flags of Alabama and the Confederacy, as well as the American flag just behind him. This was clearly the governor's territory, a place where the government Seigenthaler represented—the federal government of the United States—seemed almost like an alien force. But there were realities now that they all had to face. Seigenthaler told Patterson that if the state could not protect the freedom riders, the federal government would have to.

The governor shook his head. "Blood will run in the streets if there is a federal force," he said, and there was a flash of anger and conviction in his eyes.

Seigenthaler answered with the obvious. "Blood ran in the streets on Sunday," he said, and then he added: "Don't you want to make it Mississippi's problem?"

This was the pitch Robert Kennedy had suggested. Convince John Patterson it was in his interests to get the freedom riders safely from his state and into somebody else's jurisdiction. Patterson hesitated, and looking back on it later, Seigenthaler thought he understood why. Far more than the Kennedys, or even their emissary in Montgomery, the governor understood the magnitude of the rage—the beast that was waiting out there in the streets—for a provocation this deliberate and clear. It was more than posturing when he turned to Floyd Mann, his director of safety, and declared once again: "We can't protect them. Tell him, Floyd."

Mann, however, took them all by surprise. "Governor," he said, "you tell me to protect them, and I will protect them."

Seigenthaler looked quickly at Patterson's eyes. "What I expected to see," he remembered, "was a look that said, 'This son of a bitch has betrayed me.' I didn't get that at all. What I got was puzzlement. I think he knew the beast a lot better than I did. But Floyd said, 'We are going to do it,' and he sucked the air right out of that room."

Floyd Mann's plan, worked out with the governor, was to provide state protection on the stretch of highway between Birmingham and Montgomery. There would be patrol cars riding with the bus and others at intervals along the highway, and there would be a helicopter that followed overhead. When the caravan came to the Montgomery line, the local police would take over there. Patterson thought it was better that way, for just as there were tensions between the state and federal governments, there could be the same issues between the cities and the state. They talked to L. B. Sullivan, the commissioner of police in Montgomery, who told them flatly: "You can count on us. We'll maintain order." The governor went to bed on Friday night allowing himself a brief glimmer of hope that before much longer the Freedom Rides would be over.

There was a final glitch on Saturday morning, when the riders couldn't find a driver who would take them. As one driver told a cluster of reporters, "I don't have but one life to give, and I am not going to give it to CORE or the NAACP." Hearing that news, Robert Kennedy got on the phone with the bus company officials, and demanded that "Mr. Greyhound" find somebody who was willing to drive. The officials did, and at 8:30 A.M. on May 20, the new freedom riders embarked on a critical leg of their journey.

The ride to Montgomery was uneventful and smooth. Floyd Mann did exactly as he promised, and the bus was well guarded on the open highway. But the troopers peeled away at the city limit sign, and as the Greyhound slowly pulled into the station, the Montgomery police were nowhere to be found. There was, instead, an eerie stillness, stark, ominous, almost as if the city itself had been abandoned. When the bus finally stopped, the driver rushed away and into the station, and a howling mob appeared out of nowhere. To a person, that was how the freedom riders put it—an unnatural quiet replaced without warning by the roar of the beast.

The riders huddled near the front of the bus, gathering their nerve, and almost as soon as they stepped through the door, somebody hit John Lewis with a crate. Jim Zwerg, the young white man who had taken up the cause, knelt down to pray, and a Klansman delivered a kick to his back that was hard enough to break it. But the most horrifying image to Bernard Lafayette was his friend William Barbee lying on the ground, a white man standing with a brogan at his throat, jamming a piece of lead pipe in his ear. Even during the worst of the Nashville sit-ins, they had rarely seen this level of rage, and Bernard was sure they were all going to die.

In the midst of the chaos, he found himself near the railing of the deck, with a parking lot maybe ten feet below. With his fellow freedom rider,

Fred Leonard, he vaulted the rail and escaped without any serious injury.

John Seigenthaler was not so lucky. He had driven down from Birmingham with John Doar, another official at the Justice Department. As they came to the station, they could hear the screams, the horrible intermingling of the victims and the mob, and it occurred to Seigenthaler that even though he had been raised in the South, he had never understood it—had never really grasped the depth of the hatred, until he heard the terrible roar of that crowd. He was overwhelmed by the tragedy taking shape before his eyes, tangled together with his own sense of failure, for it had been his job to keep this from happening.

But those thoughts quickly passed, banished by the image of three freedom riders—two white, one black, all of them women—being seized by the mob. Seconds earlier, they had run for a cab, but the driver, who was black, refused in his terror to carry white women, and the black freedom rider, Katherine Burks, refused to leave the scene without her friends. As the crowd closed in, one of the women was getting the worst of it, a white kid dancing and punching at her face, jabbing like a boxer, drawing blood every time. Seigenthaler pulled his car to the curb and told the women to get in, and they might have made it if all three had obeyed, but one of them balked.

"Mister," she said, "this is not your fight. I'm nonviolent. I don't want you to get hurt."

"Get your ass in the car," Seigenthaler commanded, but that was the moment when the lights went out. There was a man behind him in bib overalls, and when Seigenthaler ordered the crowd to get back, the big man hit him across the temple with a pipe. Others in the mob began to kick him in the ribs, until he finally passed out underneath his car. He woke up once on his way to the hospital and glanced down at the shirt he had borrowed from John Doar, having failed to pack enough clothes of his own. The borrowed shirt was covered with blood, and he remembered thinking to himself through the haze, "Doar is going to be pissed."

A few hours later, he was lying in bed with a fractured skull and broken ribs, when he saw Floyd Mann coming into the room. From the moment they met, Seigenthaler had liked him. Floyd was a slow- talking native of Alexander City, a former tail-gunner on a B-17 who had served with distinction in World War II. His friends all said he was a good story-teller, even something of a practical joker, but he was also a man who was serious about his job. "The governor is terribly distressed that you are hurt," he told Seigenthaler, and at the moment that he said it there were tears in his eyes.

Seigenthaler didn't yet know that it had been an emotional day for Floyd Mann, that he had been a hero at the Montgomery station. Mann had a bad feeling about L. B. Sullivan, the police commissioner of Montgomery, and sure enough when he got to the station just to check on things for himself, it was Birmingham all over again. There was a frenzied mob having its way with the riders and not a policeman anywhere in sight. Mann immediately waded into the fray and pulled out his gun. He fired two warning shots in the air, and declared in a voice that even the people in the mob had to notice: "There'll be no killing here today." A few feet away, there was a Klansman with a baseball bat still swinging, and Mann walked over and put a gun to his ear. "One more swing, and you're dead," he said. He called in a contingent of seventy-five state troopers, and within a few minutes the riot at the Greyhound station was over.

Sometime later, a young white man by the name of Bob Zellner was wandering through the ruins. Zellner was drawn to the civil rights movement, and he would soon emerge as one of the most courageous white members of SNCC. He had grown up in Mobile, the grandson of a Klansman, and had been a student at Murphy High School when Autherine Lucy enrolled at the University of Alabama. Everybody was talking about it, and when Zellner started musing with some of his friends, suggesting that Lucy had a right to be there, people told him he ought to be careful. "People will hurt you if you say those things," one friend warned, and Zellner decided on the spot that he was different from the others. He insisted on the right to think for himself, and more and more as time went by he came to revel in his outsider's role.

Later, as a student at Huntingdon College, a small school in Montgomery, he became a supporter of Martin Luther King, and by the 1960s he was ready to make his commitment to the movement. If there was still any doubt, the scene at the bus station helped push him to the edge. It looked like a war zone. There were broken cameras and discarded lead pipes and abandoned suitcases with the sides caved in, and there were white people dancing around impromptu bonfires. To Zellner it seemed like a tribal celebration, a declaration of victory by the forces of violence.

Zellner thought they were wrong. He saw a different meaning, a different message delivered by the brave young people on the bus. With their actions that day, they had done exactly what they set out to do. They served notice to the nation that there was no place too dangerous for the movement to go—no place any longer for white supremacy to hide.

CHAPTER 8

"The Line in the Dust"

FOR ROBERT KENNEDY, THE CIVIL RIGHTS movement was suddenly more real, an issue with a face, and at the moment at least, the face belonged to John Seigenthaler. Kennedy called the hospital room to check on Seigenthaler's condition, and at the sound of the attorney general's voice, Seigenthaler broke down and wept. "I felt abject failure," he remembers. Robert Kennedy was a personal friend as well as a boss, and Seigenthaler accepted the Kennedys' definition of the civil rights issue. The new and militant demand for equality was one more item on the national agenda, a matter to be managed like anything else. It was true that there was a moral dimension at its core, but for a new administration with its mind more focused on foreign affairs, there were problems of image and national prestige if events in the country seemed out of control.

In the cool and rational calculations of the Kennedys, that was how it originally appeared, but now Robert Kennedy was starting to understand a level of urgency he had missed at the start. When Seigenthaler apologized for his failure, Kennedy told him it was not his fault. These bloody confrontations in the state of Alabama had simply been inevitable, and the moment of danger was not over yet. That same weekend on the TV news, there was the image of Jim Zwerg in his hospital bed, front teeth broken, three vertebrae cracked, declaring with an eerie self-possession and resolve: "We will continue the Freedom Ride. We are willing to accept death. . . . Segregation must be stopped."

A few rooms away, William Barbee said the same. Barbee was another of the students from American Baptist, intelligent and deeply committed to the movement, but now he drifted in and out of sleep in a haze of pain from the injury to his ear. A Klansman had jabbed him with a piece of metal pipe, and many years later his friends would say he was never quite the same, physically and emotionally devastated by his wounds. But as bad as he felt, he looked up once and there was his friend, Bernard Lafayette, standing at his bedside.

"How you doing, Brother?" said Bernard.

"Good Bro'," said Barbee, forcing a smile; "when are we going on to Mississippi?"

There had never been any doubt that they would go. They were determined to continue through the full itinerary announced by CORE when its national director, James Farmer, decided to pursue the Freedom Rides. After Montgomery, they would go to Mississippi, a state that was even more frightening than Alabama, then on to Louisiana and New Orleans. There was a mass meeting planned in support of that decision, a Sunday night rally at Ralph Abernathy's First Baptist Church. The crowd began arriving in the late afternoon, for this was Montgomery, a black community with a swagger in its step, proud of the legacy of the bus boycott, but knowing that the battle was not yet won. All over the city, people reached out to embrace the freedom riders. Doris Crenshaw, one of the young disciples of Rosa Parks, remembers how as a girl in her teens barely old enough to drive, she and a friend went cruising downtown in a borrowed Cadillac, a yellow '59, looking for freedom riders to rescue. A Montgomery pharmacist named Richard Harris, one of the strong black businessmen in the city, offered his house as a safe haven for the riders, and so did the minister Solomon Seay.

Then came the rally. Civil rights leaders from all over the country began to assemble at Abernathy's church, which had been restored from the bombing in 1957. Martin Luther King came in from Atlanta, and Diane Nash came down from Nashville, and there was word that James Farmer was coming from Washington. Fred Shuttlesworth went to meet him at the airport. He knew there were people in the ranks of southern activists who didn't really know what to make of Mr. Farmer. They found him pompous, a professor's son who seemed to wear his erudition on his sleeve. He was a large and articulate man in his forties, who had started out with the freedom riders in Washington but left the pilgrimage to attend the funeral of his father. He had missed the attacks in Anniston, Birmingham, and Montgomery, and despite the evident dangers that remained, he was eager to rejoin this noble crusade that was clearly on the verge of leaving him behind.

Curiously enough, Fred Shuttlesworth felt left out as well. He had sent out the rescue party to Anniston and harbored the freedom riders in Birmingham, and along with Diane Nash, he had coordinated the leg of the journey to Montgomery. But somehow all this was not enough. He had expected to be on the bus to Montgomery, had purchased his ticket and was walking up the steps, when he heard a policeman's voice just behind him: "Freddie Lee, where are you going?" He knew immediately it was Jamie Moore, Birmingham's chief of police, a man he regarded as more humane than the commissioner of public safety, Bull Connor.

"I'm getting on the bus," Shuttlesworth said simply, but the police chief told him he was under arrest. Later, even though it seemed unlikely, he wondered if Robert Kennedy had intervened, asking Moore to arrest him to save him from the trouble—and the possibility of death—that lay just ahead. Whatever the reason, Shuttlesworth found himself in the jail as the Greyhound bus made the trip to Montgomery. He bonded out and rushed back to his house where he shaved and dressed, then hopped in his car and headed for Montgomery. He remembered later that he was in such a hurry he shaved off a piece of his mustache by mistake. After looking at the lopsided face in the mirror, he shaved off the rest, feeling a little naked, but he shrugged and figured it would just have to do.

On his way to the airport to pick up Farmer, he was happy to be a part of the action once again—undaunted by the new and disturbing reports that a mob had assembled outside the church. There was a crowd of maybe three thousand people; it was hard to be sure, but Shuttlesworth guessed it was twice as large as the crowd in the sanctuary. The mood was getting nasty as he and Farmer drove slowly toward the scene and were suddenly trapped in the sea of white faces. There was a mixture of Klansmen and ordinary people, driven to a frenzy by the events of the last several days in Montgomery. They were even feeling righteous, Shuttlesworth thought, because of the statements of Gov. John Patterson. The governor had been hostile to the riders from the start, and there was a sense in which the mob was acting out his words, as the people in the crowd began to bang on the car, rocking it violently, until Shuttlesworth slammed into reverse and drove quickly away.

He and Farmer circled the block and stopped on the other side of a cemetery, where they left the car and made their way through the scattered tombstones, hoping to enter the sanctuary from the rear. They found it blocked by a mob as angry as the one out front. The whole church was surrounded.

To Farmer's astonishment, Shuttlesworth was undaunted. He stepped from the grove of the cemetery trees, and with Farmer in his wake, announced to the startled cluster of Klansmen: "Coming through gentlemen. Give us some room." The crowd of white people parted like the sea, and with Shuttlesworth still shouting and waving his arms, he and Farmer ducked into the church.

It was another demonstration of what everybody knew. Fred Shuttlesworth was a little bit crazy. "It takes a divine insanity," he would later explain. "I didn't think it was bravery. I was just driven by divine impulse."

Will Campbell, a white Southern Baptist supporter of the movement, had gotten to know Shuttlesworth through the years, and like everyone else he respected his courage. In the 1950s he had driven down from Nashville after one of the bombings at Shuttlesworth's church, and together they began to search through the rubble. Shuttlesworth found the remnants of a sign once posted in the church—JESUS LOVES THE LITTLE CHILDREN OF THE WORLD—and he marveled at the fact that a message so pure had survived an act as hideous as the bombing. It had to be the hand of God, he decided. As Campbell listened to Shuttlesworth's words he was struck by the depth and simplicity of his faith. This was clearly someone who believed, but there was something else also. Campbell knew people who regarded Shuttlesworth as a man with an ego the size of a bus, and he could understand that assessment as well. If Shuttlesworth saw the hand of God in the movement, he saw himself as a hand-chosen leader. He was not, thought Campbell, a man who suffered from a lack of self-esteem.

And yet with all his certainty and bombast, Shuttlesworth set the standard for courage in a movement that he knew was much bigger than himself. Once inside Abernathy's church, he huddled with the others—King, Farmer, Wyatt T. Walker, who was another of the strategists from SCLC—trying to decide what to do. Outside in the streets, the mob was getting ugly, throwing rocks, surging periodically toward the doors of the church, while a thin and haggard line of federal marshals tried to offer their protection. The freedom riders were in the choir loft, all wearing robes. In Montgomery a warrant had been issued for their arrest, and as they sang the freedom songs and old hymns, Bernard Lafayette couldn't help but reflect on how feeble and transparent their disguise must appear. There was John Lewis with a bandage on his head, the most seriously injured of the group except for Zwerg and Barbee, who were still in the hospital. Bernard himself liked being in the choir. Back in the dorm at American Baptist, he would sing the freedom songs with his friend James Bevel, working out harmonies so intricate and pure that they would one day sing at Carnegie Hall. John Lewis, however, was a whole different story. This was a man who couldn't sing a lick, and Lafayette thought if there were policemen in the church, all they had to do was listen to Lewis to know this couldn't be a bona fide choir.

As the situation grew more tense, Solomon Seay was presiding in the pulpit. He had been one of the stalwarts of the bus boycott, and as rocks rained down on the stained glass windows and the sting of tear-gas drifted through the church, he told the people in the pews to be calm. They were singing the hymn, "Love lifted me when nothing else could help," and Seay exhorted them to mean every word. Downstairs, meanwhile, Martin Luther King was on the phone to Robert Kennedy, telling him that the situation looked grave. There were black people in the church who had brought weapons with them—guns, knives, whatever they had—and there were scattered reports of Negroes outside who were armed and ready to take on the mob. King could imagine a pitched battle at the church, with massive casualties to blacks and whites—and to the fragile credibility of the nonviolent movement.

At one point during the terrifying blur of the evening, he decided it was time to venture outside. His lieutenants tried to talk him out of it, but King was determined. As people retold the story years later, there were conflicting reports about his motive. Bernard Lafayette thought he wanted to talk with a group of blacks who were ready for a fight, hoping to head off an armed confrontation. Others said he simply wanted to look around and assess the situation for himself, but a few remembered something even more dramatic—that in order to save the people in the church, King offered himself to the mob outside. Whatever his purpose, he stepped through the doors, and when the white tormentors began to taunt him, daring him to take a step in their direction, King walked right toward them. When the whites began to throw things at him, Bernard Lee and several of the others began to push him back toward the church, insisting that nothing would be served by his death. Bernard Lafayette, who never expected to see King alive, was deeply and forever impressed by his courage.

As the dangers of the evening became more intense, nerves in the church began to fray, but the leaders did their best to stay calm. When his own turn came to speak to the crowd, Fred Shuttlesworth leaned his lanky frame across the pulpit and declared in a voice that was matter-of-fact, "It's a sin and a shame before God that, in a day like this, these people who govern us would let things come to such a sad state. But God is not dead. The most guilty man in this state tonight is Gov. John Patterson."

Not far away in the governor's mansion, Patterson was feeling like a man in a vise. He knew the black leaders were holding him responsible for creating a climate of crisis with his rhetoric. He had also felt the pressure from the Kennedys, urging him to do more, treating him, he said, like "a vassal" of the federal government. But Patterson understood the political forces in his state, the masses of people who were deeply offended by the freedom riders and thought he was doing too much to protect them. Twice already—once in Anniston and again in Montgomery—the dedicated members of his public safety staff had intervened personally to save the demonstrators' lives. Privately, the governor was proud of the heroism of Floyd Mann and the others. He and Floyd had known each other for more years than they could count, their families deeply rooted in Tallapoosa County, and Mann had been a staunch supporter of his father's. In Patterson's mind he was simply the best—a country boy with sandy red hair and cool, steady eyes who was utterly impartial in enforcing the law.

Many years later, as Patterson looked back on the Freedom Rides and his days in the governor's mansion of Alabama, he remembered Mann with a special kind of warmth. He also came to respect the freedom riders, these brave young people who took their stand for changes that would make the whole country better. The Kennedys, however, were a very different matter. He still bristled at the mention of Robert Kennedy, the attorney general of the United States, and his emissary, John Seigenthaler ("They sent me a fool," he told one reporter). He was also angry with the police commissioners of Birmingham and Montgomery—Bull Connor and L. B. Sullivan—who had made their despicable agreements with the Klan, and there was one other person Patterson criticized, with words so pointed they were hard to ignore. That person, ironically enough, was himself.

"I was in a position," he remembered years later, "to bring blacks into the political process. I was in a position to do something about it, but didn't. You think about being reelected, and that's a bad mistake. I didn't get reelected anyway. So that's the biggest thing. When you are running for office the first time, you can be for segregation or you can be a martyr. But once you are elected, there are things you can do. When you think about bringing the black people of Alabama into the political process, everything changes when that happens. If I had foreseen it and had the courage to do it." His voice trailed off and he stared hard at the interrogator in his chambers. "It's one of my big regrets," he said.

But on the third Sunday in May 1961, all those reflections were hidden in the future. As the evening wore on, the governor of Alabama was simply a man with a difficult decision to make. He was caught in the grip of competing imperatives—his political career, which meant looking tough, and the need for law and order, which inevitably meant protecting the people at the church. One thing was clear. The situation wasn't getting any better. An overturned car was burning in the street, casting eerie shadows on the church, and a brick came crashing through a stained glass window, hitting an elderly man in the head. Patterson had prepared a declaration of martial law, and as he was agonizing over whether to sign it, Tom Posey, one of his aides on the scene, called to tell him it was time.

"Governor," said Posey, "you better do it."

The National Guard soon arrived under the command of Adj. Gen. Henry Graham, supported by some of Floyd Mann's state troopers, and for the first time that night the First Baptist Church of Montgomery was secure. The mob still lingered just beyond the bayonets, and it was clear to some of the reporters who were there that the troopers and the guardsmen were unhappy with their assignment. These were Alabama white men, steeped in the times, and if not for their uniforms that night some of them might have been a part of the crowd, screaming for blood.

Reporter Bob Ingram of the *Montgomery Advertiser,* who had achieved a reputation for his fairness, remembered a scene in the late-night hours when one of the bleary-eyed leaders in the church asked the authorities for an urn of fresh coffee. A few minutes later, an Alabama state trooper who was making the delivery stopped and urinated into the brew. "I didn't write that," Ingram said years later. Somehow, it seemed to be too much.

In the sweltering sanctuary, the standoff continued until almost dawn. Even after midnight, as the people in the mob started drifting away, the guardsmen maintained their vigil at the doors, refusing to let any white people in, but refusing also to let the black people out. The authorities said it was an issue of safety, but Martin Luther King and Fred Shuttlesworth saw it as a final act of harassment. There was nothing to do, however, but adjust. Under the direction of Solomon Seay, children were led to the basement of the church where they slept on tables, while old people slept on the cushions in the pews, and many others, of course, got no sleep at all.

Just before morning with the city still dark, a fleet of National Guard trucks pulled up to the church and began to transport the people back home. There was an old woman sitting next to Bernard Lafayette, and as the truck rumbled slowly through the Montgomery streets she leaned close and whispered, "You come home with me." She knew the freedom riders were still wanted men, and for the rest of the night as Bernard tried to sleep she kept a silent vigil at the window. "I never got her name," he told one reporter. "But she provided a few hours of safety."

Over the next several days, other civil rights activists began to find their way to Montgomery. James Lawson, the apostle of nonviolence, came down from Nashville, along with James Bevel and C. T. Vivian. They were ready to take part in the next leg of the journey—into the dreaded state of Mississippi. They gathered at the home of Richard Harris, the Montgomery pharmacist who supported the movement, to talk about strategy. There were more than twenty of them under one roof, and after a while one delicate issue began to dominate the rest—one awkward, excruciating disagreement about the proper role for Martin Luther King. Diane Nash and some of the others thought he ought to take part in the next segment of the ride. He had handled himself so beautifully at the church, venturing outside to confront the mob on his own, reassuring the people who were trapped in the sanctuary, delivering his sermon with an eloquence that set him apart from the rest. It was easy to see why he had become the preeminent symbol of the movement, and Nash believed that in that role he could give the Freedom Rides a credibility and a force that were simply unattainable from any other source.

King knew she was right, but he also knew that of all the people who would be on the bus he was the one with the greatest chance of getting killed—the greatest trophy the movement had to offer. He began to make excuses, and when Diane Nash continued to push, he blurted his reply, a statement he regretted as soon as it was out. "I think," he said, "I should choose the time and place of my Golgotha." In the moment of discomfort that followed his remark—his implicit comparison of himself and Jesus Christ—Wyatt Walker tried to cover. "Look," he said, "if Dr. King decides he's not going, that's it. He don't have to have no reason."

That seemed to settle the issue for a while, but in the days after that some of the young activists began to refer to Dr. King as "de Lawd," a contemptuous dismissal of his self-importance and his fear. Bernard Lafayette didn't share that view, nor did John Lewis. Whatever their feelings about King's decision, they had no doubts about his courage or character. It was the cause, not himself, that he regarded as holy, and they knew he was willing to risk his own death. They suspected, in fact, that he regarded his murder by now as inevitable. His answer at the moment was simply, "Not yet."

In retrospect, the whole discussion was one of the early indications of a strain that would soon begin to tear at the movement. For now, however, they had to put it aside. The time had come to move ahead to Mississippi.

They left Montgomery for Jackson on May 24, 1961, the first group riding a Trailways bus, heavily escorted by the Alabama state troopers. A Greyhound bus would follow soon after, and the two of them together carried twenty-seven riders. Already, there were reports of another Freedom Ride leaving Atlanta for Anniston and Birmingham, and it occurred to C. T. Vivian on the Trailways bus that their powerful message had now been delivered. Vivian, a veteran of the Nashville sit-ins, gazed out the window at the crowd along the road. Clusters of white people screamed at the bus, and blacks on porches simply watched it pass.

Much later, he remembered his own mix of feelings—the exhilaration and fear, combined with a desperate need to use the bathroom. He thought about the drama shifting now to Mississippi, but he had a feeling it would soon be back. There was something about Alabama, something in the soil, he decided later on, that seemed to be good for the civil rights movement. Ralph Abernathy came from Marengo County, and John Lewis from Troy, and Fred Shuttlesworth was born and raised in the moonshining country outside of Birmingham. And there was something also in the political climate that seemed to be different from the mood in Mississippi. There, the most visible white leader was Ross Barnett, a segregationist governor who issued his pronouncements unencumbered by the faintest trace of intellect. That was the opinion of many civil rights leaders, but it was never their assessment of Gov. John Patterson or with the man who seemed likely to become his successor, Judge George C. Wallace. Both of these men were formidable enough that they were able to participate in a clash of ideas, and in Vivian's mind that could only be good for the cause.

"The dignity of nonviolence," he said, "offered such a contrast to bigotry and hate, and the whole indefensible idea of segregation."

That was always their article of faith, a belief that the masses of Americans would eventually understand, and it seemed to be happening with the Freedom Rides. George Wallace, however, saw the opposite possibility—saw in the emerging controversy over race a new and important opportunity for himself. He still carried the wounds from his loss in the election of 1958. All his life he had wanted to be governor, even as a boy growing up in Barbour County, when others might have dreamed of being cowboys or firemen. As a teenager serving as a legislative page, he stood erect on the star near the steps of the capitol, where Jefferson Davis had taken his oath, and he dreamed of the day when he would do the same. "I knew then," he said much later, "that I would be governor."

From that day forward, what many people saw was a searing ambition that would set him apart, even from people in the world of politics. Nobody was really quite sure of the source, but it may have been his family or it may have been his place. In Barbour County in eastern Alabama, there was a faded aristocracy in the town of Eufaula, but the majority of the population was poor, divided equally between black and white. Wallace's grandfather George Oscar Wallace was a country doctor who tried to serve them all, accepting whatever payment they could muster—a potato, a chicken, it didn't really matter. He was, of course, one of the most respected men in the county, but his oldest son—another in the growing line of George Wallaces—was "something of a ne'er-do-well" as one of the family biographers later put it, a man with a temper who was given to drink. He was regarded by many of his neighbors as a failure, which was something his son did not want to be.

In the 1940s the youngest George Wallace turned to politics as his escape, his ticket out of Clio, the town of his birth, and into a world where he could be his own man. He knew from the start that he had the stomach for it, and also the talent, and he allied himself with the progressive wing of the Democratic Party—with the state's respected New Deal senators, Lister Hill and John Sparkman, and even more so, with former governor Jim Folsom, the six-foot-eight-inch giant of a man, who was widely regarded as a liberal politician, even on the delicate issue of race. In 1948, as a delegate to the National Democratic Convention, Wallace refused to be a part of the Dixiecrat rebellion against the civil rights proposals of Pres. Harry Truman, and later that year, when the Dixiecrats met as a party in Birmingham and nominated Strom Thurmond as their presidential candidate, Wallace kept his distance, and supported the national ticket under Truman.

He carried that record into the governor's race of 1958, where he ran as a populist and a moderate on race, and lost overwhelmingly to John Patterson. Seymore Trammell, the district attorney of Barbour County, remembered how Wallace came to his office a few days later and made a declaration that would redefine his life and reconfigure the shape of Alabama politics.

"Seymore," he said, "I was outniggered by John Patterson, and I'll tell you here and now, I will never be outniggered again."

It was a "Faustian bargain," concluded journalist Ray Jenkins, a compromise of principle for power, and once George Wallace made that decision, he never looked back. In the autumn of 1958, only a few months after his defeat, he found his ticket back into the headlines. The U.S. Commission on Civil Rights, established in 1957, was beginning an inquiry into voting rights abuses in the Alabama Black Belt. In some counties there, like Wilcox and Lowndes, no blacks at all were registered to vote, and in a great many others, including Bullock, Barbour, Macon, and Dallas, the barriers to the ballot were nearly as severe.

The commission met in Montgomery on December 8 in a fourth-floor room at the federal courthouse and listened to hours of eloquent testimony about the caprice and recalcitrance of county registrars. Not surprisingly, the strongest witnesses came from Macon County, where the Tuskegee Civic Association, the organization led by Charles Gomillion, had been keeping meticulous records for years. Professors and their wives from Tuskegee Institute spoke with feeling about the repeated indignity of being turned away. But perhaps the most effective witness was a Macon County farmer named Hosea Guice, who had managed in 1942 to buy his own place, 120 acres near the community of Shorter. He was proud of that accomplishment and everything it represented, and now he was ready to take the next step. He was ready to vote, to take his place among the citizens who decided on the leadership and destiny of his place. So far, however, his attempts to register, beginning in 1954, had been unsuccessful. On one occasion, he heard nothing back, on another he was told he missed a question on the test, and after that the board of registrars simply didn't meet. When the commissioners asked why he thought this had happened, Guice considered the question for a moment, then gave a simple answer.

"I was just a Negro," he said. "That's all."

For the media it might have made compelling testimony if Guice hadn't already been upstaged. Back in October, George Wallace, acting in his capacity as circuit judge, had announced that he was impounding the voting records of Barbour and Bullock counties, and that he would never, under any circumstances, turn them over to the Civil Rights Commission. After the hearing on December 8, 1958, the commission went to court and asked U.S. district judge Frank Johnson to order Wallace to give up the records. Johnson did, and gave Wallace until January 12 to comply.

As the days went by, Wallace began to contemplate his situation. He had been a friend and a law school classmate of Johnson's, and was familiar with his rulings as a federal judge—his role, for example, in the desegregation of the Montgomery buses. He knew that Johnson could be a stubborn man, the kind of judge who might throw him in jail. He could see a certain opportunity in that, the kind of martyrdom that might play well with the voters, assuming, of course that the sentence was short. But what if Johnson chose to throw away the key?

On a Sunday night in January, his collar turned up against the midwinter cold, Wallace knocked on Frank Johnson's door and asked if they could talk. "Judge," he said, "my ass is in a crack. I need some help." He explained that he wanted to run for governor and thought the current controversy would help him. He was planning, he said, to defy Johnson's order, but was hoping his time in jail would be short. "If you'll just give me ten or fifteen days," he said, "I could stand that."

Johnson stared back in total disbelief, trying to comprehend the level of presumption of this man who was now sipping coffee in his kitchen. "George," he said, after a moment of quiet, "if you don't comply, I'll pop you hard."

Knowing he could face a six-month sentence, Wallace suggested an alternative solution. He had hemmed himself in with his public defiance and couldn't back down, but he would turn the voting records over to a grand jury, and they, in turn, could make them available to the Civil Rights Commission.

Johnson shrugged. "I don't care how you do it," he said, "just so you do it before the hearing."

Wallace quickly called a jury into session and gave them the records, then made a private call to the Civil Rights Commission, telling them where the material could be found. Johnson was satisfied by that, but astonished on January 26 when Wallace began to twist the story, casting himself as the triumphant champion against the would-be tyranny of the federal government. He launched a series of public appearances insisting that Johnson and the members of the commission had simply withered in the face of his resolve.

"This Washington crowd," he declared, "and this federal judge backed down, and if and when they say they didn't back down, they're integrating, scalawagging, carpetbagging liars."

For Frank Johnson, it was a side of Wallace he had never seen, a mendacity that made him angry and sad when it seemed to be working with the Alabama voters. "The majority of white people bought every word he said," remembered the judge. "They believed it when he said he had taken on the federal government and won. George just simply misled the people." Nevertheless, it worked. In 1962 Wallace won the governor's race overwhelmingly, and on inauguration day he stood before the voters and offered a declaration of war that he had to know even then he would lose.

The speech was written by Asa Carter, a violent and enigmatic figure, born on a farm in the Appalachian foothills of Oxford, Alabama. He was a burly, dark-haired man, broad-shouldered and brooding, who gained national attention later in his life when he changed his name to Forrest Carter and wrote the acclaimed memoir *The Education of Little Tree*. As a writer he insisted he was Native American, but George Wallace knew him as a member of the Klan, founder of one of the most violent factions, the Original Ku Klux Klan of the Confederacy.

In 1956 in Birmingham, Carter and four other members of the group threw eggs at the entertainer Nat King Cole, a Montgomery native who had returned to Alabama for a concert. The following year, six of his followers kidnapped a black man, Edward Judge Aaron, on a country road outside Birmingham. In what was apparently a random act of cruelty, they beat him with a pistol, then pulled down his pants and severed his scrotum with a razorblade. They poured turpentine on the open wound—a final moment of brutality that may have saved Aaron's life, for the turpentine helped cauterize the wound. Carter said he didn't approve of such torture. The victim, he insisted, should simply have been killed.

Five years later, this was the man to whom George Wallace turned for the words he would speak on the campaign trail—and even more significantly, in his inaugural address—and whatever else you might say about him, Asa Carter rose fully to the challenge. George Wallace was a commanding figure as he delivered the speech, gazing out across the crowd on a bitterly cold January afternoon, buoyed by the symmetry and grace of Carter's words:

"In the name of the greatest people that have ever trod this earth, I draw the line in the dust and toss the gauntlet before the feet of tyranny, and I say segregation now, segregation tomorrow, segregation forever!"

Sitting a few feet away on the podium, the outgoing governor, John Patterson, was astonished. It was a brilliant performance, and George Wallace established himself that day as the equivalent in charisma to Martin Luther King or any of the other great orators of the civil rights movement. But what was he thinking? Throughout his own time in the governor's office, Patterson had pursued a very different strategy. He, too, was a staunch defender of segregation, but he knew that in the end the institution was doomed, and he was not in a hurry to speed up the day. His intention, he said, was to drag his feet, to delay the inevitable, to avoid head-on confrontations when he could.

But now George Wallace had drawn his line and dared the proponents of integration to cross it. In the escalation that he knew was sure to come, Patterson understood what the outcome would be. He would not have put any money on George.

PART THREE

THE SHADOW OF DEATH

CHAPTER 9

A History of Hate

IN BIRMINGHAM, FRED SHUTTLESWORTH thought it was time to call the question. He had been waging his one-man battle for a while, declaring his personal war on segregation, and he thought Birmingham was ready for a full-scale assault. It had in the person of Eugene "Bull" Connor a police commissioner known for his inclination to violence, a man nearly certain to cast himself as the perfect foil for the civil rights movement. But more than that, it was a community caught up in a history of hate, a smoldering, suffocating racial hostility, going back at least to the 1930s.

Shuttlesworth's memories took him back to those times, when he was still a boy and Birmingham was barely an adolescent—a depression-ravaged city, trapped in a violent and deadly dress rehearsal for the racial revolution that was coming later on. It was a steel mill town built from nothing in the 1870s, a kind of raw and elemental place where the mill owners gathered in their gated country clubs to talk about their God-given right to make money. There was one impediment they saw to that goal, a collective phobia they all shared: They were afraid of the power of the black and white masses if they came together to demand a better life. The owners had a name for the people who supported such a radical notion. They called them communists, and they were not entirely wrong.

The Communist Party was active in Birmingham in the 1930s, fueled by the energy of young organizers who came from other places—white intellectuals coming down from the North, driven by a radical understanding of justice. But there were homegrown leaders in the party also, battle-hardened black men like Al Murphy and Hosea Hudson who came to Birmingham to work in the mills and found conditions so appalling they had to take a stand. Hudson especially remembered the lessons about freedom his grandmother taught him—homespun soliloquies on the issue of justice, rooted in the promise of Reconstruction, when the era of slavery finally came to an end and black people expected something better to replace it. In Birmingham for the next fifty years, it didn't seem much better—certainly not to the men and women in the mills. The work was hard and the bosses were demanding, and when the Depression descended everything got worse. Workers unable to pay their rent were evicted from their homes, while others found their gas or water disconnected, and with the coming of the winter of 1930 a mood of desperation took hold of the city. People roamed the streets and tore apart old houses for the wood they could burn, and they came by the thousands to the Red Cross office, seeking some kind of relief. What many of them found instead was abuse.

Colonel Stone Johnson, a Shuttlesworth supporter, remembered a Red Cross visit he made in the '30s when a black woman presented a coupon for food. The clerk, a white man, was giving her nothing but tripe, or hog stomach, and the woman began to beg for something better. "Please, sir," she said, "give me something else besides tripe."

According to Johnson, the white man picked up a can of produce and hit her in the head. "Knocked her to her knees," he remembered. "My ole man had taught me to respect the ladies. I was nothing but a boy, but I turned to the room full of men, black and white, and I said, 'Y'all not gon' do anything?' Everybody was afraid in those days. Even whites with a good heart was afraid of the Ku Klux. So nobody did anything that day."

When it began to seem that almost everybody had such a story, Hosea Hudson and the resolute leaders in the Communist Party began organizing street demonstrations, some of them drawing up to five thousand people. Hudson understood that the party's converts may not have been moved by the theories of Marx. Many of them were people from the country, traditional in their values, often deeply religious, but they turned to the only group they could find that seemed to be genuinely concerned about their problems. On May 1, 1933, a crowd of several thousand gathered symbolically at Ingram Park, which would become the site of ugly confrontations in the 1960s, vowing to "stop the insults of the Red Cross." Jane Speed, a leader in the march, was standing on a car to speak to the crowd when the police moved in to carry her away. A shoving match followed and then an outright brawl, and the party leaders vowed they would come back again.

At times the confrontations turned deadly. In October 1935 a coal company owner named Charles DeBardeleben, the son of one of the founders of Birmingham, found himself besieged not by the communists but by the United Mine Workers Union. As the organizers began to march on his camp, DeBardeleben took command of his army—a group of men with machine guns and rifles—and when the shooting stopped, one union man lay dead on the highway, thirty-two bullet holes in his body.

That was Birmingham in the 1930s, but there were also the moments when the violence was personal, when the target of it was specific and clear. One of those occasions—a turning point that helped set the stage for the civil rights movement—involved a white organizer, Joseph Gelders, a Jewish intellectual who came from a prominent Birmingham family. He was a bookish man with wire-rimmed glasses who decided against working in the family restaurant. He attended MIT and the University of Alabama, and after serving in the army during World War I, became a physics professor at Alabama. He was troubled by the labor strife of the '30s and the racist rhetoric many rich people used to divide the black and white workers in the mills. He began to read the economic philosophers, from Adam Smith to Karl Marx, and he thought he found in the theories of Marx an explanation for the working conditions in his city.

As a matter of temperament and personal inclination, Gelders was not a flame-throwing radical. He had little interest in becoming a player in the brawls and shootouts and demonstrations in the streets, and yet he couldn't quite leave them alone. In the summer of 1936 he took up the cause of Bart Logan, a communist organizer sentenced to the chain gang for possessing "seditious" literature, including copies of the *New Republic*. Gelders crusaded for Logan's release, and one night in September after a meeting about the case, he was walking home alone when four men jumped him and threw him in a car. They drove him out to a dark country road, stripped him naked, and beat him nearly to death.

Four months later when his wounds had healed, Gelders testified before the Senate committee of Robert LaFollette, investigating the repression of organized labor. He identified one of his attackers as a man on the payroll of United States Steel, and in the wake of that unfortunate publicity, the giant conglomerate, for the first time in its history, officially recognized the United Mine Workers Union. It was a major breakthrough for the union and its members, and Gelders came away from his own ordeal convinced of the persuasive power of sweet reason. He set out immediately to put together a conference, a revival almost, of southern progressives who would gather in Birmingham in the fall to chart a new and democratic course for their region.

That was the dream, and it was, in fact, a remarkable cross section of people who began to assemble on November 20, 1938. From every corner of the South, they came—educators, journalists, politicians, and preachers, and the grassroots leaders of organized labor. Alabama governor Bibb Graves was there, and Hosea Hudson of the Communist Party, and fifteen hundred people in between. They mingled on the lawn of the Municipal Auditorium, chatting amiably, men in suits, women in furs, others in faded overalls and brogans. When they moved inside just a little after seven o'clock, they paid no attention to the segregation laws, sitting wherever they could find a seat, and together they listened in rapt attention as the evening's keynoter, Frank Porter Graham, issued his call for justice in the world.

Graham, the president of the University of North Carolina, was a commanding presence as he stood before the group, handsome, articulate, speaking out against the Nazi repression in Germany and the persecution of Jews in every part of the continent. But he said there were also some problems at home. "The black man," he declared, "is the primary test for American democracy and Christianity. The Southern Conference on Human Welfare takes its stand here tonight for the simple thing of human freedom. Repression is the way of frightened power; freedom is the enlightened way. We take our stand for the Sermon on the Mount, the American Bill of Rights, and American democracy."

One of the delegates, Virginia Durr, remembered years later the thunderous ovation that followed that speech and her own rush of feelings that lingered through the years. "It was a love feast," she said, "like we had crossed the river together and entered the Promised Land. It was one of the happiest experiences of my life."

In less than twenty-four hours, however, the exhilaration had faded, replaced by a gloom that would hover across the South for thirty years. The instrument of change was Birmingham's swaggering commissioner of public safety, Eugene "Bull" Connor, a man who was relatively new to his job, but who already knew what he wanted to accomplish. On Monday afternoon, when the delegates had divided into smaller committees, Connor burst into one of the meetings, backed by a squadron of Birmingham police, and ordered the participants to separate by race. Meekly and apologetically, they complied, and although they later passed a resolution taking issue with the segregation laws, for the rest of the conference they did as Connor asked. Hosea Hudson, the hard-line veteran of the Birmingham mills, thought they had made a tragic mistake. If they had only stood up to Connor, he said years later, "All that stuff that Reverend King and them went through . . . could have been stopped that day."

It may not have been that simple, of course, but it was indisputably true that Bull Connor left the Conference for Human Welfare flush with the power of his own success, and segregation became his holy crusade. Birmingham, meanwhile, remained a symbol for everything that was wrong—the segregation, the violence, the bigotry and hate, and a terrible legacy lived on in the South. As historian John Egerton would later conclude, "It would be a long, cold winter in Dixie."

It was into that history that Fred Shuttlesworth was born. He was old enough to remember the Depression and all the bitterness that went along with it, and when he became a young minister in the 1950s he could see that conditions were almost as bad. Early in his tenure at Bethel Baptist Church, a brick sanctuary on the north side of town, one of his mentors, the Reverend Charles Parker, warned him not to get carried away. Just be a pastor, the old preacher told him, and in the beginning Shuttlesworth tried. He kept his focus on the little things, the tangible realities that affected people's lives, but after a while he began to understand that so much of the hurt was a part of something bigger—part of an oppressive system of segregation that had to be overturned.

In 1956 he stepped to the center of the Birmingham stage. The immediate issue was the banning of the NAACP—the legal coup by then-Atty. Gen. John Patterson, who persuaded an Alabama judge, Walter B. Jones, to issue an injunction against any activities by the civil rights group. In Birmingham, Shuttlesworth was the membership chairman for the local chapter, and he was presiding at a meeting on Fourth Avenue North, when a sheriff's deputy appeared at the door.

"You're outlawed," the deputy announced. "I have an injunction against the NAACP."

Shuttlesworth was indignant. He asked a few questions about the scope of the ruling, then informed the deputy that it simply wouldn't stand. "You can't stop people from trying to be free," he said.

Over the next several days, people began calling from all over the state, wondering what they could do. In many ways, the NAACP had been a plodding, slow-moving organization, but it had won some important victories in the courts, and for many black Americans, it had become the preeminent symbol of hope. Now in Alabama, that fragile aspiration they were building in the '50s was abruptly replaced by a feeling of gloom. On the Friday night after the ruling was announced, Shuttlesworth lay in bed at his home, tossing and turning and praying for a sign. Finally, he said, sometime between three and four in the morning, he sat up straight, suddenly awake, knowing exactly what he needed to do. "I felt a divine impulse," he remembered, "calling me to call a mass meeting."

Arthur Shores, the great African American attorney in the city, warned him gravely that he was playing with fire. "It's an injunction," said Shores. "You could go to jail." But Shuttlesworth said it was a price he would pay, and Lucinda Robey, one of the stalwarts, told him he sounded like "the black Prince of Peace." Another of his colleagues, the Reverend R. L. Alford, offered his church as the site of the meeting, and Sardis Baptist proved to be a good choice. It was bigger than Bethel, where Shuttlesworth was pastor, and based on the number of calls they were getting, they thought they would need every seat they could find.

As the crowd began to gather on a Tuesday evening, June 5, 1956, the people filled the sanctuary and the balcony, and the rest spilled happily out into the yard, maybe fifteen hundred of them in all. It was Birmingham's answer to Holt Street Baptist. They were there, said Shuttlesworth, speaking from the pulpit, to celebrate the founding of a new organization, the Alabama Christian Movement for Human Rights. It was a name suggested by the Reverend Alford, and it was appropriate for the history they were making that night. They had gathered to declare their war on segregation, not to confront any single example—the buses, the schools, the whites-only counters—but to say to Atty. Gen. John Patterson, and to every white person in the state of Alabama, that they would not rest until the day of freedom had arrived.

Theirs would be a nonviolent war—"not one hair on the head of one white person will be harmed"—but it was a battle to the end, and if there had to be any suffering for the cause, Shuttlesworth himself would be there to lead it. "If anybody gets arrested," he declared, "it'll be me; if anybody goes to jail, it'll be me; if anybody suffers, it'll be me; if anybody gets killed, it'll be me."

One of the people in the balcony that night, a Birmingham barber named James Armstrong, said he had never heard anything like it, and he had been waiting for most of his life. Armstrong was a veteran of World War II, having landed at Normandy just after D-Day, and a few years later when he made it home alive, he, like so many other black veterans, wanted a piece of the freedom he had fought for. But in Birmingham in the 1940s, you could get arrested for vagrancy just walking down the street, and when he rode the bus to barber school every night, it could take him two or three hours to get home. Sometimes the drivers would pass him at the stop, or they would take his money and order him to reenter the bus from the rear, then drive off and leave him. But now here he was at the Sardis Baptist Church, listening to this tall, skinny preacher in the pulpit, speaking the words he was feeling in his heart. Armstrong was not a sentimental man, but he said half seriously that he "fell in love" with Shuttlesworth that night, and decided to do what he could to support him.

Within the next few months he found the opportunity. He joined "the ushers," the security force for the leaders of the movement—a cadre of men who believed in nonviolence but who were willing to stand guard duty with their guns. They soon discovered it was no easy job. For one thing, the newspaper and television reporters were constantly giving out Shuttlesworth's address—3191 North Twenty-Ninth Avenue—almost like an invitation to the Klan. That was Shuttlesworth's view, offered most often with an ironic smile, as the threat of violence became a constant in his life. There was the Christmas night bombing in 1956, when the dynamite exploded just under his bed, and he survived the experience with barely a scratch. He led an attempt the next day to integrate the buses, and the following summer, he set his sights on the schools. It was a target he regarded as critically important, the key perhaps to a different kind of world.

"When kids go to school together," he explained, "and play together, they won't be unknown and they won't be enemies."

On August 22, 1957, he put out the call for a few volunteers, families who were willing to take a risk with their children by requesting reassignment to all-white schools. Eight sets of parents stepped forward at the start, the Armstrongs among them, but James had a feeling that the number would dwindle. Some of the others were simply too vulnerable to economic reprisal, while Armstrong, fortunately enough, was not. By the 1950s he had his own barbershop on the west side of town, a tidy brick building on Eighth Avenue with his name on a Coca-Cola sign out front. There was a certain security in that, he said, and if Fred Shuttlesworth had a need for volunteers, Armstrong knew he was in it until the end.

If any of them had any doubts about the danger, they were erased on the evening of September 2. That was the night when Edward Judge Aaron, the innocent black man walking down the road, was castrated by members of the Ku Klux Klan. Aaron was not a civil rights activist. He was a mild-mannered man with no connection to the movement, but the Klansmen told him to tell Shuttlesworth: "Stop sending nigger children and white children to school together or we gonna do them like we gonna do you."

As the opening day of school was approaching, Shuttlesworth sat down with the members of his family—his wife, Ruby, and daughters, Ricky and Pat—and told them that given the level of danger, they had to be the ones to set the example. They would attempt to enroll at Phillips High School, which was still all white, instead of Parker High School, which was black. There were other school districts in the region that fall—Little

Rock, Nashville, Charlotte, Winston-Salem—that were taking the first steps toward desegregation, and Shuttlesworth wanted his city on the list.

On the morning of September 9, he and Ruby and the girls, along with two other students and the Reverend J. S. Phifer, who was driving, crowded into a car and headed for the school. A mob was waiting, descending, it seemed, from every possible direction. To everyone's surprise, Shuttlesworth got out of the car, and the angry crowd began to beat him with baseball bats and bicycle chains, while several policemen stood by and watched. The lone exception was Lt. E. T. Rouse, who waded into the fray and tried to pull the attackers off Fred, and then off Ruby, who had come to his aid.

Not far away, James Armstrong heard about the trouble, the mob that was lying in wait at the school, and with several others in the corps of bodyguards he rushed to the scene, arriving too late to do any good. They saw Shuttlesworth getting back in the car and the battered vehicle driving slowly away, and they wondered about the fate of the people inside it. Later, they were all astonished to discover that the injuries were not as bad as they had feared. Ruby had a stab wound in her hip, and Ricky's right ankle had been slammed in the car door. Fred, of course, had gotten the worst of it. He was bloody and dazed, but the hospital doctors found nothing broken, and despite the pounding he had taken with the bat, he didn't even appear to have a concussion. That same night, he addressed a rally at New Hope Baptist, a standing room crowd of more than five hundred, and told the people in the church he wasn't mad.

"I don't want any violence," he said. "We have to control ourselves and keep on fighting."

They filed a lawsuit to integrate the schools, with James Armstrong as the number one plaintiff, and it was a case that would reverberate later on, playing a pivotal role in the 1960s. But as it made its torturous way through the courts, Fred Shuttlesworth, never known for his patience, began to turn his mind to other things. In February 1960 he traveled to High Point, North Carolina, to see some of the first of the student sit-ins, and he was deeply inspired by the militancy of the young. A few months later, when the freedom riders came through the state, he was happy to play his role, but by 1962 he was worried, fearing that the movement was losing its momentum. The major headlines were coming out of Georgia, where both Martin Luther King and the students from SNCC found themselves mired in a frustrating struggle. In the town of Albany, there had been sit-ins and marches organized by a cadre of strong local leaders, but the only result was a lot of people in jail. The city fathers refused to negotiate, and police chief Laurie Pritchett, who looked like a character out of central casting—large, slow-talking, with the beginnings of a paunch—refused steadfastly to play the role of the villain.

Pritchett had studied the writings of Martin Luther King in an attempt to understand his adversary, and he decided, he said, to meet "nonviolence with nonviolence." Without allowing brutality by the members of his force, he politely and methodically arrested every demonstrator he could find. He had made arrangements to disperse the prisoners to all the jails within a fifty-mile radius, knowing that his own would quickly be full, and the small-town sheriffs were happy to be of help. King had the feeling he had stepped into quicksand, with an endless cycle of arrests and nothing to show for it except some irritating stories in the national media about his first great failure as a civil rights leader.

Shuttlesworth knew that Birmingham would be different. He knew that the movement could count on a villain, for Bull Connor was never a man of much restraint, and he began urging King to redirect his focus. Birmingham was the most segregated city in the South, the perfect backdrop, they all agreed, for a major crusade. But there were questions and complications in the plan, and one of those involved Shuttlesworth himself. Despite his bravery and a commitment rooted in the depths of his faith, he was widely regarded as a difficult man. Even his secretary, Lola Hendricks, admitted that her boss could require a little patience. They worked together in a tiny church office that was cramped and overflowing with papers, and she was constantly typing, answering his calls, making the reservations for his travels. She found him demanding—"when he wanted something, he wanted it yesterday"—and there were times when she had to bring him up short, had to look him in the eyes and tell him bluntly, "Now you just wait a minute, Reverend."

Not everybody could get away with that, and there were men in the movement who felt the occasional sting of his rebuke. The Reverend John Porter, another of the leaders, found Shuttlesworth autocratic and vain. "It was *his* movement," Porter remembered. "Get in line or get out. That was how he saw it. It may have been necessary to have a person like Fred, but he was a loner, really. He didn't mind telling Martin Luther King, 'This is my town.'"

The simple truth was, Shuttlesworth was often impatient with King. Despite a fundamental feeling of respect, he thought King was soft—an indecisive, slow-moving man who would rather spend time eating soul food with Abernathy than manning the barricades for civil rights. Remarkably enough, King didn't seem to mind. "He was the kind of person who could work with that," said Porter. "He was always surrounded by all kinds of personalities, and it was his humility even more than his brilliance that enabled him to cope. People just recognized him as the leader. How he became so secure, I don't know. He was a private person. He had no fight with anybody. Once he understood Fred's personality, he just dealt with it. It's a rare thing to find a man with that sense of satisfaction."

In the final analysis then, King had no problem with the Shuttlesworth issue and all the aggravation it entailed. Bull Connor, however, was a whole different matter, a subtler complication given the developments of 1962. It was true that Connor had his share of supporters, most of them at least as fanatical as he was, but there were some white leaders who found him embarrassing—bad for the civic image of the city and bad for business. That reality came home to Sidney Smyer, president of the Birmingham Chamber of Commerce, when he was on a recruiting trip to Tokyo. He had arrived, as it happened, at the time of the Freedom Rides, and was greeted by a front-page photo in a Japanese paper showing the Klan attack at the Birmingham station. He knew Bull Connor had a hand in the drama, either by being an active conspirator or in presiding over the incredible abdication by the city's police. Something, Smyer decided, had to be done.

A few months later, David Vann, a young attorney and former law clerk for Hugo Black, had an idea as he was driving to work. The way to rein in Bull Connor, he concluded, was to get rid of his position—abolish the city commission form of government. Connor had established his personal fiefdom as the commissioner of safety, enforced by intimidation and corruption, but if the city adopted a mayor-council arrangement, Connor at the least would have to start over. Vann, Smyer, and other city leaders pushed through a petition to get the issue on the ballot but discovered as the vote was approaching in November that there might be a problem. Martin Luther King's organization, the Southern Christian Leadership Conference, was planning to hold its annual convention in the city, and the reformers were terrified by the prospect. Smyer and the others could imagine a new wave of demonstrations and sit-ins, and therefore a backlash in favor of Connor. In a desperate attempt to keep that from happening, they agreed to do something they had never done before. They agreed to meet with Fred Shuttlesworth.

It was amazing, of course, that it had taken so long. For nearly seven years, Shuttlesworth had been the most important black leader in the city, the undisputed champion of the civil rights cause, and thousands of black people were inspired by his courage. But even in private, the white power structure had denied his significance, for to do otherwise would have been to acknowledge the depth of their mistake. All these reputable opponents of Bull Connor thought of Shuttlesworth as his opposite number, a delusional fanatic who wanted to turn society on its end. Shuttlesworth was never surprised by the snub. He understood clearly that even among the moderates in the city of Birmingham, the laws of segregation still seemed normal.

But now here he was sitting down at the table, bemused by the nervousness of his hosts, who had tried so hard for so long to avoid him. A few days earlier in one final attempt, they had asked to meet with more familiar black leaders—Lucius Pitts, the president of Miles College, and the millionaire businessman A. G. Gaston—but they had been told unequivocally that Shuttlesworth was the man. If the aim of the city fathers was to avoid demonstrations at a delicate time, only Shuttlesworth had the power to oblige.

Shuttlesworth understood his position of strength, and set out to enjoy it. He reminded Sidney Smyer of the Chamber of Commerce slogan—It's Nice to Have You in Birmingham—and wondered why it didn't apply to Dr. King. If the issue was demonstrations, he said, what were they willing to give up for a truce? When Smyer began to hedge, Shuttlesworth cut him off. "You all called me to the wrong meeting," he said, and walked out of the room.

The following morning they assembled again—Shuttlesworth, Gaston, and a larger group of whites—and after a tense and acrimonious discussion, the city leaders crumbled. They vowed to desegregate downtown water fountains and rest rooms in exchange for a promise of no demonstrations, and both sides kept to the letter of the truce. The Whites-Only signs came down in the stores, and in late September 1962, SCLC began its convention with barely a ripple in the local headlines. For one thing, the convention was upstaged by events in Mississippi—an armed insurrection by supporters of the Klan when a black student, James Meredith, attempted to enter the University of Mississippi. The reporters left Birmingham and headed for the scene, and even the members of the Birmingham Klan rushed to the aid of their brothers in Mississippi. Before it was over, 2 people were dead, and 160 federal marshals were injured, 28 of them shot.

If all that captured the attention of the nation, there *was* one moment at the Birmingham convention that remained in the memories of the people who were there. On Friday afternoon, September 28, King was speaking to more than three hundred delegates, going through a series of routine announcements, when a white man in the audience began walking toward the stage. Nobody thought much about it at first, but then the man, Roy James, an American Nazi sympathizer, made it to King and began to hit him in the face. King's lieutenants rushed to his side—Ralph Abernathy, Wyatt Walker, and others—and the spectacle on stage became even more amazing. Lola Hendricks was sitting in the crowd and had trouble believing what she saw with her eyes when King gently cradled his attacker in his arms to protect him from the wrath of the people all around. James began to weep, and Lola Hendricks, along with several hundred others, began to contemplate this display of nonviolence. It was not a tactic now, or even a theory, but an instinct that ran so deep in Dr. King that they could only consider the implications with awe.

"It gave me the faith for nonviolence," she said. "Dr. King was something special."

In the weeks after that, she found herself hoping even more than before that her city would be the place for his next crusade. She was happy in the fall of 1962 when the word finally came. Martin Luther King had decided it was time.

Bull Connor's Mistake

IT WAS LESS THAN A MONTH before the Whites-Only signs began to reappear in the downtown stores. The convention was over and so was the truce. In the city of Birmingham, segregation was still the order of the day. For Martin Luther King and Fred Shuttlesworth, it was the clear and indisputable excuse they had lacked, and they gathered in January 1963 to map out the details. They chose a setting outside of Savannah, Spanish-moss country on the Georgia coast with live oak trees and warm salt breezes even in the winter, a gentle backdrop for Project C, or Confrontation, as Wyatt Walker called it. It was only the inner circle this time—King, Shuttlesworth, and a handful of others.

Walker made the opening presentation, offering a blueprint of what they would do. It was a grand-sounding scheme, which was no surprise, given what they all knew about Walker. He was a New Jersey native who joined the Young Communist League as a high school student in the 1940s because the communists more than anybody else seemed to abhor the idea of racism. Later, he became a Baptist minister, taking a pastorate in Petersburg, Virginia, where he patterned himself, at least in part, after Vernon Johns, King's outspoken predecessor at Dexter Avenue Baptist. He was arrested once at the Petersburg library, a segregated institution, where he tried to check out a book on Robert E. Lee. When he told Johns about it, both of them were delighted by the irony of the moment—a black man jailed for trying to read about Lee, the most revered white man in the history of the South.

At SCLC, Walker was the chief organizer and strategist, and he proposed a four-tiered plan for Birmingham. They would start with a modest round of sit-ins, calling the city's attention to the cause, then move from there to an economic boycott of segregated stores, and then to mass demonstrations in the streets. Finally, if necessary, they would put out a call to activists from every part of the country, urging a national assault on the South's most violent bastion of segregation.

The idea, of course, was to build on the work of Fred Shuttlesworth and some of the younger activists in Birmingham, for many of the things that Walker was proposing had already happened. Early in 1962 the spirit of protest had stirred among the students at Miles College, a small and unaccredited black institution, struggling to survive. It had a student body of 750, an annual budget of less than four hundred thousand dollars, and a single Ph.D. on its faculty. But it had a new president, Lucius Pitts, a driven, articulate man who was proud of the mission of a college like his own. It was inherent, he thought, in the résumés of his students. There was Frank Dukes, the student body president, a thirty-one-year-old Korean War veteran who had worked in the Chrysler plant in Detroit before returning to Birmingham to complete his education. There was U. W. Clemon, the future valedictorian, the sixth of nine children in a two-room house with no running water, a young man with painful memories of his youth. Once as a teenager, he and some friends had been stopped on the street by the Birmingham police, and one of the boys was taken away in the squad car. The young man, in his fear, needed to urinate, and the policemen made him go in his pants.

Clemon and the others hated all that, hated the random cruelty of the system, and Lucius Pitts gave them his support, for his own background had been very much the same. He was a tenant farmer's son from rural Georgia, who had known the deprivations of segregation and poverty.

Now middle-aged with dark-rimmed glasses and thin gray hair, he worked in a cluttered office at the college with a picture of Jesus hanging on the wall. He moved comfortably enough in the realm of white leaders, urging them shrewdly to make their concessions in order to stave off the militancy of the young. But the white men were stubborn, and the students were determined, and during the Easter shopping season of 1962, they called for a boycott of the downtown stores.

It soon became clear that the campaign was effective, and Bull Connor, in his rage, decided to hit back. At the city commission meeting April 3, he proposed that Birmingham cut off its forty-five thousand dollar appropriation for a government food program aimed at the poor, since most of the recipients, after all, were black. The following day, he ordered the arrest of Fred Shuttlesworth for "obstructing the sidewalk," a crime that carried a sentence of six months. Shuttlesworth had not been the organizer of the boycott, but he had supported it, and had praised the leadership of Lucius Pitts. That was enough for Connor, who hated Shuttlesworth to the point of lunacy. His face turned red at the mention of his name, and at the moment of their occasional confrontations his voice would shake with the thunder of his rage.

"Are you Shuttlesworth?" he demanded when they met. "I've got something to say to you. History is going to judge you for causing one of the worst setbacks for your people."

Shuttlesworth stared back calmly and replied: "History is going to judge us both."

For Connor from that point on, it was war, and if many white people in Birmingham were embarrassed, a few were even more troubled than that. In the months that followed the Easter boycott, Murph Archibald was one of a handful of students at Birmingham Southern, a small white college in the western part of town, who went down to Miles College to offer their support. Some of them were motivated by their faith, others more purely by intellect and reason, but all were uncomfortable with the racial status quo. Archibald had grown up in Bullock County in the eastern reaches of the Alabama Black Belt—a small, dark-haired boy with a streak of stubbornness that often got him in trouble. As a child of maybe six, he was puzzled by a reprimand from his father—who had always taught him to be polite—when he said "Yes, sir" to a man who was black. Some years later at the age of sixteen, he happened to be in Montgomery on a shopping trip with his mother on the day the freedom riders were attacked. He saw Floyd Mann and his corps of state troopers breaking up a beating so vicious it was hard to comprehend, and back home in Union Springs he tried to tell his peers about the scene. Nobody would listen. The consensus seemed to be that the freedom riders had gotten what they deserved, and his friends threatened Murph with a dose of the same. He dared them to try.

In Birmingham, he found a few comrades with the same kind of history, the same kind of stories to put a face on the prejudice, and they proclaimed their solidarity with the movement. One of their group, a brave young woman named Marti Turnipseed, was suspended from school, and after one particular round of protests, there was a fear in the dorm of an attack by the Klan. There were nights in the spring of 1963 when they could hear the bombs going off in the city, and there was something else they remembered also—the shattered windshields on the cars of their friends when they were caught in the black neighborhoods at night.

It was into this environment that Martin Luther King and the movement finally came, to a city that seemed to some of its residents to be teetering almost at the edge of racial war. Even so, many people didn't want King to come. After the truce in September 1962 and the temporary removal of the Whites-Only signs, the politics of the city were still complicated. The November referendum had been successful, and Birmingham was preparing for a new form of government—a mayor-council arrangement that would soon eliminate Bull Connor's job. Connor, however, had refused to go away. In the spring of 1963, he was running for mayor, hoping, as he had so often in the past, to be swept into office by the power of the backlash. The city was bracing itself for demonstrations, and Sid Smyer, among others, thought they were just what Bull Connor needed. Smyer still nursed his visceral distaste for the tactics of King and Fred Shuttlesworth, and he was not alone. Even Emory Jackson, the outspoken editor of the *Birmingham World,* a black newspaper unequivocal in its opposition to segregation, questioned the wisdom and the timing of King's demonstrations.

So did other editors in other parts of the country. The *Washington Post* and *Time* magazine both offered warnings, and partly in response to all those voices, King and Wyatt Walker decided on a small and strategic change of plans. They would wait until after the election of April 2, the mayor's race between Connor and the more moderate segregationist, Albert Boutwell. Many people saw it as a voter referendum on the future of the city—Connor the tyrant, the hate-spewing symbol of massive resistance, and Boutwell the pragmatist, the former state legislator who favored negotiation over confrontation, and pleaded eloquently for an atmosphere of calm. The citizens were captivated by the drama, and with a voter turnout of 75 percent, the two men split the white vote evenly. But the blacks who had managed to register through the years gave Boutwell his solid margin of victory.

There were those who argued that the movement needed to give Boutwell a chance, a honeymoon period to see what he would do. King, however, believed the time for such patience had passed, for even the moderate white leaders needed prodding. The demonstrations, he said, would begin April 3.

In the weeks and months leading up to that moment, Wyatt Walker had done his best to prepare. With Shuttlesworth's secretary, Lola Hendricks, he had cased the downtown shopping district, walking the sidewalks, making his notes. He had layout charts of the downtown stores and maps of the streets and lists of people who had agreed to go to jail. Mrs. Hendricks was impressed with his attention to detail, his air of command, a level of self-confidence that rivaled Shuttlesworth's. Walker was a thin and energetic man with dark-rimmed glasses and the hint of a mustache, and he liked to think of himself, he admitted, as the movement's designated "son of a bitch."

Certainly, he was a very different man from Dr. King, who struck Mrs. Hendricks as gentle and quiet and easy to approach. She would watch him sometimes walking by himself to a little soul food place that was just up the street—the Fraternal Restaurant, tucked away in a brick storefront with plate glass windows, famous for its chicken and greens, its cornbread and pies. Along the way, King would talk to anybody he saw, oblivious to the danger, or so it appeared, and Mrs. Hendricks had to worry about him sometimes.

Even with his towering eloquence in the pulpit, there seemed to be a private uncertainty about him, a sense of the irony in what they were doing. He had talked sometimes in their strategy sessions about the labor movement in the 1930s, a force on the surface much stronger than their own, which had come up short when it tried to take on the city of steel.

Fundamentally, not much had changed in the past thirty years. White people still controlled every instrument of power—the economy, the political structure, the police—and even if there were cracks in the old monolith, political divisions, and the first hint of doubt about the moral rectitude of white supremacy, King and the others understood the odds. This was still the most segregated city in the South, and in their declaration of a nonviolent war, they were essentially taking a great leap of faith—"a cold plunge," as one historian later put it, and they had no idea what the outcome would be.

On April 3, 1963, their first group of demonstrators was small, maybe sixty-five people, barely a fourth of the number they expected. They met for a final time with James Lawson, who had been making frequent trips to the city, conducting nonviolent workshops much like those he had done in Nashville. He talked once more about the philosophy of nonviolence and the tactics that inevitably went along with it, and then the group, feeling a little wary, headed for five lunch counters uptown. Four of the five closed down immediately, leaving the protesters momentarily confused, but the management at Britt's, the fifth lunch counter, called the police. Twenty-one demonstrators were arrested, and that was it. There was no brutality, no fanfare, and very little notice in the Birmingham press.

The daily newspapers focused instead on the hometown premiere of *To Kill a Mockingbird*, which featured an Alabama actress, Mary Badham, in the starring role as Scout Finch. There was an irony in the juxtaposition, of course. The Pulitzer Prize–winning novel by Harper Lee, published originally in 1960, was a testament to racial moderation and decency, deeply rooted in the history of Alabama. In 1931, when Miss Lee was a girl in the town of Monroeville, the newspapers and family conversations were full of stories about the Scottsboro Boys—nine black hobos convicted of raping two white women. The judge in the case, James Horton, was a Lincolnesque figure with high cheekbones and piercing eyes and a firm and even-handed manner in the courtroom. Based on the flimsy evidence in the case—a doctor who doubted that the rape had taken place, a victim who ultimately admitted that it hadn't—he set aside the verdict of the jury and ordered a new trial, sacrificing his own career in the process. Some scholars later would see the similarity to Atticus Finch, the gentle hero of *To Kill a Mockingbird*, a man who never looked for controversy, but met it head on when it came his way. Harper Lee's own father, Amasa Lee, was said to be the same kind of person, and with history as her guide Miss Lee told the story of the segregated South, the hysteria and prejudice and the simple antidote of a small-town lawyer—a respect for people regardless of their color. It was a lesson Birmingham could have used, but it was swept away in the passion of 1963.

When the demonstrations started, Bull Connor was not in a mood to compromise, and he seemed disappointed by the size of the protests. By the end of the second day, barely two dozen people were in the jail, and Connor had hoped by then to have it full. He had taken his defeat in the election very badly, filing a lawsuit to overturn the result, and in the meantime he was spoiling for a fight. He was ready on Saturday, April 6, when Fred Shuttlesworth led a march of forty people to city hall. It seemed to be an escalation of the stakes, a more enthusiastic demonstration this time, led by a man who made him sputter with rage. Connor was happy to put them all in his jail.

Then came April 7, Palm Sunday, the first day of the dogs. Perhaps it was nothing more than his mood, but Connor had his corps of German shepherds waiting. The peaceful marchers were led this time by an impressive trio of Birmingham ministers, the important second tier of the leadership structure. There was Nelson Smith, the vice president of the Alabama Christian Movement for Human Rights, and John Porter, the longtime friend of Martin Luther King who was now the pastor of Sixth Avenue Baptist, and A. D. King, Martin's brother and a brave and committed man on his own. In the coming weeks, the three of them would lead several critical marches, calling themselves the three horsemen of the apocalypse, and Porter was impressed by the courage of his comrades. He found himself particularly drawn to A.D., a man he had known since his days in Atlanta, when he served as an assistant to Martin Luther King Sr. The old man was such a "bitter pill," Porter said, bombastic, overbearing, and A.D. always seemed to get the worst of it. Martin also was the occasional object of his father's tirades, but he had the ability to take it in his stride. "Aw, Dad," he would say, and simply walk away, but A.D. would fight him, and emotionally at least there was blood on the carpet.

Over the years, Porter saw the damage to the psyche of his friend, a drinking problem that slowly but surely became more serious. But in the immediate excitement of the Palm Sunday march, he was thinking more about a generational conflict of his own. His father, Robert Porter, was a Birmingham yard man, raking the leaves, cutting the grass, pruning the hedges of the people who could pay him. He encouraged the ministerial ambitions of his son, but was terrified of the civil rights movement. He was like a lot of older people that way. Based on the long experience of his life, he could hardly imagine that the changes envisioned by the movement could occur. What seemed more likely was that somebody would get killed, and he did not want it to be his son.

But as the marchers made their way up Sixth Avenue, singing "Hold My Hand While I Run This Race," Robert Porter pushed his way through the throng and fell into step, taking his place in the movement with his son. "I could have marched to New York," John Porter remembered.

In fact, they made it to Seventeenth Street, where the policemen stopped them and made their arrests. As the onlookers began to jeer in disapproval, the police dogs attacked a black teenager, Leroy Allen, and when he heard the news Wyatt Walker was ecstatic. It was precisely what they had expected of Connor—an image that made for spectacular headlines and dramatic footage on the six o'clock news.

The rush of notoriety, however, was short-lived. The subtext now on Martin Luther King, the unspoken assumption of the national press corps was that he was probably a leader who was past his prime—a failure in the Albany, Georgia, protests who was heading for the same result in Birmingham. More and more, that seemed to be the spin, and while King himself was not admitting defeat, he was aware of the obstacles that were mounting all the time. During the week following the Palm Sunday protests, an Alabama judge issued an injunction banning future marches, precisely at the time when the movement was starting to run out of bail money. King could no longer promise the Birmingham people who were willing to go to jail exactly how soon they would be getting out.

On April 12, Good Friday morning, the movement leadership gathered in Room 30 of the Gaston Motel to try to figure out what to do next. It was a more broad-based group than some of those had gathered in the past, a "central committee" from the Alabama Christian Movement for Human Rights, King's staff members from SCLC, and some of the city's more traditional black leaders, including A. G. Gaston and Lucius Pitts. Several people said King should leave Birmingham and make a fund-raising

trip through the North, and the logic of the argument was nearly overwhelming. King was the movement's most effective fund-raiser; one or
two speeches to the right kind of audience, and the money once again
would be flowing in. The problem was, he had promised to be a part of a
Good Friday march, to lead by example and take his own turn in the
Birmingham jail. He didn't much care for the whole idea. There was a
part of him that hated the inside of a jail, that recoiled from the claustro-
phobia and the fear, and there were those in his own inner circle of advisers who were giving him an out—who told him his talents were needed
elsewhere. But how could he ask other people in the city to do something
he was unwilling to do?

His spirits sank lower as he pondered the dilemma, and while the people around him continued their discussion, he retreated to the adjoining
room by himself. He stood there alone and prayed for an answer, and after
a while everything became clear. He changed from his suit to a pair of
blue jeans and a denim work shirt, his "go-to-jail" clothes, he told the others in the suite. He was still not certain what would happen to them next,
but the moment had come to move ahead on faith, for what else did they
have?

He asked Ralph Abernathy to go to jail with him, and when Abernathy
balked—he wanted to preach the Easter sermon at his church—King
repeated his request, more softly this time, but equally as firm: "I am asking you to go with me." Andrew Young was not at all surprised. Young
was another of King's lieutenants, one of the brightest and most articulate, and he knew that Abernathy was as close to King as anybody on
earth. "He was really the pastor to Dr. King," said Young, "a source of
strength," who was there at the moments of insecurity and doubt. This
was one of those moments, and Abernathy understood it, and he changed
immediately to his outfit of denim. Shuttlesworth did the same, and the
three of them left the room to lead the march—Shuttlesworth jaunty,
Abernathy smiling to lift the spirits of his friend, King still looking a little bit afraid.

By the time of his arrest, King's countenance had changed. One white
bystander remembered years later "a stoicism that seemed to shade into
sadness," but no trace of fear. He was ready for whatever Bull Connor had
in mind.

They took him away to the Birmingham jail and put him immediately in a cell by himself. It was a dismal place with concrete walls and a cold metal bed without any mattress, and he was left there alone in the fading sunlight to wonder about the future of his movement. Sometime over the weekend, he received word of an article in the *Birmingham Post Herald,* and another in the *News,* in which eight white clergymen criticized the demonstrations, calling them "unwise and ill-timed." These, he discovered, were no ordinary critics. They were some of the most prominent ministers in town—Protestant, Catholic, a Jewish rabbi—and they were anything but bigots. A few months earlier, they had issued a statement taking aim at George Wallace. They were shocked by the tone of his inaugural address, the defiant cry of "segregation forever," and they called for racial understanding and calm.

There were shades of opinion within the group of eight. Episcopal bishop Charles Carpenter was one of the most conservative, a six-foot-four-inch bear of a man, a former college wrestler who was now in his sixties but appeared, even so, like a man who could still hold his own in the ring. Episcopal young people in his confirmation classes remembered the size and strength of his hands, and many of them winced at the power of his grip. He was a son of the South, born just before the turn of the century, and while he spoke out bluntly against racial violence—the attacks on the freedom riders, for example—he never saw the harm in segregation itself. His Episcopal colleague, George Murray, was different. The youngest of the group at age fifty-four, he was a gifted orator who regarded racial segregation as a sin, a denial of the notion that all men were brothers. In 1962 he criticized Bull Connor's decision to close down the city parks rather than obey a court order to integrate, and he was not alone in the controversy that it brought him. Southern Baptist minister Earl Stallings and Presbyterian Edward Ramage both received menacing letters and calls, including death threats, when they decided to welcome black visitors to their churches.

Taken together, these were men in the moderate camp, offended by the hard-line rhetoric of Connor and Wallace, but offended also by Martin Luther King. In the spring of 1963 Murray invited King to take part in a series of interracial meetings that he had moderated since the previous year. King declined, but sent Shuttlesworth and Andrew Young in his place, and the meetings demonstrated what everybody knew—that Birmingham was divided by a chasm of mistrust that was only growing deeper and wider all the time. Murray and his seven ministerial colleagues believed King and his movement were primarily to blame. Their proclamations of nonviolence were essentially a facade, for their purpose, undeniably, was to provoke a violent response among the whites, then exploit the resulting publicity for the movement. They were provocateurs just as surely as George Wallace.

Alone in the jail, King set out to answer that charge. Writing in the margins of the newspaper story and later on the toilet paper in his cell, he began composing his "Letter from a Birmingham Jail." In the beginning it was nothing much more than a scribble, the passionate outpouring of a man who had nothing but time on his hands. For some years now, he had been deeply offended by the timidity of white moderates, particularly those in the church, who should have known better. There were exceptions, of course—the Jesuit priests at Spring Hill College who had integrated their school in Mobile without the coercion or pressure of a lawsuit, and Will Campbell, the Southern Baptist from Nashville who had made the trip to Alabama on numerous occasions, doing whatever he could for the movement. And perhaps most impressively, there was Robert Graetz, the devout and soft-spoken Montgomery Lutheran whose house had been bombed for his support of the boycott. But the very power of such witness called attention to the fact that it was rare. Far more common were these Birmingham preachers with the paternalistic arrogance to talk about patience—to set a timetable for another man's freedom.

"I guess it is easy," King wrote from his cell, "for those who have never felt the stinging darts of segregation to say, 'Wait.' But when you have seen vicious mobs lynch your mothers and fathers at will and drown your sisters and brothers at whim; when you have seen hate-filled policemen curse, kick, brutalize and even kill your black brothers and sisters with impunity; when you see the vast majority of your twenty million Negro brothers smothering in an air-tight cage of poverty in the midst of an affluent society; when you suddenly find your tongue twisted and your speech stammering as you seek to explain to your six-year-old daughter why she can't go to the public amusement park; . . . when you have to concoct an answer to a five-year-old son asking in agonizing pathos: 'Daddy, why do white people treat colored people so mean?'; . . . when you are harried by day and haunted by night by the fact that you are a Negro, living constantly at a tip-toe stance, never quite knowing what to expect next, and plagued with inner fears and outer resentments; when you are forever fighting a degenerating sense of 'nobodiness;' then you will understand why we find it difficult to wait."

When the pieces of the letter came to Wyatt Walker, smuggled out by the visitors to King's jail cell, he began to put them together like a puzzle, working with his secretary, Willie Pearl Mackey, to create a document that King could polish and review when he was free. Walker thought it was a coup, a public relations breakthrough for a movement reaching out to the country as a whole. Here was Dr. King, trapped in a dungeon for the things he believed, writing with a passion reminiscent of the prophets. Walker understood the potential over time. And certainly by the summer of 1963 the letter was assuming its place in history—reprinted in a number of religious publications, and regarded by many as one of the greatest documents in the history of Christianity.

That was how it was over time, but at first nobody was listening. After eight days, King emerged from the jail and discovered that almost nothing had changed; the movement was as shaky as it had been when he left. He called a meeting of his staff, and John Porter, who was there, remembered being shocked. "Dr. King came in," Porter told an interviewer, "and said very urgently, 'The press is losing interest; we've gotta do something to get their attention.' Well, I thought to myself, 'We're supposed to be following the Constitution. We've got *God* on our side. We don't need the press.' But of course he was right."

For Porter, it was a lesson in the pragmatism of the movement, a side of King he hadn't seen very often, and one, he thought, a little less inspiring than his steady personality or the beauty of his sermons in the mass movement pulpits. And it was one that didn't come as easily to King. There were times when he was facing strategic decisions that he agonized almost to the edge of paralysis, and one of those moments came in May 1963. The great calypso singer Harry Belafonte had helped replenish their coffers for bail, raising fifty thousand dollars after King was arrested, but even so, they were running out of people who were willing to go to jail. It was then that James Bevel, a veteran of the Nashville sit-in movement, proposed the most startling idea King had ever heard. Let the children march, Bevel said. They could demonstrate the courage that their elders seemed to lack.

It turned out that Bevel was serious about it. He was emerging by then as the mad genius of the movement, having come to Birmingham from Mississippi, where he was working in the most dangerous part of the state. He often appeared in public with a yarmulke, a "Jewish beanie," as he liked to call it, to signify his identification with the prophets—those Old Testament heroes who talked about justice raining down like the waters. There were people who compared him to Vernon Johns, a kind of John the Baptist figure in the movement, for Johns, like Bevel, was unpredictable and tough. One of his Montgomery deacons, R. D. Nesbitt, remembered the time when Johns was insulted by the driver of a bus and threatened immediately to "kick the driver's ass."

Bevel, in the end, was not like that. His commitment to nonviolence was absolute, but he was radical and charismatic, and ever since his arrival in Birmingham, he had been reaching out to students— some in college, some even younger. Many had studied about freedom in school. Under committed black teachers like Claude Wesley and Odessa Woolfolk, the students at Parker and Ullman high schools had talked about the gap between the promise of democracy and the daily realities of black people's lives. The seeds had been planted before James Bevel came and began his round of student workshops, but it was Bevel who made the teachings come alive. By the beginning of May thousands of young people were ready to march, and the elders in the civil rights movement were appalled. A. G. Gaston, in particular, was shocked, but even John Porter thought that Martin King had lost his mind.

King, in fact, was still agonizing, worried about the safety of the students and the opposition of their parents, but knowing that without them the movement would die. The hard truth was, there weren't enough adults who were willing to go to jail. On Thursday morning, May 2, the day they had promised to hold their next march, King retreated to his motel room, still unable to make up his mind, while the more decisive leaders in the movement—Bevel and Shuttlesworth, Andrew Young and Dorothy Cotton—talked to the students about the philosophy of nonviolence. One last time, they went over their expectations for the day, and just after noon young people by the hundreds burst from the doors of Sixteenth

Street Baptist Church and into Kelly Ingram Park across the street. As the policemen began to make their arrests, the squad cars and paddy wagons filled up immediately, and Connor and his forces put out an emergency call for school buses. But the children kept coming, more than a thousand by the end of the day, some of them still in elementary school, filling the jails in Birmingham and beyond.

The next day, there were more, and Connor by now had simply had enough. As the students emerged once again from the church, a phalanx of firemen turned on their hoses, knocking young demonstrators to the ground, rolling them along, as one observer put it, "like a pebble at high tide." When the protesters continued to pour from the church, Connor brought out his dogs—the canine corps he had used once before—and this time the nation was treated to the image of Walter Gadsden, a fifteen-year-old bystander, caught in the grasp of a German shepherd.

A. G. Gaston was staring at all this from his nearby office. He was talking on the phone to David Vann, one of the city's white liberals, and they were complaining as they had many times in the past about King and his tactics—an affront to the moderation that was needed if the city was ever going to solve its racial problems. Suddenly, Gaston interrupted the conversation. "Lawyer Vann," he said, in a tone of disbelief, "they've turned the fire hoses on a little black girl! And they're rolling that girl right down the middle of the street." From that moment on, the most powerful black businessman in the city put aside his ambivalence about King and Shuttlesworth and their movement. All of a sudden everything seemed simple. There were only two sides, and everybody had to choose. You could be with the movement and the children in the streets, or you could be with the police commissioner and his dogs, who were suddenly the symbols of everything that was wrong.

That was how Gaston saw it, and he was not alone. All across the country, the images flashed across the television screens, and the horror and revulsion became an epidemic. It was the lasting legacy of Bull Connor—the greatest blunder in the history of segregation—and he was not finished yet.

CHAPTER 11

"Keep on Pushing"

EVEN AFTER THE ATTACKS OF MAY 3, 1963, the young people continued to march against Connor. Freeman Hrabowski was the leader of one protest, a twelve-year-old who was pudgy and bookish and a little bit afraid. For some time now, like most of the children in the black neighborhoods, he had wanted to be a part of the civil rights movement. He had been to some of the mass meetings with his parents, who were educators committed to the ideal of freedom, and he was bitterly disappointed when they told him he was too young to march. Something might happen, they said, and they simply couldn't live with themselves if it did. "Then you're hypocrites," Freeman replied, and turned out the light in his room and went to bed.

Sometime before morning, they came to his room. They had been up all night unable to sleep, talking about the movement and their responsibilities as parents, and they had finally come to a difficult decision. "You can go," they said, and with that it was settled. He went down immediately to John Porter's church and began to take part in the nonviolent workshops, learning the philosophy and the ways to protect himself against attack. On the day of the march, the organizers put him at the front of the line, and they left Porter's church and started up the street, singing freedom songs. They made it all the way to City Hall, and Bull Connor himself was waiting for them there. "I was so scared," Hrabowski remembered, but he did his best to stare into the reddened face of this man who was staring back at him with a look of pure hate.

"What do you want, little nigger?" Connor demanded.

"We want our freedom," said Hrabowski, and with that Connor grabbed him and spat in his face. In the troubled days and weeks after that, his parents talked to him often about hate. In many ways, that had been their biggest fear—that a child at the impressionable age of twelve would carry the emotional scars all his life, a crippling anger that was nothing but a mirror image of Bull Connor's. In the spring and early summer of 1963, a lot of conversations like that took place in Birmingham. A lot of parents worried about their children, worried about the rage that was sweeping through them all.

In the first week of May the spiral of violence was only getting worse. Contrary to the prevailing image in the media, the reality in the streets was often complicated—crowds of African Americans on the sidewalks, observers at first, caught by the spectacle of peaceful demonstrators facing off against the water cannons and the dogs, and Connor speeding by in his miniature tank, a white armored car that was made just for him. There was a black German shepherd that was said to be the worst—the nastiest member of the canine corps—and the rumor quickly spread that the dog had been christened "Nigger" by his handlers and was trained to attack at the sound of his name. As Connor exhorted his troops to greater violence, the black bystanders answered in kind, raining bricks and bottles on the ranks of the officers, and the demonstrations teetered on the edge of a riot. James Bevel was often in the thick of it, and Shuttlesworth too, demanding restraint, determined to preserve the purity of the cause.

By the night of Monday, May 6, the jails were full and the imprisoned children who could no longer fit were penned outdoors at the state fairgrounds, huddled together in a driving rainstorm. Many of their parents, frantic with worry, came that night to the mass meetings at the churches—four different sanctuaries this time, filled to overflowing. King told them not to be afraid for the children; they were uncomfortable now, but they were central players in a noble undertaking, and they would be fine. The parents nodded gravely at the reassuring tone, but it was Ralph Abernathy who lifted their spirits, and he did it with humor. Abernathy had a gift for connecting with the people, and on this particular night he spoke with a merry twinkle in his eye. "Day before yesterday," he declared, "we filled up the jail. Today, we filled up the jail *yard*. And tomorrow, when they look up and see that number coming, I don't know *what* they're gonna do!"

While the audience cheered and sang freedom songs, the movement strategists were beginning a session that would last all night. With the jails overflowing and blacks boycotting the downtown stores, Wyatt Walker was ready to turn up the heat. He had noticed that white shoppers, too, were staying away from the stores, apparently afraid of getting caught in the trouble, and he was determined to bring the business district to its knees. He and the others worked until daybreak, putting together a plan for a massive operation, full of feints and diversions and all the precision of a military assault. This, he hoped, would be the movement's equivalent of D-Day.

On Tuesday morning, May 7, Martin Luther King called a press conference to announce "the nonviolent movement's coming of age." Even as he spoke, hundreds of young people made their way to downtown, moving unobtrusively in groups of a dozen, while Dorothy Cotton and other organizers waited for them with carloads of signs. Shortly after noon James Bevel sent out a group of decoys from the Sixteenth Street Baptist Church, an exuberant party of would-be picketers whose placards were confiscated by police. At precisely that moment, the hundreds of young people already downtown retrieved their picket signs from the cars and began to march through the heart of the city.

Serendipitously, that was also the moment when a group of business leaders had assembled for an emergency Chamber of Commerce luncheon to talk about the crisis. What the businessmen saw was their city overrun, blacks marching everywhere, and policemen, realizing that they had been duped, rushing uptown from Kelly Ingram Park, a distance of maybe eight or ten blocks. As soon as the policemen broke from their lines, more marchers poured from the church next door and began a "freedom dash" for downtown, adding to the mounting sense of chaos.

Back at the Gaston Motel, Fred Shuttlesworth burst into the room where King had returned from his morning press conference. "Martin," he shouted, "this is it!" But King was not in a mood to celebrate. He knew the plan was working so far, but he also knew they were inches from a riot, and he was afraid their credibility couldn't stand it. They had been so righteous in their proclamations of nonviolence, but the hard and simple truth of it was that in addition to the demonstrators who were trained, Birmingham was full of angry black people who had never been to a movement workshop and who were ready to explode at the heavy hand of Bull Connor. King understood exactly how they felt, but he also believed if they descended again and again into hate they blurred the lines between themselves and their oppressors. Such were the moral complications of the hour.

By the middle of the afternoon, King's most depressing fears came true as a pitched battle broke out in Kelly Ingram Park. It was a confusing melee, consisting of nearly two thousand demonstrators, most of them orderly, a frustrated corps of three hundred policemen, backed by their dogs, and a smaller group of city firefighters, ready with their hoses. Lining the sidewalk at the south end of the park was another group of blacks—onlookers angered by the hoses and the dogs. As they began throwing rocks, Fred Shuttlesworth waded into the fray and began to lead a group of young people back to the relative safety of the church. A firefighter saw him and in an act of disdain for this rabble-rousing preacher, took aim with his hose, knocking Shuttlesworth back against the church, breaking a rib with the first blast of water.

As Shuttlesworth lay crumpled on the pavement, a student demonstrator, James Orange, was the first at his side. "Let's go!" whispered Shuttlesworth through the pain. "I'm ready to march." But Orange and a couple of Birmingham ministers were able to persuade him to go to the hospital. When Bull Connor heard the news, he said he was sorry he hadn't been there to see it. "It must have been funny as hell," he declared. "I wish they'd carried him away in a hearse."

For Sidney Smyer, all of this was too much. He was a man who had come a long way in his thinking—from a Dixiecrat in 1948, who had walked out of the National Democratic Convention, to a committed moderate in 1963, a Chamber of Commerce leader trying to find some solution for his city. He looked like the businessman that he was, with his conservative suits and receding hairline and a smile for the camera that looked a little smug. But he was a man of courage who understood clearly the risk he was taking. Slowly and reluctantly, he had reached the conclusion that he and the other white leaders in the city had to negotiate with the Negroes, including those who made him ill at ease.

The Kennedy administration agreed with that decision and decided it was time to play a role in the process. The president had dispatched Burke Marshall to the city, putting his faith in this mild-mannered man who worked with Robert Kennedy in the Justice Department. Marshall, the assistant attorney general for civil rights, was anything but a charismatic figure. He often spoke in a monotone, almost a mumble, but his non-threatening manner proved to be effective for the job in Birmingham. He was a shuttle diplomat between the blacks and the whites, pushing both sides. Like the other members of the young administration, he thought of himself as a pragmatist, searching for a settlement that was good for the country and good for his boss. He had his reservations about King, a leader who didn't seem to know what he wanted. It was true that the movement had a few specific goals, including the immediate desegregation of downtown facilities, but King was talking about something vaguer. In his speeches and even his private conversation, he would rhapsodize about the idea of freedom and a promised land of brotherhood and justice. To the Ivy League pragmatists in the new administration, it was all too dreamy, like grabbing at smoke.

But if Marshall was unsure about the leadership of King, his sympathies increasingly were on the side of the Negroes. He was part of a gradual shift, subtle and involuntary at first, that seemed to be reaching all the way to the president—a willingness, despite their hard-headed calculations, to see not only the political implications but also the moral dimensions of the issue. On May 7, as the demonstrators poured through the city, Marshall met with Smyer and the other business leaders. He urged them bluntly to face up to the problem, which was the denial of basic rights to black citizens.

Thus prodded by Marshall, the white leaders struggled with the issue that day, and around midnight they decided to meet with Martin Luther King. Led by Smyer, they continued their discussions until nearly daybreak, and with the diplomatic help of Andrew Young, who seemed to have the gift for conciliatory language, they knew they were close to some kind of settlement.

It took three more days to work out the details, but on the afternoon of Friday, May 10, Shuttlesworth, Abernathy, and King called a press conference to announce an agreement. Sitting at the microphone in the middle and still hurting from his wounds, Shuttlesworth declared that Birmingham had reached "an accord with its conscience." He sounded subdued, and none of the leaders seemed to be overjoyed. Like all compromises, this one carried its share of disappointment, the feeling of a victory that had been watered down. Instead of the *immediate* desegregation of public accommodations, which had been the original demand of the movement, the agreement called for a phased integration within the next ninety days. Instead of the immediate hiring of Negro clerks, the agreement allowed for a wait of sixty days. Instead of charges being dropped against civil rights protesters, the compromise called for their release on bond. So it went, and Shuttlesworth was deeply apprehensive. He had little faith in the word of the whites, remembering the return of the Colored-Only signs a few months before, and he and King had quarreled at the end.

"Ain't no use scalding the hog on one side!" he thundered, contending that King was giving away too much. "While the water is hot, scald him on both sides and get him clean. If the water gets cold, you ain't *never* gonna clean off that hog."

That moment came when both men were tired, but they managed ultimately to patch things up, declaring a public victory for the cause. Both of them were facing a moral dilemma, a tug-of-war of competing inclinations. On the one hand, both the Kennedy administration and Martin Luther King needed to deliver a piece of good news, a demonstration of progress to reassure the nation. On the other hand, it was critically important to make certain it was real—a tangible improvement in the life of Birmingham—and Shuttlesworth wasn't sure that was true. With all the built-in provisions for delay, it was too soon to tell.

Such was the ambivalence the two leaders shared, but at the moment of the truce, they knew their enemies had no such problem. Bull Connor and his friends were simply irate. They rushed to denounce this act of treason by Smyer and the other white business leaders, a development they could only attribute to cowardice. Arthur Hanes, Connor's colleague on the city commission, called it "capitulation by certain weak-kneed white people under threats of violence by the rabble-rousing Negro, King."

Hanes and Connor both knew what they were doing. From years of experience, they knew their core constituency would get the message— the masses of white people out there in the hamlets, who were afraid their world was about to come apart. Some of them, particularly the men with a love of dynamite, would know exactly what to do next.

On Saturday night, May 11, Imperial Wizard Robert Shelton stood before a thousand members of the Klan, a burning cross casting shadows on their faces. The faithful had gathered in a field outside of Birmingham, and they listened resolutely as Shelton declared: "Martin Luther King has not gained one thing in Birmingham, because the white people are not going to tolerate the meddlesome, conniving, manipulating moves of these professional businessmen." When the cheers subsided, he surrendered the podium to one of his commanders who talked about the need for "stiff-backed men . . . willing to go out and fight the battle for the Lord Jesus Christ."

A few hours later, a pair of bombs exploded at the home of A. D. King. It was not yet eleven, as King steadied himself and ran searching through the wreckage for the members of his family. He found them unhurt, which was hard to imagine, given the level of damage to the house. Bombs had exploded in the front and the back, shattering windows, splintering a door, and the sound of the explosion reverberated through the black neighborhoods. Within a few minutes, a thousand people had gathered in the street, many of them screaming for revenge, threatening the policemen who arrived on the scene. King went out to confront his own people. Go home, he said. There's been enough violence.

The people in the crowd didn't leave right away; there was too much anger, too much fear, but under King's gentle prodding, their rage gave way to a haunting chorus of "We Shall Overcome."

Then came the sickening sound of another bomb. The target this time was the Gaston Motel, the place where Martin Luther King had been staying, and the bomb exploded right under his room. Martin wasn't there. He had returned to Atlanta to preach the Sunday sermon at his church, but the word quickly spread that the Ku Klux Klan had tried to kill Dr. King. A screaming mob appeared at Kelly Ingram Park, throwing rocks, setting fire to a car. Wyatt Walker and Bernard Lee, who were staying at the motel, rushed outside and started pleading for calm. As soon as he could get there, A. D. King did the same, and they were grateful for the fact that the police at the time were under the command of Jamie Moore, their well-trained chief, and not his supervisor Bull Connor. It was a curious alliance in these turbulent hours just after midnight—the black leaders trying to soothe the mob, Chief Moore working to do the same with his police.

They were making some progress around 2 A.M., when everything came apart. Just as the rioting was beginning to subside, a caravan of two hundred state troopers roared down on the park, and their commander this time was not Floyd Mann, the consummate law enforcement professional who had saved the lives of the freedom riders in Montgomery. Mann had left office with Governor Patterson, and his successor, Al Lingo, was ready to make his mark. Like Bull Connor, Lingo was the very embodiment of malice—as one historian later described him, "a tough, pot-bellied, bug-eyed archetype of southern law enforcement."

In the early morning hours of Sunday, May 12, he and his men came armed for open war. In addition to their billy clubs and handguns, many of them also carried carbines, and Lingo himself was ready with a shotgun. "Those guns are not needed," said Police Chief Moore. "Will you please put them up? Somebody's going to get killed."

"You're damned right," Lingo replied, and for the next several hours he and his men ran amok, chasing down black people in the streets, swinging their clubs, beating anybody who came within range. In response the rioting exploded once again, and before it spent itself with the dawn, fires were burning in a dozen different places, and more than sixty people had been taken to the hospital. Martin Luther King rushed back to Birmingham and began to work his way through the bars, the places where alcohol could lubricate the rage, and pleaded for the people there to stay calm. He knew it was a curious time for the movement. On the one hand, the issue of civil rights was clearly on the radar screen of the nation, and in that regard Birmingham was everything they had hoped—a powerful morality play for the nation. The television cameras had done their job, for this was the kind of story they could grasp—Bull

Connor and his dogs, and now the troopers of Al Lingo, defending a system that deserved no defense. But if you looked more closely, the purity of the nonviolent cause had been tainted, sullied by the riots, and in Birmingham itself there was a deep ambivalence about what had been accomplished. Some people said King had sold out the city, signing an agreement before it was time, declaring a victory as thin as the paper on which it was written.

Racial tensions, meanwhile, were at an all-time high, and it seemed clear enough that the segregationist leaders, including the governor, were different from those who had come just before. George Wallace was not John Patterson, and Al Lingo was not Floyd Mann. During the Freedom Rides barely two years earlier, Patterson had waged his rhetorical war against the demonstrators, and his critics understood that there were consequences to that kind of talk—people in the ranks of the violent resisters who assumed the governor was on their side. But there was a difference between the violence in 1961— the battering of the demonstrators by the Klan—and the attacks that followed in 1963. The police in Birmingham and Montgomery were the silent conspirators the first time around, willing to let the Klan have its way. Two years later, the pretense was gone. Bull Connor and his forces were leading the attack.

The state troopers, meanwhile, changed direction entirely, abandoning the role of reluctant rescuers—men who were willing, in a moment of crisis, to save the lives of black demonstrators because that was what law enforcement required. Such was Mann's understanding of the job, but now he was gone and so was Patterson, and when George Wallace handed the job to Lingo, he had to know everything would be different. Lingo came from the Barbour County town of Eufaula, just a few miles from the Wallace home place. Wallace knew him well, knew that he had only limited experience (he had been a highway patrolman in the 1930s), and his only apparent qualification for the job was his hatred of black people. But if a little head-knocking played well in the state, Lingo was only too happy to oblige.

In the weeks after his initial attacks in Birmingham, he found a place to work on his skills, to hone the art of his personal brutality, away from the prying eyes of the press. He went into Gadsden, an industrial community sixty miles to the east, a scruffy little hamlet on the Coosa River, where he believed, apparently, he could scare the civil rights movement to death.

He would fail in his effort, but it wasn't because he didn't try.

J. D. Cammeron remembered the pain of the first cattle prod—that first burning surge that was so intense, so unlike anything he had known, that it nearly made him cry. In the summer of 1963, he was part of a march of a thousand people, or nearly that many, an enormous number by the standards of Gadsden. Cammeron was a tough and hard-working man— a full-time laborer at a local pipe foundry and a part-time preacher at Mount Zion Baptist Church. Like many of the others that day, he had never been in a civil rights march, but he was tired of segregation and ready to fight it, and he discovered that it only stiffened his resolve when the demonstrators were arrested and tortured with the prods—the first test run by Lingo and his men.

The tensions in Gadsden had been building for a while, slowly pulling in people like Cammeron, ever since 1961 when a black union worker, Joseph Faulkner, filed a desegregation lawsuit. Faulkner was born in Autauga County just north of Montgomery, and in the 1940s he got laid off from a job in Birmingham and went over to Gadsden to visit his brother. During that visit, he found a job in the Republic Steel Mill, and Gadsden became his permanent home. He developed a love-hate relation-ship with it, for if Birmingham was a segregated place, Gadsden was worse, with White and Colored signs everywhere and clerks in the stores who would tell him on a whim, "We don't serve niggers here." He thought often about his boyhood days when he played with whites and sweated with them in the fields, and when they swam together in the muddy little creeks outside of Montgomery. As far as he could tell, there were no ill effects. But now here he was, a young husband and father, and they were treating him as if he were less than a boy. Finally, of course, he got tired of it, and when the sit-ins began in 1960, he and a couple of his closest friends, George Woods and Arthur Young, decided it was time to take a stand in Gadsden. They got on a bus and sat in the front, and were taken off to jail. Faulkner was exhilarated by the moment, and he and the others formed a group called the East Gadsden Brotherhood—a swash-buckling collection of grassroots activists, who kept confronting the issue of segregation, and kept getting arrested.

Through it all, he tried to keep his sense of humor. He was a stocky, round-faced man with an easy smile that made him look even younger than he was. Once in 1962, when he was in jail, Martin Luther King paid a visit to his cell. "Faulkner," he said, "God bless you for your courage," and it was like being blessed by the patron saint of the movement. But as Faulkner got to know Dr. King through the years, the thing that impressed him more than anything else was that King didn't carry himself like a saint. He was accessible and down-to-earth and funny, teasing a minister on one of his visits for wearing red socks. "Man," he said, "you couldn't get away with that in Atlanta." It made Faulkner feel like they were in it together—like their own little struggle in the community of Gadsden was tied to something much larger and more important, but something that was led by a real human being. That was the way it struck him at the time, and King's lieutenants made him feel the same. C. T. Vivian, Bernard Lee—they were all earnest men, respectful of the local movement in Gadsden, aware of the magnitude of what they were doing, but not so impressed with themselves they couldn't laugh.

For Faulkner and many others, it was easy to become energized by their presence, and by the spring and summer of 1963, he thought they were beginning to make a little progress. Their mass meetings at the churches were generally well attended, and local preachers like L. A. Warren and H. J. Hoyt understood exactly how to work up a crowd. In April many of the people had been deeply disturbed by the murder of William Moore, a white postal worker who was on a curious, one-man march for civil rights. Raised in Mississippi, later working in Maryland, Moore was walking alone through northern Alabama, wearing a sandwich board opposing segregation, when he was shot and killed just outside of Gadsden. For many blacks in the area, it was a reminder again of everything that was wrong—the official and unofficial brutality, the lack of jobs, the racial insults that became routine.

The black leaders called for an economic boycott and then in June an unrelenting string of sit-ins and marches. Richmond Flowers, the attorney general of Alabama, tried to get an injunction to shut down the protests, arguing that they were "interfering with the normal flow of commerce." As the tension continued to build through the summer, Al Lingo and his troopers came in and beat some women and children in a march, and the black community of Gadsden was enraged. Even people like J. D.

Cammeron, who had never been a part of a civil rights demonstration, except to attend an occasional mass meeting, were ready to take their place in the struggle. Cammeron remembered a meeting at the Galilee Baptist Church, where Martin Luther King had been the guest speaker. He was a man with a voice like nobody else's—a rich baritone with a hypnotic cadence and metaphors that Cammeron himself wouldn't use, but powerful images that stayed in his mind. "Freedom isn't free," Dr. King liked to say, and it was clear in Gadsden that they would have to pay a price.

They organized their massive march on August 3, 1963, and the Reverend L. A. Warren was at the head of the line as they started up Sixth Street and turned toward Forrest, where the police were waiting at the Rich Hotel. It was a daunting combination of physical force, for in addition to the specter of Lingo and his men, there were the local police and a collection of irregulars—a ragtag "posse," as somebody called them—deputized and armed to the teeth. The Reverend Warren later recalled his moment of defiance, when he informed the policemen that he and the others would not turn around. "Yes sir," he told an interviewer later, "those were some times. Those were the days when we did take a stand."

The police arrested the marchers right away, and there were beatings and proddings on the way to the jail, but it was what happened next that was hard to comprehend, and even in the telling of it forty years later, Faulkner and Warren and J. D. Cammeron felt themselves rekindling old wounds. There were, they said, too many people to fit in the jail. The women were placed in the city facility, and the men in the county, but there were not enough cells, and after an hour or two of indecision, the men were taken to the street once again and told to form a double line on the sidewalk.

Lingo was there, bullhorn in hand, his belly overhanging the belt of his pants. "Okay," he shouted, "move 'em out," and Faulkner thought he sounded like the cattle drive foreman on a television show. The similarity became even more degrading when the troopers began running the marchers up the sidewalk, beating and cattle prodding the stragglers. There were police on one side and the walls of downtown buildings on the other—no way to escape from the insults and the torture, but nobody tried. The marchers were trained in the philosophy of nonviolence, and in sharp contrast to the scenes in Birmingham, their discipline and self-restraint never cracked. They never hit back, never cried for revenge, but neither did any of them give in to panic. "We won't turn around," Reverend Warren had said, and that was how it was, even when they reached the Gadsden coliseum, the designated holding pen for the evening.

"When we got to the coliseum," remembered Cammeron, "they made everybody lie down. Those they thought were from out of town, they beat. They beat me across the legs with billy sticks and cattle prodded me all over. They beat me pitifully. It made you feel like you were nobody, like you had no rights whatsoever."

Cammeron thought later they had singled him out because the local policemen did not recognize him. He had not been a part of the earlier marches, and they assumed he was some kind of outside agitator, sent in by King for this particular demonstration. He tried to tell them that it simply wasn't true; he had lived in Gadsden all his life, but nobody would listen, and the beatings continued for the rest of the evening.

Finally, a fleet of cattle trucks appeared, big eighteen-wheelers that backed up to the door, and the prisoners were herded and prodded on board. Faulkner remembered how the trucks headed north, and as they turned off U.S. Highway 431 they passed a Klan rally out in a field. There was a burning cross and some men wearing sheets, and the truckload of prisoners pulled to a stop. Faulkner thought for a moment they would all be killed, or perhaps one or two would be pulled from the truck and lynched for the edification of the others. But it turned out to be psychological warfare, a pause for the contemplation of their fate, and then the truck moved on.

They came at last to a rural prison camp, mostly abandoned, where they were crowded into cells with concrete floors. For the next six days, that was where they slept, and the food when it came nearly made them gag—scraps of cornbread and some kind of thin, inedible soup. The beating and prodding continued off and on, and one day Cammeron was sitting on the floor and staring at his legs, bloody and infected from the pounding of the clubs. His oldest son, J. D. Junior, was there in the cell, a boy of sixteen who had been in the march, and he crawled over slowly to be with his father.

"Daddy, you hurt?"

"No, not bad."

For the next several days, they took what comfort they could from that fiction, but the truth of it was, it would be several months before the oozing and the throbbing in his legs would stop. And for a long time after the prisoners were released, when Lingo assumed that his message had been delivered, there were others who worked to underscore the point. When J.D. Sr. went back to his job at the Coosa Pipe Foundry, his boss called him in and threatened to fire him if he was ever involved in another demonstration. "I ought to do it now," he said, "so watch yourself. Not everybody feels like I do."

What the superintendent meant was that not everybody would be so forgiving, and sure enough, a short time later Cammeron found himself surrounded by a group of white workers who demanded to know what the movement was about.

"You want our women," one of them said.

"No," said Cammeron, "that's not even in it. We want our human rights."

The white workers clearly did not believe him—did not believe that the stakes were human dignity and respect and not the sexual allure of white women. Later that day, Cammeron went to the scrap yard and picked up some leftover pieces of pipe that he could use to defend himself in a fight. He thought that he and other veterans of the battle did not have a choice. Whatever it took, there was nothing to do now but "keep on pushing." But he knew they still had a long way to go.

CHAPTER 12

The Schoolhouse Door

THE EVENTS IN GADSDEN MIGHT have made the national news—the drama and the violence were certainly that intense—if they hadn't been upstaged by the governor himself. As the pressures in Gadsden were beginning to build, George Wallace was preparing to make good on a promise, a campaign pledge that he had delivered in 1962. When he launched his race for governor in Montgomery, he promised to resist integration to the end, even specific court rulings that required it.

"I shall refuse," he said, speaking with that defiant curl of the lip that was about to become his political trademark, "to abide by any such illegal federal court order even to the point of standing in the schoolhouse door, if necessary."

There were reporters who thought Wallace never meant it, that he was caught in the rush of his campaign rhetoric until the summer of 1963, when he found himself held to his promise by the press. But in Wallace's mind, there was no way around it. The governor was emerging in the state of Alabama, as he would later in the nation as a whole, as a man with a gift for political symbols. He was like a distorted mirror image of Martin Luther King, a leader with a rare and compelling ability to put his stamp on the public debate. If King used biblical allusion and metaphor, a rhetoric that soared to the realm of the spirit, Wallace was the master of the visceral truth—the symbolic act or the hard-edged phrase that tapped the roiling core of emotion, particularly the anger, that many white people felt.

In the South especially there was still an inferiority complex, a Lost Cause rage and sense of persecution that had its roots in the Civil War and Reconstruction. Win or lose, what mattered was the fight, and Wallace understood that as well as anybody. The schoolhouse door that he picked for his stand was one at the University of Alabama, which was still all-white and, more than ever, a place of mythic implications for the state. By the summer of 1963, the university was home to a folk hero, a football coach named Paul "Bear" Bryant, who had been a solid, dependable starter on a Rose Bowl team in the 1930s and had come back home to his alma mater to restore the fortunes of a losing program. He had won five games in 1958 and a national championship three years later, and the people of Alabama were enthralled. On Saturday afternoons, Bryant prowled the sidelines in his houndstooth hat, growling at everybody who came within range, and his mumbling mystique was southern to the bone. He was humble in victory, gracious in defeat, praising his players whenever they won, and blaming nobody but himself when they lost. His earliest teams consisted most often of overachievers, players who were not that flashy or big, but who quickly developed a national reputation as the greatest giant-killers in college football.

All of that was important to the people of Alabama, a powerful tonic for the delicate and troubled psyche of the state. By now, many white people were deeply ambivalent, uncomfortable with their image as a national pariah, troubled by a nagging sense of injustice and the fundamental truths of the civil rights movement. And yet if an era was careening toward an end, and many people knew it was, the shape of the future was difficult to see. Except for a handful of whites who were moved by the rhetoric of Martin Luther King, even those who saw that segregation was doomed could not quite imagine what system would replace it. Nobody seemed to be offering that vision. The past, meanwhile, was like an old shoe, and the aging university in the city of Tuscaloosa, with its magnolia trees and great spreading lawns, embodied the very *idea* of tradition. If racial integration could come to such a place, nothing was safe, and nothing was quite as familiar anymore.

Such were the feelings of the state's racial moderates, a queasy intermingling of embarrassment and dread, but there was something else as well—a feeling they shared with those more extreme. They were tired of being the nation's whipping boy. As their governor was fond of making them see, there were racial problems everywhere in the country, and yet the people in the North and the nation's capital seemed to be obsessed with the state of Alabama. Once again in the Heart of Dixie, there was that old, familiar feeling of invasion, and Wallace was orchestrating the resistance. Somehow, he was able to roll into one the heated racism of his hardcore constituency, including the Klan, and the angry populism of a people under siege. He was brilliant and ruthless in the pursuit of that goal, and nobody seemed to know how to stop him.

There were a few who tried, including George LeMaistre, a white business leader from Tuscaloosa. LeMaistre was a tall and handsome man, a law professor turned bank president, who saw George Wallace as the state's most visible impediment to progress. In November 1962 he spoke at a Civitan Club in Tuscaloosa, and his delivery at first was so low-key that one of his friends later said, "I think he took public-speaking lessons from Calvin Coolidge." LeMaistre, however, slowly warmed to the subject, and his pitch on the surface was a hard-headed plea—a warning against the economic ruin that was waiting down the road of massive resistance. But LeMaistre was also a Presbyterian layman who saw the moral dimension of civil rights, and his passion seemed to flow from that source.

"No state official," he declared with an edge, "has the right to put himself above the law. . . . And that includes the governor."

There was, as one historian later put it, "an audible gasp" in the room full of business leaders and peers, and then, remarkably, almost everyone rose to applaud. Over the next several months, LeMaistre continued making his case, speaking to business groups around the state and finally sitting down with Wallace himself. To no one's surprise, the meeting with the governor did not go well. Wallace was never very gracious in dealing with opponents. He was always more of a street fighter at heart, not a counter puncher or an artist, but a bare-knuckled brawler who believed in the value of a good offense. When LeMaistre pointed out that the Supreme Court had ruled on the issue of integration and it was the duty of American citizens to obey, Wallace dismissed the argument with a wave.

"Law and order is a communist term," he said. "Every time the communists take over they clamp down with law and order."

LeMaistre was astonished. For a split second, the words wouldn't come, for what could you say to this scowling little man, this midget of a leader who was winning the loyalty of the Alabama masses by appealing to the absolute worst that was in them? The maddening thing was, LeMaistre understood that Wallace wasn't stupid. He had to see the wreckage he was about to create, and yet he was willing to do it anyway. LeMaistre felt the anger rising through his body, starting somewhere near the tips of his toes, as he leaned forward across the desk in the governor's office and uttered the only words he could find: "That's bullshit, George. That's bullshit!"

LeMaistre was not alone in his dismay. In the weeks leading up to the stand in the schoolhouse door, Wallace received letters and telephone calls from other business leaders who counseled moderation, but the governor was simply in no mood to listen. In Wallace's mind, the University of Alabama was the state's most sacred symbol of segregation, and he had promised segregation forever. There was no choice now but to dig in and fight.

Black citizens, meanwhile, were just as determined. In the years since the Autherine Lucy disaster, literally hundreds of African Americans had applied for admission to their state university, but all had been dismissed, intimidated, or evaded, until the summer of 1963 when it came down to three. Perhaps the most resolute was Vivian Malone, a young woman from Mobile who had been an outstanding student at Central High School. She was quiet and reserved, almost regal in her bearing, with her high cheekbones and soft brown eyes, and some people said she looked like a model. She dressed conservatively in the Villager outfits that were popular at the time, her blouses buttoned all the way to her collar, and in the media interviews that came later on, she presented herself with extraordinary poise.

As a teenager she lived near the Warren Street Methodist Church, where the minister, Joseph Lowery, was a civil rights champion and a friend and confidant of Martin Luther King. Vivian sang in the choir on one of King's visits, and she was eager to find her place in the movement. She had already caught the eye of John LeFlore, Mobile's most visible civil rights leader, who saw her as a conscientious, level-headed girl who came from a family of high moral character. She wanted to study personnel management, but there was no such major at Alabama A&M, the all-black college she initially attended. There was, however, an excellent program at the University of Alabama, and Vivian Malone decided to apply.

Meanwhile, in Gadsden, the former student body president at Carver High School was ready to do the same. James Hood had been a high school athlete, a football player who had run a hundred-yard dash in less than ten seconds. Off the field, he could be a flashy dresser with his plaid sport jackets and dark-rimmed glasses and a multicolored feather in the band of his hat. He was funny and outgoing, known for his ability to make friends easily, and he was proud of his role in the civil rights movement. He had been an organizer in Gadsden, and when he went away to Clark College in Atlanta, he spent time in the meetings of civil rights groups, including SNCC, SCLC, and CORE. Some people wondered about his stability, for he suffered occasionally from anxiety and depression, but he was an A-minus student who couldn't be dismissed when he decided to transfer to the University of Alabama.

The third student, Dave McGlathery, also presented a strong application. He was the oldest of the three, a twenty-seven-year-old sharecropper's son who lived in Huntsville and worked in the space program. He had served with distinction in the U.S. Navy and graduated magna cum laude from Alabama A&M. In October 1962, when he accepted his job at Redstone Arsenal, he thought it might be good for his career if he added a few more courses in math. He applied for admission at the University of Alabama branch in Huntsville.

State officials responded to these applications as they had since the days of Autherine Lucy. They tried to dig up some dirt to disqualify the applicants. Vivian Malone knew it was happening, and she denounced the "iniquitous means" employed by the state, but in her case it didn't really matter. Ben Allen, one of Al Lingo's detectives, was a tenacious man who dug through her background and found nothing incriminating in his search. "Vivian was good people," he told the Alabama journalist Howell Raines, but it was not what Lingo wanted to hear. As Allen remembered it, the public safety director ranted and fumed, saying things that "wouldn't be fit to print," for in Lingo's understanding of the world there was not a black person anywhere who couldn't be discredited by a detective who was diligent enough at his work. Vivian Malone defied that racist article of faith, and so did Dave McGlathery and James Hood. Their applications survived, and the stakes were beginning to rise for George Wallace.

On Wednesday, June 5, U.S. district judge Seybourn Lynne issued an injunction against the governor, forbidding interference with the immediate admission of the three black students. The judge had come a long way on the issue of civil rights. He was a gray-haired patrician who had graduated from the University of Alabama law school, and he had seen himself for most of his career as a judicial conservative. Seven years earlier, he was the minority vote on the three-judge panel that overturned segregation on the Montgomery buses. He didn't believe in 1956 that the courts should interfere in the issue, but now he accepted—indeed he welcomed—the inevitable doom of official segregation. In addition to that, he was deeply offended by the governor's promise to put himself above the law.

"Thoughtful people," he wrote, "if they can free themselves from tensions produced by established principles with which they violently disagree, must concede that the governor of a sovereign state has no authority to obstruct or prevent the execution of the lawful orders of a court of the United States."

Judge Lynne also let it be known that if Wallace decided to defy the injunction, his contempt citation could put him in jail. These were formidable forces the governor was facing—the threat of jail time, a clear and unequivocal ruling by the court, the vocal opposition of some strong business leaders. But Wallace believed in his own instincts, and he remembered the exhilaration in the crowd on that cold inauguration day in January when he vowed to defend segregation forever. Six months later, in the early summer of 1963, the mail continued to pour into his office, and it came from people all over the country. Wallace, whose ambition burned as fiercely as any other man's, was starting to consider the larger possibilities, and he thought a lot would depend on the next several days. With the whole country watching, he had to create a dramatic confrontation, casting himself as more than a southerner who was worried about race. He had to be the little man facing Goliath.

That was how he would play it, as a new aspiration began to take flight, taking him to places he had never been before—perhaps one day to a run at the White House. Why shouldn't he consider it? Lesser men had made that trip, and despite the odds, his journey would begin in the schoolhouse door.

In Washington, the Kennedy administration was worried. The president and his brother didn't want to play the foil to this maddening bantamweight from Alabama, but their memories were raw from the University of Mississippi. It had been less than a year since 2 people died and 160 federal marshals were injured in pursuit of the admission of a single black student. The Kennedys, above all, did not want a repeat.

On April 25, 1963, knowing that a confrontation with Wallace was near, Robert Kennedy made a trip to Montgomery to try to determine what the governor had in mind. When he arrived for his appointment at 9 A.M., he found the capitol ringed with Alabama State Troopers. They were there for security, George Wallace insisted, but Kennedy took away a different message. As he was walking through the lines toward the governor's office, one of the troopers jabbed his stomach with the end of a nightstick. The attorney general of the United States was sure that the trooper would just as soon have killed him.

Things were not a lot better inside. Kennedy found the conversation bizarre, a series of jousts and non sequiturs that left him confused. Wallace, he thought, seemed to be living in a whole different world, not hallucinatory or insane, but in a state of denial about the historical realities that all of them faced. Because he saw no validity in the civil rights cause, Wallace lacked any sense of its inevitability, which his moderate opponents in the state clearly grasped. But did he really think he could win? And how far would he go to get what he wanted? Those were the questions the Kennedys had to face, and their answers, unfortunately, were only a guess.

As the summer session approached at the University of Alabama, the attorney general was working overtime. He kept in touch with the university administration, particularly Frank Rose, the charismatic, dark-haired president who had taken the job in 1958, and who after a resolute struggle against integration, now seemed ready to accept the inevitable. Kennedy's other contact was Jefferson Bennett, who served as a special assistant to the president and was a man who did whatever needed doing. Bennett was a handsome, square-jawed educator, tough and humane and a veteran of the earlier integration wars. (He was the driver of the car in 1956, when Autherine Lucy made her escape from a rock-throwing mob.)

On June 10, 1963, the day before the final showdown, Bennett called Robert Kennedy to tell him what he knew. He had come from a meeting between Wallace and the board of trustees, and he said Wallace clearly intended to stand in the door. He would appear the next morning at Foster Auditorium, the site of registration for summer school classes, and he would bar the admission of Hood and Malone. Bennett reported that the governor seemed nervous, which Kennedy regarded as a piece of bad news, for if Wallace was feeling unsure of himself, that could make him even more unpredictable. The good news was that Wallace seemed genuinely opposed to any violence, and if confronted by a show of federal force, would almost certainly be willing to step aside.

That was Bennett's assessment, and Kennedy took what encouragement he could from it. He had decided that his deputy attorney general Nicholas Katzenbach, a tall and balding former Ivy League football player, would be the one to confront the governor in the door. They had gone over every possible contingency. Should Katzenbach shake hands? Should the students be with him or should they stay in the car? What would they do if Wallace, backed by Alabama State Troopers, decided to stand his ground and fight?

On the morning of June 11, Kennedy thought they were as ready as they could be. The day was already hot and sticky, the temperature hurtling toward the upper nineties, when Wallace arrived at the Tuscaloosa campus. Bob Ingram thought the governor looked nervous, and Ingram knew him as well as anybody. He was the capitol correspondent for the *Montgomery Advertiser*, regarded by many as probably the most capable reporter on the beat. Ingram was a physically unimposing man, dark-haired, medium build, recognizable by his glasses with a dark plastic frame. As a reporter he was always folksy and bold with his own special sense of how to draw the line—of how, for example, to cast himself as one of the good old boys in the George Wallace orbit, while retaining enough independence to do his job. In the minutes just before the stand in the door, Ingram hovered at the edge of the Wallace inner circle, and he could see immediately it was not an ordinary day. The governor was not in a wisecracking mood, which was often his habit when he was filled with adrenaline. On this occasion he merely seemed tense, fretting, pacing, worrying about whether he would wind up in jail. John Kohn, a Montgomery lawyer and Wallace confidant, was there at his side, offering reassurance. Kohn had been the primary author of the statement that Wallace would deliver that day, and he genuinely regarded the moment as historic. "You have divine blessing today," he said. "Good luck and may God bless you."

As Wallace waited in an air-conditioned office, Bob Ingram was certain of one thing. There wouldn't be any violence on the campus that day. Wallace was absolutely serious about that. In the weeks leading up to the moment of truth, the governor and Al Lingo had put out the word to the Ku Klux Klan: troublemakers would not be tolerated on the campus. A few days before the schoolhouse stand, a carload of Klansmen, heavily armed, had been arrested and jailed on their way to Tuscaloosa, and the word went out again among the faithful. The governor was serious about it this time.

At Foster Auditorium, a drab and nondescript brick building except for six white columns that gave it a neo-Classical facade, an army of state troopers sweltered in the sun, their tension overtaken by their misery and boredom, until a three-car caravan finally arrived. It was 10:48 A.M. when Nicholas Katzenbach stepped from his car, a government sedan with no air conditioning that he shared with Vivian Malone and James Hood. Katzenbach was already sweating, and while he knew it was hot in the car, he asked Hood and Malone to stay behind. He didn't want them humiliated by the governor or personally insulted by the little man's charade. Katzenbach felt nothing but contempt for George Wallace, a visceral distaste for his politics and churlish ambition, and everything about this day made it worse. Wallace was waiting at a podium as Katzenbach approached. There was a white semicircle painted on the ground, like the tape on the stage of a Broadway play, showing the actors exactly where to stand. Katzenbach was astonished at the unreality, and when he stepped deliberately across the line, Wallace raised his palm in a signal to stop, like a crossing guard at an elementary school, annoyed by the presence of an unruly child.

Katzenbach, who had not slept in thirty-six hours, began to speak, and his hand trembled slightly from nervousness and rage. "I have come here," he said, "to ask now for unequivocal assurance that you will permit these students who, after all, merely want an education at a great university—"

But Wallace cut him off. "We don't need a speech," he said, and then he proceeded to make one of his own. For nearly seven minutes he read from a statement, denouncing an "illegal usurpation of power," while Katzenbach could only stand there and sweat. When he finally finished, Wallace took a step back from the small wooden podium and stood in the doorway, flanked by his troopers, his chin thrust upward in a look of defiance.

With his arms folded patiently across his chest, Katzenbach tried once again. "I do not know what the purpose of this show is," he said. "From the outset, Governor, all of us have known that the final chapter of this history will be the admission of these students. . . . I ask you once again to reconsider."

When Wallace only stood there, refusing to reply, Katzenbach turned and walked away, and he and the other federal agents at the cars led the two black students to their dorms. Vivian Malone was greeted warmly by her new house mother and again by a group of a half dozen coeds when she sat down to lunch. Back at Foster Auditorium, Wallace also settled in for lunch—a steak and fries both smothered with ketchup—while he waited quietly for the other shoe to fall. The Kennedys had federalized the National Guard, and sometime after 3 P.M., a line of infantrymen carrying M-1 rifles took up position outside the auditorium.

At exactly 3:30 Gen. Henry Graham, followed by Katzenbach and two other officials, confronted the governor once again in the doorway. Graham did not relish the assignment. He was a Birmingham businessman who had made a career in the National Guard, and he was a distinguished-looking officer at the age of forty-seven with his silver hair and stiffly pressed fatigues. He had a reputation in the ranks of the guard as a man of impressive dignity and calm, a general whose authority came not from his bluster but his sense of resolve.

"It is my sad duty," he told George Wallace, "to ask you to step aside, on order of the President of the United States."

And that was it. Within a minute or two it was over, and it was difficult at first to say what it meant. Reporter Bob Ingram concluded years later that it was all a charade, an act of theater, and he used to tease Wallace about it in private.

"Hell," he would say, "you never even intended to stand in the door. You just got caught in your campaign rhetoric and the fact that the press would not let it go."

"I meant it all the time," Wallace would insist, but Ingram would laugh.

"Wallace, you're lying. You know it and I know it."

And the governor of Alabama would look at him and grin.

Back in Washington, John and Robert Kennedy were relieved. The two black students were now in school, and the following day the third student, Dave McGlathery, enrolled without incident at the Huntsville campus. James Hood wouldn't make it beyond the summer, withdrawing with signs of a nervous breakdown, but Vivian Malone saw it through to the end, setting new standards for dignity and courage, as she became, in 1965, the first black graduate of the University of Alabama.

For the Kennedys during the same stretch of time, the events in Birmingham and Tuscaloosa marked a turning point in their level of engagement. On the night of June 11, 1963, John Kennedy accepted his brother's advice and addressed the nation on the subject of civil rights. It was a remarkable week of oratory for the president. On the day before, he had delivered the commencement address at American University, and many people said it was Kennedy at his best. His subject that day was foreign affairs, particularly the Cold War tensions with the Soviet Union, and he said it was time for a new way of thinking. "No government or social system," he said, "is so evil that its people must be considered as lacking in virtue. . . . If we cannot end all our differences, at least we can help make the world safe for diversity. For, in the final analysis, our most basic common link is that we all inhabit this small planet. We all breathe the same air. We all cherish our children's future. And we are all mortal."

In his civil rights address the following night, Kennedy took his place before the television cameras with a text that was still in bits and pieces—

pages reshuffled just minutes before with notes and scribblings still in the margin. He seemed awkward at first, a little too stiff, but after a while he spoke more confidently from his heart: "Every American ought to have the right to be treated as he would wish to be treated, as one would wish his children to be treated. But this is not the case." The nation, he said, was "confronted primarily with a moral issue. It is as old as the Scriptures and as clear as the American Constitution." And if anyone doubted the reality of prejudice confronting the black man, "who among us would be content to have the color of his skin changed and stand in his place? Who among us would then be content with the counsels of patience and delay? One hundred years of delay have passed since President Lincoln freed the slaves, yet their heirs, their grandsons, are not fully free. . . . And this nation, for all its boasts, will not be fully free until all its citizens are free."

He was introducing, he said, a civil rights bill to end discrimination in all facilities that were open to the public—hotels, restaurants, theaters, and stores, all those places where segregation delivered its daily insult. The legislation, said the president, would simply provide "an elementary right," the denial of which was "an arbitrary indignity that no American in 1963 should have to endure."

In the ebb and flow of historical analysis, later generations would seek to pick apart the record of the Kennedys, particularly with regard to civil rights, but for the generation that heard him that night, there was, without question, a shimmering new sense of possibility and promise. That was especially true in the South, for in the collective memory of black Alabamians, no other president had ever spoken this way. No white official that they could remember had allied himself more completely with the cause.

As he so often did, Martin Luther King captured the feelings of many thousands of others when he sent a telegram to the president, complete with the errors of his own hasty typing: "It was one of the most eloquent profound and unequival pleas for Justice and Freedom of all men ever made by any President. You spoke passionately to the moral issues."

The jubilation, as pure and intense as any in the turbulent history of the movement, lasted less than twenty-four hours. The gratitude toward the president remained, along with a towering sense of satisfaction that events from the Freedom Rides through the spectacles in Birmingham and

Tuscaloosa had slowly, but surely, gotten Kennedy's attention. Yet it almost seemed to be a law of nature that every moment of triumph was followed by a tragedy, and once again, the old pattern held.

Shortly after midnight in Jackson, Mississippi, Medgar Evers came home from a meeting. His wife and children were waiting up for him, still excited by the president's address, when they heard his station wagon coming up the drive. Evers was a field secretary for the NAACP, a resolute veteran of the civil rights struggle and a villain in the eyes of the Ku Klux Klan. As Evers got out of the car and stepped into the glaring light of his carport, he made an easy target for Byron de la Beckwith, a Klansman hidden in the nearby shadows. Beckwith took aim through the scope of his 30.06 Winchester rifle, and squeezed the trigger. The bullet tore through Evers's back, leaving a massive exit wound at his sternum, and the civil rights leader died within the hour.

Evers was not the only target on this mission of revenge that included Klan organizations in three different states. In Selma, Alabama, on the night Evers died, Bernard Lafayette was also coming home late from a meeting. Lafayette, the freedom rider and sit-in veteran, was now an organizer for SNCC, an organization that grew from the student sit-ins and took its place on the cutting edge of the movement. By the summer of 1963 the group was sending its field organizers to places nobody else would go, and one of its more revolutionary goals was to register the masses of potential black voters. It was dangerous work in the rural back-waters of Alabama and Mississippi, for there were counties where blacks were in a majority, and white control of the political system depended entirely on disenfranchisement.

When Lafayette came to Selma in 1962, the little river town was emerging as a symbol of everything that was wrong. Only a handful of blacks were registered to vote, and the overwhelming majority had simply given up. "Well, son," a retired postal worker told Lafayette, "you came to the wrong place. You're not going to get much done around here." But Lafayette kept at it, wandering through the county and talking to people, and after a while a few began showing up at his meetings. That alone was reason to celebrate, for apathy and fear were the first adversaries the move-ment had to conquer. Lafayette was feeling pretty good on the night of President Kennedy's address, when he stopped outside his apartment building and reached for some flyers in the back seat of his car.

Back in those days, Lafayette was driving an old '48 Chevy, solid black, with fluid drive and no clutch, a humble but somewhat conspicuous machine that his white adversaries were learning to recognize. In addition to that, the *Selma Times-Journal* had published his address on the front page of the paper, almost like an invitation to trouble. Despite those things, and despite his perpetual awareness of the danger, Lafayette wasn't worried when he saw another car parked hood-up in front of his apartment. There was a white man standing in the shadows beside it and another man inside, but in a town like Selma, small and intimate in so many ways, the white and black neighborhoods were never far apart, and a broken-down car didn't seem out of place.

"How much would you charge to give me a push?" one of the white men asked.

"No charge," said Bernard, and he backed his car behind the other one. One of the white men stared at the bumpers as if he thought they didn't quite fit, and when Lafayette got out to see for himself, the man suddenly clubbed him in the head from behind. Lafayette rose to face his assailant, who hit him again, and after a few more blows Bernard was getting woozy. Still he remembered his nonviolent training: Never back down. Always look your assailant in the eye. There was always the hope of a human connection, a spark of conscience that might take an adversary by surprise.

This time, however, the only thing Lafayette saw was a gun, and he was sure that the white man was ready to shoot him. He called for help, and suddenly his neighbor, a black man that everybody called "Red," appeared on the balcony, a rifle in his hand. He began taking aim, using the banister railing as a prop, when Bernard called out and told him not to shoot. The last thing they needed was a dead white man in Selma, Alabama.

In the moment of distraction, the white men fled and Lafayette survived. It took eleven stitches to close up the gashes, but all in all it could have been worse. An FBI agent down in Mobile told him later that according to informants there were supposed to be three murders that night—Evers, Lafayette, and a veteran CORE organizer in Louisiana, who was simply not there when the killers came to get him.

At his home in Atlanta and in the course of his travels for the next several weeks, Martin Luther King tried to take it all in. He had to believe they were making some progress. The civil rights bill that Kennedy was proposing might be one that would really make a difference, and in his June 11 speech, the president had embraced the morality of the movement in a way that was new and long overdue. But the violence continued in many parts of the South; the battered walls of segregation still stood, and nobody knew what Congress would do.

King liked an idea that was circulating among civil rights leaders, a plan for a massive march on Washington probably sometime later in the summer. It could be a way to build on momentum established in Alabama that spring and to remind the Congress and even the president that the civil rights movement would not go away. As the summer unfolded, those were King's hopes. He had no way of knowing that the March on Washington would be the shining moment of his life.

CHAPTER 13

"I Have a Dream"

THE IRRESISTIBLE FORCE BEHIND THE MARCH was A. Philip Randolph, the grand old man of the civil rights movement. For more than twenty years, Randolph had dreamed of a national gathering in Washington, a great outpouring of Negro Americans and their white allies demanding a national commitment to justice. As the veteran leader of the Pullman Porters Union, he had been thinking recently about a march in the fall of 1963, seeking job opportunities for blacks. He readily agreed to combine that effort with a late summer march for human freedom.

On June 22 a group of civil rights leaders met with President Kennedy, who lobbied them mildly against such a protest, fearing a backlash that could damage the chances of the civil rights bill. With characteristic dignity, Randolph rose to take on the president. He was a tall, impressive, gray-haired man who always spoke with a slight British accent, adding a touch of elegance to everything he said. "The Negroes are already in the streets," he explained, and there was no way to change that fundamental fact. Nor should there be. As the president himself had acknowledged in his speech, black Americans had waited a hundred years for the freedom that was promised by Abraham Lincoln, and there was no harm now in a well-led march that would dramatize the issue.

Kennedy acquiesced gracefully to a demonstration that he could see was inevitable, and as the officially designated leader of the march, Randolph committed himself to a peaceful protest. The civil rights leaders decided on a date of August 28, and there was a united front behind the idea. Martin Luther King was clearly on board, and so were Roy Wilkins of the NAACP and Whitney Young of the Urban League and Alabama's John Lewis, the newly elected chairman of SNCC.

The formidable task of pulling things together fell to Bayard Rustin, a civil rights veteran with a résumé unlike anybody else's. He was a pacifist, socialist, homosexual who was a former member of the Young Communist League and a backup vocalist to the blues singer Leadbelly. Born in 1910, he was raised in Pennsylvania as a member of a large extended family that included a stepfather of West Indian descent, whose accent Bayard decided to adopt. As an adult, Rustin was a tall, angular man with flyaway hair, gray by the time he organized the march, and he was proud of an ancestry that included both American Indians and blacks. He was the original eccentric, but a man of great skill, admired by Philip Randolph and Martin Luther King for his towering intellect and his deep and passionate commitment to the movement.

His handling of the march was nothing less than brilliant. Working out of an old church building on 135th Street in Harlem, he put everything together in less than three months. Rustin understood the delicacy of the task. A crowd of 100,000, the minimum number the leaders were expecting, could become surly and restless for the smallest of reasons—not enough bathrooms, perhaps, or not enough food. By August 28, when the people gathered on the Washington Mall, Rustin had arranged for the installation of several hundred portable toilets, twenty-four first aid stations, more than twenty new drinking fountains and a place to distribute 80,000 bag lunches. There were 4,000 volunteer marshals trained to keep order, but the most important thing, Rustin believed, was to make sure everything ran on time. He wanted the march to be over by dusk, for when the sun went down, funny things could happen to the mood of a crowd. The problem was, he had to pare down the list of speakers, which led inevitably to bruised feelings and egos.

One of those he planned to leave out was Fred Shuttlesworth, which was a stunning omission to anyone from Alabama. Nobody was braver or more committed; nobody had accomplished more for the cause. Martin Luther King was particularly concerned, for there was a simmering rivalry between the two friends, and he didn't want to see it get any worse. He was relieved when Rustin changed his mind and sent Shuttlesworth out to deliver the first in a day's worth of speeches. It was a beautiful after-noon in the nation's capital, eighty-four degrees with bright blue skies and a rustling breeze, and a crowd so large it was hard to take it in. There were estimates as high as a half million people, and Shuttlesworth could believe it. "We came here today," he declared, caught in the vast emotion of the moment, "because we love our country, because our country needs us and because we need our country. . . . Everybody in America ought to be free."

As Shuttlesworth spoke, there was a backstage drama that the crowd couldn't see, an emergency meeting in a security guard's office tucked away at the base of the Lincoln Memorial. John Lewis found himself sur-rounded by leaders who were worried about the tenor of his speech. Based on copies that had been circulating since the day before, Lewis was ready with a verbal hand grenade. As he tried to explain, this was a speech not only for himself, but for his increasingly militant colleagues in SNCC and for the powerless people in the Mississippi Delta and the Alabama Black Belt, whose lives were in danger if they dared take a stand. For too long, he thought, the Kennedy administration had been of little help, and even the president's civil rights bill, belated as it was, did not address itself to the issues of voting or police brutality or the wanton bombings and mur-der by the Klan. As the ones who were living on the cutting edge of dan-ger, who were absorbing every day the unspeakable cruelties of life in the deepest backwaters of the South, the SNCC workers were the angriest people in the movement. John Lewis wanted to give them a voice, while affirming his commitment to nonviolence. Even if he would never pick up a gun or raise his hand to harm another person, he thought of himself as a revolutionary, a nonviolent crusader against the status quo.

Calling President Kennedy's civil rights bill "too little too late," Lewis intended to declare at the Lincoln Memorial that an increasingly militant civil rights movement would "march through the South, through the heart of Dixie, the way Sherman did. We shall pursue our own 'scorched earth' policy and burn Jim Crow to the ground—nonviolently."

The Kennedy administration was appalled, and so were Roy Wilkins and many of the movement's white allies. Even Randolph and King were worried about metaphors that sounded that abrasive, that certain to offend. "John," said King, remembering the gentle farm boy from Alabama, "that doesn't sound like you."

Legendary for his stubbornness, Lewis at first refused to change a word, but then he was faced with A. Philip Randolph. The old man looked tired. "I've waited twenty-two years for this," he said. "I've waited *all my life* for this opportunity. Please don't ruin it." And of course that was it. This was the man, after all, who had confronted Franklin Roosevelt in the White House and made him back down, relying on nothing much more than his eloquence. It happened in 1941, with a war coming on and black people barred from the best defense jobs. Randolph had called for a march on Washington, and for the sake of national unity, Roosevelt asked him to call it off. Randolph refused until the president agreed to an executive order ending discrimination in hiring. Randolph had never been a man to beg, but he was close to it now at the Lincoln Memorial, and the look on his face broke Lewis's heart. There was nothing to do but tone down the speech.

Working with James Forman, SNCC's fiery and impatient executive director, Lewis struggled to preserve the integrity of his message without becoming the sour note for the occasion. In the end, he was happy. "We will march through the South," he said, "through the streets of Jackson . . . through the streets of Birmingham. . . . We cannot stop, and we *will* not be patient."

The words were softer than he originally intended, but he had sounded his note of militant resolve, and now he was ready to hear Dr. King. More than most of his colleagues in SNCC, Lewis was still a little bit in awe of a man who had been his mentor and friend. There was nobody like King on occasions such as this, and Lewis had the feeling they were in for something special. King, however, didn't begin his address with poetry or fire. He was plodding almost, feeling his way, and the substance was more important than the style. It was a more militant speech than history has remembered, for in addition to the dreams of brotherhood and peace, there was a demand for justice, and in its absence, the threat of greater disruption in the streets. King made it clear that the patience of black America was exhausted.

"In a sense," he said, "we have come to our nation's capital to cash a check. When the architects of our republic wrote the magnificent words of the Constitution and the Declaration of Independence, they were signing a promissory note to which every American was to fall heir. This note was the promise that all men—yes, black men as well as white men— would be guaranteed the inalienable rights of life, liberty and the pursuit of happiness. . . . We refuse to believe that the bank of justice is bankrupt. We refuse to believe there are insufficient funds in the great vaults of opportunity of this nation. . . . And so we have come to this hallowed spot to remind America of the fierce urgency of now. . . . There will be neither rest nor tranquility in America until the Negro is granted his citizenship rights. The whirlwinds of revolt will continue to shake the foundations of our nation until the bright day of justice emerges."

As he moved through the text, gazing out across the sea of jubilant faces, King became caught in the moment himself, and he reached for a whole new level of emotion. He remembered a passage he hadn't thought to include, one that had gone over well in Birmingham and Detroit, "and I just felt," he said much later, "that I wanted to use it here." So he pushed his printed text aside, and simply let the words pour out in a rush:

"I say to you today, my friends, even though we face the difficulties of today and tomorrow, I still have a dream. It is a dream deeply rooted in the American dream. I have a dream that one day this nation will rise up and live out the true meaning of its creed—we hold these truths to be self-evident, that all men are created equal. I have a dream that one day on the red hills of Georgia, the sons of former slaves and the sons of former slaveowners will be able to sit down together at the table of brotherhood. . . . I have a dream that one day down in Alabama—with its vicious racists, with its governor's lips dripping with the words of interposition and nullification—one day right there in Alabama, little black boys and little black girls will be able to join hands with little white boys and little white girls as sisters and brothers.

"I have a dream today!"

It was a vision that became his gift to the country, an antidote to the bleak realities they still had to face. "He's damn good," said President

Kennedy, watching on television at the White House. And there in the audience at the Lincoln Memorial, Fred Shuttlesworth also listened in amazement. Unlike many others in the civil rights movement, he had never been a man who looked up to King, a leader whose style was a little too soft, too indecisive, for Shuttlesworth's taste. But everybody had their gifts, and this quite clearly was Martin Luther King's.

"Every once in a while," Shuttlesworth said, "God intervenes in such a way that you know that only God could do it. That was God preaching to America through King."

Back in Alabama, there were a few signs that people were listening. In the town of Anniston, where the freedom riders were attacked in 1961, there were now the first intimations of progress. The changes began with a cautious initiative from two black ministers, N. Q. Reynolds, a Baptist, and William B. McClain, a United Methodist. They decided in 1962 to approach their white ministerial counterparts to try to generate a racial dialogue. They found no takers on their first couple of stops, but then they came to Phillips Noble, the soft-spoken minister at First Presbyterian. As a matter of theology, Noble had long been interested in the issue of race, and as a citizen of Alabama he was troubled by the burning of the freedom riders' bus and the disturbing headlines coming out of Birmingham.

One of the members of his church was Miller Sproull, a business leader and aspiring politician, who would soon be elected to the city commission. Both as a businessman and a Presbyterian layman, Sproull thought bigotry was bad for his city, and he and Noble would talk about it some, often on quail-hunting trips to the country. There was a feeling of perspective in the cool autumn woods, a gathering certainty that things had to change. They agreed some kind of instrument was needed, perhaps some kind of interracial commission, to guide the community in an era of transition. But the timing of it never seemed right, until Mother's Day 1963. That was the Sunday when a group of local hoodlums, probably members of the Ku Klux Klan, fired several shots into the homes of local blacks.

Sproull called Phil Noble at once. "It's time to establish the commission," he said. "I want you to be the chairman." Noble decided he could not refuse, and over the next several weeks, he began to hold meetings of a nine-member body—five whites, four blacks—appointed by Sproull, as city commissioner, and Anniston's like-minded mayor, Claude Dear. The group started slowly, negotiating with national chain stores about desegregating their rest rooms in Anniston. The change was made with little fanfare, and then the Human Relations Council, as the new group was known, turned its attention to the public library. On a late summer Sunday in 1963, after church had been dismissed, N. Q. Reynolds and William McClain became the first black patrons to try to check out a book. But the Ku Klux Klan was waiting in ambush, and with the Anniston police nowhere to be found, they beat the ministers with clubs and chains, severely injuring Reynolds.

The following morning, Sproull, Noble, and a small group of blacks, including McClain, entered the library together, serving notice to the people of Anniston that the moderate proponents of desegregation would not be deterred by the violence of the Klan. Many years later, Noble remembered the threatening phone calls and the worry every time he started his car that maybe somebody had planted a bomb. But he knew his community was moving forward as it should.

A similar story was unfolding in Huntsville, a growing city of more than eighty thousand people, where the movement had been a quiet, persistent undertaking. In September 1963 a black first-grader named Sonnie Hereford IV was about to enter an integrated school, which was uncharted ground in the state of Alabama. The young boy's father, Sonnie Hereford III, was a Huntsville doctor who had scrambled to get an education of his own and wanted only the best for his children. With his brother, Thomas Hereford, Sonnie III had sharecropped his way through college at Alabama A&M, raising enough cotton, cattle, and swine to pay the tuition of twenty-two dollars per quarter. After two years, he went away to Meharry Medical College in Tennessee, and on October 8, 1956, he opened a practice in his hometown of Huntsville.

Almost immediately, he came face to face with the issue of race. There was a meeting of doctors at the local hospital, which began with dinner at 6:30 P.M., but Hereford, the only Negro, was told to come at 7:00 when the dinner was complete. One of the items on the agenda that night was a surgeon's decision to remove the womb of one of his patients, only to discover from the pathologist's report that the organ was healthy. Asked to defend his decision, the doctor said simply: "This was an ignorant nigger woman." That seemed to settle it, and many years later, Hereford remembered his helpless indignation. "It was as if I wasn't even there," he said. "I had no voice. I had no vote. There was nothing I could do."

The racial insults, petty and otherwise, continued through the years, and Hereford was ready when the civil rights movement came. He read the news reports coming out of Greensboro, North Carolina, when the sit-in protests began in that city, and he found himself wishing for the same in Huntsville. So did his friend, John Cashin, a Huntsville dentist who chafed under the daily weight of segregation, but both men were busy with their medical careers, and not until 1962 did they find themselves swept along with the tide. That was the year Hank Thomas came to Huntsville. Thomas was a young organizer working with SNCC, and he had had his own baptism in Alabama. He had been a freedom rider, the youngest of those on the original ride who were attacked in Anniston and Birmingham and barely escaped with their lives.

In Huntsville he began to meet with local high school students, as well as those from Alabama A&M, and they started sitting in at the downtown stores. When the students were jailed, Sonnie Hereford stepped forward to post bond money, and after a while he and other adult leaders in town began to join in the student demonstrations. One of the turning points came on March 19, 1962, when Martin Luther King came to Huntsville and addressed a crowd of three thousand at Oakwood College. King spoke with passion about "a victory for justice, a victory for freedom," and more than a year before the March on Washington, he ended his sermon with words that were soon to become immortal: "Free at last, free at last. Thank God almighty, we're free at last."

The demonstrations got a little bigger after that, and more creative. Faced with a virtual blackout by the local news media, the Huntsville leadership decided to try for national publicity. They picketed the New York Stock Exchange, warning the business elite of the country: "Don't Invest in Huntsville—It's Bad Business." And even more dramatically, Hereford's wife, Martha, and Cashin's wife, Joan, decided to get arrested at one of the protests. Mrs. Hereford was seven months pregnant at the time, showing visibly, and Mrs. Cashin had a baby barely four months old. And when the two young mothers were taken to the jail, the news reports spread quickly across the country.

The white leaders in Huntsville were deeply embarrassed. The demonstrations were happening at a time of buoyant optimism for the city, when the economy was strong and sure to get better if nothing happened to ruin it. Huntsville was home to Redstone Arsenal, a critical ingredient in the space program in a country embarked on a race to the moon. It was an economic anchor as solid as any in the state, and Huntsville nurtured an image of itself as a progressive American city on the rise. The movement, of course, was a threat to that image, and the city began to make its adjustments. In July 1962 restaurant owners agreed to integrate their facilities, and a biracial commission began to wrestle with a host of other issues, including job opportunities for the city's black residents.

The movement then turned its attention to the schools, filing a desegregation lawsuit with Sonnie Hereford as the lead plaintiff. Four black families offered their children as the city's pioneers, and in August 1963 the case was heard in U.S. District Court in Birmingham. Judge Hobart Grooms delivered his opinion straight from the bench. The situation, he said, was so cut and dried there was no need to pause and deliberate about it. The four black children would be admitted immediately to formerly all-white schools, and by January 2, the board of education would come up with a plan for desegregating all the schools in the county.

On the Tuesday after Labor Day, the scheduled opening day for the schools, Sonnie Hereford held tightly to the hand of his son, as they approached Fifth Avenue Elementary School, ready for a whole new era to begin. They discovered, however, that the school had been closed. Twenty-four state troopers had descended that morning on orders from the governor to block the operation of an integrated school. It was yet another stand in the schoolhouse door, by proxy this time, with the troopers taking the place of the governor. And there were similar scenes in Tuskegee and Birmingham.

Once again, even many white leaders thought Wallace was wrong, and some who had worked for a peaceful transition, including Huntsville's chief of police Chris Spurlock, were visibly enraged. If it wasn't clear by now that the governor of Alabama was "a sick man," said the chief, "then by God none of us are discerning enough to read the facts."

Down in Tuskegee, Allan Parker felt the same. Parker was part of a dogged cadre of white liberal leaders in a town where whites were in a minority. He was a sharecropper's son from Coffee County in the far southeastern corner of the state, and he had worked his way through school, and then through the ranks of American business, to become president of the Alabama Exchange Bank. He was a short, shy man, a leader in the Macon County Church of Christ, who believed that his faith had moral implications. It taught him inevitably that all men were brothers, even if people didn't act that way. It was clear to Parker that the racial order in America was changing, and the tranquil college town of Tuskegee, where Booker T. Washington had built his institute, was coming face to face with integration.

On August 13, 1963, U.S. district judge Frank Johnson had ordered the immediate desegregation of Tuskegee High School. School superintendent C. A. "Hardboy" Pruitt, a former football player at Auburn, had resisted desegregation in the past, but now he could see that change was unavoidable, and he worked to persuade the community to accept it. He was an impressive man, stocky, plain-spoken, a gray-haired educator in his sixties, and he thought he was making a little bit of progress as he began to lobby the local leadership. He had strong support from people such as Parker, and he was feeling optimistic when the PTA from Tuskegee High met at the school on August 29. There were maybe four hundred people in the small auditorium, a good turnout, but almost immediately the mood of the gathering began to turn sour, as a few of the parents invoked the name of George Wallace. Let's call the governor, one of them said, and ask him to intervene against the courts.

Allan Parker was amazed. How could people really think that would help? The grandstanding in June at the University of Alabama had delayed the inevitable for less than four hours, and if Wallace had the nerve—the unvarnished presumption—to claim victory for his cause, it was completely astonishing that anyone believed him. This was an exercise in massive self-deception, but when Parker made that case before the PTA he could see that he wasn't changing any minds. Over the next several days, some of the parents did go to Wallace, and the governor was only too happy to intercede.

At dawn on Monday, September 2, a state trooper appeared at the home of Superintendent Pruitt and delivered an executive order from Wallace, requiring the closing of Tuskegee High. At 6:30 A.M., more than six hundred troopers formed a ring around the school, turning everyone away. All of this was necessary, said Wallace, to protect "the peace and tranquility of this State."

In Tuskegee, however, any sense of tranquility was a thing of the past. The white community was now deeply divided between those who favored a graceful acquiescence and those who drew their encouragement from Wallace, and vowed to resist integration forever. When the high school opened on September 9 after a week of futile maneuvering by Wallace, less than a fourth of the 565 white students showed up for class. The rest were seeking special transfers to other public high schools in the county or to a hastily established private school that came to be known as Macon Academy. In the coming months, private school enrollment would soar, as whites abandoned the public high school entirely. One Methodist minister, an outspoken liberal named Ennis Sellers, preached against this development, and he became so disheartened by the divisions in his church that he decided it was best to leave Tuskegee. As soon as he was gone, the Methodist lay leaders adopted a new policy. They locked the doors during Sunday morning worship to protect the racial purity of the service.

However disheartening all this may have been, particularly to the moderates in the city of Tuskegee, the situation in Birmingham was worse. There, the resistance to school integration flared quickly into violence, culminating eventually in the greatest tragedy the movement had yet known. James Armstrong had a feeling it was coming, a sickening dread that some kind of terrible reprisal might occur. He just didn't know what form it would take. Armstrong was the lead plaintiff in the Birmingham case, a civil rights veteran who had braved the occasional threats on his life, and the poisoning of his dog, a mixed-breed chow, and the night some boys raced by in a truck and smashed the windows on his Buick Riviera. During the weeks leading up to the opening of school, he posted armed guards outside his house, which was now a common ritual in Birmingham. Ever since the bombings that started in the '50s, Armstrong himself had been a designated guard, as the black community rallied around the obvious targets—the homes of Fred Shuttlesworth and attorney Arthur Shores and the movement pioneers such as Autherine Lucy. This particular stretch in 1963 was as bad as any that Armstrong could remember, with a half dozen bombings since the spring demonstrations.

John K. Wright was a boy of thirteen when the protests started, and many years later, as a distinguished educator, he remembered the nights on the porch of his home, sitting there with his brother, shotgun in hand, watching for strangers. Neighbors up and down the block had worked out a system— blinking porch lights when an unknown car would appear on the street. But even with these extraordinary precautions, the terrorism could not be stopped. On the night of August 20 bombers hit the home of Arthur Shores, the attorney who was handling Armstrong's case, and two weeks later they attacked him again. It was 9:40 P.M. when Shores told his wife he thought he might sit on the porch for a while. As he was walking toward the cabinet where he kept his double-barreled shotgun, an estimated four sticks of dynamite exploded near the front of his brick ranch house, buckling the aluminum door, shattering windows, and gouging an ugly crater in the lawn. The force of the blast knocked Shores to the floor and threw his wife out of bed. Shores was only bruised, but his wife was rushed to the Holy Family Hospital, where she was listed in fair condition overnight with a shoulder injury and a concussion.

Within minutes, an angry mob gathered outside the house, calling for revenge and throwing rocks and bricks at police. Hearing the news, Fred Shuttlesworth hurried to the scene, and as he had so many times in the past, pleaded with the people in the crowd to go home. But the rioting was out of control this time, and it grew even worse when police began firing their weapons in the air—pistols, rifles, submachine guns. On one occasion, they fired too low, killing John Coley, a twenty-year-old black man, who died from a bullet to the back of the neck. The police reported that Coley had a gun, but Shuttlesworth insisted that he didn't. Coley, he said, was running from the scene when the fatal bullet hit him from behind.

Whatever the truth, the violence on the night of September 4 gave George Wallace the ammunition he needed to close down the schools, or more precisely, to bully a reluctant board of education into making that decision. But it wasn't just the bombing or the deadly confrontation that followed, for in the same ugly span of twenty-four hours, there was rioting by white Alabamians as well. A group of more than a hundred demonstrators from the National States Rights Party scuffled hand to hand with the Birmingham police. By anybody's standards, these were people from the lunatic fringe. They operated out of Bessemer, a Birmingham suburb, in a large stone house where a Confederate battle flag flew from the porch and literature denouncing Communists and Jews was available to anybody inside. The party's leader, Edward Fields, was a handsome thirty-year-old chiropractor who published a monthly newspaper called the *Thunderbolt,* where among other things, he called for the murder of the members of the U.S. Supreme Court.

Fields saw himself as a friend of George Wallace, and not without reason. On the evening of September 1, Wallace addressed a crowd of ten thousand people at a segregation rally in Birmingham, and he invited Fields to a place of honor on the platform. Several days later, when Fields's men battled with the Birmingham police, Wallace defended their actions in an interview with the *New York Times*. These, he said, were "not thugs," but "good working people" who had simply gotten mad at the specter of integration. "It takes courage," he added, "to stand up to tear gas and bayonets."

The interview with reporter John Herbers offered remarkable insight into the mind of George Wallace. It was one of several Alabama stories that day in the *Times*—stories about Wallace and the States Rights Party and rioting outside the house of Arthur Shores. For coming generations, the dispatches from Herbers and his two colleagues, Fred Powledge and Claude Sitton, would become the backbone of history, a vivid word picture of the civil rights movement and the righteous certainty of the people who opposed it.

"The society," said Wallace in the interview with Herbers, "seems to be coming apart at the seams. What good is it to force these situations when people nowhere in the South want integration? What this country needs is a few first-class funerals, and some political funerals too."

And there it was—a startling, explicit call to arms by the governor of Alabama, a defense of the violence by the States Rights Party, coupled with a plea for some well-placed funerals. Did Wallace really mean it? Was the highest official in the state of Alabama really advocating murder? One of the reporters who knew him the best, Bob Ingram of the *Montgomery Advertiser,* believed there was never a time when Wallace really wanted to see people killed, or even hurt, in the war for segregation. It was, for Wallace, a high stakes game of political theater, driven by the naked power of ambition. But whatever the motive, the rhetoric was out there, and there wasn't any doubt that some people in the ranks of the true believers took the governor quite literally at his word.

So did the people in the civil rights movement. For James Armstrong, everything he needed to know about Wallace was there in the presence of the Alabama State Troopers blocking the entrance to Graymont Elementary. For nearly six years, ever since he had volunteered to put his name on the lawsuit, Armstrong had waited to see his children admitted. He lived a block and a half from the three-story schoolhouse, and the exclusion of his daughter and three young sons was one more absurdity of a segregated world. Since the 1950s he had lived through the legal feints and delays, all those sophistries that lawyers could employ, but finally in the summer of 1963, U.S. district judge Seybourn Lynne issued his clear and unequivocal ruling. Graymont Elementary and two high schools, Ramsay and West End, would be desegregated in the fall. On Wednesday morning, September 3, his two youngest sons, Dwight and Floyd, had actually managed to register for their classes, but then the troopers closed down the school. They were led by Col. Al Lingo himself, and they were a menacing presence with their guns and batons, infamous now in the ranks of the movement for their use of the cattle prods in Gadsden.

Eventually, of course, their mission proved futile. Lawyers for the black students in Birmingham (as well as those in Tuskegee and Huntsville) went back to federal court and secured injunctions against further interference by the governor. President Kennedy federalized the National Guard, and Wallace backed off, saying he couldn't "fight bayonets with my bare hands." On Monday morning, September 9, Sonnie Hereford IV and three other black students entered formerly all-white schools in Huntsville, and on the following morning, September 10, the barriers finally fell in Birmingham. For the most part in Huntsville, the change was handled with civility and grace, but Birmingham would be a different story. On their first day of classes, Dwight and Floyd Armstrong were hit with a barrage of racial epithets— "adult obscenities," as one reporter put it, "in the soft treble voices of little boys."

Every morning after that, James Armstrong would drive the boys to the school and see them safely inside the doors, then retrieve them again at 2:45. In between times, at his barbershop, his heart would leap every time he heard a siren, but the boys, he said, gave him the courage he needed to continue. At the end of each day, they would tell him about the harassments they endured—petty assaults at the water fountain, a baseball bat thrown at them on the playground—but they always told their stories with a smile. They had been many times to the mass meetings of the movement and had met Dr. King, who was a regular customer at their father's barbershop. Through it all, they had been well schooled in the theory of nonviolence, and they were ready, they said, to do what it took.

A father could wonder sometimes if it was worth it, but the proof would come later in an integrated world. In the meantime, they had to have faith, had to believe in the dreams of Martin Luther King, for he had the gift that was missing in ordinary people to see the possibilities and put them into words. For Armstrong, however, one test of his faith overshadowed all the others, one moment so bleak that it shattered every piece of optimism he could muster, and it was true for people at every level of the movement. It was a moment that came on a Sunday morning, September 15, five days after the desegregation of the schools. Armstrong had been afraid of some kind of tragedy, for the governor was talking about blood in the streets, and it had the terrible ring of a prophecy. And yet on this particular morning, his mind for once was on other things. He had driven to Selma, the site of the Armstrong family homestead, where he was planning to visit his sister and his cousin. As soon as he got there they told him the news. They had seen it on the television, they said, a sketchy report about the bombing of a church— Sixteenth Street Baptist, the primary staging ground for the movement. According to the report, four children were dead, and nobody knew if there were others in the rubble.

Armstrong didn't wait to hear any more. He and his family didn't belong to the church, but his daughter Denise had been invited to visit the service with her friends. Fearing the worst, Armstrong raced north on Highway 22, driving eighty miles an hour on the backcountry roads, through the blur of the rolling Alabama hills, trying to focus his mind enough to pray. The prayers somehow would not take flight, and all he could manage to do was just hope—hope that his daughter might still be alive, hope that the television might have it wrong.

When he finally arrived, he discovered that Denise was safe at their home, but the scene at the church was as bad as he had feared. Four little girls, all friends of the family, had been killed in the blast, and the black community in Birmingham—one of the most violent cities in the nation—had never confronted this level of horror. Neither had Martin Luther King in Atlanta. When he heard the news, the shock gave way to a depression so deep his family wondered if he could pull himself together. These were children barely older than his own, killed because the civil rights movement—*his* movement—had used their church as its base of operations. He had spoken so grandly in many of his sermons about the idea of suffering and the great, redemptive power that it held. But he didn't mean this—not the sacrifice of little girls.

As the reality overtook him, it was hard to believe that it had been less than three weeks since the March on Washington, with all those people out there in the streets in peaceful solidarity with the civil rights cause. It was easy to speak of dreams on that occasion. But on the morning of the bombing of the Birmingham church, nothing else in the world could seem quite as real—not the march, not the success of the movement in Huntsville. Birmingham again was center stage, and there was nothing to do now but pull himself together and go back to that city, and try to make some sense of what had happened.

CHAPTER 14

The Patent Leather Shoe

IT WAS A MORNING THAT BEGAN with such promise. The weather was beautiful, sixty degrees and bright blue skies, just a touch of autumn in the September air. The Reverend John Cross was looking forward to the service, for September 15 was the Youth Day worship, when the older children in their white Sunday finest came upstairs after Sunday school classes to act as ushers or sing in the choir at the eleven o'clock service. Cross had been at the church for a little over a year, and he had grown quite fond of Sixteenth Street Baptist. The building itself was such a handsome presence just across the street from Kelly Ingram Park—a large brick structure with a stone foundation and a pair of towers overlooking the entrance, and it was particularly beautiful on mornings such as this when the sunshine poured through the stained glass windows.

Cross had come to Birmingham from Richmond, Virginia, where he had been minister at a church of two hundred people—"hard-working people," he told one reporter—and an active participant in the civil rights movement. The search committee at Sixteenth Street asked him less about the movement than about the depth and subtle dimensions of his faith. When was he called to preach, one church leader wondered, and how did he know that the call was authentic? Did God really speak to him from the heavens? Cross said no, it was an inner voice, reassuring and strong, for that was the way God moved in the world. But he believed also that God was present in the civil rights movement, and particularly in the leadership of Martin Luther King. He had heard King speak at a meeting in Richmond, and he never forgot the power of that occasion. In April 1963, when the demonstrations began in Birmingham, Cross was happy to offer his church.

A few people asked him about it, leaders in the church who were afraid of some kind of act of reprisal, but Cross quickly brushed their objections aside. "I thought y'all wanted to see things change in Birmingham," he would say, and that seemed to settle it. Cross played a personal role in the protests, helping to coordinate the nonviolent workshops and the other logistics that went with the marches, and he allowed his seventh-grade daughter, Barbara Cross, to join the ranks of the children's crusade. Many years later, Barbara would recall the exhilaration of the moment, the young people chanting together as they marched: "What do you want?" "Freedom!" "When do you want it?" "Now!" There was an innocence about it, and a purity of hope, that survived the jailings, fire hoses, and dogs, but died on the morning of September 15.

Barbara Cross remembered her Sunday school class that day, a lively discussion on the designated topic, "The Love That Forgives." As soon as it was over, she started off to the rest room with several of her friends— Addie Mae Collins, who was quiet and serious, her closest friend in the group; and Cynthia Wesley, a generous, open-hearted girl who seemed to have a natural gift for leadership. Denise McNair was there also, and Carole Robertson, and Addie Mae's little sister, Sarah Jean. They were a happy troop as they set off together to do a little primping before the big service, and Barbara felt a flash of disappointment when her Sunday school teacher asked her to wait. The teacher, Ella Demand, needed help completing a list of students who were ready for promotion to the next grade level. As Barbara was busy writing down the names, there was a loud explosion that made the whole building shake, and she thought immediately that it must be the Russians. It had been less than a year since the Cuban missile crisis, and these were the days of Cold War terror, with civil defense drills in every school in the country—students crouching under their desks, or evacuating their buildings single file. It always seemed a little unreal, which was not the case with whatever was happening that morning at the church. People were screaming, running everywhere, and after a while somebody told her that four of her friends had been killed in the rest room. For a girl of thirteen, it was hard to know how to process the news or the sudden realization that she would have been there with them if the Sunday school teacher hadn't asked for her help.

Her father, meanwhile, was trying to take charge in the middle of the chaos, relying on nothing but the strength of his instincts. He had been in the women's Sunday school class, up in the sanctuary level of the church, when he first felt the terrible force of the bomb. Like his daughter, he ran through the most preposterous explanations. It's the hot water heater in the kitchen, he thought, for they had been having trouble with it. But then he knew in the hazy aftershock that this was the familiar sound of dynamite. He ran to the lower level of the building, glanced into several of the Sunday school classrooms and saw no injuries. "Thank God," he whispered, and rushed outside.

There was a crowd already, angry and afraid, and he did everything he could to keep them calm. "If you want to help out," he said, "clear the vicinity—and say a prayer on your way home." Then he turned and saw a hole in the side of the building, a gaping chasm at the base of the wall that was almost big enough to walk through. The rescue workers were afraid of collapse, but Cross agreed to go in first, followed soon after by M. W. Pippin, whose granddaughter, Denise McNair, had been in the rest room. They started digging through the plywood and rubble, and almost immediately found a patent leather shoe.

"That's Denise's shoe," the grandfather said.

"Mr. Pippin," said Cross, "that could be anybody's shoe. A lot of little girls wear shoes like that."

But then they came to the tangle of bodies—Denise and then the others, Cynthia Wesley, Addie Mae Collins, and Carole Robertson. Addie Mae's little sister, Sarah Jean, was there also, still alive, but partially blinded by the flying debris. She was one of fourteen among the ranks of the injured.

For the next several minutes, Pippin walked in a daze among the people at the church, crying out in his anguish and stricken disbelief, "I'd like to blow the whole town up!" His brother, F. L. Pippin, was there also. The two of them owned a dry cleaning place not far from the church, close enough, in fact, that its windows were shattered by the force of the blast. There were images later of F. L. Pippin, carrying the patent leather shoe in his hand, tears of grief and horror on his face, as he wept for a loss he could barely comprehend.

The word spread quickly through the black neighborhoods, and Birmingham was convulsed once again in the familiar cycle of atrocity and riot—black people throwing rocks at police, and some of them roaming the streets with their guns. As the feeling of savagery swept through the city, there were two Eagle scouts—both of them white—out riding in their car, and for reasons they were never able to explain, they shot and killed a black child on a bicycle. When Virgil Ware died in his brother's arms, he became the fifth and nearly forgotten victim of the hatred that had overtaken Birmingham.

Martin Luther King was afraid of racial war. When he rushed back to the city from Atlanta, the situation was as dangerous as any he had faced. By Sunday afternoon George Wallace had sent in three hundred state troopers, whose swaggering brutality only added to the atmosphere of tension, and the Birmingham police were not any better. One of their officers, Jack Parker, shot and killed Johnnie Robinson, a black teenager who threw a handful of rocks at a passing car and then tried to run. In response, the black neighborhoods were brimming with weapons, the people preparing themselves for attack.

King asked Kennedy for federal troops to help put an end to the "civil disorder," but the president was reluctant. In Birmingham he was represented uncertainly in the person of Burke Marshall, the Justice Department emissary on the scene. Marshall had handled himself with distinction in the spring, a middleman in the delicate negotiations between the business community and the civil rights movement. But now in a moment of deepening crisis, he seemed to be suddenly out of his depth. When he arrived in Birmingham Sunday night, he had scheduled a meeting with Martin Luther King and other black leaders at the home of John Drew, a black insurance executive who had offered his house as a temporary headquarters. The FBI, however, said it was dangerous for a white man to travel in a black neighborhood, and Marshall initially accepted that verdict. He finally agreed to make the trip, hiding face down in the back seat of a car, and he was "shivering," when he eventually arrived at the meeting, according to one black leader who was there.

"Even though he had been afraid to come," scoffed attorney Oscar Adams, "he said he didn't think it was serious enough to merit use of federal troops to restore order."

Despite his trembling and unimpressive presence, Marshall's instincts may have been right. The violence in Birmingham eventually subsided, leaving the community exhausted and trying to come to terms with its conscience. Mayor Albert Boutwell, whose defeat of Bull Connor in the mayor's election had eventually been validated by the courts, spoke from his heart about the loss of life and what it meant for the city. "It's just sickening," he said, "that a few individuals could commit such a horrible atrocity. All of us are victims, and most of us are innocent victims."

When he heard that statement, Charles Morgan, a white civil rights attorney in Birmingham, found himself seething. The proclamation of innocence was clearly overblown, and once again, the city's white leaders seemed more concerned with their civic image than with the realities of hatred that had to be addressed. Twenty-four hours after the bombing, Morgan spoke out at a civic club meeting.

People were asking who did it, he said, as he gazed at the mass of white faces in the room, and the answer to that question was not very pretty. "The 'who,'" he argued, "is every individual who talks about the 'niggers' and spreads the seeds of his hate to his neighbor and his son. The jokester, the crude oaf whose racial jokes rock the party with the laughter. . . The 'who' is every governor who ever shouted for lawlessness and became a law violator. It is the coward in each of us who clucks admonitions. . . . Who did it? The answer should be, 'We all did it.'"

A short time later, also speaking at a Birmingham civic club, Alabama attorney general Richmond Flowers, a handsome, silver-haired man who was beginning to chart his own course on the issue of race, gave an overlapping answer to the question of guilt. "In their way," he said, "the individuals who bombed the Sixteenth Street Church were standing in the schoolhouse door." That was the emerging consensus in the country. The rhetoric and reckless example of George Wallace made him the implicit perpetrator of the crime. *Time* magazine, for its cover that week, featured a photograph of the stained glass window above the altar in the church, the face of Jesus blown away by the bomb. Superimposed above that image was the scowling countenance of Wallace, his expression the very embodiment of malice. And Martin Luther King sent the governor a telegram, telling him simply: "The blood of our little children is on your hands."

For King, the swirling aftermath of the attack seemed to pull him from his personal despair. His private emotions now felt like a luxury, and for the moment at least he had to shove them aside. Strategically, he was groping for exactly what to do, but one of the realities that was bearing down quickly was the terrible necessity of the little girls' funeral. King wanted all of them buried together, but the Robertson family would not agree. "We realize Carole lost her life because of the movement," explained Mrs. Robertson, "but we feel like her loss was personal to us."

She was buried on Tuesday, September 17, with John Cross and Fred Shuttlesworth each preaching a part of the eulogy at her funeral. The following day King preached the funeral of the other three girls, and John Porter was happy to offer his church. He knew there was a lingering risk of reprisal, for nobody could say if the lunatic fringe was now running scared or proud of itself and just getting started. But Porter had known King since their days in Montgomery, and as the respected pastor of Sixth Avenue Baptist, he had emerged as a leader in the Birmingham movement, a man who was willing to take risks for the cause. Beyond that, he was a friend of John Cross. The two of them looked enough alike to be brothers, and even their churches bore a striking similarity, having been designed by the same architect. Porter didn't hear the Sunday morning bomb, but word traveled quickly and he dismissed his own service and rushed to the hospital. "I got there," he said, "as they were bringing the babies in."

On the morning of the funeral, his role was to lead a delegation of clergy who had assembled initially at a Catholic church some two blocks away. They walked together to Sixth Avenue Baptist—white, black, Catholic, Protestant, Jew, Greek Orthodox—and as they entered the church through the great stone arches, Porter was struck by a feeling of hope. Given the fundamental grimness of the day, it took him by surprise, but there seemed to be something in the coming together, and he began to wonder if there might be a measure of redemption in the deaths.

Certainly, that was the theme of King's sermon—redemption, forgiveness, and the need, in the end, to keep on pushing. "History," he said, "has proven over and over again that unmerited suffering is redemptive. . . . So in spite of the darkness of this hour, we must not despair. We must not become bitter, nor must we harbor the desire to retaliate with violence. We must not lose faith in our white brothers. Somehow we must believe that even the most misguided among them can learn to respect the dignity and worth of all human personalities."

John Porter listened to the words with a familiar sense of awe, a respect for King and his gift for the language, and his rejection of the first impulse of human nature. Revenge, in a way, would have been so sweet, an eye for an eye in response to the murder of four little girls, but for Martin Luther King, strategically and morally, it was simply not an option. Porter thought of the families of the four murdered children and what it must be like to hear such a message, what strength it took not to give in to rage, or even to a raw and elemental hate. But these were people of extraordinary character, and they showed it now in this massive outpouring at the Sixth Avenue Church.

A few years later, a reporter came to town, working on a story about the legacy of Birmingham. Porter sent him to see Claude Wesley, whose daughter, Cynthia, had died in the bombing. "If you want to understand the movement," Porter said, "I think you ought to talk to Mr. Wesley."

The reporter wrote later about the portrait of Cynthia that hung on the wall—the permanent smile on her round, pretty face, and the response of her father every day when he saw it. "She was a very happy child," he said. "She always liked to be in the forefront. Her teachers would say if they could get Cynthia on their side, they could get the whole class."

Wesley smiled and fell silent for a time. He was an educator by trade, a thin and wispy, gray-haired man, who was first a teacher and then a principal in the Birmingham schools. His students remembered the lessons he taught about the role of the Negro in American history, about the inescapable link between the generations, and the taproots of freedom going back a hundred years. He saw the death of his daughter that way— a terrible, heart-breaking, personal loss that was nevertheless part of a much bigger story.

"We never felt bitter," he told the reporter. "That wouldn't have been fair to Cynthia. We try to deal with her memory the same way we dealt with her presence, and bitterness had no place in that. And there was something else we never did. We never asked, 'Why us?' because that would be the same thing as asking, 'Why not somebody else?' But as far as the movement went, we continued to feel about it the way we always had. We supported it. We felt it was seeking necessary change."

For the people who planted the bomb at the church, this was the most perplexing thing, the fact that the movement could not be cowed. All along, these underground warriors for white supremacy shared an article of faith with George Wallace—a grim and ugly but heartfelt belief in segregation now and segregation forever. They could not imagine another kind of world.

On the day before the bombing, Birmingham Klansman Robert Chambliss told a member of his family, "You just wait until after Sunday morning and they will beg us to let them segregate." Such was the fatal self-delusion of the Klan.

For every agency investigating the bombing—the FBI, state troopers, and police—Chambliss was high on the list of suspects. "Dynamite Bob," as everybody called him, was an Irish American who had been in the Klan since the 1920s. He was a ruddy-faced, blue-eyed street-brawler with a deep and abiding hatred of black people. Back in the '20s, he had labored in the squalor of the Birmingham mines and was once a member of the United Mine Workers Union, but by the 1930s, his allegiance was solely to the Ku Klux Klan. He reveled in the mission of the Klan at that time— intimidating black workers and stirring the racial passion of whites— which was precisely the division the mine owners needed to weaken the union and keep it at bay. Chambliss was not concerned about economics. For whatever dark intermingling of reasons, he was preoccupied only with the divine right of whites to occupy a rung on the ladder above blacks.

He had learned about dynamite in the mines, and he began to use it as a tool of warfare sometime late in the 1940s. As later investigations would reveal, it was Chambliss who, on Christmas night, 1956, bombed the home of Fred Shuttlesworth, an attack that only stiffened Shuttlesworth's resolve. But Chambliss, too, became more committed to the battle through the years, and he operated until the 1960s with the support and approval of his friend Bull Connor. During that time, there were forty-seven bombings in greater Birmingham, and these most often were guerilla attacks—not bombs with timers left to explode, but sticks of dynamite thrown by Chambliss or some of his cronies as they crept through the shadows or roared through the neighborhoods in their cars.

The bombing of the church was a break from this pattern—the bomb exploded at least eight hours after it was planted—but a lot of things had changed by the troubled autumn of 1963. For one thing, Bull Connor was no longer in power and no longer able to offer his protection. For another, it was clear to everyone—even to the Klan—that segregation was crumbling, which drove Chambliss to a whole new level of fury. On Saturday morning, September 14, he told his niece Elizabeth Hood that Connor and Wallace and all but a handful of people in the Klan were simply not tough enough to take a stand. How else could anyone account for the fact that the "goddamn niggers" seemed to be winning? But all that was about to change. After Sunday morning, he said, the black community in Birmingham would beg.

When the black community didn't, more bombs exploded in the next several weeks. The most significant of those came on the night of September 25, a double hit in a black neighborhood in the south part of town, which had never been a primary target in the past. The first bomb exploded around 2 A.M., gouging a hole in the ground and shearing a utility pole at its base. Thirteen minutes later, a second bomb went off in the same location, this one spraying nails and jagged pieces of scrap metal in a pattern that was obviously intended to kill. The police were astonished. Thirteen minutes was plenty of time for them to arrive on the scene to investigate a bombing, which meant that the terrorists intended to kill not only the bystanders in a black neighborhood but some of Birmingham's finest as well.

Remarkably, nobody was hurt. Somehow the shrapnel missed its human targets and spent itself in the dense underbrush of a vacant lot. This was, however, a new chapter in the war, and for the Birmingham police it had the effect of undergirding their resolve to find the church bombers.

Their investigation was moving forward slowly, still in its tentative, embryonic stages, when the governor of Alabama made a startling announcement. On September 29 he reported that the state police under Al Lingo had broken the case. Robert Chambliss and Charles Cagle, another notorious Birmingham Klansman, had surrendered to authorities. The announcement quickly made national headlines, as Wallace bragged to reporters at the capitol, "We certainly beat the Kennedy crowd to the punch." In the Justice Department, Robert Kennedy and Burke Marshall were shocked. They knew there was no way that Lingo, even if he had been serious about it, could develop a murder case in so short a time. What was going on here? Was it an attempt to muddy the real investigation or simply more political theater by Wallace?

Nine days after the flurry of headlines, Chambliss and Cagle both came to trial. They pled guilty, not to murder, but to the misdemeanor charge of possession of dynamite without a permit, a conviction that carried a one hundred dollar fine and a suspended sentence of six months in jail. In the wake of the murder of four little girls, such was the governor's understanding of justice.

Diane Nash was not surprised. She had been in North Carolina with her husband, James Bevel, when she first heard about the bombing of the church. Bevel was working in the eastern part of the state as an organizer for SCLC, and Nash was busy being a young mother, working off and on for the movement. On September 15 she was at the home of Golden Frinks, one of the leaders in North Carolina, when Bevel burst through the door with the news. He told her about the dynamite and the girls, and as they contemplated the enormity of the crime, their reaction went beyond either rage or grief. What they felt was a fusion of the two and all the explosive energy it implied. They felt responsible for the crime in a way, for they had both worked hard on the Birmingham protests, and it was Bevel's idea, when the movement was struggling, to let the schoolchildren march.

As they began to talk about what to do next, they discovered that the magnitude of the bombing tore at their basic faith in nonviolence, a faith unshaken since the movement began. They had endured the brutality of the Freedom Rides, and later the attacks of the Birmingham dogs, without ever doubting the power of their approach. But now they found themselves talking about murder, about tracking down the perpetrators of this crime and bringing them personally to a vigilante justice. They knew they could do it. The identity of people like Robert Chambliss was a poorly kept secret, and if they chose this tempting path of revenge—a path intoxicating in its pull—they could do it unencumbered by the rules of evidence or the sophistry of lawyers or the maddening twists and turns of the courts. The bombers, they decided, were already doomed.

And yet as they talked, a second option began to take shape, and the more they thought about it the more they knew that it was a far more radical idea than the first. Without any question, the time had come to escalate the war, but not with violence or an eye for an eye. They were talking now about the cold practicality of political change—about what it would take to create a world in which even the most vicious, hard-core racist would have to think twice about bombing a church; in which the governor of Alabama, no matter his level of naked ambition, would have to think twice about a rhetoric of hate. What it would take, they decided, was the right to vote and the willingness to use it, and it was a change that needed to come right away.

They were suddenly excited, driven by the fury that only moments before had them contemplating murder, but now they were talking about political tactics—about bringing the state of Alabama to its knees. They would assemble a massive, nonviolent army, something much closer to the March on Washington than the level of protests they had seen in the past, and they would descend on Wallace, who had the blood of children still dripping from his hands. They would surround the capitol, and clog the streets, and block the runways out at the airport. As the condition of a truce, they would call on President Kennedy in Washington to declare the government of Alabama illegal.

Early in the week of September 16, just before the funerals of the four little girls, they took their idea to Fred Shuttlesworth. They wanted to make an announcement at the service, building on the immediacy of the grief, but Shuttlesworth said no, it would not be appropriate. "Right now, Diane," he told her sternly, "we're going to express our grief by mourning. And if you get out here and do other things that would take away from the sacredness and sanctity of the funeral, then I will have to call a press conference and say that I asked you not to do this for the sake of the family, for the sake of the occasion. . . . A funeral is not the time to do what you are talking about."

Nash was impressed by the gentle sensitivity of a man that most people regarded as a warrior. It was a reminder of the depth of Shuttlesworth's faith and his calling as a pastor that, instinctively and emphatically, he put the feelings of the families ahead of the strategic interests of the movement. Nash could understand that decision, but she was not about to let the idea drop, to treat it as some kind of cathartic fantasy that helped to get her through a moment of anger.

A few days later, she brought it up again, and her target this time was Martin Luther King. It was a role she had played on other occasions, pushing Dr. King to be bolder. She remembered the day when she had tried to persuade him to join the Freedom Rides, and she remembered the cynicism in SNCC when King had refused. Many of the young activists out there in the field, the people in Selma or the Mississippi Delta who confronted the possibility of death every day, regarded King as far too timid and soft, too caught up in the perks of leadership to get himself dirty on the barricades. Nash did not quite share that opinion. Like her friends John Lewis and Bernard Lafayette, she had always felt great affection for King, almost a tender inclination to protect him, and the affection clearly went both ways. King listened patiently to her plans for George Wallace, for this massive, Sherman-like assault on Alabama, and although it struck him as completely impractical, he tried to be gentle in his words of rejection.

"His response was kind," Nash remembered years later, "but the bottom line was, 'Get real, Diane.' He just didn't buy it."

So Bevel and Nash made a decision on their own. They would go to Alabama, to the heart of the Black Belt, and they would stir such fervor among the citizens there that King would have to follow the lead of the masses. Their goal in the end was the right to vote—a right still denied to the majority of blacks in the Deep South states—and this would be the final, revolutionary push, the great and necessary victory for the movement.

Before it was over, things would happen almost as they planned, but it would be a few months—very *difficult* months—before all the pieces would fall into place.

CHAPTER 15

Eyes on the Prize

ON SEPTEMBER 19, 1963, FOUR DAYS after the bombing of the church, Fred Shuttlesworth made a journey to Washington. He was still reeling from the horror of the past several days, and it tempered the rush he might otherwise have felt in meeting with the president of the United States. Not that Shuttlesworth was easily impressed. He was always the ultimate self-made man, essentially unmoved by the trappings of power or erudition or wealth, all of which John Kennedy possessed. Many of the leaders in the civil rights movement were deeply ambivalent about the young president. Privately at least, they agreed with John Lewis, who had wanted to say at the March on Washington that Kennedy was offering too little too late. But Shuttlesworth had a slightly different view. He thought he detected something in Kennedy, some spirit of sympathy for the cause of black America that couldn't be contrived, and his feeling was confirmed once again at the White House.

Sitting on one side of Kennedy with Martin Luther King on the other,

Shuttlesworth asked what he and other leaders could say to people who were trying to come to terms with the tragedy. These victims, he said, were "four innocent little girls, not in war, but just studying a Sunday school lesson, and they're blown away." Was there really an answer that made any sense? Kennedy's reply was immediate. "I know exactly how you feel," he said. "But you have to tell your people that in every situation there are some innocent people who get killed. In a war, more bystanders get killed than those on the battlefield. And somehow you have to communicate that this happens."

There was nothing profound about the president's reply, but neither was it inappropriate or shallow, and Shuttlesworth found himself thinking again that this was a man who was on their side. He knew that King was not quite as sure, that he regarded Kennedy as far too tentative, which was doubly ironic since King, unintentionally, had been a key player in Kennedy's election.

The story went back to October 1960, when King decided to join a student sit-in, subjecting himself to arrest in Georgia. He expected to serve a brief time in jail, demonstrating his solidarity with the students, but Judge Oscar Mitchell sentenced him to four months of hard labor on a Georgia chain gang. The police came to get him in the middle of the night, leaving Coretta King, who was six months pregnant, frantic with worry about the fate of her husband.

When word of all this reached the candidate John Kennedy, he picked up the phone and called Mrs. King to express his sympathy and to offer to do what he could to help. The election was less than three weeks away, and from all indications, was going to be close. Some of those on Kennedy's staff, including Robert Kennedy, were afraid the call would cost Kennedy the South. But the more Robert learned about the sheer outrageousness of the sentence, the angrier he became. Finally, he called Judge Mitchell in Georgia, and persuaded him to set King free.

All this came at a delicate time, when black America was divided in its political affiliations. The Republicans were still the party of Lincoln, and racial liberals such as Nelson Rockefeller occupied prominent positions in the party. But the Democrats had been moving in the right direction ever since Eleanor Roosevelt spoke out strongly for civil rights, and Pres. Harry Truman began to desegregate the military. Among black voters, the presidential election of 1960 appeared to be a dead heat until the word began to spread about Kennedy's telephone call to Mrs. King. Martin Luther King Sr., a Republican and a Baptist, had planned to vote against Kennedy, a Catholic Democrat, but now he spoke in Kennedy's behalf. Meanwhile, the senator's campaign sent out more than 2 million pamphlets, telling black churchgoers of the act of compassion on behalf of Dr. King.

The result was astounding. In an election decided by 100,000 votes out of more than 68 million cast, Kennedy won the black vote by a margin of 70 percent to 30 percent. Four years earlier, the Republicans had won by nearly that much. Without question, Kennedy would never have been elected without the Negro vote, and King believed that the president had never quite delivered on his debt. Kennedy's calculations, once he made it into office, seemed to be more political than moral, and his general support of the civil rights movement, though a matter of record, was tempered by his constant political hedging. It was true he had delivered a powerful speech following Wallace's stand in the schoolhouse door, but he had taken more than two years to submit a civil rights bill, and King wasn't sure how hard he would push it.

For all these reasons, King was strangely cool and pragmatic in late November 1963 when Kennedy was murdered on a trip to the South, plunging the country into a state of disbelief. When a white graduate student working on a dissertation asked about the meaning of Kennedy's death, King called it a blessing for the civil rights bill. "I'm convinced that had he lived," King said, "there would have been continual delays, and attempts to evade it at every point, and water it down at every point. But I think his memory and the fact that he stood up for this civil rights bill will cause many people to see the necessity for working passionately. . . . I think we have some very hopeful days ahead."

Whatever the rationality of that assessment, other black leaders, including Shuttlesworth and John Lewis, were far more inclined to lead with their hearts, to offer more open expressions of grief. Lewis, especially, responded to the assassination of Kennedy with a depth of emotion that took him by surprise. Like King, he had always been ambivalent about the president, and he thought even now that his civil rights legislation was simply inadequate. It made no mention of voting rights or police brutality, which were life and death issues to the people in SNCC and the local blacks they sought to organize. Still, Lewis felt an admiration for Kennedy, not only for the grace that most people saw but for his quick intelligence and his willingness to listen. Somehow, he seemed to be growing with the movement, and it was with an honest and heartfelt sense of loss that Lewis proposed to his friends in SNCC that they hold a vigil at Arlington Cemetery. He was startled by the vehemence of their response. Hell no, many of them said. Kennedy had never been a friend to the movement. He was just another in a line of white politicians who couldn't be trusted, and his death in the end wasn't worth the trouble. For Lewis, the cynicism was startling, one of the early signs, he said, that the movement could self-destruct on its anger.

Back in Alabama, Fred Shuttlesworth agreed with Lewis. He was as tough and militant as anybody else, as instantly contemptuous of the feeble gestures of white politicians, but he was not contemptuous of John F. Kennedy. Here was a man who came from one of the wealthiest families in the country, who could have wrapped himself in a cocoon of arrogance, but who had struggled instead with the issues of justice and who "wanted to do good." That was Shuttlesworth's view, going back at least to the inaugural address of 1960 when Kennedy had talked about an era in which "man holds in his mortal hands the power to abolish all forms of human poverty and all forms of human life." This was a president who was bold in his thinking, who didn't shrink from the opportunities and the dangers, and Shuttlesworth always admired that trait. And if there were the inevitable moments of disappointment when Kennedy clearly could have done a little more, Shuttlesworth compared him not to some ideal of perfection but to all the presidents who had done even less.

"I really believe," he said years later, "that if the Kennedys had not been in the White House when we were in the streets, we would be in a terrible fix in this country today."

Certainly, that view was prevalent in the South, particularly in the cabins in the heart of Alabama, where rural black families by the hundreds and thousands offered their private and personal tributes. These took the form most often of roughly framed pictures hanging from the walls—Jesus, John Kennedy, and Martin Luther King—a kind of holy trinity of justice for people with instincts honed by oppression. They knew without analyzing the details that their freedom was tied to the work of these men, and if historians or movement militants disagreed, it was not a matter even worthy of debate.

The odd thing was, some people on the other side were just as sure. In Tuskegee, Alabama, on November 22, the radio bulletin about Kennedy's assassination drew cheers from the whites who worked at City Hall. And over in Montgomery, George Wallace's legal adviser, John Kohn, author of the governor's statement in the schoolhouse door, rushed from his office when he first heard the news to cheer for the bullet of Lee Harvey Oswald—a dance of joy on Dexter Avenue.

Wallace himself was far more subdued. He heard about the murder as he was getting ready to speak at a high school dedication in the town of Haleyville. "What are we coming to," he said, "when a president cannot ride down a street of an American city without being shot." And he began to stammer and fumble for his words before sitting down. Shortly afterward, he declared a thirty-day period of mourning, ordered the state flags flown at half-mast, and wrote a warm, personal letter to Jacqueline Kennedy, expressing his sorrow about what had happened. Despite their disparate views on race, Wallace secretly admired John Kennedy, a man who seemed so sure of himself, who lacked the massive need for affirmation that occasionally made Wallace tremble with insecurity.

Lyndon Johnson understood that feeling. Now suddenly and tragically elevated to the White House, the former vice president and senator from Texas had his own ambivalent feelings about Kennedy. Like Wallace, he admired the president for his dignity and grace. But like many vice presidents down through history, he seldom felt a part of the inner circle, and as a man of massive ambition himself, he chafed at the slights inherent in the job. He thought in particular that he could have helped on the issue of civil rights, for as a native southerner he understood all its murky complications, and certainly he could grasp, far more naturally and instinctively than Kennedy, the mind-set of Wallace and the southern demagogues.

In the closing days of the Kennedy administration, Johnson was finally pulled into the civil rights deliberations, and he urged the president to be bolder—to go on television, for example, and speak from the depths of his conscience and his heart about the urgent necessity of righting old wrongs. Equivocation, said Johnson, only encouraged people like Wallace, and did nothing to soothe the hostility of his followers.

Once in the White House, Johnson was determined to follow his own counsel. He would pursue the passage of the civil rights bill with all the arm-twisting vigor he could muster, and he would cast John Kennedy as the fallen martyr to the civil rights cause. Many black southerners were skeptical at first. In an essay in *Look* magazine, the great black journalist Louis Lomax, a native of Georgia, wrote about seeing the new president on television, and the immediate misgivings in the Negro community: "As we listened to him talk, the cracker twang in his voice chilled our hearts. For we know that twang, that drawl. We have heard it in the night, threatening; in the day, abusing; from the pulpit, sanctifying segregation; in the market place, denying us opportunity; everywhere, abrogating our human dignity. Yes, we know that twang. And we reacted."

But Lomax predicted, long before the passage of the civil rights bill, that Johnson would emerge as a champion of justice. He thought the new president and his wife, Lady Bird, who was descended from the Alabama aristocracy, were the kind of southerners who might be liberated by the movement. They were "the good white people," who were never inclined to lynch or abuse or discriminate personally but whose decency was circumscribed by the times. As a politician with national ambitions, Johnson had been caught in a terrible dilemma. If he said too much about civil rights, he threatened his political base in Texas, but if he didn't, the country would see him as one more in a galaxy of southern politicians, and he would never be president. Now in a horrifying irony, the murder of John Kennedy had finally set him free, and Lomax was sure that Johnson would use his personal liberation to do what was right, and to carve his own place in the history of the nation.

By the summer of 1964, history made it clear that Lomax was right. These were still troubled times for the country, with the murder of three civil rights workers down in Mississippi, their bodies discovered in an earthen dam in the swampy backcountry of Neshoba County. And late in June, in the ancient city of Saint Augustine, Florida, weeks of demonstrations finally culminated in an ugly attack, a scene reminiscent of Birmingham and other places, with mobs of whites beating peaceful demonstrators and the unlucky journalists assigned to the story. To Fred Shuttlesworth, a leader in the marches, it was déjà vu, and to Martin Luther King, who was also there, the intensity of the violence was worse than Birmingham.

But there was a piece of good news that summer. On July 2 President Johnson signed the civil rights bill, passed with the help of the NAACP and other national civil rights groups. It was, perhaps, the most sweeping piece of legislation of its kind since the days of the Emancipation Proclamation. There was much that the bill did not accomplish, but Johnson was certain, as Kennedy had been, that this was a law with powerful implications—that it could help change the tenor of life in the South. It banned segregation in public schools, libraries and playgrounds, and in places of public accommodation, including theaters, restaurants, hotels, and waiting rooms, and it outlawed racial discrimination in hiring. Johnson signed the law within hours of its passage, flanked by many of the giants of the movement, including Martin Luther King and Rosa Parks.

Shuttlesworth was not on the guest list, which was a galling oversight, given the historical importance of Birmingham. One year earlier, John Kennedy had called a meeting of the leaders to strategize about the civil rights bill. "But for Birmingham," he said, "we wouldn't be here." Shuttlesworth was certain that was true, and he thought it was appropriate, when the bill finally passed, for the first test of it to come in his city. On Thursday evening, only a few hours after the signing, he and a small group of activists quietly entered the Parliament House, one of Birmingham's finest hotels, and asked to be seated in the dining room. They were treated with respect, and there were similar reports from other restaurants in other parts of town.

Elsewhere in the state, there were the occasional exceptions to that optimistic pattern. Down in Selma on July 4, Sheriff Jim Clark used a cattle prod on a young black man who asked to be served at a drive-in restaurant. But even in some of the most difficult places, the movement activists began to see a difference. In Gadsden, J. D. Cammeron, one of the black demonstrators beaten and prodded by Al Lingo in the summer of 1963, noticed a change of mood in the place where he worked. It had been an uncomfortable year at the Coosa Pipe Foundry, with Cammeron's white coworkers threatening him physically for his role in the protests. But almost as soon as the civil rights bill passed, the word went out from the plant superintendent—a new man on the job—that he would not tolerate any further harassment.

"He said if he caught them," Cammeron remembered, "they would not work there no more."

Gradually, the compliance became less grudging, and for the movement's foot soldiers like J. D. Cammeron, life was different in subtle and unremarkable ways that were nevertheless profound. If nothing else, the physical danger that went with being black was slowly but surely beginning to subside.

On the other side of the chasm, however, the forces of segregation had not given up. If anything, the governor of Alabama was moving with a new, invigorated swagger, the result of his decision to run for the presidency. The idea began to take shape around the time of the stand in the schoolhouse door. On June 2, 1963, Wallace was invited to appear on *Meet the Press,* the nationally televised interview show, and he was happy about the chance for national exposure. Bob Ingram, political reporter for the *Montgomery Advertiser,* flew to New York to cover the event, and he remembered that Wallace was in high spirits. There was a band of Greek musicians on the flight, and they offered a brief, impromptu concert in honor of the governor, playing a rendition of "Dixie" with traditional Greek instruments. Wallace was delighted. But about the time the plane touched down, he began to fret, worrying about whether the *Meet the Press* panel would grill him on things like foreign policy. A presidential candidate ought to have one, he said, and he had never given it much thought. Bob Ingram tried to be reassuring, telling Wallace he would do just fine, and Ingram was right.

When the telecast began, Wallace took a deep breath and presented himself as a man who was fully and comfortably in command. "The tremble left his hands and the quaver left his voice," one reporter noted, and what the nation saw was a man who was calm and gracious under fire. He intended to stand in the doorway, he said, to raise an important constitutional question. One member of the panel, Anthony Lewis, the eloquent columnist for the *New York Times,* pushed Wallace hard, suggesting that the constitutional issues were already settled and the stand in the door was "a political gesture to try to arouse violence." Wallace deftly sidestepped the challenge. There would be no violent resistance, he said. "I am against that as much as anybody."

And so it went for most of the hour, and when it was over, the governor of Alabama was giddy with his triumph. It had almost been too easy, he thought. There had been no questions about foreign policy, and he handled everything else with aplomb. "All they wanted to know about was niggers," he told one member of his entourage, "and I'm the expert."

That November he headed north for the Ivy Leagues and an appearance at Harvard, and once again he played the matador to his challengers. One of the people in the audience that night was Gordon DuBois II, the grandson of W. E. B. DuBois, the great black thinker who had challenged the accommodationist policies of Booker T. Washington. True to his heritage, the younger DuBois tried to goad and provoke, telling Wallace he intended to run for president someday. Wallace only smiled. "Between you and me both," he said, "we might kick out that crowd down in Washington. Maybe we should run on the same ticket."

Seeing that the Harvard audience was charmed, Bob Zellner was fuming. Zellner was a white Alabamian, who regarded his governor with a seething contempt. Zellner had grown up in Mobile, and as a college student in the 1950s, had become a supporter of the civil rights movement. He had been radicalized by the Freedom Rides and the image of the beatings by the Ku Klux Klan, and he had become an organizer for SNCC, deeply respected by his black colleagues for his unflinching bravery in the toughest situations. Clean-shaven with neatly cropped hair, he didn't really look the part of a radical, and there was almost nothing in his personal background to suggest the direction his own life had taken. His grandfather and his uncle were unrepentant Klansmen, and Wallace, who had long been a friend of the family, was contemptuous of this young prodigal who had given his comfort and support to the enemy.

He was surprised to see him in the audience at Harvard and startled momentarily when Zellner rose to ask him a question. "How do you square what you say about civil rights with your police brutality?" Zellner began. But Wallace cut him off, lapsing briefly into the street-brawling persona that played so well to the crowds in Alabama. "Oh, I know you," he said. "You're Bob Zellner and you are a renowned Alabamian. In fact, you have been in a number of jails in Alabama."

The two of them sparred back and forth for a while, debating the Wallace civil rights record, and as the governor quickly regained his composure, the crowd responded with a standing ovation—for Wallace, according to the Alabama papers, but Zellner thought he saw something different. "The place exploded in an ovation," he said, "for everyone who had fought for civil rights."

Whatever the case, Wallace, on balance, clearly held his own. For the most part, he had kept his bantamweight temper in check, and he was much more the charmer than the Alabama rube. He was beginning to believe in his national appeal, and the feeling grew stronger on a tour of the western part of the country. Throughout the trip, Wallace cast himself as the intrepid champion of the little man in America, feisty but gracious, a battler to the end. He was careful never to talk about race, at least not directly, and the western journalists were impressed by a man who confounded their negative expectations. The *Tacoma Tribune* called him a "mild-mannered person with a sense of humor and a message. His message is mainly a firm belief in states' rights."

In the winter and spring of 1964 Wallace entered three presidential primaries—Wisconsin, Indiana, and Maryland—all outside the South. He hammered away at the civil rights bill, which was currently making its way through Congress, calling it a "nefarious piece of legislation." But he was careful never to speak ill of blacks. He talked instead about the growth of the central government in Washington and the destruction of the property rights of individuals. When he spoke in white suburban neighborhoods, he raised the specter of open housing, and in the union halls he talked about quotas and jobs taken away from hard-working whites who had labored to earn their positions of seniority. Overlaid against all those intertwining themes were the strong and disturbing intimations of conspiracy—some overt but unspecified link between the civil rights movement and the communist party. When his opponents attacked him or became too shrill about his dubious civil rights record at home, Wallace struck a posture of injured innocence. "I have tried to speak the truth," he said, "nothing more."

All in all, it worked. In Wisconsin, the Democratic governor, John Reynolds, had declared early on that a vote of 100,000 for Wallace would be a "catastrophe." When the votes were counted, Wallace had polled some 266,000, more than a third of the total number cast. In Indiana, he took more than 30 percent, and in the border state of Maryland, he took nearly half. It was more than a moral victory for Wallace; it was a clear demonstration of his national appeal. He became the candidate who spoke in code, wrapping the reality of racial animosity in a rhetoric that had nothing to do with skin color. People's darkest fears became something righteous, and all their resentments and misunderstandings took on the cast of a noble crusade. And at last, improbably, they had discovered a champion.

That was how it looked to Martin Luther King, as he contemplated the star that was now George Wallace. In a curious way, he and the governor were competing exports from the state of Alabama, and he had no illusions about the strength of his opponent. In King's estimation, there had never been anybody like Wallace, nobody in the ranks of southern segregationists who possessed the same level of political brilliance. Even before the presidential primaries, King regarded Wallace as "perhaps the most dangerous racist in America today," a politician whose speeches were polished and honed to the point that they became "minor classics." Now, it seemed, Wallace presented an even greater danger, for he had learned to reach out to a national audience and to make the reality of a racial backlash feel not only respectable but righteous.

The odd thing was, King's own appeal was growing also, at least by the measure of international renown. Early in 1964 he was chosen by the editors of *Time* magazine as their Man of the Year, and then in October he won the Nobel Peace Prize. The news reached King in a hospital bed, where he was suffering from high blood pressure and exhaustion, but somewhere in the haze of his fatigue and medication, he began to sort through his mix of emotions. The symbolism of the Peace Prize was important, for it made the point, often overlooked in the American South, that the pursuit of justice was the pursuit of peace, and the two, in the end, could not be separated. But the truth of it was, they were still a long way from justice in the South, and there was an irony, therefore, in this moment of triumph that made it a double-edged honor at best.

In Oslo, Norway, where he accepted the prize, not for himself, but on behalf of the movement, King spoke in a somber and understated tone. "I am mindful," he said, "that only yesterday in Birmingham, Alabama, our children, crying out for brotherhood, were answered with fire hoses, snarling dogs and even death. I am mindful that only yesterday in Philadelphia, Mississippi, young people seeking to secure the right to vote were brutalized and murdered. Therefore, I must ask why this prize is awarded to a movement which is beleaguered and committed to unrelenting struggle, to a movement which has not won the very peace and brotherhood which is the essence of the Nobel Prize."

Such was King's state of mind at the time. His personal accolades were flattering, and the Civil Rights Act had clearly made a difference. But it was also clear that his brothers in the southland were still not free. Down in Selma, a segregationist sheriff was using cattle prods in his personal repudiation of the new federal law. And over in the town of Philadelphia, Mississippi, a segregationist judge had freed the killers of the three civil rights workers buried in a dam. What was needed now, King thought, was not an appeal to the national conscience, which was caught in a pull between himself and George Wallace. What they needed instead in the Heart of Dixie was a fundamental shift in the balance of power. They needed the ballot as their ultimate weapon of self-defense, to rid themselves of all the petty tyrants who ruled in the same old climate of fear.

The time had come to pursue that goal, and King had chosen a little-known place for what could be the final crusade of the movement. They would go to Selma, the antebellum town on the Alabama River, and they would settle the voting issue once and for all.

PART FOUR

REVOLUTION

CHAPTER 16

The Battle Plan

JAMES BEVEL AND HIS WIFE, Diane Nash, had been lobbying hard for more than a year, pushing the battle plan they had developed after the bombing of the Birmingham church. They had gone to Selma to build on the efforts of Bernard Lafayette and other SNCC organizers working with local leaders in the town.

Nash understood that it was almost an act of insubordination, this plan of theirs to drag Dr. King into a confrontation he rejected when they first brought it up. But she also knew that her husband didn't care, and the truth of it was, neither did she. The time had come, she thought, not only to pursue the right to vote for every black person in the state of Alabama but to transform the meaning of the Birmingham bombing. Somehow the deaths of the four little girls had to stand for something more—something *finer*—than the racist depravity of the Ku Klux Klan. There had to be some sense of *resurrection*, some feeling that a triumph worthy of these children had sprung from the senseless horror of their deaths.

That was the fundamental hope that sustained them as they began to map out a hard-headed plan. They went into Selma late in 1963, determined to stir the local rebellion so that King himself would have to come in. In the first few months, they came face to face with the crippling inertia of the southern Black Belt, the age-old feeling that nothing would change because nothing ever had. But they also discovered the handful of heroic people who were like those in every other corner of the movement. These were the ones with the ability to hope, to believe in things they had not yet seen, and they were led in Selma by Sam and Amelia Boynton, two people with such deep roots in the South that they were essentially a part of the black aristocracy.

Going back all the way to the 1930s, the Boyntons had struggled for the right to vote, not only for themselves but for the thousands of other black people in their county. Sam was an agricultural agent who traveled the back roads and knew every farmer, every tenant and sharecropper on the lands of white planters, and knew the conditions under which they lived. He knew about the poverty and the quiet desperation, but he believed also that these were people who would do well enough in a democratic world, and he was determined somehow to bring that about. He knew they still had a long way to go, for in the 1930s, there were hardly any black voters in the county, and even as late as the 1960s, there were only a few—maybe two or three hundred out of a black population of more than sixteen thousand. The obstacles were fierce, and the indignities inherent in the Dallas County system were sometimes more than a proud man could bear. There were the poll taxes and the unrelenting hostilities of the white registrars, and there was the fact that in order for a Negro to register, a white person had to vouch for his character.

Despite all this, the Boyntons were gradually making some progress, until sometime late in the 1950s and the white backlash against the civil rights movement. They worked as a team, Sam and his pretty young wife, Amelia, whom he had met in Tuskegee where both of them were students. As they built their life together in Selma, they understood that this freedom they were seeking came at a price, and they endured the threats and the callers in the night, and sometimes a danger that was even more direct. One day in Selma in the 1960s, a stocky white man maybe sixty years old stormed into their office and began to threaten Sam Boynton with a club. The Boyntons by then were selling insurance, and the white man, who was an agent himself, was irate over the loss of some of his business. As he screamed his threats and racial epithets, Amelia stepped forward in a rush of adrenaline and tore the brandished weapon from his hands. She was a trim and dignified woman, but in her moment of fury she drew back the club and was ready to use it, when she heard the steady voice of her husband. "Don't hit him," said Sam, and Amelia caught herself in midswing. About that time two black men passing by on the street saw what was happening and came in the door. "Get out of here," they said, and the white man did, smashing the Boyntons' front window as he left.

Amelia thought later about the depth of hatred she saw in his face, which was flushed and contorted, transformed, she said, "into the very Devil himself." She knew that he stood at the threshold of murder, and at the very least had assumed they would cower, for that was the way of the world in Dallas County. Every form of power was in the hands of the whites, and black people were caught in an undertow of fear, a knowledge perpetually in the back of their minds that one wrong move, however innocent or unintended when it started, could carry the most catastrophic results. Consequently, most black people set out to please, to live their lives "at a tiptoe stance," as Martin Luther King had so often put it. But Amelia understood that there was also a certain reservoir of courage—like that of the black men passing on the street, who saw the threat to the safety of their friends and quickly found a way to take a stand.

Amelia thought that was something they could build on, particularly with the coming of the young organizers, including the Bevels and Bernard Lafayette. Lafayette was the first, and when he arrived in Selma in 1962, he was a person unlike anybody they had seen. He seemed to be easygoing enough, with his quick-witted humor and his sly, impish grin, but perhaps the most important quality he brought was something endemic to the SNCC organizers. He seemed to be unafraid. Early on, he went to see Jim Clark, the Dallas County sheriff who aspired to be the Bull Connor of the Black Belt. He explained his mission and presented Clark with his home phone number, and when he asked for the sheriff's home number in return, Clark told him mildly to call at the office. Lafayette immediately took his measure of this man, who was taller and more physically imposing than Connor, and perhaps more intelligent with a college education. Lafayette thought this might set him apart and make him more vulnerable to the pressures of the movement, for in a standoff that was partly a war of intellect, Clark was certain of his own superiority. In Lafayette's estimation, this was a hard and violent man whose indignation would sweep him away if he ever found himself out-maneuvered. He decided immediately that if eyes of the nation were ever focused on Selma, Clark would be a villain as compelling as Connor.

The movement needed people to play that role, but at the moment it also needed foot soldiers, and as late as 1963, there were only a few of such people in Selma. There were the Boyntons, of course, and there was a Selma teacher named Margaret Moore who gave Lafayette a room in her house, even though she knew it could cost her her job. There was Marie Foster, a dental hygienist who conducted citizenship and voter education classes, and there was the Reverend L. L. Anderson, a Baptist minister who seemed to have more courage than most. Lafayette quickly found other recruits—students at Selma University and the public high schools, and dirt-poor farmers in the Dallas County countryside, who decided they simply had nothing to lose.

He worked slowly for a while, holding small meetings, giving little talks about the possibility of freedom, and then in April 1963, he saw the opportunity for a breakthrough. It came ironically with the passing of Sam Boynton, the soft-spoken, sad-eyed champion of the cause, who had told his wife that he didn't mind dying but he didn't want his death to be for nothing. "I want you to see that all Negroes are ready to vote," he said.

To Bernard Lafayette, the final wishes of this good man, who was respected universally in the black community of Selma, cried out power-fully for some kind of memorial, some fitting tribute to the meaning of his life. Lafayette went immediately to L. L. Anderson, pastor of the Tabernacle Baptist Church, which was one of the handsomest structures in the city, with its stately columns and high, vaulted ceilings, and a curved wooden balcony that could accommodate a crowd. He suggested that they hold a mass meeting at the church, which would be part funeral and part voting rights rally, and Anderson readily agreed to the plan. His deacons, however, were not quite as sure. They had read about the rash of bombings in Birmingham, and it was easy to imagine that outcome in Selma, the seat of government in a racially charged county where the black and white populations were the same—approximately sixteen thou-sand each. Whites held tightly to their monopoly of power, primarily by assuring that blacks couldn't vote, and a memorial service with political overtones could invite a retaliation by the Klan. The deacons spoke reverently of the building of the church and the sacrifices of the past generations for whom this stately edifice in the heart of downtown had become a symbol of their own sense of worth.

Anderson listened patiently to what they were saying, frustrated by their sense of priorities, for how could a building compare with being free? Finally, he told them with a shrug of his shoulders that he accepted their verdict and there would be no political meeting at the church. They would hold it instead on a strip of land just beyond the church grounds, and he would tell the people who assembled that night that they were not welcome at Tabernacle Baptist because the leaders of the church were afraid.

The deacons were startled, caught in a moment of uncertainty and shame, and they quickly relented and agreed to allow the service in the church. The occasion, in the end, proved to be at least as tense as they had feared. There were 350 people in the crowded sanctuary, and there were more outside, blocked by Sheriff Clark and his posse. That was what people called his ragtag assembly of deputized white men, poorly trained and heavily armed, with a mission that was easy enough to understand. They were to crush the civil rights movement in its tracks.

It was an eerie scene from inside the church—the police lights flashing through the stained glass windows, and the sound of windshields smashing outside, as the members of the posse and a crowd of bystanders vented their fury on the black people's cars. After a while the sheriff himself came into the building, flanked by his deputies, and dared the participants to say anything subversive. The featured speaker that night was James Forman, the fiery executive director of SNCC, who was not a man to be intimidated easily. He said it was good that Sheriff Clark was there, for he stripped away any trace of easy courage, making it clear to everyone in Selma what it would eventually take to be free. But freedom, he said, was waiting for them there in Alabama if all of them together could muster the will.

It was a performance that left the whole city buzzing, particularly the blacks, who were beginning to understand the possibility of defiance—who could see that the boldness of Forman and Lafayette, and later James Bevel and Diane Nash, was something accessible to the people of Dallas

County. These organizers who came into the community were people who were willing to put down roots, to move in with the people they were seeking to befriend, and to look a man like the sheriff in the eye.

In the weeks and months after that, hundreds of black citizens started going down to the registrar's office, seeking to add their names to the rolls. One of the bravest and most determined of that group was a sturdy black woman named Annie Cooper, a native of Selma who had moved away when she was fourteen, living first in the coal country of eastern Kentucky, then in Pennsylvania and Ohio. She married a miner and registered to vote in every place she lived, accepting it simply as an elemental duty. But then in 1962, she came home to Selma to take care of her mother, and within a few months, everybody was starting to talk about the vote. She was astonished at first that it was even an issue. Of course people voted; it was part of being an American citizen, and she went down immediately to put her name on the rolls. Three hundred people were in line that day, and she was surprised to see her employer, Dr. Dunn, surveying the line and writing down names. Dunn was a smallish, middle-aged man, the eccentric proprietor of a Selma rest home, and as Mrs. Cooper would soon discover, a rabid defender of the segregated order. Already, it had struck her as odd that whenever there was any kind of civil rights news, Dunn would order the televisions turned off so that none of the black people who worked on his staff would become contaminated by the movement.

On the day Mrs. Cooper attempted to register, Dunn wrote her name in his little notebook, and the following morning she learned she was fired. As the word began to spread, forty-two staff members—mostly maids and janitorial workers—walked off the job with her, protesting intimidation this crude. For their troubles they were fired also and blacklisted in Selma, and for the rest of the year most of them tried in vain to get a job.

It was only one example of a pattern of suffocating repression, rooted in the faith of the white leadership that if they were tough and unrelenting enough, the movement would die, and the natural order of things would prevail. In July 1964 one of Selma's white judges, James A. Hare, issued an injunction forbidding any "assembly of three or more persons," even to *talk* about the issue of civil rights. The movement dwindled in the months after that, shrinking finally to a core group of eight—"the courageous eight," as they became known in the black community of Selma. There was Mrs. Boynton, who was never one to flinch, and Marie Foster, the citizenship instructor, and F. D. Reese, a teacher and minister who was the newly elected president of the Dallas County Voters League. They were professionals mostly, and black business people—all in all, a solid collection of Negro citizens who continued to meet wherever they could: in barbershops, church offices, or each other's houses.

One day in December 1964 they gathered at the home of Amelia Boynton, 1315 Lapsley Street, and they drafted a letter to Martin Luther King, inviting him to bring his movement to Selma. Mrs. Boynton had written him a letter already, telling him the story of the Dunn rest home and the gratuitous punishment of Annie Cooper and the others, and it was not a report that King could take lightly. He had the greatest respect for the Boyntons, this family that had persevered for so long. In addition to the work of Sam and Amelia, their son Bruce Boynton had triggered the Freedom Rides with his landmark case of *Boynton vs. Virginia,* a kind of one-man stand against segregated travel. For Martin Luther King, if people like this were asking for his help, it was difficult indeed to say no.

But that was not the only source of pressure. The final push came from James and Diane Nash Bevel, who had been in and out of Selma for a year, and who knew it was ready for a major campaign. At an SCLC retreat late in the fall of 1964, James made another of his passionate appeals, supported strongly by Ralph Abernathy, and all of a sudden the issue was settled. King was to send his lieutenant, C. T. Vivian, into Selma to meet with Mrs. Boynton and the other local leaders, and King would hold his first mass meeting on January 2, 1965.

The Selma crusade was about to begin.

It was a cold winter's day, a Saturday morning, and John Lewis awoke to a light snowfall, much like the one they had seen in Nashville when the sit-in movement began years ago. He had come to Selma to hear Dr. King and to do what he could to soothe the feelings of his fellow SNCC workers, who believed once again that they were being upstaged. For some time now, there had been a simmering rivalry between SNCC and King's organization, SCLC, even though the lines between the two groups were blurry. James Bevel, for example, though now on the staff of SCLC, had been among the founding members of SNCC, and Lewis, though a prominent leader with SNCC, held a seat on the board of SCLC. Lewis saw no problem with such a casual arrangement; they were, after all, on the same side of the war, but he knew there were others who didn't feel the same. Worth Long and John Love were among the SNCC organizers who had been in Selma for more than a year, digging into the community, living with the fears and hopes of the people, and they saw a contrast between their own careful work and the headline-grabbing approach of Dr. King. Lewis, however, reminded them gently that the local black leaders had invited King in, and whatever their private opinions might be the Selma project was now a joint operation.

Lewis was reflecting on all these things as he made his way through the streets of Selma. It was a town that was quite familiar by now, like a lot of little hamlets in southern Alabama with its brick storefronts and cotton warehouses. But Selma's identity was shaped in part by the Alabama River, which meandered its way, dark and muddy, in a curve around the southern boundary of the town. Selma itself was nestled on the bluffs, connected to the distant shore of the river by the curious hump of the Edmund Pettus Bridge, a high-arching structure with four lanes of traffic and broad sidewalks for people who needed to cross it on foot. On January 2, 1965, John Lewis didn't pay much attention to the bridge, for it had not yet achieved its place in history, but he did have the feeling—a certainty, in fact—that one way or the other, history was being made.

More than seven hundred people had gathered that day to hear Dr. King. They crowded together at Brown's Chapel Church, a red brick sanctuary on the edge of the Carver housing projects, a development named for George Washington Carver, the renowned black scientist and Tuskegee researcher. Selma's black population didn't have far to go as they streamed from the drab expanse of public housing, but they had to be a little bit nervous. Judge Hare's prohibition against public assemblies was still in effect, and nobody knew if there would be mass arrests or more bloody retributions from Sheriff Clark and his posse.

Surprisingly enough, there was neither. Clark, apparently, was not even there for reasons the black leaders came to understand. Selma had elected a new mayor in October, a tall, skinny, crew-cut man named Joe T. Smitherman, a refrigerator salesman thirty-five years old, who was not a part of the Selma aristocracy. Like most white people who lived in the city, Smitherman believed in segregation, but he seemed to be a moderate, pragmatic man whose priorities as mayor leaned toward the practical, paving roads, putting in street lights. He appointed Wilson Baker, a former police captain so well trained in the art of law enforcement that he taught criminology at the University of Alabama, chief of police for the city of Selma. Baker, like Smitherman, was a moderate segregationist who was not only offended by gratuitous violence but understood clearly that it simply didn't work. If the movement needed villains to help make its case, Baker was determined not to play that role. Along with Smitherman, he negotiated a jurisdictional compromise with Clark. The sheriff would deal with issues that arose outside the city limits and immediately outside the county courthouse, where his own office was. The rest of the city, including the area around Brown's Chapel Church, belonged to Chief Baker and the city police.

On January 2, 1965, the chief decided to ignore Judge Hare's injunction, a ruling so blatantly unconstitutional that it was almost silly. His policemen were present for the rally at the church, but they were professional and polite, and the drama for the most part came from inside. King made a powerful speech that day, talking about the vote and the symbolism of Selma and the victory that waited at the end of their struggle. If the leaders of the city didn't listen, he said, "We will appeal to Governor Wallace. If he refuses to listen, we will appeal to the legislature. If they don't listen, we will appeal to the conscience of the Congress in another dramatic march on Washington." But whatever it took, they would have to persevere, for this was the moment of truth for the civil rights movement, its line in the dust.

John Lewis listened as he always did, a little awestruck, proud of his own association with King, but he also knew that this was always the easiest part—gathering together with the people in the churches, singing the songs, listening to the inspirational speeches. The hard part would come in the cold winter months, when they would march together to the county courthouse, leaving the safety of Wilson Baker's domain to confront the unpredictability of Sheriff Clark.

The first march came on January 18, a Monday, led by John Lewis and Martin Luther King. There were four hundred people in the line that day, moving quietly toward the county courthouse, where Sheriff Clark waited on the green marble steps, billy club in hand, flanked not only by his own core of deputies but also by a seedy-looking group from the American

Nazi and States Rights parties. Nothing much happened for the next several hours. The demonstrators waited, and the registrar's office remained off limits. At the end of the day, the weary protesters marched back to the projects, and King set off on a corollary mission—to register for the night at the Hotel Albert, Selma's finest, which had never before admitted a black guest. In the hotel lobby, a young white man attacked him, a raw-boned member of the States Rights Party who managed to land several good punches and one or two kicks before Wilson Baker rushed forward to stop him.

King was startled, though essentially unhurt, but it was clear by now that the battle lines were drawn, and the national media began to pour into town. On the following morning, Clark seemed tense as the line of marchers came again to the courthouse and demanded this time to be admitted inside. He grabbed Amelia Boynton by the collar and led her roughly to the jail, where she joined more than sixty of the other demonstrators. On Wednesday morning, when the tantrum predictably made national headlines, Wilson Baker confronted Clark on the steps and demanded bluntly that he show some restraint. This, he said, was the perfect street theater for the civil rights movement, precisely the kind of heavy-handed show that would make Selma a laughingstock or worse. The two of them argued about it for a while, and Baker could see that he was getting nowhere. Jim Clark was determined to be Jim Clark, and the only question now was how bad it would get.

The answer emerged over the next several weeks, little by little, in a slow escalation of the big man's temper. On January 22, a Friday afternoon, F. D. Reese led a march of teachers, an act in which he took great pride. A teacher himself, Reese was a tall and dark-skinned man in his thirties, the elected president of the Dallas County Voters League. He had been inspired by the coming of the SNCC organizers—"the modern day pioneers," he called them—people who seemed both militant and wise, and who channeled the simmering rage of the Negroes into a relentless pattern of nonviolent protest.

In the beginning, however, many of the teachers were still hanging back, afraid of everything they could lose, and Reese could understand their hesitation. For the most part, these were people like himself, refugees from the cabins and the shotgun houses of rural Alabama who had built their careers and a place of honor on their own side of town, but who could be fired on the whim of the white school board. Of all the black citizens of Dallas County, they were some of the most vulnerable to economic pressure. And yet it was true that they were still not free, and in their classrooms, how could they teach about citizenship when they had never claimed the most basic rights for themselves?

That abstract question began to take on an urgency with the arrest of Amelia Boynton that week, for they all had to live with the image of Clark dragging this good woman away by her collar. With their apprehensions muted by their new indignation, they gathered on Friday at a local elementary school and began to march double file toward the courthouse. There were parents on the sidewalk, weeping with admiration for their stand, and there were cheering students who fell into line, and Reese couldn't help but smile to himself as he took his place at the head of the procession. He was marching next to his former homeroom teacher, A. J. Durgan, proud of their generational alliance but wondering what dangers were waiting just ahead.

Sheriff Clark was stationed at the door of the courthouse, on the Alabama Avenue side of the building, and as Reese and Durgan led the group up the steps, Clark gave them sixty seconds to disperse. When they refused, he shoved them roughly down the steps with his nightstick.

"What shall we do?" asked Durgan.

"We are going back up the steps," said Reese, and twice more a group of them made their ascent, as the sheriff's warnings became more impatient and his handling of them rougher as he pushed with his club.

Finally, they agreed that the point had been made. Despite his seething contempt, they had stood toe to toe with Sheriff Jim Clark, and they had let it be known that the most respected black professionals in the city were squarely on the side of the civil rights movement. As for Clark, the confrontation was another indication that his mood was growing surlier by the day.

The following Monday, another group of demonstrators came to the courthouse, four hundred strong, like a plague of locusts in the sheriff's estimation—these once docile residents of Dallas County, stirred to a fever by people who didn't even live in the area. Sometimes it was almost more than he could stand. They kept coming back, kept defying his orders to move away from the steps, and when it happened on Monday he grabbed one demonstrator by the collar and pulled her out of line toward the jail. His target this time was Annie Cooper, the defiant Selma native who had lost her job at the Dunn rest home for trying to register in 1964. Mrs. Cooper was a woman of some heft, and on this particular day, she was in no mood to be bullied by the sheriff.

"Don't jerk me like that," she hissed, wrenching free of his grip.

Clark hit her in the back of her head with his hand, and she was caught in a feeling she couldn't quite define, a mixture of anger and simple resolution. But whatever it was, she knew she wasn't going to take it anymore. "I went to fighting him," she explained years later, and as she began to flail away at the sheriff, she put her weight of two hundred pounds into every roundhouse blow she could land. Clark staggered backward, clearly taken by surprise, and he turned for support to a small group of deputies who seemed to be frozen in a state of disbelief.

"You see this nigger woman," he snarled. "Do something!"

Three of the subordinates rushed immediately to the aid of their boss, throwing Mrs. Cooper to the sidewalk pavement, then hitting her with a billy club in the eye. They rolled her over and handcuffed her wrists behind her back—handcuffed her twice, according to one newspaper account—but Mrs. Cooper was not yet ready to surrender. "I wish you would hit me, you scum," she yelled at Clark, and the sheriff was only too happy to oblige. As John Herbers reported in the *New York Times*, writing with a chilling, antiseptic precision: "He then brought his billy club down on her head with a whack that was heard throughout the crowd gathered in the street."

Clark and his deputies dragged her away, and despite her pain, Mrs. Cooper's epithets gave way to a hymn, "Jesus Keep Me Near the Cross." She stayed in jail eleven hours that day, singing more hymns, and one of the white jailers told her later that Clark was drinking heavily in his office, threatening to kill her. About eleven o'clock that evening, the worried jailer came to her cell and set her free. "He told me," remembered Mrs. Cooper, "he didn't want my blood on his hands."

At the mass meeting in Selma on the following night, the leaders of the movement weren't sure what to say. Mrs. Cooper's outburst had been, without question, a lapse in the collective commitment to nonviolence, and James Bevel felt compelled to remind everybody that theirs was a struggle requiring great discipline. But the national headlines and the photo of Cooper, blood streaming from her wounded right eye, were precisely the kind of publicity they were seeking. At that same mass meeting at Tabernacle Baptist, the Reverend L. L. Anderson presented Cooper as a victim, a courageous woman "who took a beating today for you and me."

The truth of it was, no matter how the leaders might try to spin it, in the Negro community of Selma, Alabama, Annie Cooper was suddenly a folk hero—not the martyred victim of a beating by the sheriff, but a woman who decided it was time to fight back. As one protester would put it years later, "This was the lady who beat the hell out of Clark."

It was about this time that the dignitaries began to stream into Selma. All over the nation people were transfixed by the melodrama that was taking shape there. A group of congressmen and political figures, led by Michigan representative John Conyers, toured the city with Martin Luther King, and Malcolm X, the fiery Black Muslim, made a speech to the faithful at the Brown's Chapel Church. He shared the podium with Fred Shuttlesworth and Coretta King, two of the staunchest apostles of nonviolence, but Malcolm himself had a slightly different view. Their movement, he said, was part of a worldwide struggle against oppression, a war to be won by any means necessary.

"I think the people in this part of the world," he said, "would do well to listen to Dr. Martin Luther King and give him what he's asking for and give it to him fast, before some other factions come along and try to do it another way."

Even in Selma, there may have been people who were willing to listen, white people ready to consider a compromise, but they were swept from the stage by the bombast of Clark. Wilson Baker, among others, was appalled by the sheriff and his strategy of swagger, and Mayor Joe Smitherman thought that Selma was caught in a vise between the excesses of Clark and the pressures of the movement. But if the sheriff had his doubters, he also had every reason to believe he had the support of Gov. George Wallace. At the end of January, Wallace sent in more than fifty state troopers commanded in person by Al Lingo, and they took their places with Clark and his posse.

And so it was that on the morning of February 16, 1965, Clark appeared at the courthouse door with a button pinned to his uniform lapel. NEVER, it read, and if there was any ambiguity in the meaning, it disappeared in a face-off with C. T. Vivian, a senior staff member for SCLC. Vivian was a veteran of the Nashville sit-ins and the leg of the

Freedom Rides from Montgomery to Mississippi, and he had been in Birmingham also. He was a tall, slender man with a little mustache, a minister who was resolutely nonviolent, but whose temper was nearly a match for Jim Clark's. He was a leader who was easily drawn to debate, reflective and passionate, determined to win through the power of sweet reason. On February 16, confronted by the sheriff and his cadre of deputies, Vivian was caught in the absurdity of the moment. Here were the deputies, these stoic white men who were probably good people in other situations—good to their families, honorable most often in their dealings with their neighbors—but they were blocking the door to the county courthouse, denying the elemental rights of democracy.

As the television cameras captured the exchange, Vivian began a stern and unrelenting lecture, the words pouring out in a cogent, mesmerizing barrage. He told the deputies that there were people who had followed Adolph Hitler, much as they were following Jim Clark, blindly, oblivious to the consequences of their behavior. But the day of reckoning always came, and it would come in Selma, for the black people there would not go away, and they were determined to acquire the rights of other citizens. To the astonishment of many of the people in the crowd, including the reporters and the television cameramen, the deputies stood in rapt fascination, listening to Vivian as they might to the preacher in their own Sunday pulpits, not comprehending every word he was saying, but demonstrating by the looks on their faces that this was a message that could not be ignored.

Finally, Sheriff Clark heard all he could stand. He stepped forward suddenly and hit Vivian squarely in the mouth with his fist. Clark said later he didn't remember the punch, but the force was enough to send Vivian to the pavement and to break a bone in Clark's own hand. Vivian rose, blood streaming from his nose, and continued his sermon. "We are willing to be beaten for democracy," he said. "You can't turn away."

But Jim Clark did, a look of elemental hatred on his face, and he stalked back into the county courthouse. In the days after that, there were those who wondered if he was losing his grip, slipping like Bull Connor before him in the direction of his fatal mistake.

CHAPTER 17

Bloody Sunday

IN FEBRUARY 1965 THE VOTING rights movement spread from Selma to the surrounding countryside, particularly to Perry and Wilcox Counties. Martin Luther King visited both places, addressing mass meetings in the town of Marion and the tiny backwoods community of Gees Bend, then walking the voter registration lines, encouraging the farmers and small-town workers not to give up now. The day of freedom was coming, he said, and they were the ones who would soon make it happen.

King sent James Orange, an SCLC staff member, to Perry County to support the local leadership there, and Orange, who had been a student demonstrator in Birmingham, helped organize a march of young people that led to more than seven hundred arrests. The students were driven like a herd of cattle to a high-walled stockade where they slept together on a concrete floor and got their drinking water from a trough. A few days later, on February 18, Orange himself was arrested and charged with contributing to the delinquency of a minor for his part in leading the young people's march.

Albert Turner, a leader in the Perry County Voters' League, had lived for years with the vagaries of life in rural Alabama. He had seen the cruelties that occurred now and then, and he understood that any black person caught rocking the boat would almost inevitably have to pay a price. But he had never seen anything like this—never the retribution on a massive scale with young people bearing the brunt of the revenge. He called down to Selma on February 18 and asked if the leaders of SCLC could send a speaker to Marion, the county seat, to lead a rally that evening at a church. He asked especially for C. T. Vivian, for he knew of the confrontation with Sheriff Clark, and he thought Vivian might provide a little fire.

C. T. at first was reluctant to go. He had just gotten out of jail, and that weekend he was in charge of the SCLC office in Selma. But he found Albert Turner difficult to refuse, and he agreed to deliver a quick speech at the church. Many years later, he remembered the curious twist of perspective as he made his way to the pulpit and gazed out across the faces in the crowd. Zion Chapel Church looked huge that night, teeming with people whose courage had become intertwined with their faith, and who were starting to believe that life in rural Alabama could change. Later, when Vivian saw the church standing empty, it didn't look much bigger than a box, but there was something about the night of February 18, some magical spirit set free in the church, that made everything a little larger than it was.

Vivian was eloquent that evening as always, and when he had finished his speech he rushed out the door and started back to Selma on the long straight road through the Alabama night. He was feeling guilty as the miles clipped away on a desolate stretch of Highway 14. He knew that Marion was sure to be a dangerous place that night. With a population of thirty-five hundred, it was smaller than Selma and by some accounts a little rawer, and there had never been a time that anyone could remember when racial tensions were running quite as high. Nevertheless, the people in the church had decided to march. They were angry about the jailing of their children, and they were worried about the fate of James Orange, the youthful organizer sent in by King. The charges against him, though clearly absurd, could easily lead to some hard prison time. They knew that Orange himself was afraid, and they decided to march from the clapboard church to the city jail just a few blocks away. They would sing freedom songs and let Orange know—and the authorities of Perry County as well—that he had not been forgotten.

C. T. Vivian admired their bravery and the spirit of unity that he saw in the church, but he also knew that this was a perilous thing they were doing. Nighttime marches in the movement were rare, for too many things could happen in the dark. Traditionally, of course, these were the hours that belonged to the Klan, but things were different in the Alabama Black Belt. Here, there wasn't any need for the sheets, for the men who were willing to do what they must—to kill if they had to—often wore the uniforms of the state, and they assumed in the winter of 1965 that they were acting on the orders of Gov. George Wallace.

Vivian understood that all this was true, and when he saw the flashing police car lights, maybe twenty or more racing in the opposite direction toward Marion, he was filled immediately with a deep sense of dread. He turned around and followed the lights back to town, annoyed with his initial lapse of priorities and determined now to do what he could for these courageous people who were trying to take a stand.

As he pulled into Marion, the city square was dark, and he found the black people huddled at the church. He began asking questions, trying to piece together what had happened, and the people told him that it had been bad. They had left the church marching two by two, led by Albert Turner and another of their local leaders, James Dobynes. They had made it less than half a block when Marion police chief T. O. Harris ordered them to stop. Harris had plenty of muscle to support him, for he was backed not only by his own small force but also by the battle-hardened troopers of Al Lingo, and even Sheriff Clark, who had come up from Selma, saying it had gotten "too quiet" in his town.

When the marchers were ordered to return to the church, James Dobynes knelt for a moment to pray, and that was when everything broke loose. One of the troopers hit Dobynes in the head, and in the darkening shadows of the town hall square the others assaulted anybody they could find. "Negroes could be heard screaming, and loud whacks rang through the square," wrote John Herbers of the *New York Times*. Some people ran to the safety of the church, but others found themselves cut off and fled in search of some other shelter. Cager Lee, an eighty-two-year-old farmer who aspired to be a voter before he died, ducked into Mack's, a little cafe, but the troopers followed him and continued to beat him, along with his daughter, Viola Jackson.

The old man's grandson, Jimmy Lee Jackson, was there also and tried to intervene. He was a strapping young man, twenty-six years old, an army veteran and the youngest deacon in his small Baptist church. As he rushed to the aid of his mother and his grandfather, one of the troopers shot him in the stomach at point-blank range and shoved him out the door to the street, where he collapsed in a growing puddle of his blood. He was not the only victim that night. At least ten people needed medical attention, including Richard Valeriani, a news reporter for NBC, who was bloodied with a club. But Jackson's condition was much worse than the others. He was taken to Selma to the Good Samaritan Hospital, where he continued to hover between life and death.

When he died on Friday, February 26, it was an excruciating moment for the civil rights movement. For a decade now, the leaders had seen the mounting toll of atrocities, and if the movement was slowly making some progress, any feeling of accomplishment was simply overwhelmed, and all that was left was a sickening sense of rage.

On the following morning sometime around three, James Bevel left his room at the Torch Motel and came down to the lobby. Annie Cooper was working at the desk, her first job in Selma since being fired from the Dunn rest home. She liked the work well enough, for the motel was home to the civil rights leaders, and they were a colorful and fascinating lot. Especially Bevel. Most often he was wearing his little skullcap, a symbol of his Judeo-Christian heritage, and he always had something interesting to say, often something borderline outrageous. On this particular morning he was talking about a vision, a blinding epiphany in the middle of the night that the time had come to talk to George Wallace—to march by the thousands from Selma to Montgomery and confront this Alabama tyrant with the truth. Maybe they would carry the body of Jimmy Lee and lay his coffin on the steps of the capitol. Or maybe they would simply march in his spirit, and he would become yet another martyr to the cause, like the four little girls who had died in Birmingham.

That was the way Bevel talked, in a tumble of metaphor and sweeping revelation, and if some people thought he was a little bit crazy, the idea of a massive march to Montgomery took hold quickly among the people in the movement. They had to do something with their anger and grief, and they were drawn to this notion of a showdown with Wallace. For Bevel, of course, it was not really new. With his wife, Diane, he had talked about it now for a year and a half—some cataclysmic act of civil disobedience that would bring the state of Alabama to its knees.

Wallace vowed that he would never let it happen. In the governor's mind, things were quickly getting out of control, and this was not a time he intended to waver. If the civil rights leaders were planning their assault, his troops would be waiting at the Edmund Pettus Bridge. The marchers wouldn't make it past the city line.

The moment of decision came on Sunday, March 7, the day the leaders had talked about a march. As the day drew near, Martin Luther King was filled with a debilitating sense of dread. There had been some death threats, which was not unusual, but they seemed to be more disconcerting this time. It may have been the murder of Malcolm X, a grisly execution in New York City, carried out by members of the Black Muslim sect. It had happened on Sunday, February 21, and for King it was a time of complicated emotions. He had always been ambivalent about Malcolm, having been the object of his stinging rebuke. In the early years of the civil rights movement, the Black Muslim leader seemed to be saying that non-violence was soft, the path of a coward, and King took it personally. But they met briefly in Washington in 1964, and Malcolm couldn't have been more gracious. Again in Selma the following year, less than three weeks before his death, Malcolm had come to the Brown's Chapel Church and offered nothing but support for King and his movement.

This was clearly a man on a journey of his own, the master of his rage and not the other way around, and whatever their disagreements may have been, King was horrified by the murder. He shared the assessment of C. Eric Lincoln, an Alabama native and the prize-winning author of *The Black Muslims,* the story of the movement out of which Malcolm came. Lincoln was convinced that both personally and politically, Malcolm was never inclined toward aggression. He was a model of discipline, willing to strike back if the occasion required it, but he had no interest in initiating violence. It was easy for King to understand that position, and he was sure that Malcolm could never be replaced.

His feelings about the murder, however, were far more personal than a simple sense of loss. The identity of the assassins didn't really concern him; they were simply the people from the lunatic fringe, and if it could happen to Malcolm, it could happen to anyone. King had long been certain that his own day was coming, and now the possibility was even more real.

All this was on his mind in late February when he preached the funeral of Jimmy Lee Jackson and led a thousand mourners in a march through the rain. As they were leaving the church, he turned to Joseph Lowery, one of the board members of SCLC, and joked about the dangers waiting just ahead. "Come on and walk with me, Joe," he said with a smile. "This may be my last walk."

King did his best to sound light-hearted, but beneath his bantering exterior he was troubled. When March 7 came, he was not in Selma. He was back in Atlanta, preaching the Sunday morning service at his church, which was what the people in his inner circle had advised. But he was brooding about it, and he suggested they delay the march for a day. The problem was, the word of the protest was spreading through Selma and early in the day, more than six hundred people began to assemble at Brown's Chapel Church. Andrew Young, one of the SCLC staffers on the scene, could see already that there was too much emotion in this particular crowd for King or anyone to ask them to wait. He talked about it with Hosea Williams, one of the toughest members of King's entourage, and with the local leaders, including F. D. Reese, and everybody agreed. The people had to march.

Certainly, John Lewis concurred in that decision. He had driven over from Atlanta the night before, officially representing himself and not SNCC. For most of Saturday, March 6, he and a dozen of his SNCC colleagues had met at a little soul food place in Atlanta, a cafe called Frazier's, which was famous for its vegetables, especially the yams. The SNCC leaders debated the merits of the march, and most of the group, including Jim Forman and Silas Norman, the project coordinator in Alabama, thought it was another case of grandstanding, more publicity mongering by King. Lewis didn't agree. For one thing, he was weary of the organizational jealousies that seemed to be sapping so much of their energy, and for another he respected the people of Selma. The evidence was clear that they were ready to march, *needed* to march, as an expression of their grief. Jimmy Lee Jackson was the *people's* martyr, a young man of great promise who had never assumed a leadership role but had joined the movement on behalf of his community. His death resonated through the Alabama Black Belt, for everybody knew it was merely the random hand of fate. The trooper who executed Jimmy Lee could have chosen anybody.

In addition to that, there was the heart-breaking story of Cager Lee, Jimmy's grandfather, who was beaten by the troopers on the night of the shooting. Some time later, as the plans for a march were beginning to take shape, Bernard Lafayette and James Bevel went to see him. He lived in a shack with no running water, as he had all his life, and now he was coping with a new kind of loss. They talked for a while, and then Jim Bevel asked him a question.

"Mr. Lee," he said, "I was thinking we might try to march again, and I was wondering if you'd be willing to march at the head of the line with me."

"Oh yes, Reverend Bevel," the old man replied, "I'll walk with you. I've got nothing to lose now, Reverend Bevel."

All around Selma, that seemed to be the feeling. With the coming of the movement in the past several months, segregation had been stripped of its pretense, of the white man's fiction that it was somehow benign, and the evil of it, the caprice and malevolence, were now laid bare. Against the clarity of that understanding, most people grimly agreed with Cager Lee. Whatever might happen on the road to Montgomery, there was nothing left to lose.

For all these reasons, John Lewis decided to march with the people, and Bob Mants, another SNCC staff member, decided to go with him. Mants, like Lewis, had little patience with the jurisdictional disputes of the civil rights movement. Out there in the field, with their lives on the line, nobody cared if you worked for SNCC or SCLC. What mattered was the people who wanted to be free. But Mants understood, perhaps more than Lewis, the bitter disillusionment of his friends in SNCC, for most of them now were battle-scarred veterans. They had lived through the Mississippi summer of 1964 and had seen people killed and twenty-six churches burned to the ground, and they were "terribly disillusioned with the democratic process." These were young people, not especially patient, and their idealism was turning into anger—a rage, in fact, that was almost paralyzing in its force.

Mants himself was a little more resigned. He was raised in the South, and he understood the pace at which things moved, and given the glacial evolution of the past, he could see at least a faint glimmer of hope. In any case, he knew he needed to be there to march.

On Sunday afternoon, March 7, they set out in pairs just a little after four, with Lewis and Hosea Williams in the lead. Williams had lost a coin flip with Andrew Young and James Bevel, the representatives of SCLC who were present at the strategy sessions for the march. They agreed in advance that two of the three would be held back to deal with the aftermath of an emergency. When Williams was the odd man out in the three-way flip, Young and Bevel both teased him about it, gloating about sending him out to his doom. The assumption they shared going into the march was that Sheriff Jim Clark was certain to block it.

"We weren't equipped for a march of that distance," remembered the Reverend L. L. Anderson. "We said we were going all the way to Montgomery, but I don't think we would have made it more than a mile or two down the road." Some of the women just out of church were still wearing heels, and John Lewis, who was only a little more prepared than the others, carried a backpack over his coat, equipped with a toothbrush and a book he was reading by the monk Thomas Merton.

They started out slowly on a dusty back road that cut through the heart of a public housing project, and then turned right on Water Street, which ran by the river. After a mile or so, they came to the foot of the Edmund Pettus Bridge. As Lewis remembered the scene years later, it was not a typical civil rights march. There was no laughter or talking, no freedom songs to lift people's spirits, just the shuffling of feet as they started up the steep incline of the bridge. They stayed on the sidewalk, moving double file—Lewis and Williams, Mants and Albert Turner, Marie Foster and Amelia Boynton—and then a line of maybe six hundred people.

When Lewis and Williams came to the summit of the hump-backed bridge, they stopped in their tracks. Waiting for them on the other side was a mass of uniformed troopers and deputies that looked like an army. The troopers were dressed in blue; Sheriff Clark and his men, in khaki. Some were on horseback and all were armed, many with clubs in addition to their guns. Hosea Williams looked down at the river, the dark, swirling waters a hundred feet below.

"Can you swim?" he asked John Lewis.

"No," said Lewis, his voice deadpan.

"Well," said Williams, forcing a smile. "Neither can I, but it looks like we might have to."

They continued down the other side of the bridge to the bank of the river outside the city limits. When they were fifty feet from the ranks of the troopers, Maj. John Cloud, the man in command, raised his bullhorn and told them to disperse. "You have two minutes," he said, "to turn around and go back to your church."

Lewis and Williams thought about the options. They couldn't go back, for it would look like cowardice, and in any case, the logistics of retreat were nearly impossible. There were too many people in line on the bridge. They *could* march forward straight toward the ranks of the troopers and their guns, but that seemed somehow to be too provocative. Lewis turned to Williams and suggested, "We should kneel and pray."

One minute had elapsed after Major Cloud's warning. Lewis was careful to keep track on his watch, as he turned to pass the word down the line that the people should kneel or simply bow their heads. The message hadn't made it very far through the ranks when they heard the sound of Major Cloud's voice: "Troopers, advance!"

"And then," recalled Lewis in his autobiography, "all hell broke loose."

Reporter Roy Reed of the *New York Times* was one eyewitness who recorded the scene. "The troopers," he wrote in the May 8 *Times,* "rushed forward, their blue uniforms and white helmets blurring into a flying wedge as they moved." John Lewis stared for a moment in dismay, his hands in the pockets of his tan overcoat, even as one of the troopers approached him and hit him across the left temple with his club. A few feet away, Amelia Boynton tried to take it all in. "I just couldn't imagine," she said years later, but she didn't have long to contemplate the insanity. One of the troopers hit her in the head, and when she didn't fall, he hit her again. This time she crumpled to the pavement unconscious, and sometime later in the bloody aftermath, people told her what had happened next—how the trooper continued to pound her with his club, screaming as he did it, "Get up, nigger! Get up and run."

Finally, somebody called for an ambulance, concluding from the amount of blood on the pavement that Mrs. Boynton and some of those around her were dead.

"Let the buzzards eat them," muttered Jim Clark.

By this time, everything was chaos, and somewhere back near the summit of the bridge, JoAnne Bland was caught in the middle of it. JoAnne was eleven. It was not her first civil rights protest, for she was like a lot of other children in Selma who had listened to the exhortations of James Bevel and reveled in their role as the movement's foot soldiers. James Perkins, who would later become the city's first black mayor, remembered being a "seasoned protester" at the age of twelve. JoAnne herself had already been arrested thirteen times, and she had come to enjoy it. At least as ardently as any of her peers, she detested the practice of racial segregation, the glib assumption by every white person she had ever known that black people simply didn't matter as much.

Once, her grandmother had sent her to the grocery store for some food, and the clerk was weighing her packet of ground beef, when he stopped in the middle to wait on a white woman. JoAnne was worried because her grandmother had told her not to "tarry," and she was afraid she would lose the old woman's trust. But when she got back home, her grandmother didn't scold. "Don't worry, baby," she said with a sigh. "Soon we won't have to do that anymore."

So JoAnne was happy to be a part of the movement, and until that moment at the Edmund Pettus Bridge, she thought it was the greatest adventure of her childhood. But now all of a sudden, she was caught in a horror she could barely comprehend, trapped on a bridge a hundred feet above the river, with people screaming and Sheriff Jim Clark and his posse on horseback lashing out blindly at everybody who was black. She thought at the time that some of the men had "horrible faces," like monsters almost, as they galloped through a cloud that was making people choke. Later, somebody explained what had happened—how the troopers had fired their canisters of tear gas, and how they were wearing gas masks to protect themselves from the power of the fumes.

As JoAnne was watching all this unfold, she saw an old woman trying to get away and a mounted deputy bearing down upon her. JoAnne tried to call out a warning, but it was too late. The woman was trampled and as her head hit the pavement of the Edmund Pettus Bridge, JoAnne heard the sickening crack of her skull. Somehow she was sure that must have been the sound, and she could hear it clearly above all the screams. But later she wondered if it had been her own head, for she fainted dead away from the terror of the scene.

Back at the church, Annie Cooper wandered in a daze among the wounded. Earlier in the day when she was nursing a cold, she thought about not going to the march, but in the end she knew she couldn't stay away. Just a few weeks earlier, she had gained a measure of renown in Selma for her physical confrontation with Sheriff Jim Clark, and as the hour of the demonstration was approaching, she knew in her heart she needed to be there. Like everybody else, she found it nearly impossible to comprehend. The police chased people all the way to the church, clubbing, cursing, spoiling for more. "They were like savages," Mrs. Cooper remembered, and though she escaped the worst of it herself, she found Marie Foster and Amelia Boynton, two of her friends, lying unconscious.

"The only way you could tell they were alive," she told one reporter, "was by the quivering of their skin."

There were also a handful of SNCC people there, young organizers familiar with Selma, who called in reports to the SNCC office in Atlanta. The majority of the calls, made from a pay phone, came from Lafayette Surney, who was watching the march from a street corner downtown. SNCC's telephone log offers a commentary on the day:

> 4 P.M. About 2,000–3,000 people are marching. Mr. Turner of Marion is also leading. They are on the bridge now . . .
> 4:15 P.M. State Troopers are throwing tear gas on them. A few are running back. A few are being blinded by tear gas. Somebody got hurt—don't know who . . .
> 4:16 P.M. Police are beating people on the streets. Oh, man, they're just picking them up and putting them in ambulances. People are getting hurt pretty bad . . .
> 4:18 P.M. Police are pushing people into alleys. I don't know why. People are screaming, hollering. They're bringing on more ambulances. People are running, hollering, crying.
> 4:26 P.M. They're going back to the church. I'm going too.

When he came to the chapel a little after 4:30, Surney and another SNCC staffer, James Austen, found state troopers continuing their assault, beating people at random, even throwing rocks at those who were running. It was about this time that Wilson Baker intervened. The police chief of Selma had been worried precisely about such a scene. He knew

Jim Clark was out of control, and the state troopers under Lingo were not any better. The night before, Baker had threatened to resign, warning Mayor Smitherman that a bloodbath was likely. He wanted to arrest the marchers before they made it to the Edmund Pettus Bridge, while they were still in the city limits of Selma, in order to protect them from the lunacy of Clark. But the mayor and other city leaders were reluctant, and Baker eventually agreed to a compromise. He would let the march go forward, while keeping his own men out of the fray. Now, however, at the Brown's Chapel Church, he was faced with the bloody reality of his fears. He cursed the sheriff, this bloodthirsty fool who had made such a mockery of enforcing the law, and finally persuaded him to pull back his posse. But he knew the damage was already done.

On national television that night, ABC was showing the film *Judgment at Nuremberg,* the story of Nazi racism against the Jews, when network officials decided to interrupt with the footage from Selma. News anchor Frank Reynolds introduced a tape of the carnage, and even for a nation that had lived through the Freedom Rides and seen the film clips coming out of Birmingham, Selma was exponentially worse—official violence on such a massive scale against a group of demonstrators who were utterly peaceful. "I did not understand how big it was," Mayor Smitherman later confessed to journalist Juan Williams, "until I saw it on television."

Gov. George Wallace was equally as stunned. "I was with him when he saw the TV coverage," remembered Bob Ingram of the *Montgomery Advertiser*. "He was berserk. That was not supposed to happen."

What Wallace expected is a little unclear. In the strategy sessions before the demonstration, one of his aides, Bill Jones, made a case against interrupting the march. Jones was certain, as many black leaders admitted later on, that the logistical groundwork had not been laid and the march would fizzle of its own accord somewhere east of the Edmund Pettus Bridge. Let the demonstrators look foolish, Jones argued, but Wallace in the end rejected that advice. According to one theory, he was afraid of violence if the marchers made it as far as Lowndes County, generally considered the toughest piece of terrain in Alabama. Physically, it was a haunting, sparsely populated stretch, a natural prairie through much of its breadth, with grass-covered hills that gave way occasionally to blackwater swamps. It was a place where white supremacy was unchallenged—where not a single black person in the twentieth century had ever even *tried* to register to vote. It was a place, Wallace knew, where people got killed.

But the governor's biographer Dan T. Carter believed there was another, more powerful reason why Wallace rejected Bill Jones's advice. What it came down to was this: He simply couldn't stand the idea of a march, of a group of black people from Selma, Alabama, thumbing their noses at the authority of the state. There may have been a time in the governor's life when he wanted to be known for his racial moderation—when he proclaimed it proudly in his first race for governor and showed it clearly as a circuit judge in his treatment of the people who came through his courtroom. But when he made his promise in 1958 never to be "outnig- gered" again, it was a decision that seeped all the way to his core. He was constantly in the company of unapologetic racists, including the leaders of the Ku Klux Klan, one of whom had written his inaugural address. And certainly, Al Lingo never had any doubts, as he established a consistent track record of violence, that he and George Wallace were on the same side.

At a hearing soon after the attack at the bridge, Lingo testified in fed- eral court that his instructions from Wallace had been crystal clear: "There was to be no march. I interpreted this to mean that I was to restrain the marchers."

"Regardless of what it took to do it?" asked U.S. District Judge Frank Johnson.

"Yes sir," said Lingo.

It was true with Wallace that there were also the occasional flashes of humanity that made people wonder. Once, in Birmingham in 1963, he addressed an audience of Alabama conservatives that included Imperial Wizard Robert Shelton and a number of his followers from the Ku Klux Klan. Making his way to the hotel ballroom, Wallace stopped to greet an old friend, a black man from Barbour County who happened to be serv- ing as headwaiter for the evening. The governor walked over and hugged his neck.

"Doc, I'm so glad to see you," he said.

"I'm glad to see you, Judge," the black man replied.

There were people in the crowd who were deeply offended—Klansmen and members of the States Rights Party who wondered if Wallace was soft around the edges. Probably in those days, the governor was not. He was fiercely committed to the idea of segregation and comfortable in the company of the advocates of violence, including those on his staff.

But it didn't take a liberal to see what had happened at the Edmund Pettus Bridge. Faced with the terrible television footage, George Wallace was appalled. He knew it would not be good for his cause.

CHAPTER 18

"The Arc Is Long"

AMONG THE RANKS OF THE WOUNDED back at the church, the anger for a time was threatening to explode. There were people who were talking about getting their guns, and as Andrew Young remembered it later, the high-minded arguments would not have dissuaded them. There could be no talk about the theory of nonviolence or the redemptive power of unmerited suffering—all those refrains in the message of Dr. King. For the moment, the arguments had to be purely practical: There were not enough black people and not enough guns to win an all-out war in the state of Alabama.

As Young and James Bevel worked their way through the crowd, trying to prevent a catastrophic confrontation, they understood how fragile everything had become. Martin Luther King understood it also and rushed quickly to Selma after putting out a nationwide call for reinforcements. It didn't take long for the call to be heard, and within the next several days it seemed to many of the people of Selma, black and white, that the whole country was suddenly descending on the town.

"That saved the nonviolent method," said F. D. Reese, one of the local civil rights leaders. "After the beatings on the bridge, when I got back to the church, I looked into the eyes of those marchers and I could see a question mark. Should the nonviolent method really be pursued? But that same night, when we were still in the sanctuary, a group of people arrived from New Jersey. They said, 'We have heard the call of Dr. King. We are here.' That was the most exhilarating thing. I looked into the eyes of the people again, and I saw renewed hope."

Reese knew it was not the first time that people from the outside had come into Selma, bringing encouragement to the black citizens of the town. The SNCC organizers were the most important, of course, and then Dr. King, but now and then, there were white people too. On the Saturday before the Bloody Sunday march, a group of seventy white Alabamians, many from Birmingham, came into town and marched to the courthouse in support of civil rights. They endured a few taunts as they sang a stanza of "America the Beautiful" and joined a group of blacks singing "We Shall Overcome."

There was also the time, during a children's march in 1964, when one of the black mothers, Theoda Smith, watched in horror as a Klansman in a car gunned his motor and headed straight for a group that included her daughter. "He was going to run them down," Mrs. Smith remembered. "But this nun, I don't even know her name, had come in from out of town, and she stepped between the car and the kids. The driver didn't want to run over a white lady, a nun at that, so he stopped. Well, I figured then, 'If these people I don't even know can take that kind of risk for my children, it's time for me to do something myself.'"

After Bloody Sunday, those same feelings took hold again. But inter-mingled with the exhilaration and the hope was a level of anger and inter-nal tension that the civil rights movement had never seen, and the next several days unfolded in a blur. On Monday morning, March 8, Martin Luther King and an all-star cast of civil rights lawyers—Fred Gray, Arthur Shores, J. L. Chestnut, and Orzell Billingsley—asked U.S. District Judge Frank Johnson for an injunction against further state interference. The black people of Selma and their supporters in the national civil rights movement were determined somehow to make it to Montgomery, and there was talk of a march on Tuesday afternoon.

King had faith in the sympathies of Judge Johnson. Beginning with the bus boycott in 1956, the judge had ruled consistently in favor of civil rights, and King was sure he would do so again. He was disappointed late Monday when word came back that Johnson wouldn't issue any kind of decision until after a hearing that would start on Thursday. In the meantime, he issued a restraining order against a march.

King was in a quandary when he heard the news, for there was mounting pressure to march right away. The black community of Selma was impatient, and the leadership of SNCC had descended on the town—one delegation rushing over from Atlanta, another from Mississippi, all of them angry and ready for a fight. Cleveland Sellers led the Mississippi group, four carloads of young organizers, who headed east from Jackson at 4:05 on Sunday afternoon, the moment they heard what was happening at the bridge. Sellers, like Jim Forman in Atlanta, was fed up with the pattern of the white man's atrocities; the police, the Klan, it didn't make any difference who the perpetrators were. The brutality cried out for a different kind of response, something more pointed than the patient forgiveness of Martin Luther King.

As soon as the SNCC people made it to Selma, their anger immediately focused on King, who was—predictably enough, they decided—waffling once again. King said he understood the need for a march, but he had never defied a federal court order, and he didn't want to start now. After a hearing that was only three days away, Judge Johnson was certain to rule in their favor, and that probability was worth a little patience. The leaders from SNCC did not want to hear it. *To hell with the courts,* they said, and to hell with the fickle support of any whites, even that federal judge in Montgomery. It was time to march.

King was not immune to such anger, and he thought if he ignored the SNCC position the civil rights movement would begin to come apart. By late Monday night, he was leaning toward a march, but he was feeling the pressure from the other side as well. President Johnson had sent in LeRoy Collins, the former governor of Florida and head of the Community Relations Service, a federal mediation agency created by the Civil Rights Act of 1964. Collins was making the case against a march. There was simply no reason, the president's emissary argued, not to wait until Judge Johnson ruled.

At a tense negotiating session Tuesday morning, King and several others, including Fred Shuttlesworth, listened to the case that Collins was making, and Shuttlesworth said it was Collins, not King, who was being illogical. He ought to be talking to Lingo and Clark, the architects of violence at the Edmund Pettus Bridge, not to the people who were protesting peacefully. It was then that Collins came up with a solution. King could lead a march that same afternoon, a symbolic face-off at the base of the bridge, and Collins would secure from Lingo and Clark a promise that there would be no attack, no repeat of the events of Sunday afternoon. King, in return, would agree to turn around at the east end of the bridge, leading the demonstrators back to the church, instead of trying to push ahead to Montgomery.

"I cannot agree to do anything," said King, "because I don't know what I can get my people to do. But if you can get Sheriff Clark and Lingo to agree to something like that, I will try."

Collins went immediately to Lingo and Clark, and that afternoon he was holding his breath, wondering if the tenuous agreements would survive. The marchers came quietly over the bridge, more than two thousand strong with King in the lead. They stopped at the bottom, fifty yards from a line of Alabama State Troopers, and King informed the state officials on the scene that he and his followers intended to pray. The troopers stood silently through the round of prayers, and then through the singing of "We Shall Overcome," and finally to the palpable relief of Collins, King and his marchers headed back to the church. As they began their retreat, the troopers on the highway did a curious thing. They backed away from the road, opening a path where the marchers could have gone. It was a moment orchestrated by Governor Wallace, intended apparently to make King look foolish, for he had announced his intention to march to Montgomery, but was turning back now from an open highway. Many of the marchers in the line were confused, and the leaders in the SNCC delegation were livid. They had no knowledge of the agreement King had made, and they denounced his "trickery," referring to the aborted march ever after as "Turnaround Tuesday." Some of them vowed not to work with him again.

The exception to that proclamation was John Lewis, who was hospitalized with a fractured skull. Of all the injuries at the Bloody Sunday march, his were the worst, more serious even than those of Marie Foster and Amelia Boynton, the two Selma women who were marching just behind him. He lay in his hospital bed for three days, and despite the terrible throbbing in his head, he could hardly wait for the doctors to release him. He felt cut off at a critical hour, and there were things he wanted to say to his colleagues. He wanted to tell his old friends in SNCC that they were running out of patience at an ironic time. They needed to step back, to reflect for a moment on the larger opportunities, not on the tactical decisions of Dr. King, which in Lewis's mind were not a retreat but a necessary tack. The big picture, Lewis thought, was really pretty good. In more than eighty cities nationwide, there had been demonstrations in support of the movement, a national outpouring greater than anything Lewis could remember, and two days after the attack at the bridge, people were still pouring into Selma, ready to march when King gave the word.

On Tuesday night, Lewis checked himself out of the hospital and went to the meeting at the Brown's Chapel Church. He said he was "overjoyed" to be there, and when reporters asked about a split with Dr. King, Lewis simply refused to discuss it. "SCLC is not the enemy," he said. "George Wallace and segregation are the enemy."

That night when the singing and the preaching were over, a joyous occasion that obscured the simmering feud within the ranks, three white ministers who had come from out of town decided to go get something to eat. They had heard of a place called Walker's Cafe, a little soul food diner that was popular among the veterans of the civil rights movement. They ate their fill and started back toward the church but lost their way on the back streets of Selma and wound up passing another restaurant that was the opposite number of the Walker's Cafe. It wasn't that the food was all that different, but the Silver Moon was the white people's turf. F. D. Reese, one of the local leaders in Selma, remembered the protocol when he was young—how black people were not allowed in the door, but had to order their food, takeout style, from a window at the side. On Tuesday evening, March 9, the Silver Moon was home to a surly clientele, a group of white toughs who recognized the preachers for exactly who they were—out-of-town supporters of Martin Luther King.

Within a few seconds, the ministers were surrounded, and one of them, thirty-eight-year-old James Reeb of Boston, was clubbed in the head with a baseball bat. The roundhouse swing caught him squarely from behind, driving fragments of his skull through the base of his brain. He was taken by ambulance to Birmingham, where doctors at University Hospital said they were not at all optimistic. It was only a matter of time, they feared, until the civil rights movement would have another martyr.

On Wednesday as the minister hovered near death, there were demonstrations in Montgomery sponsored by SNCC. Many of the protesters came from Tuskegee, led by a vocal group of students who were fascinated by the SNCC organizers. Gwen Patton was one of those students, an intense young woman who had grown up in Montgomery, where both of her grandparents were active in the movement and her father worked as a union organizer. At the family dinner table, the topic most often was current events, and Patton needed little prodding to take her personal stand for civil rights. When she came to Tuskegee, she read Ralph Ellison's *Invisible Man,* written and published some fifteen years after Ellison himself had been a student at Tuskegee. Patton was stirred by the haunting power of that novel, the disturbing portrait of what it meant to be black. There were a great many ways, she was beginning to discover, for a student at Tuskegee to feel as invisible as Ellison's protagonist. Because you were black, she said, your humanity was invisible to the white world around you, and because you were young, Charles Gomillion and the other civil rights leaders in Tuskegee were clearly skeptical of your value to the movement.

"We respected Dr. Gomillion," said Patton, the elected leader of Tuskegee's student government, "but he also wanted to make us invisible."

And then came SNCC. Late in 1964 Bob Mants, Stokely Carmichael, and a handful of other charismatic organizers began coming to the campus, sleeping in the dorms, going to the classes, talking to the students about the possibility of freedom. Patton didn't agree with everything they said. Some, for example, wanted the students to drop out of school and commit themselves full time to the cause. Patton thought that was foolish. Someday, she reasoned, this movement they were building would win, and when that happened and it was time to take their places in society, they needed to be ready.

"I fought very hard for the concept of scholar-activist," said Patton, who would later emerge as one of the great black scholars in her state. But whatever her reservations about SNCC, Patton and hundreds of Tuskegee students were deeply moved by the message of defiance, and the feeling that they didn't have to wait to play a part.

In February 1965 they established the Tuskegee Institute Advancement League, a student-led group that, among other things, supported the voting rights movement in the Black Belt. They were aware of the tensions that were building in Selma, and after the beatings at the Edmund Pettus Bridge, they decided, said Patton, to become the "east flank" of the Montgomery march. Tuskegee and Selma were equidistant from the capital, give or take a few miles, Tuskegee to the east, Selma to the west, and on Wednesday morning, March 10, seven hundred students set out from the campus. Supported by members of the Tuskegee faculty, they chartered buses for the forty-mile drive, and faced off at the capitol with another contingent of Alabama State Troopers.

The student spokesman that day was George Ware, a graduate student in chemistry, who had become one of the strongest supporters of SNCC. Ware was older than many of the others, a slightly built man in his early twenties who struck some observers as affable enough, but who was also developing a militant edge that would take him deep into the Black Power movement and a philosophical mistrust of anybody white. In Montgomery he was the portrait of militancy and pride, telling a group of black ministers who wanted to lead the march that this was a student protest, and students, not the ministers, would make the basic decisions about strategy. He was also unafraid of the troopers, despite their reputation for violence, and he was reading from a petition when a Montgomery policeman moved in to arrest him. The other students sat down on the spot, blocking the sidewalks in front of the capitol, and there they stayed for the rest of the day. They rejected the pleas of the Montgomery ministers and Tuskegee's dean of students, P. B. Phillips, that they get up quietly and return to the campus.

They braced themselves for the inevitable attack, but on this occasion it did not come. The policemen instead made a circle around them, and as the hours crept by, the students quickly learned that if any of them left the group for any reason, the policemen would not let them return. The problem became the need to use the bathroom. When the urge was simply too strong to resist, they began to urinate in the middle of the circle— "as modestly as possible," according to one historian's account—and the demonstration went down in the annals of SNCC as "the great pee-in" on the steps of the capitol.

Some of the organizers laughed about it later, but at the time it was happening, nothing about that week was very funny. James Reeb died on the following night, and for Martin Luther King, the roller-coaster ride was beginning once again. He was used to it now, this old familiar pattern of highs and lows and tantalizing hope, and the tragedies that continued to tear at his heart. The movement itself lurched forward through it all—including the hearing on Thursday in Judge Johnson's court, where it was clear from the tenor of the questions from the bench that the judge would bestow his blessings on a march. On Saturday in Washington, Pres. Lyndon Johnson called a press conference to announce the submission of a voting rights bill, and on Monday evening, March 15, he addressed a joint session of Congress, delivering a powerful speech on civil rights— more explicit and passionate even than John Kennedy's.

Martin Luther King was watching from Selma, huddled with his aides and other civil rights leaders in the living room of Sullivan Jackson, a Selma dentist who had offered his home to the people in the movement. John Lewis was there, and C. T. Vivian, and they remembered the look on King's face as the president stood before the members of Congress and spoke of the historical significance of Selma:

"At times," said Johnson, "history and fate meet at a single time in a single place to shape a turning point in man's unending search for freedom. So it was at Lexington and Concord. So it was a century ago at Appomattox. So it was last week in Selma, Alabama. . . .

"Rarely in any time does an issue lay bare the secret heart of America itself. . . . The issue of equal rights for American Negroes is such an issue. And should we defeat every enemy, and should we double our wealth and conquer the stars and still be unequal to this issue, then we will have failed as a nation. . . .

"It is wrong—deadly wrong—" the president concluded, "to deny any of your fellow Americans the right to vote in this country." And for those left out of American democracy, Johnson proclaimed that "their cause must be our cause too. Because it is not just Negroes, but really it is all of us who must overcome the crippling legacy of bigotry and injustice. And we shall overcome."

When the president ended to thunderous applause, choosing the words of the greatest civil rights anthem of the times, John Lewis glanced across the room at Dr. King and saw the glisten of a tear on his cheek. Nobody in the room had ever seen King cry. They had seen him depressed, worried, fearful, overwhelmed, and they were even more familiar with his humor and his courage and his gift with the language that set him apart from every leader in the movement. Certainly, thought Lewis, King's abilities in that regard were far greater than the president's, but Lyndon Johnson was a southern white man in the 1960s, speaking with the kind of deep Texas twang, a cadence that was common among the people of Dixie, that was most often tied to the cry for segregation. Martin Luther King was deeply moved by the moment, and by the clear-cut endorsement from the president of the country, and for an instant his emotions spilled out of control.

Joe T. Smitherman wanted to cry also, or curse, or perhaps throw things at the television screen. The mayor of Selma was watching that night, and if he was braced for the condemnations of brutality and all the stupid excesses of Jim Clark, he was also a man still committed to segregation. He could hardly believe it when the president of the United States adopted as his own the most famous slogan of the civil rights movement. "It was like you'd been struck by a dagger in your heart," he said.

For reasons very different from Smitherman's, many of the people in SNCC also reacted negatively to the president. Danny Lyons, a staff photographer for the civil rights group, said he "wanted to puke," and executive director Jim Forman thought the speech sounded empty and hollow, and he resented the president's ending most of all. "Johnson," he said, "spoiled a good song that day."

The following day, Forman's disillusionment became more intense. At another SNCC demonstration in Montgomery, a group of student protesters from Alabama State College, supported by student volunteers who came from the North, set out on a half-mile march to the county courthouse. They were protesting that morning without a permit, and the police intercepted them at the downtown corner of Adams and Decatur, a block or two from their final destination. The students sat down again on the sidewalk, much as they had the previous week at the capitol, and for an hour and a half, they sang freedom songs, becoming, in the words of one reporter on the scene, "increasingly loud and restless."

At exactly 1:12 P.M. troopers on horseback moved in suddenly to break up the protest. With their billy clubs and heavy pieces of rope, they flailed at the students, who screamed their epithets in return, a trial run for rhetoric that would soon reverberate through the nation: "Pigs!" they yelled. "Fascist pigs!"

The standoff soon became more violent, as a group of maybe a dozen demonstrators retreated to the wall of a nearby house and the mounted policemen followed close behind, using their horses to push people from the wall. According to accounts in the *New York Times,* one of the possemen who was dressed in green with a ten-gallon hat approached the demonstrators and, hiding from the cameras behind a wall of mounted deputies, he began pounding away at the students with his club. Reporter Roy Reed gave this account: "There was a moment of freakish near-quiet, when the yells all seemed to subside at once, and in that instant the man in green struck hard on the head of a young man. The sound of the nightstick carried up and down the block."

For James Forman, it was too much. If Lyndon Johnson meant anything he said, these kinds of scenes would not be happening. The message would have gone out loud and clear to officials at every level in Alabama that the days of gratuitous violence were over. But the violence continued as it had for many years, and there was no reason now to believe it would end. The following day, March 17, King and John Lewis came over from Selma to lead a march of solidarity with the student protesters. Institutionally, King and Forman were still bitterly at odds, with John Lewis caught somewhere in the middle, but for the moment their common enemy was clear. It was not simply the policemen out there in the streets, wallowing in the primitive inclination to bully; it was the idea that survived among the people of Alabama that police brutality was a necessary tool.

At a mass meeting that night, Jim Forman stared out from the pulpit of the church and made no attempt to edit his rage. "There is only one man in the country," he said, "that can stop George Wallace and those posses. These problems will not be solved until the man in that shaggedy old place called the White House begins to shake and gets on the phone and says, 'Now listen, George, we're coming down there and throw you in jail if you don't stop that mess.'

"I said it today, and I will say it again. If we can't sit at the table of democracy, we'll knock the fucking legs off."

In the startled silence that followed his remarks, even Forman knew he had gone too far. "Excuse me," he said, for this was a church, and many of the people in the crowd that night were the old-line veterans of the Montgomery movement. They prided themselves on their dignity and decorum, as well as their determination to succeed, and they had never heard that kind of talk from the pulpit. In the excruciating moment of awkwardness that followed, it fell to Martin Luther King to clean up the damage. He was feeling uneasy as he walked toward the podium, and so was John Lewis just a few feet away. Lewis thought they were starting to lose something precious, that impeccable aura of dignity and restraint that set the movement apart so dramatically from all the ugliness at the heart of segregation. Lewis had always admired Jim Forman. He knew him as a man of charisma and courage, and even on Tuesday when the police had attacked, Forman and Jim Bevel were there in the streets, pleading for calm among the youthful demonstrators. But Lewis could see in Forman, and more generally in the passionate membership of SNCC, an anger at the pattern of official violence that had to find some way to escape. In this case it was merely profanity in the pulpit of a church, but Lewis had to wonder what was coming next.

For King, meanwhile, the ambivalence about Forman was even more double-edged, for the young executive director of SNCC had criticized King as harshly as any black leader ever had. In public and private, King was gracious about it, for that was his style. But the awkwardness had to be on his mind as he approached the pulpit, wondering how he could cover the faux pas. As John Lewis remembers it, somebody called King aside just before he spoke and told him that Judge Frank Johnson had ruled. He had issued his opinion just a few minutes earlier, granting permission for a march to Montgomery. Suddenly, the awkwardness was swept away, not only for King, but for the people in the church, and jubilation replaced it. Ever since the Bloody Sunday attacks, the march on the capital had loomed as a piece of unfinished business, a moral imperative for the people in the movement, and now after the days of waiting it would happen.

Judge Johnson barred all law enforcement officials in Alabama—particularly Jim Clark and Al Lingo, whose actions, he said, had been indefensible—from "harassing or threatening" peaceful demonstrators.

"The extent of the right to assemble, demonstrate and march peaceably along the highways and streets in an orderly manner should be commen-surate with the enormity of the wrongs that are being protested and peti-tioned against," Judge Johnson concluded. "In this case, these wrongs are enormous."

George Wallace immediately denounced the ruling, and refused to spend state money to protect the marchers, but Lyndon Johnson federal-ized the National Guard. The day of the march to Montgomery was at hand.

They gathered in Selma on March 21, 1965, a Sunday afternoon, two weeks after the attack at the bridge. James Armstrong couldn't help but feel a little nervous. He had come down from Birmingham to his home-town of Selma, having experienced so many of the ups and downs, the tri-umphs and tragedies that made up the movement. In the public schools of Birmingham, his children had been the integration pioneers, and for most of a decade beginning in the '50s, he had guarded the houses of civil rights leaders, including his own, from late night attacks by the Ku Klux Klan. He had come to Selma for the Bloody Sunday march, and now he was back for the moment of triumph. He was given a place of honor in the march, carrying the American flag behind a front row of dignitaries that included Dr. King and Rabbi Abraham Heschel, the great Jewish scholar who had written a book called *The Prophets,* and with his air of solemnity and long, flowing beard, reminded some of the marchers of God.

As they stepped off together toward the Edmund Pettus Bridge, thirty-two hundred strong, protected this time by the Alabama National Guard, Armstrong felt that rush of apprehension that he had known as a soldier during World War II. First in Selma, and later in the patchy swamplands of central Alabama, he found himself looking for snipers in the trees. He did his best not to think about it much but to focus instead on the better days ahead. It did give him hope to see these people from all over the country, who had accepted the civil rights cause as their own, and he was happy again to be with Dr. King, who, in the days of the Birmingham demonstrations, had been a regular customer at the Armstrong barber-shop.

For John Lewis, who was marching nearby, there was something absolutely right about the scene, this egalitarian mingling of those who were famous with those who were not. In Lewis's mind, the greatest dignitaries in the column that day were not Ralph Bunche, the Nobel laureate; or Dick Gregory, the comedian; or even A. Philip Randolph, the grand old man of the civil rights movement. The biggest celebrities were the everyday people, the veteran foot soldiers who had struggled through the dark and difficult days, when triumph seemed like a distant possibility. There was Cager Lee, the ancient grandfather of Jimmy Lee Jackson, whose murder at the hands of an Alabama trooper had triggered the whole idea for a march. And there was Amelia Boynton, the unofficial first lady of Selma, whose only regret was that her late husband, Sam, couldn't be there with her. The Boyntons together had battled for the right to vote since the '30s, and now as the marchers moved out of Selma, she knew they were on the threshold of winning.

They covered only seven miles that Sunday, stopping at a prearranged campsite, the Dallas County farm of David Hall, a maintenance man for Selma public housing. The weather turned bitterly cold that night, as two thousand marchers bedded down in tents and the rest were ferried back to Selma in cars. Those at the camp woke up shivering, to continue their trek, covering sixteen miles on Monday. They were in Lowndes County now, trudging along a narrow stretch of road where Judge Johnson had ordered that the number of marchers be reduced to three hundred. It was a route that took them through an eerie bottomland, where Spanish moss rustled in the branches of the trees, and danger seemed to lurk at every turn.

But they encountered no violence, and they came at dusk to the farm of Rosa Steele, who had given them permission to pitch their tents. Mrs. Steele was a large and formidable woman, a gray-haired widow in her seventies who had long been known as a pillar of the community. She ran a mom-and-pop store on Highway 80 and owned more than two hundred acres nearby, and when the march organizers asked for her help, she immediately agreed. She knew she would pay a price for the gesture, for this was Lowndes County, a place so oppressive that no black people were registered to vote, and only a few had even tried in more than sixty years. Mrs. Steele, however, said she was ready for whatever came.

"I've lived my three-score and ten," she explained.

With the passing of the marchers, the reprisals did come—an economic revenge that took the form of food vendors refusing to sell to her store, a policy intended to drive her out of business. The intimidation failed when SNCC organizer Bob Mants and another black store owner, William Cosby, persuaded the struggling black merchants in the area to boycott the vendors until they started selling again to Mrs. Steele.

It was one of the side dramas obscured by the march, which forged ahead from the Steele home place, through a driving rain that lasted most of Tuesday and soaked the demonstrators to the bone. They spent that night in a sea of mud and pressed on Wednesday along the broad expanse of the four-lane highway, past cattle herds grazing on the distant hillsides, and clusters of black people cheering them on. Finally at dusk, they came exhausted to the outskirts of Montgomery and stopped to rest once again for the night.

Sonnie Hereford was one of the doctors on call, and he made his rounds through the blisters and sprains and even the occasional diabetic seizure. Hereford, a longtime leader of the movement in Huntsville, was impressed by the cheerful spirit of his patients, and like many of the others who were there that day, he was a little wide-eyed at the spectacle that was beginning to take shape around them. Celebrities seemed to be everywhere. There was an evening concert with Odetta, Joan Baez, Harry Belafonte, and Peter, Paul, and Mary, all of whom had long been supporters of the movement. But there was also the host of Johnny-come-latelys, including the nightclub crooners such as Tony Bennett. In a way their presence was a tribute as well, if not to the fundamental idea of justice, then at least to the popular perception of who was winning.

The crowd continued to grow that night, and by morning the estimates ran to more than twenty-five thousand as they set out on the six-mile walk to the capitol. F. D. Reese was filled with pride, not only for himself but for the people of Selma, when he was asked to walk in the line with Dr. King. Mrs. King was there also, and Ralph Abernathy and his wife, Juanita, and Rosa Parks, whose act of defiance nearly ten years earlier had set this chain of events in motion. As they came up the hill on Dexter Avenue, past the little brick church where King had been the pastor, Amelia Boynton was marching near the leaders, carrying a petition to read to George Wallace.

The governor, however, did not show his face. Instead, he was peeking through the blinds at the capitol, watching with his aides, muttering occasionally about the size of the crowd. "My God," he said, "it looks like an army." Reporter Bob Ingram was there at his side, and he remembered somebody saying half-seriously that the marchers outside might be the future shape of the electorate. Twisting the barb, another friend said if Wallace ever learned to speak like King, he might be successful one day himself. It was, of course, a grudging salute to an adversary's triumph, to this man outside on the steps of the capitol who was also stirred by the size of the crowd, and who delivered a speech that Thursday afternoon that was at least the equal of "I Have a Dream."

"I know," said King, in the cadence that had become so familiar through the years, "that some of you are asking, 'How long will it take?' I come to say to you this afternoon, however difficult the moment, however frustrating the hour, it will not be long, because truth pressed to earth will rise again. How long? Not long, because no lie can live forever. How long? Not long, because you still reap what you sow. How long? Not long, because the arc of the moral universe is long, but it bends toward justice!"

Annie Cooper, one of the Selma heroes, was watching from the crowd, and she thought King was better than she had ever seen him. She had heard him many times in the pulpits of her town, exhorting people like herself to keep pushing. But there was something different about him that day. "His eyes were just a'twinklin'," she remembered, and thirty-five years later with a catch in her voice, she repeated her favorite line from the speech: "The arc is long, but it bends toward justice."

She knew they had seen some difficult times, but everything moved in God's own time, and there on the steps of the Alabama capitol, she thought, at last, that the day of justice might be at hand.

PART FIVE

BLACK POWER

CHAPTER 19

The Martyrs and the Law

THAT SAME NIGHT, MARCH 25, as they slipped into bed, Arthur Gamble turned to his wife and told her with a heartfelt sigh of relief, "Well, they made it through Lowndes County." Gamble, a tall and distinguished-looking lawyer, was a state prosecutor in central Alabama, and though he wished it could have been different, a part of his jurisdiction was Lowndes. He understood its reputation for violence, and it was hard to imagine during all the tensions of 1965 that the civil rights marchers had not been attacked.

But on Friday morning, March 26, the telephone rang a little after midnight, and Roberta Gamble knew the news wasn't good. She could hear the tension in her husband's voice, and he rushed from the house and didn't return until well into the day. He said he had learned that Viola Liuzzo, one of the white volunteers on the march, had been murdered Thursday night on Highway 80. She was a mother of five who had come from Detroit, and according to the early accounts of the crime, she was using her car, an Oldsmobile sedan, to ferry some of the marchers back to Selma. She had made one trip and was starting a second, when she was shot and killed by the Ku Klux Klan.

Liuzzo had been in Alabama for a week, having heeded the call of Martin Luther King. Because she had a car, her primary job before the march was transporting people from the airports to Selma. Bernard Lafayette was one of those people. He had been in Chicago at the time of the Bloody Sunday attacks, and he rushed south again to try to be of help. He had tried and failed to get a plane to Montgomery, and had to fly into Birmingham instead. Mrs. Liuzzo drove up to meet him, and he enjoyed her company on the two-hour trip. She was a cheerful woman, not yet forty, friendly, smiling, eager to do what she could.

"She was dedicated," Lafayette remembered. "There were a lot of people like that in the movement."

On the last day of the march, Mrs. Liuzzo drove again to Montgomery and made the final trek up Dexter Avenue, where she listened to the powerful words of Dr. King. In the late afternoon when everything was over, she drove a carload of people back to Selma, then turned around and started back east on Highway 80. Leroy Moton, a black teenager, was riding with her. It was about eight o'clock on the outskirts of Selma when a carload of Klansmen saw the two of them together. The white men immediately began to give chase, and the two cars raced through the Alabama darkness, reaching speeds of 100 miles per hour, until the Klansmen finally pulled alongside, and shot Mrs. Liuzzo in the head.

Moton grabbed frantically for the steering wheel, but the car went careening out of control and into the steep embankment of a ditch. Moton lay still. He was a resourceful young man, a movement volunteer who had carried an American flag on the march. He had not been hit by either of the bullets, and remarkably enough, had not been seriously injured in the wreck. He held his breath as he heard the shuffling approach of the Klansmen, and he knew that his survival depended on his ability to play dead. The white men glanced at the bodies in the car, and seeing no signs of life, mercifully enough, they all turned away.

It didn't take long for Arthur Gamble to learn these things. The crime, in fact, was an easy one to solve. One of the Klansmen was Gary Thomas Rowe, an FBI informer, who had amassed a violent résumé of his own. In the spring of 1960 he had signed on as a paid informer with the bureau, and in June of that year he joined the Klan's most violent klavern, East-view 13, in Birmingham. He was there for the beating of the freedom riders, getting in a few blows of his own, and by his own admission he shot a black man during the Birmingham riots of 1963. Now here he was at the scene of a murder. He called his handlers at the FBI and identified the shooter as Collie Leroy Wilkins, a burly, crew-cut mechanic, twenty-one years old, who was eager to prove his mettle with the Klan. An arrest quickly followed, and a trial was set for the first week of May.

As word of the killing swept quickly through the country, Lyndon Johnson knew that as awful as it was, it was another strong argument for the voting rights bill. The march to Montgomery may have been a triumph, and the people in the crowd may have seen it as a towering moment of hope, but the simple truth was, the white supremacists had not given up. They were still out there, still ready to kill, and still confident of the fact that they could get away with murder.

Turning up the pressure on Congress, and not incidentally on the Ku Klux Klan, Johnson went on national television to denounce the killing and the men who had done it. Mrs. Liuzzo, he said, "was murdered by the enemies of justice. . . . They struck by night as they generally do, for their purpose cannot stand the light of day." *Time* magazine reported that week that "the word from the White House to Capitol Hill was perfectly plain: Don't mess around with the new voting rights bill, just pass it fast. Sentiment in Congress was for doing just that."

As the president was sending his message to Congress, George Wallace also made a TV appearance and set the tone for the official response in Alabama. "I regret this incident," the governor declared, "but I can say with 25,000 marching in the streets and chanting and maligning and slandering and libeling the people of this state . . . I think the people of our state were greatly restrained." The Alabama legislature, at about the same time, passed a resolution that condemned the Selma to Montgomery march and cited "evidence of much fornication."

John Lewis replied on behalf of SNCC: "All these segregationists can think of is fornication, and that is why there are so many shades of Negroes."

As the political sparring dominated the headlines, prosecutor Arthur Gamble was getting ready for the trial. This was the thing he had dreaded from the start, a media circus in the Alabama Black Belt. It was not his nature to be a part of such a thing. He was an Alabama patrician, dignified and reserved, the son of a judge and a pillar of the social order of the South. But if he was a conservative man and even a segregationist at the time, he did not care for the Ku Klux Klan and its ugly invective and periodic violence. "He was a Southern gentleman," said one family friend, and another described him as a "very proper man, very dignified and very kind."

He knew that his wife was a little bit different. Roberta Gamble was born to an immigrant family in Florida, a dour and close-knit group of Scots, and she had little knowledge of the racial peculiarities of the segregated South—not until she married Arthur Gamble and moved to his antebellum house in Alabama. By the 1960s she was a closet supporter of the civil rights movement, having been a social worker and a teacher, and having seen firsthand a level of poverty and deprivation that most people simply could not have imagined. She yearned to be a part of the demonstrations and the marches, and in particular that mass of humanity that followed Dr. King to the steps of the Capitol.

She had resisted the urge for the sake of her husband, a man of quiet and stoic ambition who had recently been elected to the prosecutor's office. But in the first week of May, the opening of the trial of Collie Leroy Wilkins, the lure of the action was finally too strong. She drove up to Hayneville, the county seat of Lowndes, and she was impressed as she had been many times in the past by the stark and haunting beauty of the land—the rolling hills without a lot of trees—prairie country that might resemble something in South Dakota or Kansas. The town itself was pure Alabama with its oak-shaded square and the ancient-looking courthouse gleaming just behind it, and she remembered one of the first times she had seen it. She had come there with her husband, probably sometime in the 1940s, and she was startled by a cage in the back of the courtroom— a rectangle of iron where the violent offenders were kept before trial. There was a young black man clutching at the bars, the anger flashing in his dark brown eyes, and she remembered how he had made her afraid.

She was uneasy again in 1965. From the moment she arrived, there seemed to be a pervasive feeling of fear, a physical danger that was almost casual in the languid heat of a summer afternoon. For one thing, the whole courthouse was crawling with Klansmen, including Robert Shelton, the imperial wizard, who said he had driven down from Tuscaloosa "in the interest of seeing that these men get a fair trial." Shelton was a slender, sandy-haired man, and Roberta Gamble thought it was strange that he always wore a white trench coat, even when the courthouse temperature was stifling.

But then again, everything about the trial was surreal. There were journalists who had come from every part of the world, from the London *Times* to the Associated Press in Montgomery. Mrs. Gamble took a seat next to Jimmy Breslin, a flamboyant reporter for the *Herald Tribune* in New York, who was once described by journalist Tom Wolfe as "a good-looking Irishman with a lot of black hair and a wrestler's gut . . . a bowling ball fueled with liquid oxygen." On the morning of May 3, before the start of the trial, Breslin regaled everybody with his stories and his astonishment at finding himself in such a place. Over the next several days, the images that made up the backcountry South became a cornerstone of his dispatches—a mule that was grazing in a field near the courthouse, a deputy sheriff spitting out the window. But even for Breslin, the trial was memorable less for its color than the dramatic testimony in the case.

Young Leroy Moton gave a terrifying account of the fatal car chase, from the outskirts of Selma down Highway 80 to a moss-shrouded area that was known as Big Swamp. Mrs. Liuzzo, he said, was humming "We Shall Overcome" at the moment she was shot.

On cross-examination, the defense attorney, Matt Murphy, a curly haired Klansmen in his early fifties, stalked back and forth in front of Moton and demanded to know if he had been the killer. Murphy was a massive presence in the courtroom, six-feet-three and more than two hundred pounds, with a Klan insignia on one of his lapels and a button proclaiming NEVER on the other. He came to court every morning with a pair of handguns, and his style most often was loud and overbearing. His strategy quite clearly was to counterattack, to question the credibility of the prosecution witnesses, and perhaps even more, to question the character of the dead woman herself.

"I suggest," he said to Moton, "you fired two shots, then rifled her pocketbook."

"I did not," Moton replied.

"Did you have relations with Mrs. Liuzzo?"

The prosecution objected, and Judge Werth Thagard, a white-haired jurist who seemed to work hard at being even-handed, agreed that the question didn't have any relevance. Murphy, however, was not finished yet. Cross-examining a policeman who had been at the murder scene, the attorney demanded: "Did you see a Communist membership card in her pocketbook?"

The policeman said that he did not.

For Arthur Gamble and the other prosecutors, Murphy's intentions seemed obvious enough, to inflame the passions of the all-white jury and make the case that Liuzzo had it coming. Gamble knew the strategy could work, but he also knew the prosecution's case was a strong one, particularly the testimony of Gary Thomas Rowe. The star witness was a stocky, red-haired man who wore dark glasses and a dark blue suit, and seemed proud of his assignment with the FBI. He recounted how he and three other Klansmen were driving around in Selma when they spotted Mrs. Liuzzo and Moton.

They had been inspired, Rowe said, by a chance encounter at a Selma restaurant with a man who said he had murdered James Reeb. Rowe didn't name the killer of Reeb, but quoted him as saying: "God bless you men; you do your job—I've already done mine." According to Rowe, his companions in the car—Wilkins, William Eaton, and Eugene Thomas— were hungry for blood as they chased Mrs. Liuzzo for more than twenty miles. About halfway to Montgomery, they finally caught up with her, and Wilkins "put his elbow outside the window and fired two shots." Rowe thought at first that Wilkins must have missed, for the car continued in a straight and steady line before veering off suddenly into the ditch.

As the testimony continued, Roberta Gamble glanced occasionally at Collie Leroy Wilkins and the other two men who were still awaiting trial. Wilkins seemed to be so young, baby-faced at the age of twenty-one, with his crew-cut hair and his muscular physique, but there was something frightening about him also. He gave a little smirk when Rowe took the stand, but most of the time he sat stone-faced, devoid of any emotion at all. During one of the breaks, a child belonging to one of the Klansmen declared tight-lipped to nobody in particular: "My daddy says he's gonna git Tommy Rowe." It was startling to realize in that moment that there was a twisted innocence at the heart of this scene, an indestructible assumption among the members of the Klan that they really were waging some kind of holy war, and despite all the mounting evidence around them, most of them still seemed to think they would win.

Matt Murphy certainly gave that impression. On May 7 he stood before the jury and offered an hour-long closing harangue, disjointed and rambling, though the message could not have been clearer. "*That white woman,*" he called Mrs. Liuzzo, then caught himself as if the adjective didn't really apply. "She started out with this nigger," he thundered, pausing to let the image sink in before he declared: "I'm proud to be a white man. I'm proud to stand on my feet and say I'm for white supremacy!

"The Communists are taking us over," he concluded. "I say *never!* Gentlemen, we shall die before we lay down and see it done."

It was on that basis that he asked for acquittal, and however preposterous it may have seemed on the surface, Arthur Gamble knew it would not be an easy appeal to undo. The issue, in the end, was rationality versus passion, and Gamble was as rational as Murphy was the opposite. He told the jury he didn't agree with Mrs. Liuzzo or her reasons for being in the state of Alabama.

"But gentlemen," he said, "she was here, and she had every right to be here on our highways without being shot down in the middle of the night."

Then, according to the *New York Times,* "The square-jawed solicitor, drawing himself up to his full 6-feet-3 inches, urged the jury in a slow, commanding voice: 'Don't put the stamp of approval on chaos, confusion and anarchy.'"

Roberta Gamble thought her husband had done pretty well. She had winced just a little when he qualified his assessment of Mrs. Liuzzo, saying that he did not approve of her purposes. But of course it was necessary to say that, to ally himself as much as he could with what he knew were the prevailing sentiments of the jury.

Once it was done, there was nothing left to do but wait for a verdict. The jury got the case at 3:40 P.M. on May 6. Twenty-four hours later, they informed the judge that they could not agree. The deadlock was hopeless, and Judge Thagard reluctantly declared a mistrial.

Mrs. Gamble thought it was a heartbreaking moment, particularly because they had come so close. The vote was 10–2 for conviction, which meant that ten white men in the most segregated county in Alabama had listened to the evidence and tried to do what was right. But the bottom line was, there had been no conviction, and Alabama once again was the pariah. The nation had been horrified by the murder, and the media coverage of the trial had been intense, and as Collie Leroy Wilkins had expected all along he was still a free man.

Arthur Gamble didn't say much about it. For more than thirty years after the trial was over, he refused to be interviewed on the subject. But there was one exception, one brief snippet of on-the-record conversation in which Gamble made it clear he understood the irony. In a racist, emotional appeal to the jury, attorney Matt Murphy had urged these men from rural Alabama to join him in a proclamation of "Never." They would take their stand against the power of communism and civil rights, and they would draw a line in the sand for white supremacy. But the effect, said Gamble, was exactly the opposite. If there had been any doubt about the passage of the voting bights bill, it was obliterated by the outcome of the trial. The act passed quickly in both houses of Congress, and on August 6, 1965, Lyndon Johnson signed it into law.

"The vote," said the president, "is the most powerful instrument ever devised by man for breaking down the walls of injustice."

Even the angriest activists in SNCC thought that was true, and they regarded the Voting Rights Act of 1965 as the most tangible accomplishment in the history of the movement. As John Lewis put it, "This law had teeth." Among other things, it ordered the suspension of literacy tests, and where there was a history of voter discrimination, it sent in federal examiners to replace the recalcitrant local registrars. Lewis understood that in the darkest, most forgotten corners of the South, including the state in which he was born, the era of democracy was finally at hand. But he also knew that a lot of difficult work still remained, and he suspected, in fact, that danger and disappointment were waiting just ahead.

The events of the summer quickly made him a prophet. By the time it was over at least two things were clear: There were places where the attitudes of blacks were getting harder, and the white supremacists were not finished yet.

In the town of Tuskegee, the students who had demonstrated in Montgomery began to step up the level of protest. They challenged the hiring practices of local merchants and began to picket stores, banks, and other institutions where blacks had been excluded. The pattern was pervasive. Even Allan Parker, who was widely regarded as one of the most liberal white men in the city, had no black people working at his bank. The student picketing brought the promise of reform, and the protesters moved on to the public swimming pool, which was still segregated despite the Civil Rights Act of 1964. On May 31 twenty-five SNCC students descended on the pool, and more the next day, but on June 2, they found piles of garbage floating in the water, and shortly after that, a live alligator. The city fathers shut down the pool.

In June, with local tensions on the rise, Tuskegee president Luther Foster called Gwen Patton into his office and urged her, as the elected leader of student government, to persuade the demonstrators to back off. Tuskegee, he said, had been a model of race relations in the South, with a tradition of civility between black and white, and the students were stripping away that veneer. Patton reported the conversation to her friends, and SNCC's George Ware led the chorus of disdain. "If this is such a model city," he said, "if blacks and whites get along so well, let's go to the churches."

Ware was like a lot of young people that way, his antennae attuned to the hypocrisies and fictions of the older generation, black or white, and he began to organize Sunday morning demonstrations at the churches. The protests in the beginning were small, but as the tensions grew, so did the number of student demonstrators. On July 11 more than five hundred people marched on the Methodist church in Tuskegee, and when they returned the next week, several black students were attacked by whites.

Charles Gomillion regarded all of this with despair. From the time he arrived on the campus in the '30s, he had worked every day for a different kind of world. His primary focus was the right to vote, which he viewed as the key to an interracial democracy, a political system in which people were no longer judged by their color. By 1964 the relentless efforts of his own organization, the Tuskegee Civic Association, had achieved a watershed moment in Tuskegee history: The number of black voters finally exceeded the number of whites—3,733 to 3,479. With the impending passage of the Voting Rights Act, the ratio was likely to become even better, but in the election of 1964, as a foreshadowing of his own biracial inclinations, Gomillion had supported a Democratic slate that included only two black candidates for the five-member city council. His aim, he said, had never been a black monopoly of power, but the opportunity for blacks and whites to work together.

In Gomillion's mind, the student protests had become an impediment. These graceless confrontations at the Tuskegee churches were immature and destructive, serving only to stir ill will. For Gomillion, the irony of it was staggering. At the moment black citizens were on the threshold of victory, the dream they had struggled to attain was being lost—abandoned, even, by a new generation that didn't understand what to do with its rage.

In the summer of 1965 the students in SNCC, and some of their younger supporters on the faculty, felt a deep ambivalence about Dr. Gomillion. On the one hand, they couldn't help but admire him; he had been a warrior for longer than most of them had been alive. But despite his intellect and commitment they found him naive, too trusting of whites when he should have known better. It was a habit going back to Booker T. Washington, who assumed that white people holding power in the South would accept the Negro as soon as he established himself educationally. In Gomillion's twist on the same understanding, if the black majority demonstrated its restraint, the white community would be reassured, and the day of reconciliation was at hand.

Paul Puryear, one young member of the Tuskegee faculty, called it "the politics of deference," and Stokely Carmichael, one of the SNCC organizers who came to the campus, maintained it was time for a new way of thinking—a radical redefinition of the issue. In the national best-seller *Black Power,* coauthored with former Tuskegee professor Charles Hamilton, Carmichael would argue that whites were not interested in the sharing of power, and appeals to the conscience of white people in the South—and indeed in the country—were self-demeaning and absurd.

"The black people have nothing to prove to the whites," he wrote. "The burden is on whites to prove that they are civilized enough to live in the community and share in its governance."

By the summer of 1965 Carmichael was part of that vanguard of militancy that was sweeping through SNCC. He was a veteran of the wars in the Mississippi Delta, a lanky, good-looking man of twenty-five, with pointed features and a flash of anger in his soft, brooding eyes. Around the time of the Montgomery march, he had moved to Lowndes County where he was confronted again with the kind of mind-set he had seen in Mississippi—a vicious, unrelenting opposition to even the smallest gains for civil rights. His own cynicism was now running deep, and as one of the gifted speakers in SNCC, with his high-pitched voice and his hard-headed logic, he spoke less and less about racial integration, and more about the need for political power.

Within a year, he and another of the SNCC organizers, Willie Ricks, would popularize a cry for Black Power, an intoxicating slogan that swept through the country from the rural outback of Alabama and Mississippi to the steaming ghettos of the big-city North. There was some disagreement about exactly what it meant, but it seemed clear enough that Stokely Carmichael and his corner of the movement had departed not only from Charles Gomillion but from the dreams of John Lewis and Martin Luther King, who were driven by the vision of the "beloved community." Carmichael was no longer talking about love and justice and reconciliation. He was interested in "the politics of liberation," in breaking the bondage that had changed very little since the coming of the seventeenth-century slave ships—and it was something, he thought, that black people had to do for themselves.

Even so, there were the occasional white people who broke through his shell, and if they did not change his philosophy, they won his respect and even, on rare occasions, his affection. One of those people was Jonathan Daniels, a young Episcopal priest from New England who came south around the time of the Montgomery march, going first to Selma and then to Lowndes County. By the account of virtually everybody who knew him, Daniels was a difficult man to dismiss. He was still in his twenties, tall and slender and visibly warm-hearted, and the people in the black community talked about his smile. He was a student at the Episcopal Theological School in Cambridge, Massachusetts, when he saw the footage from the Edmund Pettus Bridge. The following evening, he and ten classmates flew to Atlanta and caught a bus to Alabama.

Daniels had had a brief encounter with the South; he had gone to undergraduate school at Virginia Military Institute, but he had never seen any place like Selma. Superficially, it may have resembled his hometown in New Hampshire, with its quaint storefronts and old wooden houses, but in the early spring of 1965 the racial nerve in Selma was exposed. On the Tuesday after the attack at the bridge, Daniels marched with King to the scene of the crime, where they sang and prayed and then turned around. With Judy Upham, his friend from the seminary, he was also there for the triumphant march, ferrying the demonstrators back to Selma, much as Viola Liuzzo had done.

He had not expected to stay very long, but there was something about the spirit of the place that he couldn't put aside. Perhaps it was the rhetoric of Martin Luther King, made real in the example of the people he was meeting. He was staying in the Carver housing projects, and he was deeply touched by the kindness of his hosts, and their bravery in the face of brutality and oppression. He talked about it with Father Maurice Ouellet, who ran a Catholic mission in the town that included the Good Samaritan Hospital. Ouellet had been in Selma since 1960 and had become an active supporter of the voting rights struggle. He said he thought it was important to put down roots.

Daniels decided to try to do the same and to find his own way to work for reconciliation and justice. As a devout Episcopalian himself, he began leading integrated groups every Sunday to Saint Paul's church, where the prosperous and segregated congregation responded with a mixture of hostility and anguish. Daniels had hoped it would be very simple, a black and white witness for the brotherhood of man, but as he began to talk to white leaders in the town—lawyers, ministers, newspaper editors—he slowly and reluctantly began to understand that this was a complicated struggle he had entered. The victories were not going to come overnight, but there were some tangible things he could do. For one thing, he could follow the example of Father Ouellet and immerse himself in the life of black Selma. He could try to be a pastor as well as an activist, building friendships, playing with the children, talking to people about the problems in their lives.

He was staying at the home of Lonzy and Alice West, both of whom had been active in the movement, and one day he saw their young daughter, Rachel, who was also active at the age of nine, standing at the edge of the housing project and staring toward the town.

"Why aren't you playing with the others?" he asked.

"I don't know why."

"You afraid of something?"

Rachel said she was thinking about the sheriff and his posse "and some of the bad things that had been happening." Daniels picked her up and tossed her in the air, and when she began to giggle he told her not to be afraid anymore.

"I'll watch you," he said, "and make sure nothing or nobody bothers you."

JoAnne Bland took all this in. At the age of eleven, she was two years older than Rachel West, and was another in the ranks of seasoned demonstrators. She lived in the projects, and for all her life, her encounters with white people had been disappointing. Once when she was little, she had gone shopping with her grandmother and saw a pair of patent leather shoes. Impulsively, she rushed to try them on, and the sales lady shrieked, "That little nigger put her feet in those shoes." The clerk insisted that JoAnne and her grandmother buy the shoes, now unfit to sell, even though JoAnne's feet were too small.

Such were the lessons she had carried through her life, but suddenly here was Daniels taking the children for ice cream cones, giving them piggy-back rides on his shoulders, making them feel a little safer in the world. Many years later, JoAnne Bland recalled the fundamental nature of her amazement: "Jonathan was white and he was also nice."

Stokely Carmichael saw these qualities as Daniels broadened his attention from the town of Selma to the area just around it. He began to join the voting rights struggles that were gaining momentum in Lowndes and Wilcox Counties. Not all the SNCC workers were happy with his presence, but Carmichael noticed a few things about him. First of all, Daniels seemed to be a person of humility, more interested in listening than dispensing advice, which was not always the case with the young white activists coming in from the North. There were those who harbored their own kind of prejudice, their private and poorly concealed condescension for the rural people they had come down to help. Daniels clearly was not like that. He was friendly and careful with other people's feelings, and Carmichael had to respect that about him. But there was something else that was nearly as important, nearly as valuable to the civil rights movement as the qualities he may have possessed as a person. Jonathan Daniels had a car—a rented Plymouth that he was willing to make available to the Lowndes County movement, which certainly beat traveling on the back of a mule.

By the summer of 1965 that was often what the SNCC workers did, for their funding support was drying up steadily in proportion to their militance. But with the coming of Daniels, they found themselves with greater flexibility, and they traveled through the distant reaches of the county, visiting the fields and the shacks with no plumbing, trying to persuade people to register to vote—or at least to come to the meetings every

Sunday. Daniels occasionally spoke at those meetings, standing in the pulpits of the little wooden churches, comparing the civil rights movement to the biblical stories about the children of Israel. But most of the time, he was simply one more person in the church, as unobtrusive as a white man could be, casting his lot with the people of Lowndes County.

On Saturday morning, August 14, he and Father Richard Morrisroe, a Roman Catholic priest from Chicago, joined a group of SNCC demonstrators in the town of Fort Deposit, a Klan stronghold that was generally considered the toughest corner of the toughest county in the state. The tension that morning was reminiscent of Selma, and perhaps in a sense it was even rawer, for there wasn't any massive media presence, any feeling of connection with the outside world. This was a town of fifteen hundred, where the white minority was angry and alarmed and rapidly arming itself to the teeth. Eight days earlier, Pres. Lyndon Johnson had signed the Voting Rights Act into law, and the people in control of Fort Deposit understood immediately that this was a law with revolutionary implications. In addition to that, the television news was now full of stories about the rioting in Watts, a black ghetto in the city of Los Angeles, where the years of frustration were exploding into violence. The whites in Fort Deposit could imagine that this was their future playing out on the screen—masses of black people out of control, looting, burning, taking what they wanted.

For the members in the Klan, and even the ordinary citizens of the town, it was hard that morning to see the distinction between the looters in Watts and the group of demonstrators, most of them young, who had assembled at a church just north of the town. There was, of course, all the difference in the world. The Fort Deposit demonstrators merely carried picket signs, protesting the rude and discriminatory treatment they had often received from the Fort Deposit merchants. They had taken a vow to remain nonviolent.

Jonathan Daniels supported the protests, though he hadn't planned to march or carry a sign. But given the tension that was building in the town, he and Morrisroe changed their minds, and marched with the others toward a group of armed whites. The police intervened and took them to jail, then drove them to Hayneville in the back of a truck that was used ordinarily for the collection of garbage. The jail in Hayneville, the county seat, was larger than the one in Fort Deposit, but it was a sweltering place without any air conditioning or fans. The plumbing in the barren cells was unreliable, flowing sometimes in the wrong direction and dumping raw sewage on the concrete floors.

Daniels had never been in any kind of jail and never contemplated one as primitive as this. But for the next six days, he endured the hardships along with his friends and often led the freedom songs or the prayers. The occasional visitors who came to his cell were surprised to find him both cheerful and relaxed.

One of those visitors was Francis Walter, an Episcopal priest from Mobile, who had been an active supporter of the civil rights movement. Walter came to the jail with another priest, Henri Stines, who represented a national organization called the Episcopal Society for Cultural and Racial Unity, a group that was able to raise bail money. Walter thought Morrisroe and Daniels were in greater danger than any other prisoners, more visible obviously because they were white. As a southerner himself Walter understood the level of hatred among the members of the Klan toward people they regarded as traitors to their race.

Daniels and Morrisroe, however, refused to post bond and leave their friends in the Lowndes County jail, this little brick dungeon in the heart of the Black Belt. Finally, on Friday, August 20, the authorities announced that all of them were free. Civil rights lawyers had filed a motion in federal court challenging the arrests, and officials in Hayneville didn't want to argue the case in that venue.

Just a few minutes after their release, Daniels, Morrisroe, and two young women, Ruby Sales and Joyce Bailey, walked up the street toward a little country store, looking for soft drinks. When they came to the store, Tom Coleman, a white man from a prominent Lowndes County family, was waiting at the door with a .12-gauge shotgun cradled in his arm. Coleman, who worked for the highway department, was like a lot of other people in the county. He hated the demonstrators in the civil rights movement, and in particular he hated the white people who were drawn to their cause. He confided later to one local activist that he could nearly understand the motive of the blacks, who were, after all, looking out for themselves. But when he saw the two priests with their clerical collars walking up the road with a couple of black girls, he felt something snap.

"Get off this property," he screamed, "or I'll blow your goddamn heads off."

Apparently seeing the shotgun rise, Daniels pushed Ruby Sales to the side, just as the buckshot tore through his chest. He died on the spot. The others ran, and Coleman opened fire on Father Morrisroe, wounding him seriously in the back. He threatened to kill a group of bystanders, before he put down the gun and drove away in his truck.

The word quickly spread through the Lowndes County movement, and Stokely Carmichael seemed to take it hard. Until a short time earlier, he and Daniels had shared a cell at the jail, and their mutual respect had grown even deeper. There were differences, of course. Daniels was white, Carmichael was black; Daniels was religious, Carmichael was not. But even as he wrestled with his mistrust of whites and the toll of atrocities they had all had to face, Carmichael mourned for this good and decent man, who had put his own life on the line for the movement.

On Tuesday, he flew to New Hampshire for the funeral, and when the service was over and the people in the crowd began to drift away, he joined hands at the grave with a few of Daniels's friends, and as they started the chorus of "We Shall Overcome," Stokely Carmichael wept.

CHAPTER 20

The Black Panthers

BELOVED AS HE WAS, JONATHAN DANIELS was a Lowndes County foot-note, an ancillary player in one of the toughest chapters in the civil rights struggle. His martyrdom added momentum to the cause, but the irre-placeable characters in the story were black—homegrown activists who were ready to die for the idea of freedom and SNCC organizers who were ready to do the same.

They came together at the time of the Montgomery march, when Stokely Carmichael moved to the county with his friend Bob Mants, another of the battle-tested veterans of SNCC. Mants was a southerner, a native of Georgia who grew up knowing that the world wasn't right. As a boy of twelve, he saw the picture of Emmett Till in *Jet* magazine, and the image stayed with him for the rest of his life. Till was only two years older, a teenager from Chicago who was more streetwise than some of his cousins from rural Mississippi. On a visit to the South, he whistled at a white woman or said something fresh, and for that crime he was mutilated beyond recognition, and his body was tossed into the Tallahatchie River. Bob Mants at the time was still a few months short of his teenage years, and he listened intently as the adults in his family's circle of friends warned their children about the dangers of the world.

For Mants and a lot of young men his age, all those dangers now had a face—the battered, misshapen visage of Emmett Till—and the fear became like an undertow for them, a force of nature that never went away. For Mants, however, there were other realities in his young life as well, far more sustaining and pleasant to recall, including the visits he made to his great-aunt Molly's home. His earliest memories went back to her house, where she took in ironing from the white folks around her and his job was to fold the handkerchiefs and socks. Aunt Molly was a talker. She told him about her own coming of age, what it was like growing up in Troup County, Georgia, and the boy was amazed by her resiliency and strength. He was still a child when he began to think about changing the world, as if his own generation had a special obligation, and a few years later as a SNCC organizer, he had a simple definition of his role: "We were trying to build on the struggle of our ancestors."

Wherever he went in the course of that work, he would seek out the elders, the people who gave him that sense of connection and helped him remember why he did what he did. In Lowndes County, at least two stood out from the rest. The first was Aunt Ada, an ancient black woman who was probably in her nineties and lived in the tiny community of Trickum, not far from Whitehall in western Lowndes County. She was mostly bedridden by the time Mants met her, but she heard him talking to her daughter, Dessie Bowie, and asked Mrs. Bowie to bring him to her room. She must have thought he was a fine- looking man, young and slender ("120 pounds soaking wet," as Mants remembers it), with dark brown skin and large, steady eyes, and she was deeply and immediately touched by his presence.

"Boy," she said, pointing a bony finger in his direction, "I been pray-ing y'all would come here. I seed y'all marching 'round Abraham Lincoln's grave."

Mants was amazed by the old woman's courage, her ability to hope, even as her own life slipped toward its end, that better times were ahead. Nearly two years earlier, she had seen the television footage of the march on Washington and the masses who gathered at the Lincoln Memorial, and she had done the only thing she could do. She had set about praying that one day they would come.

Mants came back to visit whenever he could, and he made arrangements to get her a wheelchair so she wouldn't have to spend all her hours in the bed. And sometimes at night when the fear overtook him, the certainty that the vigilantes were out there, he would think of this old woman, he said, and draw a little bit of strength from her own.

Nor was she the only one. Another of the elders was a man who lived on the other side of the county, not far from the farming community of Hope Hull, which straddled the Lowndes and Montgomery county lines. Lemon Johnson had also been an organizer in his day, one of the stalwarts of the Share Croppers Union in the 1930s, battling for living wages in the fields. Thirty years later, he lived by himself in a wood-frame house, and when Mants and Stokely Carmichael went to see him, he offered them lemonade and talked about history. He was a wispy-looking man with gray hair and glasses, and in one photograph taken later in his life, there seemed to be a certain fastidiousness about him—a neat wool sweater, a white shirt buttoned all the way to the collar. He remembered the strikes of 1935, when the union organized in at least seven counties, demanding a dollar a day in wages, a ten-hour workday, and equal pay for black and white workers.

There was a strike in the spring at cotton-chopping time, and another in August at the time of the harvest, and everybody knew this was a dangerous business they were in. The union was supported by the Communist Party, the only ally the field workers had, and the leadership often met deep in the woods, seeking to avoid the sheriff and his posse. Johnson said later that he generally went armed and was ready to shoot back whenever he had to.

"The only thing to stop them from killing you," he said, "you got to go shooting."

In the end, however, it was a one-sided fight, and it came to a head on August 19, 1935, on the massive plantation of J. R. Bell, where the cotton fields looked like a vast sea of snow and there was not a single cotton-picker in sight. Charles Smith was one of the pickers on strike, a teenager at the time, who would emerge again in the 1960s as one of the leaders of the voting rights struggle. He was a little bit younger than Lemon Johnson and more active in the battle the second time around, and he knew from his experience in the '30s that the struggle in the '60s would be bloody and hard. He still remembered that morning in 1935 when the sheriff and his deputies and the plantation overseer confronted the workers and ordered them all at the point of a gun to return to the fields.

Willie Witcher was the leader of the strike that day, a young, powerfully built man who had always made his living with his hands. He was polite, but firm, for the stakes had to do with dignity and survival. Witcher told the overseer that until the workers could make a living wage, they would not go back. They wanted a dollar for every hundred pounds of cotton they picked, instead of the forty cents they were making at the time, and considering the back-breaking nature of the work, that didn't seem to be too much to ask. Witcher said his piece in his soft-spoken way, and then started walking slowly toward his cabin.

"He was shot on the spot," remembered Charles Smith. Witcher became the first of at least a half dozen casualties at the hands of the Lowndes County sheriff and his posse.

Bob Mants was fascinated by the stories, and he thought about Smith and Witcher and Johnson in the way that he thought about the runaway slaves—the anonymous heroes who were willing to risk everything for their freedom. In Lowndes County in 1965 there seemed to be a lot of people like that, their desperation transformed by a glimpse of something better. They had been meeting since the winter, and the de facto leader of the group was John Hulett, a Lowndes County native who moved away for a while in the 1940s and took a factory job in Birmingham. He didn't care much for that kind of work, remembering later that he labored at the Birmingham Stove and Range Company for "six years, four months and two weeks."

"It was like a prison," he told one reporter, but his time in Birmingham was beneficial. He joined a union and later the NAACP, where his mentor was the state president, W. C. Patton. He was also a follower of Fred Shuttlesworth, and soon took his place in the ranks of the "ushers," the men who guarded the churches and the homes of the civil rights leaders. Three or four nights a week, he would sit quietly in the darkness with a .12-gauge shotgun, battling sleep and waiting for a visit from the Ku Klux Klan. One night at the home of Arthur Shores, a car pulled up with the lights turned off, and when Hulett went out to see who it was, it turned out to be the Birmingham police.

"We were just checking on you," one officer insisted, and everybody immediately understood the lie. Hulett was sure they were casing Shores's home, and the policemen seemed to know that Hulett understood. In a way, of course, that was probably the point, and the message couldn't have been clearer: when the bombers finally came to Arthur Shores's house, they, not the leaders of the civil rights movement, would be the ones who enjoyed the support of the police.

None of this surprised John Hulett. When he was a teenager growing up in Lowndes County, the person he feared most of all was the sheriff. Otto Moorer was his name, a swashbuckling man who hated black people and didn't need a lot of provocation for his violence.

"If you were walking at night," said Hulett, "and you saw some car lights, you better hit the ditch. It could be the sheriff. More than one time, I've laid down to hide. I ain't gon' lie. Those were some pretty sad times, you know."

Despite those memories of brutality and violence, Hulett went home in 1959. His father was ill and that gave him his excuse, but the truth of it was, he wanted to be back. His family's roots ran deep in the Lowndes County soil, going all the way to his grandfather's time, when Hilliard Hulett, who was born a slave, scraped together enough money to buy a piece of land. John Hulett was one of the heirs to that land and also to his grandfather's level-headed gumption—a fierce assumption somewhere near his core that despite the evidence that white people offered, he was just as good as anybody else.

In Birmingham, that assumption was shaped and hardened by the courage of Fred Shuttlesworth and W. C. Patton, and Hulett could hardly wait for the day when the civil rights movement would finally come to Lowndes. He also knew that he and the others who lived in the county would have to be the ones to make it happen, and one night in the winter of 1965, they met at the home of the Reverend J. C. Lawson. There were five or six of them that night, an intrepid handful who talked about the power that went with the ballot. They lived in a county where 81 percent of the people were black, but every instrument of power, political and economic, was in the hands of the whites. The average black citizen subsisted on $985 a year, and if that reality was unlikely to change, the political system was a whole different issue. There, all they needed to do was vote.

As the six of them talked about these things, John Hulett noticed a curious thing. The Reverend Lawson, who was elderly and blind, kept talking in a whisper, and Hulett realized after a while that the old man was terrified. With the nearest white person two miles away, he was still so afraid of being overheard that he could barely bring himself to speak aloud. It soon became apparent that his paranoia was not out of place. When they met the next time at a different location, a white man crept to a corner by the chimney, and they found him there when the meeting dispersed. There was no need now to try to be discreet. On the first Tuesday in March, a group of black citizens—more than three dozen, according to one account—gathered at the courthouse to register to vote. It had been a long time since a Negro had even attempted that feat, and they realized when they came to the square that nobody was really quite sure where to go.

After a while, they found Harrell Hammonds, the white-haired probate judge in the county, who was regarded by some of them as friendly and kind. He was one of the biggest landowners in the area, a powerful member of the rural aristocracy, but Hulett knew of black people down on their luck who had been allowed to live on his property for free. Hammonds told them where to find the registrars, but the courtesies dried up quickly after that. Carl Golson, one registrar who lacked the patience and civility of the judge, turned all of them away, dismissing their aspirations as "dumb."

Two weeks later, they were back again with an even bigger crowd, and despite his fears a few weeks earlier, the Reverend J. C. Lawson was at the head of the line. This time, he and Hulett were allowed to register, becoming the first black voters in more than sixty years. It was, of course, only the most rudimentary tokenism, but it was a start. On March 19, 1965, seventeen black leaders met in Trickum at Bud Haralson's store and established a new civil rights organization, the Lowndes County Christian Movement for Human Rights. The name was taken from Fred Shuttlesworth's group, the Alabama Christian Movement for Human Rights, founded nine years earlier in Birmingham. There was something appropriate about that choice. Shuttlesworth was known throughout the state as the preeminent symbol of militancy and courage. Despite the misapprehensions of many whites, he was not a loose cannon, but a minister of steely purpose and resolve. John Hulett knew that in the next several years those were the qualities they would need in Lowndes County.

It was about this time that the SNCC workers came in—Mants, Carmichael, and a handful of others—and the chemistry from the very beginning was impressive. In later years Mants was quick to point out that SNCC leaned hard on the wisdom of the locals. Wes McCall, who ran a store in Hayneville, talked about the dangers they could face in Fort Deposit, and in the earliest days, when they were sleeping in Selma, he told them to stay off the roads after dark. Soon after that, a Lowndes County farmer, Matthew Jackson, offered them the use of a house on his land—a "freedom house," they started to call it, and it became the place where the SNCC workers stayed. They spent many hours visiting with Jackson, a man in his fifties with a weathered face and faded overalls, and an air about him of wisdom and strength. He seemed to know every inch of the county, and many of its people, and he became a welcome source of advice.

There was one topic that came up often, not only with Jackson, but with civil rights supporters all over the area. Tied to the frequent warnings about danger was a dismissal of the basic idea of nonviolence. Mants was uncomfortable with it at first, for he had steeped himself in that particular philosophy, not only as a tactic but as a way of life. The people in the county, however, were emphatic. As one of them put it, "You can't come here talking that nonviolence shit. You'll get yourself killed, and other people too."

With the murder of Jonathan Daniels in Hayneville, the warning rang true, and when one of the longtime residents of the county offered Mants a pistol, he decided to take it. A few months later, in January 1966, there was another killing in the neighboring county of Macon—a black SNCC worker named Sammy Younge, murdered by a white man—and for Mants that finally erased any doubt. He came at last to the difficult conclusion that in the hardest counties of the rural areas of Alabama, nonviolence was a theory that no longer worked. The white people took it as a license to kill.

Certainly, John Hulett thought that was true, and with the murder of Daniels he put out the word, relying primarily on the pure, inflammatory power of the message: "You kill one of us, we'll kill three of you." Then as later, he was not a man who was looking for a fight. He was physically unimposing, slender and less than six feet tall, but in Birmingham he had spent a whole string of sleepless nights standing guard duty with a .12-gauge shotgun. He thought it was something the Klan understood.

For more than a year, they worked at it together—SNCC and the Lowndes County Christian Movement for Human Rights—offering to the country a kind of living laboratory for black power. Among the people caught up in that effort, Stokely Carmichael was the most flamboyant. Still only twenty-four years old, he was a native of Trinidad who had grown up in New York and graduated from Howard University. He had been a freedom rider and an organizer in the Mississippi Delta before coming to Lowndes, and within the next two years, he would replace John Lewis as chairman of SNCC and explicitly renounce the philosophy of nonviolence. Some people saw him as the next Malcolm X, whose cry for black power stirred the adrenaline of blacks in every part of America. Charles Hamilton, his collaborator on the book *Black Power,* said later that by the time it was published in 1967, Carmichael was "a full-fledged proponent of violent revolution." But Hamilton thought he saw an incongruity between Carmichael's rhetoric and his private personality. He remembered a time when they were working on the book and had gotten together in southern Pennsylvania. Ivanhoe Donaldson was there also, an old SNCC hand, and Carmichael had taken center stage, regaling his friends with tales of Lowndes County. After a few minutes, the telephone rang, and it was James Reston of the *New York Times,* looking for Stokely. When the interview was over, Carmichael returned to the group, looking pensive and subdued.

"What's the matter, fellow?" Hamilton asked him.

"I'm too young for this," Carmichael muttered. "I don't know enough yet."

That was how Charles Hamilton saw him, a young man deeply committed to the cause who was also aware of his own limitations. His rhetoric would take on a life of its own, particularly the media catchphrase Black Power, and his political theories would continue to evolve, moving eventually down an esoteric path that took him far from the American mainstream. But in the year or more he spent in Lowndes County, what Carmichael wanted was to get people to vote, and within the local black leadership, he was widely regarded as one of the heroes. John Hulett saw him as a warm-hearted man who was bold in his confrontations with power and quick on his feet, but not an advocate of violence—not in public, and not in their long and private conversations. Hulett did see him with a gun at least once. The two of them had driven to Selma, and after they had parked their car, Stokely was reaching to put coins in the meter when a .25 pistol fell out of his pocket. Hulett didn't think much about it. He had gone armed on many occasions himself, and he knew that his purpose was self-defense, not aggression. He was sure the same thing was true of Carmichael.

Bob Mants agreed. "Stokely's public persona," Mants remembered, "was this hip, articulate, fear-nothing guy. But he was not the violent radical he was perceived to be. He would rather talk his way out of a situation than fight."

Francis Walter, a white Episcopal priest from Mobile, came to the Black Belt about that time, the official replacement for Jonathan Daniels, and he found Carmichael one of the most compelling figures in the movement. In his civil rights diary that he kept in those days, Walter took note of Carmichael's "eloquence," even in the private meetings about strategy, and like John Hulett, he never heard him advocate violence. What he did see clearly was Carmichael's feeling for the people of the Black Belt.

"Stokely could be very gentle with black people," said Walter. "He had an intense respect for rural folks, almost like a Russian writer's view of peasants. He saw them as a source of wisdom and strength."

Walter saw Carmichael as the driving force behind a plan to get black people registered to vote, and then to form their own political party. In Lowndes County it was working. With a handful of SNCC workers canvassing the county, the people were gradually overcoming their fear. By the time the Voting Rights Act was enacted, at least fifty Negroes had managed to register, and when the federal examiners arrived in the county, replacing the recalcitrant local registrars, the floodgates opened and blacks began to step forward by the hundreds.

With elections looming in 1966, the question was how they should exercise power. Should they ally themselves with the Democratic Party, the dominant force in Alabama at the time? Or should they follow the advice of Carmichael and form a political party of their own? Hulett said the choice was made easier when the Democrats, still mostly white, increased the filing fee for their candidates to five hundred dollars—a prohibitive sum for blacks who might aspire to public office. There was nothing to do but form their own party, and in March 1966, the Lowndes County Freedom Organization was born. The founders of the group, including John Hulett, chose a black panther as the emblem of the party, and Hulett thought there was poetry in the choice. "A panther," he said, "won't bother anybody, but push it into a corner, and it will do whatever it takes."

In the spring of 1966 SNCC organized voter education workshops, explaining the duties of the county officeholders—the sheriff, the coroner, the members of the school board—and little by little, the idea of holding elective office became less intimidating to the people. On May 3, 1966, more than nine hundred blacks from every corner of the county voted in the primary of the Black Panther party. For the vast majority, it was the first time they had voted for anything before, and in Carmichael's mind that very fact represented a kind of existential triumph. The black population in this harsh and repressive bastion of white supremacy had proclaimed its right to citizenship, and in that moment, had redefined its humanity. Such were the stakes in the Lowndes County election.

As they began to prepare for the November vote, Carmichael was caught more and more in his national celebrity and the demands that went with the chairmanship of SNCC. As a result, the hard and tedious work fell to Mants, which did not surprise him. When he came to Lowndes County, there were many times when he and Carmichael would stay up talking until well after midnight, and he would try to tell Stokely that a radical organizer in the Alabama Black Belt should be "like a termite and not a woodpecker"—relentlessly undermining the walls of injustice without ever calling much attention to himself. But Carmichael had a different set of gifts, both as a theoretician and a speaker, and when he began to spend less time in the county, somebody had to get out the vote.

For weeks leading up to November 8, Mants and the other organizers from SNCC, along with Hulett and the local leadership, traveled the back roads and knocked on the doors, explaining the voting procedures to the people. They arranged for transportation to the polls, and they put up a sign out on Highway 80—the image of a panther followed by the words: PULL THE LEVER FOR THE BLACK PANTHER AND GO ON HOME.

One of the supporters of that organizing effort was Huey Newton, a young Californian who came to Alabama captivated by the symbol of the panther. Newton was a law student who lived near San Francisco Bay, and like many black men in the city of Oakland, he nurtured a deep dislike for the police. They were racist and brutal in Newton's estimation, and he was inspired by the people in the Black Panther movement, these hard-working farmers from rural Alabama, who had taken up weapons for their own self-defense and put out the word that they would no longer tolerate any violence.

After a few weeks, Newton returned to California, and with his friend Bobby Seale he established the Black Panther Party for Self-Defense, a group of young men who brandished their weapons on the streets of Oakland and challenged the power of the city police. As their militancy began to draw national attention, John Hulett and his friends were not at all happy with this use of their symbol. They never said much about it, but they thought these swaggering young men in the ghettos, who some-times seemed to be spoiling for a fight, were caught in a different under-standing of black power. To them, as far as Hulett could tell, the panther was primarily an emblem of rage. In Lowndes County, Alabama, it was a symbol of democracy, and the militancy that burned at the heart of that struggle was simply a refusal to be pushed aside.

That was the way John Hulett understood it, and he knew they still had a long way to go. Despite the gains of the past several months, there were a lot of black people who were not yet registered, and after the pas-sage of the Voting Rights Act, there had been a curious countermove by the whites. Plantation owners, bowing to necessity, helped to register the blacks who lived on their land, then let it be known how they wanted them to vote. For the Lowndes County farmhands, the penalty for failing to do as they were told was finding themselves without a place to live. Already, it was happening. Already, there were people who were living in tents for daring to proclaim their political independence.

Hulett didn't know what the effect of that intimidation would be. Would it stir the resolve of the masses of black people, or would it rein-force old habits that held people back? When the votes were counted, the news wasn't good. Sidney Logan, the black candidate for sheriff, got less than 42 percent of the vote. The figures were similar for the other six can-didates, and the pattern held true all over Alabama. In places where blacks had never voted before, they ran the most spirited campaigns for public office, but in nearly every case, they came up short. There were a handful of glorious exceptions. In Macon County, Lucius Amerson, a thirty-two-year-old Korean War veteran, became the first black sheriff in the state of Alabama, and in Dallas County eleven thousand newly registered black voters helped assure the defeat of Sheriff Jim Clark. Wilson Baker, the moderate and professional police chief of Selma, ran successfully against him, promising an end to the era of brutality. But in the state primaries and the general election, these were the aberrations, not the norm. There were charges of fraud and clear examples of voter intimidation. In Lowndes County, for example, a black poll worker named Andrew Jones, a respected man who, as one leader put it, "didn't raise no sand," was attacked in the town of Fort Deposit, adding to the level of tension and fear. But in the end, of course, there could be no excuses. There were too many blacks who had failed to vote, or who had voted for whites, and for the SNCC organizers and the people they served, there was nothing to do but keep on trying.

"We won't quit," John Hulett promised. "We won't give up."

Four years later in the sheriff's election, Hulett personally made good on his promise. He decided to run for office himself, and by then there wasn't any doubt that he would win. Too many Negroes had registered to vote.

Not long before the ballots were cast, Tom Coleman approached Hulett near the Lowndes County courthouse. Coleman was the killer of Jonathan Daniels, and barely one month after the shooting he had been acquitted by a jury of his peers. The trial had occurred in this same court-house, just a few hundred yards from the scene of the crime—the little tin-roofed store where Coleman had confronted the young priest and his friends. The prosecution presented at least five eyewitnesses, all of them black, including the feisty and articulate Ruby Sales, whom Daniels had saved by pushing her aside. But the mood of the jury, and indeed of the white population of the county, was revealed during an early piece of testimony. Another eyewitness, Joyce Bailey, described the standoff at the door of the store—how Coleman had told them, "Get off this property or I'll blow your goddamn heads off." The spectators twittered at this unexpected repetition of profanity, then burst into uncontrollable laughter, joined by the jury, when the black teenager described her response to the first blast of gunfire: "I was running."

It was downhill from there. The jury took less than an hour and a half to deliver its verdict as a cold autumn rain lashed at the windows of the Lowndes County courthouse. *Newsweek* journalist Marshall Frady was there, and he offered this epitaph on the trial: "It was like a second, formal, larger crime of extinction and effacement—in a sense, in that courtroom, Daniels died a second and more final time, became no more than the empty and meaningless clothing lifted out of the coroner's cardboard box, and a garishly sinister caricature in the recollections of his executioner's friends."

A few years later, when Coleman stopped John Hulett at the square, there was no way for Hulett to be anything but wary. Coleman felt vindicated, or so it appeared, affirmed by his neighbors in the community of Hayneville—those on the jury and those who were merely spectators at the trial—as a man who had done what he needed to do.

"John," said Coleman, "how about taking a ride up to Lowndesboro?"

Hulett knew the route, north on state Highway 97 as it twisted its way through the vast pastureland, rolling and empty except for the white-faced cattle on the hills. A person could disappear in those hills, but Hulett had made it his personal policy never to back down from the challenge of a white man. Once in Fort Deposit, the Klan stronghold, Hulett had gone to see about Stokely Carmichael, who had been arrested and charged with reckless driving. There were maybe a dozen armed white men milling around outside the town hall when Hulett and his cousin John Brooks arrived. Hulett and Brooks were both unarmed, and for Hulett, especially, that was unusual. He rarely went anywhere without a weapon, usually a .12-gauge shotgun—"something to keep people off me, you understand." But he knew this time that a gun would make it worse, that his best defense was an air of authority and self-confidence. He nodded casually as he stepped through the crowd, as if it were a typical summer afternoon, and it amused him to see how well it worked, how tentative and nervous these white men became at the sight of a black man totally unafraid.

So he decided to get in the car with Tom Coleman, and they set out slowly through the Lowndes County countryside. As Hulett remembered it many years later, Coleman didn't seem hostile that day, just a little uncertain about all the changes that were taking place around him.

"John," he said, "what are you and your folks going to do?"

"Well, Tom," said Hulett, "I'm running for sheriff, and I think I'm going to win."

"That's okay," said Coleman, "I'm leaving the county."

Hulett stared at the white man for a moment, then told him simply, "We didn't leave when you were in charge." He went on to say that the electoral victories now looming for blacks would not usher in an era of revenge, just an era of fair dealing and equality, and he wondered if Coleman could handle such a thing.

Sometime later, after Hulett had won and assumed the mantle of Lowndes County sheriff, his telephone rang in the middle of the night. It was Tom Coleman, who had been listening, he said, to his police scanner. There had been an accident on I-65—a truck overturned near Fort Deposit, its contents scattered all over the highway. Coleman offered to meet Hulett at the scene and help with the cleanup. Once again, Hulett had to wonder. This was a dark and lonesome stretch of road in a place where blacks had reason to be afraid. But he told Coleman fine, please come on down, and the two of them worked until it was almost morning, cleaning up the debris.

A curious realization began to dawn after that. This middle-aged killer of Jonathan Daniels, this dour and unremarkable white man with lines on his face and a furtive hint of sadness in his eyes, was becoming one of Hulett's most dependable supporters. Not everybody saw him that way, of course. In the eyes of many black people in the county, Coleman remained an unrepentant racist and a reminder of those dark and terrible days when white people, literally, could get away with murder. But Hulett thought Coleman was trying to reach out, trying in his gruff and uncertain way to seek forgiveness for this thing he had done.

Charles Hamilton, the political scientist who had written the book *Black Power* with Stokely Carmichael, thought the story of John Hulett and Thomas Coleman was important mostly for what it said about Hulett. The new black sheriff of Lowndes County, Alabama, possessed a quality that Hamilton had seen many times in the Black Belt, and had seen later on in the nation of South Africa. From Mandela to Hulett, these were people with no hatred in their hearts and no interest in revenge. "None whatsoever," said Hamilton, and that was the truly remarkable thing.

But did their victory really change anything?

A couple of years after John Hulett's election, a reporter from one of the national magazines ventured into Lowndes County and began asking people about the legacy of the movement. One of his subjects was Earvin Hinson, a burly, truck-driving farmer who lived at the end of a rutted dirt road. He owned his hundred acres of land, a product of the toil and sweat of his family who had lived in the county since before the Civil War. Hinson was wary of uninvited white strangers, but he and the visitor settled into a pair of flimsy metal chairs and talked about life in that part of Alabama. There was still a lot of prejudice, Hinson declared, and times were as hard as ever economically, but there was one difference from the way things had been.

"John Hulett," he said, "is the sheriff."

When the reporter stared at him blankly for a moment, Hinson told a story: "A few years back, I was driving home one night and my car broke down. It was late and while I was sitting there trying to decide what to do, these white guys came by and gave me a hell of a head-whippin'. They tied my hands behind my back and stuffed me into the trunk of a car. They must have driven around for hours, and when they stopped, my shirt and everything else was covered with blood."

When they opened the trunk, Hinson discovered that one of his tormentors was a highway patrolman, and for the men who had chosen that night to beat him at random and threaten him with death, there was the collective certainty that they would not pay a price. Now, he said, that was no longer true.

"We have a black man for sheriff," he explained. "You don't have to worry as much about the head-whippin's."

Hinson thought about the moral of his story for a moment, then offered this assessment: "No," he said, squinting at the fading afternoon sun, "it ain't justice, still a long way from it. But it's better than it has been."

CHAPTER 21

"A Messy Business"

FOR FRANCIS WALTER, EVERYWHERE he looked against the familiar backdrop of Alabama poverty, there were also the tantalizing glimmers of progress. He was happy about that. For almost as long as he could remember, the civil rights movement had given a shape and a definition to his life. Long before he came to the Black Belt to pick up the work of Jonathan Daniels, he had waged his own struggle with the issue of race. Growing up in Mobile, he developed a deep ambivalence toward the church, and the role it played in the life of the South, even as he was called to the Episcopal priesthood.

In many ways, it began with his mother. Martha Walter, as Francis remembered her, was "an intellectual and a rebel" from an old southern family with roots in the Louisiana low country. She went away to college at MIT, then returned to Mobile where she started a family and moved to the elegant suburb of Spring Hill. She developed breast cancer in the 1940s, and the disease seemed to deepen her religious inclinations. She became a leader in her own congregation, and one day at a Lenten service at the church, she noticed a black man sitting in the back. He was a smallish figure, maybe five-feet-seven, but good-looking and trim, and to Mrs. Walter's surprise, he was wearing the clerical collar of a priest.

"Hello," she said, when the service was over. "I'm Martha Walter."

The black man nodded and shook her hand. "I'm Father Cole," he said, "from the Church of the Good Shepherd."

"I didn't know there was a colored Episcopal church."

"Since 1859," he said, softening her embarrassment with his smile.

Soon after that, Mrs. Walter paid a visit to his church, and set out to develop a relationship between the women's auxiliaries. She took her son to meet Father Cole, and even as a boy, Francis Walter admired the intelligence of this soft-spoken priest and his gentle understanding of the irony of the world. A few years later as a freshman at Spring Hill College, the Jesuit institution that was the first in Alabama to desegregate, Francis became an adviser to an Episcopal youth group. He invited Father Cole to speak to the group, which was considering a question that Francis had posed: "If you were on a bus in Mobile, and a Negro sat down next to you, would you get up and move away? Would Jesus?"

The all-white vestry at Saint Paul's Episcopal, an assembly that included many of the most distinguished business leaders in the city, took a dim view of this kind of program, and refused to allow Father Cole at the church. It fell to Francis to deliver the news. He felt himself flush with embarrassment and shame as he entered the study of Father Cole's church and told him what the members of the vestry had decided. The priest was gracious. "Don't worry about it," he said. "I didn't think I'd be allowed to come."

Unsure how to respond to such kindness, Francis glanced for a moment around the room, and he noticed the range of the books on the shelves—much broader certainly than those at his home, or those in the study at Saint Paul's Episcopal. The arrogant stupidity of the Saint Paul's vestry hit him, he said, with a force that was unfamiliar in his life. He left the church and was gazing at the ground as he walked toward his car, moving slowly up the brick walkway, staring idly at the moss on the bricks and the crosshatched pattern in which they were placed. Angry and dazed, he said he kept asking again and again: "What in the world is going on here?"

Many years later, he remembered the experience as his moment of conversion, and he knew other southerners who had been through it too—"the moment when the scales would fall from your eyes." He wasn't sure what to do about it yet, but he knew he was living in "a horrible society," and he knew he would have to be a part of the change. By 1965, when he came to the Black Belt, that conviction had only gotten stronger, tested by years of struggle as a priest. He was fired from his pulpit in Eufaula, Alabama, when he helped draft a statement by Episcopal activists expressing their approval of interracial marriage. From that point on, he was a thorn in the side of the Episcopal bishops, Murray and Carpenter, who presided over the church in Alabama, and they did not approve in the summer of '65 when he decided to take the place of Jon Daniels.

He went first to Selma, where he lived for a while in the Roman Catholic mission, and then in the Carver housing projects. His host in the projects was Lilly Walker, a lady who walked with a crape myrtle cane and cooked him sumptuous breakfasts every morning—sausage and eggs, biscuits and grits, topped on occasion with her sand-pear preserves. He called her Miss Lilly, and she called him her child, and one day she gave him an old hickory-backed chair that had belonged to her mother, who had grown up a slave.

Such were the bonds he discovered in the Black Belt, the feeling of connection with these people whose struggle he had chosen as his own. Walter never saw himself as a leader; it was not his style and not his place, and everywhere he looked the people were doing well enough on their own. He remembered a time in Wilcox County when he was driving to a meeting at a wood-framed church, a little white-washed building set deep in the woods. His car bounced slowly down a primitive road that curved and slashed its way through the trees, and every few feet there were men with guns who would step out and wave to the people they knew. "Revolution was in the air," said Walter, but it was not the destructive, nihilistic kind. These were solid communities, he thought many times, where the people were caught in a whole new sense of dignity and purpose.

There was a middle-aged woman he met in Gees Bend, a tiny hamlet maybe forty miles southwest of Selma. She had been in a march in the county seat of Camden, and when the police in the town quickly moved in to stop it, the marchers knelt to pray. The police backed cars to the edge of the crowd and blew exhaust on this kneeling mass of black people—a sort of primitive substitute for tear gas—but the marchers held steady. "I had been afraid of white people all my life," the black woman said, "but in that moment, I stopped."

Walter did his best not to idealize the people he met in the Alabama Black Belt. They had their frailties like anybody else, drinking problems, petty jealousies, fears that were sometimes hard to overcome. But there were some who had such a gift for leadership that he wondered what celebrity they might have attained with a little education and a little bit of luck. In Wilcox County, the Witherspoons were those kind of people. Eugene and Estelle had been married for as long as anybody could remember, and they lived in a tin-roofed cabin with a crumbling chimney and a rickety porch and daffodils resolutely blooming in the yard. They rented from a white man for ten dollars a month, and they scratched out a living the best way they could. Eugene Witherspoon, a gray-haired man who wore an old felt hat, had fallen out of a tree when he was younger, and he still walked with a terrible limp. He hunted, he trapped, he fished on the river, and he rode an old mule to tend to his chores. Whenever the white postman was called out of town, Mr. Witherspoon delivered the mail on his mule.

When nightfall caught him in Wilcox County, Francis often stayed in the Witherspoon's cabin, and in the long and reflective hours of conversation, he was even more impressed with Estelle. She was a short, round woman with a third-grade education, a commanding figure in a self-help effort called the Freedom Quilting Bee. It began in 1966, when Walter was surprised by the prevailing art form near the community of Gees Bend. It seemed that all the women made quilts, patching together little pieces of cloth in intricate colors and intricate patterns that seemed to be purely a matter of instinct. Their purpose, of course, went beyond aesthetics; it was chilly in the cabins on the cold winter nights. But Walter saw the beauty in what they were doing, and with a grant of $700 from the Episcopal Society of Cultural and Racial Unity, he bought up some quilts for $10 each and took them away for sale in New York. For a while at least, they were all the rage, bringing in $50, $100, $150 apiece, and when he had sold the first batch, Walter brought the money back to Wilcox County, and asked the quilt-makers, "What do you want to do with it?"

They decided to start a quilting co-op, and with Estelle Witherspoon as manager, it became a long-running industry in the county. "It brought a lot of money into these black households," said Walter. "It sent kids to college."

All over Alabama in the latter half of the 1960s, this became the pattern—a frenetic, surging, grassroots energy channeled most often toward the twin frontiers of political power and economic freedom. Legal segregation was already dead, doomed by the passage of the civil rights laws, and the struggle was now in a difficult phase, often unnoticed by the rest of the country. Beginning late in 1965 activists in a half dozen Black Belt counties, mostly led by SNCC, picked a battle that was far too obscure—and too complicated—for the national media. They worked to get black farmers involved in the local elections of the Agricultural Stabilization and Conservation Service (ASCS), a federal agency that played a critical role in the economy of agriculture. Among other things, it reimbursed farmers for part of the cost of soil conservation, planting grass and trees, for example, to cut back on erosion. It also oversaw acreage allotments for many cash crops, and then paid farmers who were willing to plant less in order to keep from overwhelming the market. And finally, it made loans to farmers and bought some of their crops in an effort to keep the market more stable.

As arcane as it sounded, the county committees of the ASCS determined how much money a farmer could make, and not surprisingly in most of the South, the committees were dominated by whites. As always, the people in control had no intention of letting go of that power. In some of the counties, when it was time to elect the new committee members, the incumbents disqualified the black nominees; in others, they flooded the ballots with the names of black farmers, thus diluting the vote.

Despite the efforts of the SNCC organizers, when the votes were counted in 1965, the results were disappointing. There were only a handful of blacks elected to their community committees, and the price of that modest success was high. In Wilcox County, thirty-two tenant families were evicted from their homes, and there were at least thirty more in three other counties, Greene, Lowndes, and Hale. In the Alabama Black Belt, any attempt to tinker with the economic order was grounds for the harshest form of reprisal.

In many cases, the evicted families spent the winter in tents, shivering against the winds that swept across the picked-over fields, and wondering sometimes if things would ever change. They knew, however, that the battle was joined, and there was simply no way to back away from it. They could leave their counties or the state of Alabama, but if they stayed there was nothing they could do but battle for the power to control their own lives. In Lowndes County, where the number of evictions eventually swelled to at least forty families, Bob Mants and the other SNCC workers set out to ease the suffering in the tents. Mants was moved by the courage of these tough rural people, who had been willing to risk everything for their freedom, and even now, were demonstrating a level of resolve that he knew would have made their ancestors proud. One frigid night in the dead of winter, a young black woman, Josephine Mays, gave birth to her baby, and Mants couldn't help but think about the slaves, particularly the runaways and the rebels, whose will to survive was a part of the strength on which the current generations could draw.

With some of the local civil rights leaders, he set out to raise money for basic needs such as food. But they all knew it was also important to think about the future, to find money for land so the evicted families and those still living in the wretched tenant shacks would eventually have livable houses of their own. Among other things, they established a lifeline to people in Michigan. There was an organizer there, a union man named Simon Owens, who had gone to Detroit from Lowndes County to work in the plants. He wanted to do what he could for the people back home, and Mants went up to talk to him about it. Before he left, when he would mention his plans for a trip to Detroit, everybody would tell him about their relatives there. "People would say, 'I got a son there, I got a daughter there, I got a cousin.' I had a long list of people by the time I left, and I decided to put together a meeting. I called Simon Owens. We met at the union hall, and it took off. They would send food, and they got some of the top guys in the union to support the efforts of the people back home. Some of them came down to see for themselves, and they took some pictures of the conditions we faced. They raised money and bought some land for people who needed a place to build a home."

Before it was over, everybody in the tents, and many of those still living in the shacks, were able to build decent houses of their own—"thanks," said Mants, "to the efforts of the movement." There was nothing simple or tidy about the process—no federal program, no single phi-lanthropist to put up the money. "It was just the people in the commu-nity," said Mants, "looking out for each other."

In Wilcox County the story was similar. As the evictions mounted in 1966, Francis Walter and Everett Wenrick, an Episcopal seminarian who worked with Walter at the Selma Inter-Religious Project, began traveling through the county and taking depositions from those who had been summarily displaced. They found, among others, an eighty-year-old woman who was living in a shack on a white man's place, too old to work on the farm anymore, with no family of her own to take care of her. The white man let her stay in the cabin for the token rent of five dollars a month, but when he learned she had voted in the Democratic primary, he demanded to know which candidates she supported. She told him proudly that she had voted for Richmond Flowers for governor—the state attor-ney general who had stood up on occasion for the rights of black people. The white man told her she had a month to move out.

Another black tenant said the white landlord for whom he had worked seemed to go crazy when the voting rights movement came to the county. "There wasn't a better man to work for," the black farmer said, "but since this registration he's been like a wild man." Before the 1966 elections, the landlord appeared at his tenant's cabin in a fury. "Get out of this house by sundown," he screamed, "or I'll tear the roof off."

Working with civil rights attorney Charles Morgan, Walter took these stories and more than sixty others, and sent them off to the U.S. Department of Justice. Atty. Gen. Nicholas Katzenbach made a vague promise to investigate the charges, but nothing ever happened. In the meantime, there were others who did reach out to the families. The Reverend John Prince, an Episcopal priest in Birmingham, raised money to start a factory to build inexpensive bricks made out of concrete, which the people then used to build their own homes. The Freedom Quilting Bee sold lots from a seven-acre tract that it owned to families who had no place to go.

Before all this happened, many of the families were forced to move away, sometimes going to live with relatives or moving to the cites where there might be jobs. But for those who stayed, the houses they were able to build for themselves were far more livable than the ones they had lost.

All across the Black Belt, this was the pattern—the people straining toward an uncharted future, unsettled sometimes by the changing of the rules, but determined to find a way to move ahead.

In Hale County, northwest of Selma, Lewis Black, a schoolteacher and farmer, was working to build a credit union—a source of self-help funding for businesses and families in one of the poorest counties in the state. Black was a dedicated civil rights activist, part of the voting rights struggle in 1965. Along with the Reverend A. T. Days, he helped lead a series of summer demonstrations, protesting the caprice of the voter registrars. On July 15 a mob of whites attacked a group of peaceful demonstrators, sending seventeen people to the Good Samaritan Hospital in Selma. On July 17 two black churches, including Reverend Days's, were burned to the ground. By the end of July, there had been more than 435 arrests—of demonstrators, not their attackers—and for Lewis Black, all this made him wonder if democracy was possible in a county like his own. The reprisals seemed to be unrelenting.

He was convinced, however, that blacks could develop their own economic base, and the credit union was a step in that direction. In the early 1960s, he and seven other people put up the initial deposit of $42.50, and by May 1966, the once-fledgling alliance now had a thousand members and liquid assets of $80,000.

Black was also part of a grassroots effort, spreading rapidly through the counties all around him, to bring War on Poverty money to the Black Belt. There had been a time early on in the Johnson administration when the president saw the struggle against poverty as potentially the finest legacy of his career. It was a noble idea, eradicating economic suffering in the richest, most powerful nation on earth, but the war in Vietnam was sapping resources and adding new tensions at a time when the nation had been through a lot. In addition to that, the War on Poverty itself was a messy business in many parts of the country, and rural Alabama was certainly no exception. There were divisions of every shape and variety.

In Dallas County, there was a battle for power between a group of poor and radicalized blacks, operating under the acronym SHAPE (Self-Help Against Poverty for Everyone), and an interracial coalition forged by Mayor Joe T. Smitherman. In a county where nearly 70 percent of the people were poor, the SHAPE coalition was pushing for control of antipoverty grants, arguing that poor people understood their own needs better than anyone else ever could. Smitherman wanted no part of that. As a master politician (an opportunist in the eyes of his critics), he foresaw the possibility of a federal windfall—millions of dollars flowing into Selma, with all the power and patronage that implied. He intended to control it.

In his quest for money from the Office of Economic Opportunity, the national antipoverty agency in Washington, Smitherman won the support of more traditional black leaders, including F. D. Reese of the Dallas County Voters League. Francis Walter, among many others, thought the struggle between the factions in Dallas County revealed an added layer of complication in the South—a chasm not only between black and white but a painful division in the black community itself. He remembered an antipoverty meeting in Selma in which a black farmer rose to ask a question and was scolded by a black schoolteacher for the flaws in his grammar. Enraged by this public display of condescension, the rural contingent got up and left.

"This had a thrilling effect on me," said Walter. "These were people standing up for themselves, demanding to be treated with respect, not only by white people for the first time in their lives, but by the middle class members of their own race."

In the end, the Smitherman faction won the battle for the money, and the antipoverty grants began to pour into Selma. The mayor used the first grant of $256,000 to install a citywide drainage system, improving the infrastructure all over town, and not incidentally, his standing in the eyes of many black voters. He may have been a segregationist at heart, but he was also a pragmatic politician who understood the changing reality of the times. Following the passage of the Voting Rights Act, he knew he needed black support to keep his job, and the War on Poverty gave him his chance. As the grants kept coming, he told a reporter a few years later that the use of federal money in black neighborhoods was one of the reasons he kept getting reelected.

"If you want to improve the quality of this whole town," he said, "you take the worst parts of it and work from there. We've had a lot of tangible changes."

In other areas, the poorest of the poor in the rural countryside were more successful than their counterparts in Dallas County. In Lowndes and

Wilcox, coalitions of farmers, supported by SCLC and SNCC, pitted themselves against the power of the governor in pursuit of money for adult education. George Wallace, at the time, was looking for an issue. He was nearing the end of his first term as governor, forbidden by the state constitution from succeeding himself. He had decided, therefore, to run his wife, Lurleen, as a stand-in candidate, even though he knew she was stricken with cancer and might not live to serve a whole term. Even for Wallace, a man legendary for his political nerve, this was a breathtaking plan. In order to sell it, he needed once again to stir the passions of the people in the state.

In the summer of 1966 he thought he saw his chance. On June 28 Sargent Shriver, director of the Office of Economic Opportunity, announced the approval of two federal grants—one of $240,640 to the Lowndes County Christian Movement for Human Rights to teach the basic skills of reading, writing, and math; the other of just over $300,000 to the Wilcox County SCLC for a similar project. Wallace immediately went on the offensive, denouncing the Lowndes County Movement as a "group which advocates 'black power,' violence, turmoil and disorder, bordering on treason, in this nation." In the governor's mind, SCLC was almost as sinister—"a group which has created turmoil, strife and disharmony since its organization."

For the next several days, he continued to heap scorn on the Lowndes County leaders, focusing especially on Robert Strickland, who was widely regarded as one of the bravest men in the movement. Ten years earlier, he had lived in Montgomery, where he worked in construction and supported the Montgomery bus boycott, driving regular shifts for the car pool. Strickland was a large and powerful man who was convicted of murder when he was still a teenager. He said he was attacked by four white boys who threw rocks at him and chased him into a neighbor's house. He grabbed a shotgun and fired two shots, killing one of his attackers. An all-white jury, disregarding his claims of self-defense, convicted him of murder and sentenced him to life in prison. He served five years before he was paroled, then pardoned in 1957 by Gov. Jim Folsom.

In his attack on the Lowndes County Christian Movement, Wallace dredged up Robert Strickland's record and, ignoring the pardon, called him "a convicted murderer [who] has served time in the penitentiary." For Sargent Shriver, the charges were too inflammatory to ignore, and he promised to investigate the situation. But on November 17, 1966, just a few days after the governor's election, which was won overwhelmingly by Lurleen Wallace, Shriver approved both grants, one to Lowndes, the other to Wilcox.

As the autumn slowly gave way to the winter, Francis Walter would drive over periodically to a Lowndes County church, where the people would gather to learn how to read. They would come together every afternoon at four o'clock, huddling close around an old wood stove, studying in the glare of a hundred-watt bulb. Five nights a week, they would pore over the pages until it was almost ten, a voracious group, grasping for a chance that had long been denied.

For Walter, it was one more sign of the times.

A few weeks after the start of those classes, in January 1967, Lewis Black presided over a meeting in Selma. The agenda for the day was more ambitious than anything that had happened on the economic front—more far-reaching in its untapped potential than the Freedom Quilting Bee or the Hale County credit union or any of the self-help housing initiatives. Black, in 1966, became director of the Rural Advancement Project (RAP), an initiative of the Alabama Council on Human Relations designed to help small farmers stay on the land. He had seen the growing number of evictions, not only in Lowndes and Wilcox Counties, but in Choctaw, Sumter, Greene, and many others. Part of it was a simple matter of retribution, the price for supporting the civil rights movement. But there were systemic factors at work also, changes in the structure of southern agriculture. Some of the largest landowners now had machines that would do the work of a field full of tenants, while others were moving from cotton to cattle, which required fewer hands.

Given these irreversible realities, Black saw the need for new institutions. Early in his tenure with RAP he helped a group of farmers in Sumter County put together a housing cooperative, and now he was thinking about something much bigger—a farmers' alliance stretching across the heart of central Alabama. There were farmers he knew, nearly all of them black, who understood what it meant to work with the land but needed both technical and marketing support to succeed independently of their white landlords. In a ten-county area, stretching from Hale County just northwest of Selma to Monroe County northeast of Mobile, there were farmers and veterans of the civil rights movement who were eager to apply for a federal grant to underwrite the startup costs of a co-op. The idea was simple. Small farmers, black and white, would switch from cotton to produce, which could be grown on smaller plots of land, and they would market them together to vegetable buyers in Montgomery and other places.

They were optimistic early in 1967 that the Office of Economic Opportunity would support the idea, for this was a way to keep farmers on the land—to keep them from fleeing to the big city ghettos, which were already starting to erupt into riots. For Lewis Black and the other co-op leaders, it was hard to imagine anything controversial about black people growing cucumbers and peas. But Selma mayor Joe Smitherman saw the Southwest Alabama Farmers Cooperative Association (SWAFCA) as a threat to the social order of his state. It was a grassroots alliance that he had no chance of controlling, and by the spring of 1967, Smitherman was leading the chorus of opposition. Fearing this fledgling group of small farmers would "take over agricultural operations in the Black Belt," the Selma mayor denounced its leadership as an incendiary group of "professional troublemakers" with long-standing ties to the Black Panther movement.

In a sense, he was right. Charles Smith, one of the SWAFCA supporters from Lowndes County, had been active in the Lowndes County Freedom Organization, which ran candidates for office under the Black Panther logo. And there were other civil rights leaders in the co-op, ranging from Lewis Black to Albert Turner, the new state president of SCLC. But the SWAFCA supporter who seemed to enrage Joe Smitherman the most was Shirley Mesher, a white woman from Selma who had come to the city in 1965 to participate in the march to Montgomery. An energetic woman in her early thirties, Mesher had stayed on to work in the movement, and in Dallas County alone, she had helped register more than eleven thousand black voters. She worked in an office not far from SNCC's, and as Smitherman noted, she had Black Panther emblems on the windows and the door.

The mayor's rhetorical attack on Mesher—a "radical . . . who openly espouses black power"— seemed to be part of a larger phenomenon, for among the ranks of the ardent segregationists, there was a visceral hatred for these white outsiders who came to Alabama to work in the movement. The killers of James Reeb and Viola Liuzzo saw them ultimately as traitors to the race, and perhaps as masterminds of the cause, for how could blacks, without any help, orchestrate such a massive undertaking? In his verbal assault on Shirley Mesher, Joe Smitherman never put it that way, of course, but his attack clearly resonated through the state and, before it was over, had spread to the legislature and members of Congress.

All this delayed the antipoverty grant, as the Office of Economic Opportunity considered the charges of subversion in SWAFCA. The farmers, however, simply pushed ahead. Down in Monroe County, a grassroots leader named Ezra Cunningham offered more than a hundred acres of his land to nineteen families who were members of the co-op. "I had land available," he said, "I had the tractor, I had a little credit that I could get the fertilizer and seeds and stuff like that." When the crops came in, Cunningham and another farmer, Prince Black, hauled the produce to Selma in their trucks, where it was graded and shipped to the national markets. "We would be there all night," Cunningham remembered, "sometimes through the next day trying to get it graded. It was a religion kind of thing."

On July 5, 1967, just a few weeks after the first SWAFCA harvest, Sargent Shriver announced a $400,000 grant to the co-op. Sounding like anything but the violent revolutionary who danced through the imagination of his opponents, SWAFCA board chairman Joe Johnson sent letters to churches across the ten-county area asking for their prayers of thanksgiving.

"We want to SHARE OUR JOY WITH THE ENTIRE COMMUNITY," the board chairman wrote, "and GIVE THANKS TO GOD."

But even then, the attacks on the Alabama farmers didn't stop. Within a week of Sargent Shriver's announcement, the Alabama State Troopers stopped a pair of trucks carrying SWAFCA cucumbers to the market. The troopers detained the trucks on the side of the road until they ran out of gas and their cooling mechanism shut down, ruining the produce before it was sold. There were fertilizer suppliers who refused to deliver and companies who promised to buy the produce but reneged under pressure from Alabama officials. None of this, however, could kill the momentum. In its first four months the co-op sold more than a million pounds of vegetables, including cucumbers, okra, snap beans and peas, butter beans and crookneck squash. The prices were higher for the cucumbers and peas than the individual farmers had been getting on their own, and they found new markets for the sale of their okra.

They were looking forward to 1968, especially when the Office of Economic Opportunity announced a new grant of nearly $600,000. But the opposition remained unrelenting, especially in Selma, where Mayor Smitherman managed to get a court injunction against the spending of the federal grant money. Eventually, all this began to sap the organization's energy, and there were well-publicized accounts of mismanagement and corruption. In the summer of 1968 one senior staff member failed to order seeds in time for the planting and siphoned off $75,000 in co-op money to an account he had set up for himself. The money was recovered, but the damage to SWAFCA's reputation was done.

The co-op continued to operate for a while, lasting well into the 1970s, but it never lived up to the hopes of its founders. Certainly, in terms of its agricultural mission, it was never the revolutionary force that Lewis Black and many others had foreseen. But there were people who refused to dismiss it as a failure.

"It was growing an awful lot of cucumbers for Whitfield's Pickles," said Francis Walter, who did some organizing for the co-op. But more than that, SWAFCA was part of "the great upsurge, a growing sense of dignity, a feeling of people overcoming their fear." In many ways, said Walter, the civil rights struggle was "a messy business," a great, untidy movement of the masses toward a redefinition of what it meant to be alive. In Walter's mind, it was hard to overstate the importance of the change.

He also knew there were places in the Black Belt—the state's final bastion of white supremacy—where the results were cleaner and much easier to judge; where the civil rights leaders were steady and focused in their pursuit of the inevitable moment of triumph.

CHAPTER 22

The Sheriff without a Gun

IN FEBRUARY 1965 THOMAS GILMORE came back home. He had gotten tired of Alabama for a while, the meanness of it, the rigid segregation, and in 1963 he had moved his family out to California. But he discovered early on that he couldn't run away, and in any case, the city of Los Angeles was not a happy destination for his flight. "The bigness of it and the wildness of it" were a little too much for a country boy from Greene County, and he decided he missed those swampy bottomlands, where he had fished and hunted and learned to be a man.

The civil rights movement was gaining momentum at the time of his return, even making its way to those Black Belt counties where it sometimes seemed as if nothing ever changed. Gilmore hadn't really thought much about it, not in terms of his own participation, for it was a distant reality from his life in California—and certainly it had never even crossed his mind that he would one day become a symbol of liberation. He was simply homesick, lonesome for the sight of Forkland, Alabama, where he had grown up poor on a patch of land that had been in his family for five generations.

He began his life in a rough wooden cabin, which was later replaced by a white frame house, down in the southern end of the county. The Warrior River was just a stone's throw away, and he and the others who lived in the area were known as "swamp people." They were an independent lot, especially the Gilmores, who traced their ancestry back to Joe Winn, a slave who managed to buy enough land, in the days just after emancipation, to give his six children eighty acres each. Clara Gilmore, Thomas's grandmother, was still a farmer on one of those plots, raising a little bit of everything—pigs, chickens, milk cows, and vegetables.

Overlaid against the strength of his family and the legacy of independence going back a hundred years was the specter of racism. Like virtually every black southerner his age, Gilmore carried a picture in his mind of the horrible, misshapen face of Emmett Till, and there were lesser cruelties in Alabama as well. As a child on shopping trips to Demopolis, the nearest town with a store, he was troubled by the segregated drinking fountains, for what difference did it make where a child got his water? Later as a teenager, he could see the purpose of the segregated order, how it was not a simple matter of separation, polite and benign, as many whites insisted, but a tool for keeping black people in their place.

Once, in a field not far from his house, two young men, one black and one white, got in a good-natured wrestling match that abruptly turned dark and almost deadly when the black youth threw the white boy to the ground. Sometime later, this young black man was paddling across the Warrior River in his skiff, when the same white boy and several of his friends rowed out to meet him. Somewhere out near the middle of the river, they flipped his boat and threw him in the water, and the black youth had to swim for his life.

Gilmore absorbed these lessons of the times, and as a young man early in the 1960s, he was torn between the pull of being a minister in Forkland or getting as far away from it as possible. In 1963 he left for Los Angeles, where he never felt at home, and when he returned to Alabama after only two years his life took a sudden and unexpected turn. On a gray and dreary February day, he had driven to Demopolis to pick up some baby formula for his child, and he saw an old friend at a service station. He pulled in to greet him, and as he did so, he hit a mud puddle and splashed dirty water on a state trooper's car. He immediately got out and told the trooper, "I'm sorry about that." The officer, however, took one look at this tall and gangly black man in his twenties, with his big-city beard and his California plates, and he immediately assumed this was an agitator looking for some trouble. He and his partner made Gilmore stand with his palms on the gas pumps while they frisked him for weapons.

"You are going to wash this car yourself," the trooper informed him, with a look of Alabama meanness in his eye. Gilmore was startled, but kept his composure. "Officer," he said, "I will pay to have your car washed."

The policeman was not impressed by the courtesy. "I'll get your ass," he said. "I know where you're headed."

Gilmore assumed that the trooper meant Selma, where the voting rights protests were in full swing, and although it had not been a part of his plans, it occurred to him then that he ought to go to work for the civil rights movement. He decided to look up an old mentor and friend, the Reverend William McKinley Branch, who was the founder of the fledgling Greene County movement. Reverend Branch, as it happened, had long been one of Thomas Gilmore's heroes. He was a smallish man in his forties, dark-skinned, with a merry disposition and an air of authority, and not even the trace of a wrinkle in his face. He had been a child in Greene County in the 1930s, when the times were as hard as anybody could remember. His father was a sharecropper trying to pay off a five hundred dollar loan from a white man. Mr. Branch put up a share of his cotton every fall, but no matter how many acres he plowed or how many cotton bales he produced, he always seemed to fall a little short. "Boy," the white man said every year, "if you had just made one more bale."

They subsisted many days on parched corn and water, and "were glad to get it," William Branch said later. But one day when there wasn't any meat in the house, William prayed to the heavens for some kind of relief. "Lord," he said, "let a turtle come up in the yard." He was maybe eleven years old at the time, and could imagine the savory tang of turtle soup; and thirty minutes later, when a turtle, in fact, came crawling toward the house, it was easy to see it as the answer to a prayer. Having already heard the call to be a preacher, he decided he was ready to give his life to the Lord.

He knew he needed some more education, and before he had graduated from high school he set out one day for Selma University. He caught a milk truck to the town of Demopolis, paid a driver a quarter to take him to Uniontown, then walked the rest of the way to Selma. It was another thirty miles or so, he guessed, and he made it to the outskirts of town around dusk. With no place to sleep, he sat up all night in a Selma juke joint, and the following morning, he appeared on the doorstep of William Dinkins, the president of the college. Dinkins was impressed with this tenacious young man, polite and disheveled, who was standing at his door, and he gave him a piece of hard-headed advice.

"Finish high school," Dinkins told him, "and then come back."

In 1941 Branch did, and after earning his two-year degree, he went back to Greene County and accepted the pastorate of a small Baptist church, working for the salary of twelve dollars a Sunday. He was never at ease with the racial order in the South, and as the civil rights movement gained momentum, he dreamed of the day when it would come to Greene County. He knew the resistance was sure to be fierce, for this had been, as Branch often put it, "a slave county" before the Civil War—a place where blacks outnumbered whites, and a hundred years later, the ratio was the same. If Negroes ever registered to vote, they would hold a majority of nearly two to one.

Sometime early in the 1960s Branch set out to try to make it happen. He set up a chapter of the NAACP, and many years later, he remembered the tension when the word got around. Before one of the organizational meetings, "my people heard a whisper," he said—a rumor that the Klan was planning an attack. That night at the church, ten or twelve of Branch's supporters came with their guns and slipped out to the graveyard just behind the building. They crouched in the bushes and hid in the trees, and after a while the Kluxers did come—a group of armed men crawling toward the church on their stomachs. They were inching toward a window at the back of the building, which looked in on the pulpit where Branch was already starting to speak, when the Negro sentries took them by surprise.

"Stick 'em up!" they commanded from the darkness, using a phrase that was popular in the cowboy movies, and the startled Klansmen ran howling for the trees.

"The Lord took care of me," said Branch.

By 1965, when Thomas Gilmore returned from California, Branch had amassed a solid group of followers, but he was happy for the new addition to the ranks. He thought of Thomas as one of the brightest young men in the county, recently married, devoted to his family, a quiet and reflective person overall, who was also comfortable among the ranks of the militants. In the winter and spring of 1965 Gilmore began to make the connections between the Greene County movement and the efforts of SCLC and SNCC. He got to know James Orange, Dr. King's representative in Perry County, and Stokely Carmichael over in Lowndes, and like a lot of people out in the trenches, he was indifferent to the organizational disputes that seemed to be attracting the attention of the media.

Officially, he worked for SCLC, a contact point for King in Greene County, but whenever Carmichael came in to visit, Gilmore was always happy to see him. "He was the kind of guy you would want to be around," Gilmore remembered. "He was smart, tough, daring, a lively companion. He thought he could change this place, and he was willing to die for the change; that much I know. I said, 'Man, you're reckless, a reckless thinking fellow.'" Sometimes when Stokely would stay at his house, sleeping on the floor when he slept at all, they would stay up talking about the shape of the movement, about the Black Panther party gaining strength in Lowndes County, and Gilmore thought that Stokely and his theories were "changing the very connotation of blackness." Carmichael had little interest in whites, none at all in friendship or appeasement, and Gilmore was sure that Stokely would turn to violence if he had to.

"But he was not mean," Gilmore decided. There were others in SNCC that he wasn't as sure of, men with a fundamental hardness in their eyes. "But Stokely's eyes," he said, "were not like that."

If Gilmore absorbed some of Carmichael's fire, he was also the protégé of William Branch, a gentler spirit and an old-school preacher, who never had an inkling of hatred in his heart. Together, they were committed to the cause of nonviolence, and they worked to get people registered to vote, and addressed other issues that came up as well. It gave them comfort to know they were not alone, that in counties all over rural Alabama, from Choctaw to Lowndes, Monroe to Dallas, people were throwing off the shackles of fear and stepping forward to register. They were encouraged by SCLC and SNCC, but in the end every person had to muster the nerve.

Once in Greene County, during a voting rights march, a young woman was struck by a deputy sheriff, and Gilmore tried to have the deputy arrested. When the authorities treated the suggestion as a joke, he brought thirty people to the district attorney's office, and they refused to leave until their grievances were heard. The police came quickly, and as Gilmore remembered it, "They beat us up pretty badly." He talked about the beatings with William Branch and his friend James Orange of SCLC, and Orange came up with a radical suggestion.

"You be the sheriff," he said.

For the next several months, Reverend Branch refused to let it go. He talked about the aura of repression and fear that hung over the lives of black people in the county, and although it was true that the incumbent sheriff, a former football player by the name of Bill Lee, was a kinder, more complicated man than Jim Clark, he was also a segregationist at heart. He had played in the Rose Bowl for the University of Alabama, and his father and brother had both been sheriff. The office, in fact, had been in the family since 1922, and when Gilmore finally decided to run, Lee was heard to vow that "a cotton patch nigger" would never take it away.

He was a large, beefy man with thinning hair and a plain-spoken manner that was most often affable enough on the surface. Just before the election in 1966, he told *Newsweek* magazine's Marshall Frady that he had generally gotten along well with black people. "I don't think no more of walking into one of those nigger joints without a gun, and a hundred liquored-up niggers in there, than I would think of walking into a church," he said. "Because they know ol' Bill's gonna be fair with them."

But there were growing chinks in Lee's armor of amiability as the civil rights movement turned up the pressure. William Branch remembered the time when a white man known for his violent ways threatened Branch with a gun. The minister reported the threat to Bill Lee, but the sheriff had little sympathy for this boat-rocking preacher who was turning life in Greene County on its end. When Branch insisted that the man had tried to shoot him, Lee told him in a rage: "You goddamn jughead son-of-a-bitch, I'd be glad if he did."

A few weeks later, Branch came home from a trip to Demopolis, and his wife told him warily that the sheriff had been there asking to see him. Reluctantly, Branch went down to the office where Lee had cursed him, and the sheriff said he needed to get something off his chest. "Reverend," he said, "I told my wife I cussed the preacher. She told me I should not have done that. I want you to forgive me."

Such was the enigma of Sheriff Bill Lee.

Branch forgave him, and the two men embraced, but it didn't alter the fact that Lee was a part of the old social order, a cornerstone of Greene County segregation, and for the blacks and whites who lived in the county, Thomas Gilmore's challenge to his office was a revolutionary moment. Gilmore ran as a Democrat, which was part of the strategy of SCLC. After the passage of the Voting Rights Act, the organization had sent volunteers to 113 counties in the South, 15 in Alabama, to try to get black people registered to vote. Once that goal was accomplished, the question was how they should exercise power, and the organization's strategists, including Hosea Williams, emphatically rejected the third party theories of Stokely Carmichael. The realistic option was to use black power—the power of the vote—to transform the Democratic Party in the South.

In the spring of 1966 Gilmore was willing to accept that strategy, and along with the candidates for several other posts, he hit the campaign trail—the churches, the farms, the juke joints on the weekend. Some of the people seemed to be excited, nursing the hope that things would really change. But Gilmore discovered a frustrating thing. There was still a vast residue of fatalism, old feelings of resignation and defeat, that took many forms. He went one morning to speak at a church, and a black deacon told him, "I'm not gonna vote for you. If I vote for you and you win, they'll kill you. It's a nail in your coffin. I'm not gonna help kill you."

Another time at a little juke joint on the road to Greensboro, Gilmore went in on a Saturday night and asked to put a poster behind the jukebox. "There was this brother standing there," he remembered, "wearing bib overalls. I said, 'I sure need your vote, man. We got to bring down Mr. Bill Lee.' He said, 'Man, why don't you cut out that bullshit?' This was such a new idea for black folks. There was such cynicism built up over time that people just couldn't conceive of the difference."

Still, he knew that the overall numbers were strongly in his favor. By election day, May 3, there were thirty-four hundred black people registered in the county and only two thousand whites, and if the blacks turned out and there wasn't any fraud, the results were virtually a foregone conclusion. But then the stories began to trickle in—white people voting who were not on the rolls, people who had moved from the county years ago either coming back to cast their ballots themselves or designating somebody else to do it for them. One black lady told Gilmore later that when she went to the polls, the white election worker asked her, "Do you want to vote for Sheriff Lee or Bill Lee?"

The reports were disturbing, but on that warm Tuesday evening as he waited for the count, Gilmore refused to give up hope, refused to listen anymore to those cynical voices he could hear somewhere in the back of his mind. "I just can't believe," he told Marshall Frady, "they'd actually take this thing away from me now. . . . Not even them."

The whites, meanwhile, gathered at the courthouse, as they might at a high school football game. It was a Greene County tradition—the people coming together at dusk, assembling at the square in the county seat of Eutaw, and waiting for the returns. The actual count took place in a second-floor office, hidden away in a stucco building at the back of the square. There was a wrought-iron staircase leading to the door, and on the night of May 3, the people glanced anxiously in that direction. Ordinarily, there were running tabulations posted through the evening, scribbled on a blackboard in the hall of the courthouse, and it was part of the suspense and anticipation that could make election night one of the most festive occasions of the year. But not this time. There was no blackboard, no attempt at entertainment, for in the first week of May 1966, most of the people who gathered at the square thought the stakes were too high—nothing less than their whole way of life. They could hardly imagine a black man as sheriff, as the ultimate symbol of small-town authority, and rumors early in the evening were grim. Gilmore was said to be in the lead.

But then came the total from the absentee ballots—only one black vote among the two hundred cast—and Sheriff Bill Lee back in front, back where his followers thought he should be. When the evening was over, and the tension finally died, Lee won by a total of three hundred votes, and as he made his way through the slap-happy throng, shaking their hands, thanking them graciously for all their support, he seemed to know even then that it was only temporary. The white minority, he told Marshall Frady, could not hold off the majority forever.

For Thomas Gilmore, it was only after he knew he had lost, when the cold reality of it set in, that he knew how badly he wanted to be sheriff. All along, he thought it was important, and he would talk philosophically about giving his children and the others in the black community of Greene County "somebody they can look up to without being afraid." But those, he discovered, were the reasons in his head, the intellectual understanding of the need for a change. Now in defeat, he was coming to terms with a level of yearning that he hadn't really grasped. His ambitions for himself and the people of the county were abruptly and exponentially magnified.

He helped initiate a lawsuit, citing irregularities in the primary, and as the case made its torturous way through the courts he prepared for the election of 1970. There was, however, one event that intervened, a deeply moving interlude in his life that made him reexamine his commitment to the office; made him wonder, in fact, if he could really be a sheriff.

The event was a visit from Martin Luther King, early in the spring of 1968.

King, by then, was in a difficult place—a moment in his life and public career that was probably more exhausting and more ambitious than anything else that had happened through the years. On April 4, 1967, he had appeared at the Riverside Church in New York and denounced the war in Vietnam. It was not the first time. He had also spoken at his own church in Atlanta, but the media was listening at the Riverside service, and the word went out across America that the greatest civil rights leader in the land had now waded in on the issue of foreign policy. The denunciations were swift and unrelenting. From Senator Barry Goldwater on the right to Senator Edward Brooke of Massachusetts—the first black senator since Reconstruction—there were suggestions that King had stepped out of line, putting the civil rights movement at risk by breaking with a president who had been its friend. But King held fast to his antiwar position.

"The bombs of Vietnam explode at home," he said. "They destroy the dreams and possibility of a decent America."

More specifically, they were sapping the resources of the War on Poverty at a time when the country was exploding in rage. In the summer of 1967 there were riots in a hundred American cities, and eighty people died. King was convinced that poverty in a land of plenty was to blame— the grinding, soul-numbing daily existence of people in the cities and people in the rural backwaters of the South who didn't have jobs or food for their families. In August 1967 a young black activist named Marian Wright, who had worked in Mississippi and seen the terrible poverty of the Delta, came to King and suggested a poor people's pilgrimage to Washington. King immediately agreed, and with his staff in Atlanta he began to make plans.

On March 20, 1968, he came to Alabama, following stops in Mississippi and Memphis, stumping for support for the poor people's march. Gilmore was his driver, and happy to serve, for he and King had been friends for several years. In 1966 King came to Greene County to campaign for him, and two years later he asked Gilmore to help coordinate the march. On March 20, as the evening shadows settled on the highway, King and his inner circle of advisers were driving from Eutaw to Greensboro and Marion, and as usual they were late—a time-honored habit of King's through the years. As luck would have it, they were caught on a curving road behind a truck, six of them crowded into Gilmore's car, a '63 Chevy, two-tone green. In the front seat with Gilmore were Abernathy and King, Abernathy in the middle, and in the back seat were Bernard Lee, Dorothy Cotton, and Hosea Williams. They were talking about the Poor People's March and their plans for a mule train out of Mississippi, picking up people as it made its deliberate journey through the South. As the conversation bounced from seriousness to banter, Gilmore thought King looked tired. It was clear he was worried again about the movement—about the future of nonviolence in an era of riots, about the specter of poverty, and the fading commitment of the United States government, and about his own ability to set a new agenda. King had battled for integration and the ballot, but there was still so much that needed to be done, and he was not a man to rest on his laurels.

On the road to Marion, as Gilmore was listening to the stream of conversation, he was grumbling to himself about the eighteen-wheeler, grinding its gears as it slowed for the curves, making King later than he already was. Finally, he thought he saw an opening, and whipped out to pass—a dangerous maneuver, he thought when it was over. But everybody laughed, and there was a sudden burst of hard-edged teasing about Gilmore trying to kill Dr. King. About that time, the road straightened out, and the eighteen-wheeler pulled back alongside and turned deliberately into their lane. At the moment they were passing a tiny gas station, and Gilmore swerved from the path of the truck and pulled to a stop not far from the pumps.

The driver of the truck, a white man in his twenties, jumped from his cab and stalked to the driver's window of the car. "Nigger," he said, "get those lights out of my rearview mirror."

"Can you believe this?" mumbled Ralph Abernathy, and in the back seat Hosea Williams was telling Gilmore to roll his window up on the truck driver's throat. Only King seemed calm. "Young man," he said, in that baritone voice that was always serene, "get in your rig and go ahead now. You're starting trouble, and you don't need to do that."

The white boy stood frozen as he recognized King, then slowly backed away.

As Gilmore started again down the highway, King began to talk about the state of the nation, how troubled it was, and how the sickness now was even closer to the surface. Two weeks later, on April 4, 1968, Gilmore remembered that curious episode when he heard the news flash coming out of Memphis—the terrible, unbelievable report that King had been murdered on his hotel balcony. Only a few minutes earlier the most gifted civil rights leader in the nation had been in a pillow fight with his friends, but then the rifle bullet tore through his neck, leaving the country and the movement with a new kind of martyr—a man who was always larger than life, even to those who saw his humanity.

All over America, as the news quickly spread, the inner cities erupted into riots, and for thousands of African American people, nonviolence died on the balcony in Memphis. For Thomas Gilmore the effect was just the opposite. He found himself haunted by the greatness of King, a man with his frailties like anybody else, but a leader with a powerful vision for his country. His stubborn, unflinching proclamations of nonviolence were clearly no contrivance, as Gilmore had seen on the highway to Marion. Over the next several weeks, as he struggled with his grief, Gilmore decided to pay honor to the memory by adopting nonviolence as his own way of life. Before, he had always seen it as a tactic, a sensible approach to the goal of liberation, but now it needed to be something more.

The decision, however, raised a fundamental question. Was it possible to be a nonviolent sheriff? In a rural community as tough as Greene County, could you enforce the law without carrying a gun? With the approach of the 1970 elections, Gilmore decided he would give it a try. The ambition still burned, along with the steady realization that in a county like his own there was no other office more important than the sheriff.

He decided this time to run under the banner of the National Democratic Party of Alabama (NDPA), founded by Huntsville dentist John Cashin, a longtime supporter of the civil rights movement. Cashin was a black man, and there were ways in which his third-party effort, unveiled in December 1967, resembled Lowndes County's Freedom Organization, which ran its candidates under the emblem of the panther. Certainly, one of Cashin's primary goals was to get black people elected to office. But there were also a couple of noteworthy differences between the new organization and the third-party theories of Stokely Carmichael. For one thing, Cashin was deliberately biracial, cofounding the party with a couple of white men, Alvis Howard and Charles Morgan. In addition to that, the NDPA proclaimed its allegiance to the national slate of Democratic candidates, thus becoming a curious kind of hybrid—part mainstream, part third-party boat-rocker.

In the breakthrough campaign of 1970 the NDPA elected twelve candidates across the state, while another black, civil rights attorney Fred Gray, who had been active since the Montgomery bus boycott, ran as a Democrat and was elected to the Alabama House of Representatives. But the greatest vindication came in Greene County, where blacks won every governmental seat, making Greene the first county in the country with an all-black government. William Branch, the respected elder statesman of the movement, was elected probate judge, the first black since Reconstruction to hold that position, and Thomas Gilmore became the new sheriff.

As Gilmore saw it, the challenge now was to govern with integrity. He allowed his deputies to carry handguns, a concession, he said, to the reality of the job, but Gilmore himself remained committed to his oath of nonviolence. There were some dicey moments in the course of his thirteen years in the office. There was an armed black man on an Alabama back road, threatening violence, and Gilmore, who never carried a gun, trying to talk him out of it. "Man," he said, in a soft, easy voice, "it would do me good if you would put that gun down."

There were white people, too, who drifted near the edge, and Gilmore would spend a lot of time in conversation—in kitchens and living rooms sipping cups of coffee—telling a man who was having trouble with his wife: "Man, I'm trying to work this out so you don't go to jail. That'll just end up costing you money. I don't know about you, but I'm a country boy from down in the swamp. I don't have money to waste."

The key, he said, was to respect the humanity of the people in trouble, and it was one of the things he had wanted all along, to soothe the irrationality and the fears that had gotten so inflamed by the issue of race. He wanted the people of Greene County to see that there wasn't any reason anymore to be afraid.

By the end of his term, he thought they had made a little bit of progress. He said it was the least he could do for Dr. King.

CHAPTER 23

Unfinished Business

THE CIVIL RIGHTS MOVEMENT BEGAN to lose momentum sometime early in the 1970s, slipping away, in the words of one writer, like a piece of driftwood beneath the surface of the water. But before the tumult subsided altogether, there were a few pieces of unfinished business.

The University of Alabama was no longer the place it had been in the 1950s, when Autherine Lucy tried to integrate the campus, or even seven years later, when George Wallace stood in the schoolhouse door. Following in the dignified footsteps of Vivian Malone, blacks were now a common sight in the classrooms, and even among whites the attitudes were different. One measure of the change came on March 21, 1968, when Robert Kennedy paid a visit to the campus. In 1963, when he had come to negotiate with George Wallace, an Alabama State Trooper had threatened his life, and for many of the white people living in the state, he was as much a pariah as Martin Luther King.

Now, however, he was running for president. He came to Alabama on a swing through the South, and nine thousand students turned out to hear him. For Kennedy, this was happening all over the country. He was a politician who had struggled with his own identity, struggled to find a definition of himself in the wake of his brother's assassination in Dallas. By the early spring of 1968, it was clear that he had found it—a message of indignation and hope and a deep, instinctive identification with the poor. Some people said the empathy was rooted in Dallas, in his own encounter with the agony that followed, but wherever it came from, he gave it a voice, and became a national icon of compassion.

John Lewis, who went to work for Kennedy in 1968, said his reasons for that decision were simple: "The man really grew. You could *see* him growing."

The irony of it was that as Kennedy electrified crowds around the country, so did George Wallace. The former Alabama governor, whose wife Lurleen held title to the office, was dividing his time in 1968 between running for president on a third-party ticket and dealing with the harsh, inevitable truth that his wife was slowly dying of cancer. His time on the stump seemed to be a necessary diversion, a source of energy and purpose for a man who had always reveled in the chase. From California to Michigan and many places in between, he delivered his familiar campaign address—an attack on civil disorder and street crime, blurring any distinction between the two. "You work hard," he told one audience of blue-collar workers. "You save your money, you teach your children to respect the law," while "the pro-communist, long-haired hippies" were running amok in the streets of the country.

The message of Robert Kennedy couldn't have been more different. At the University of Alabama he spoke of a time when "our great nation is troubled, divided as never before in our history; divided by a difficult, costly war abroad and by bitter, destructive crisis at home; divided by our age, by our beliefs, by the color of our skins. . . . But for my part, I do not believe these disagreements are as great as the principles which unite us. . . . History has placed us all, Northerner and Southerner, black and white, within a common border and under a common law. All of us, from the wealthiest and most powerful of men, to the weakest and hungriest of children, share one precious possession: The name American."

The message drew cheers in the heart of Alabama, and there were those who thought that Kennedy and Wallace were now in a battle for the conscience of the country. If that was the case, the contest ended on June 4, when Kennedy was shot after winning the California Democratic primary. After he died on June 6, 1968, a Mobile songwriter named Dick Holler, a young white man, wrote a tribute to Kennedy and the other great martyrs—a simple, heart-rending anthem of grief called "Abraham, Martin, and John." From the very beginning, music had played a critical role in the movement, and now it seemed to be the epitaph.

Didn't they try to find some good for you and me?

And yet there was nothing to do but press ahead. There were elections to win in the Alabama Black Belt, and voters to register all over the South, and at the University of Alabama, there was also a lawsuit—a dispute that might have seemed trivial on the surface, except for the symbolism of the issue. The Afro-American Association at the school, represented by U. W. Clemon, a Birmingham civil rights attorney, filed a federal lawsuit against the legendary football coach Paul "Bear" Bryant. As the decade of the '60s drew to a close, Bryant's teams had no black players at all, remaining, in a sense, the last visible and celebrated bastion of whiteness.

For the university's black students, that statement of exclusion had to be offensive, and Clemon was happy to take their case. Now twenty-seven, he had been a student activist himself just a few years before, a leader at Miles College in the battle against the Birmingham establishment. He didn't know what to expect from Bryant, but the coach was gracious when Clemon came by to take his deposition. He made his excuses about recruiting a black player here and there, only to lose him to other schools in the region, and promised to try to do better in the future. Clemon decided to give him a chance, and agreed to postpone a hearing in the case until late in the spring of 1971. If there was any doubt about Bryant's good faith, it vanished in the fall of 1970 when Alabama played Southern California in Birmingham, and lost 42–21, mostly because of the opponent's black players.

"There was no problem with black recruitment after that," remembered Clemon. "Coach Bryant never acknowledged it to me in so many words, but I think he appreciated the fact that our lawsuit was filed. I never thought he was prejudiced. He never seemed that way. But I believe he felt, initially, he would have to sacrifice some of his immense popularity among Alabama whites if he voluntarily integrated his team."

Whatever the intricacies of Bryant's motivations, Alabama football reached its greatest heights in the 1970s. With the team integrated, Bryant coached Alabama to three national championships and an astonishing record of 107–13 in the decade beginning in 1971. And there was something else as well. In a time when black athletes across the country were protesting unfair treatment at the hands of their coaches, there were no such complaints at Alabama, but rather a consistent affirmation from the players that the coach was color-blind.

And so it was that Alabama's last public symbol of segregation became, in the end, the symbol of its opposite. When Bryant retired from coaching in 1982 and died of a heart attack a few weeks later, U. W. Clemon led the chorus of sadness. "At a time when Alabama's stature in the eyes of the nation was at an all-time low," Clemon said, "he was one person— probably *the* one person—all Alabamians could feel good about."

In the same decade, a friend of Bryant's, a University of Alabama graduate named William Baxley, was addressing another piece of unfinished business—an issue this time much grimmer than football. Baxley was a student in 1963 when the Sixteenth Street Baptist Church was bombed, and he made a vow at his fraternity house that he would one day track down the bombers. In 1970 he was elected attorney general of Alabama, and he set out immediately to make good on his pledge.

Baxley was part of the generation of converts, the son of an aristocratic family from Dothan, his father a judge, his grandfather the mayor. By 1970 there were many others like him in the state of Alabama—young white people who were touched by the power of the civil rights movement. They believed in the justice that lay at the heart of it, and were troubled by the tragedy and turmoil around it. Baxley made no secret of his liberal opinions. At the age of twenty-eight, he was an ambitious man who wanted to be governor, but his ego told him he could do it his way. He wore his dark hair fashionably long, and in his Montgomery office there was a framed photograph of U.S. district judge Frank Johnson, the archenemy of Wallace, flanked by a bust of Abraham Lincoln.

As soon as he took the oath of office, Baxley hired black lawyers to work on his staff and set an activist agenda for his term—among other things, blocking oil companies who wanted drilling rights to Mobile Bay. But he made it clear from the start that nothing was more important than the church bombing. He wrote the names of the four little girls on his telephone calling card issued by the state, a place he knew he would see them every day, and he assembled a team to investigate the case. Their first suspect was J. B. Stoner, always a prime candidate in the solution of hate crimes. Stoner was a leader in the National States Rights Party, a man who wanted to ship all blacks to Africa and who worried that Hitler was soft on the Jews. Everybody knew that Stoner was violent, but in the case of the church the trail went cold. From the very beginning, the primary suspicion had focused on the Klan, particularly a violent fringe from the Eastview Klavern, and Baxley knew that the FBI had interviewed some potential suspects. The problem was, the federal agency under J. Edgar Hoover refused to cooperate with the state or to allow the attorney general's new team any access to the FBI files.

For most of his first term in office, Baxley badgered and pleaded and cajoled, but even with the death of Hoover in 1972, the agency was perversely unwilling to help. Nobody could say whether it was simply a territorial imperative or something more sinister, but Baxley knew he needed the files to help jumpstart his own investigation. Finally, he went to a journalist in Washington, Jack Nelson, a native Alabamian who worked in the capital for the *Los Angeles Times.* After hearing Baxley's story, Nelson went to U.S. attorney general, Edward Levi, and threatened to write a story about the FBI blocking the investigation of the bombing. A few days later the FBI began turning over files. Much of the information was useless; in some cases, the names of potential witnesses had been blacked out. But the bureau provided an office in Birmingham for one of Baxley's investigators, Bob Eddy, and over time the level of cooperation increased.

It would take more than six years to finally break the case, but the turning point came in 1977, when Eddy once again was searching through the files. He came to a statement by Elizabeth Hood, a niece of Robert Chambliss, one of Birmingham's most notorious Klansmen. Eddy, at first, could hardly believe it. On October 11, 1963, Ms. Hood, an attractive, sandy-haired woman in her twenties, told the FBI of a conversation with her uncle. She said on the morning of September 14, the day before the bombing, Chambliss was railing about his hatred for blacks and offered a self-incriminating boast: "You wait until after Sunday; they will beg us to let them segregate." On other occasions, according to Hood, he had said many times, "We ought to blow that church up." And when the TV reported the killing of the children, Chambliss declared with some agitation, "It was supposed to have gone off earlier."

All of it was there in the files, and there was more—an interview with a black woman from Detroit, Kirthus Glenn, who was visiting Birmingham in 1963 and passed by the church early on the morning of September 15. She saw three white men sitting in a car, parked in the shadows on Seventh Avenue, just a block or so north of the building. From pictures shown her by the FBI, she identified one of the men as Robert Chambliss.

Eddy was astonished. These were the building blocks for an indictment, and in the altered racial climate of the 1970s, the testimony of these two women might even be enough for a conviction. But would they tell their stories under oath? Would they risk the wrath of the Ku Klux Klan and this violent man who already had the blood of children on his hands? Eddy wasn't sure, but his boss, Bill Baxley, was not a man to take no for an answer. When Mrs. Glenn was reluctant, the attorney general flew to Detroit with the distinguished civil rights attorney Fred Gray, and together they persuaded her to testify. Elizabeth Hood was a much harder sell. Recently married, she was now the Reverend Elizabeth Cobbs, a Methodist minister in Birmingham who understood her moral obligation to the case. But she told Bob Eddy she wasn't sure she could do it.

"I'm really afraid for my life," she said.

She knew Robert Chambliss, had personally witnessed the ferocity of his temper and the depth of his hatred, and she had no doubt about his urge for revenge. Nevertheless, she eventually agreed to testify as well, and on November 14, 1977, Robert Chambliss went on trial. Baxley wasn't sure what to expect. Two months earlier, according to the accounts of journalist Frank Sikora, he had called Chris McNair, whose daughter, Denise, had been killed at the church. McNair in 1977 was a newly elected member of the Alabama legislature, a widely respected, level-headed man, whose opinion Baxley valued. The attorney general confided to McNair that the case against Chambliss was mostly circumstantial and could easily be lost.

"The next attorney general," he said, "may be able to get a stronger case and win it. But if we go ahead now and lose it, it'll be gone and over for-ever."

"I want you to go ahead," said McNair, "because once you leave office, no one will ever try."

"That's what I need to know," said Baxley.

When the trial began, the testimony at times was intense. John Cross, the soft-spoken senior pastor at the church, recounted again the horror of the bombing and his own desperate search for the bodies in the rubble. Chris McNair recalled his last conversation with his daughter, and Sarah Collins, who was also seriously injured in the blast, remembered her sis-ter Addie Mae tying the sash on Denise McNair's dress only seconds before the bomb went off. But the most damaging testimony came from Cobbs, who presented a portrait of her uncle Robert Chambliss as a vio-lent racist who talked authoritatively about the bombing—both before and after it happened.

The jury of nine whites and three blacks began deliberations on November 17, Denise McNair's birthday, and on the following morning reached a verdict of guilty. Still protesting his innocence, Chambliss was sentenced to life in prison, and according to one cellmate he went to bed every night asking God never to forgive Bill Baxley.

Baxley, for his part, knew there were others involved in the bombing, and he even thought he knew who they were. In a memo written in 1965 the FBI named four men as the primary suspects— Chambliss, of course, and three of his friends from the Eastview Klavern: Tommy Blanton, Bobby Frank Cherry, and Herman Cash. But as Baxley was leaving office in 1978, he concluded reluctantly that there was not enough evidence to convict the other three. He wondered if their day would ever come.

Some twenty years later he was happy to learn that U.S. Attorney Doug Jones, a Birmingham native who was nine years old at the time of the bombing, had reopened the case. In 1963 when it happened, Jones didn't pay a lot of attention to the crime. He was only a boy, and his mind, he said, was on other things—whether the New York Yankees would make it to the World Series, whether Bear Bryant and his football team would win another in a line of national championships. But then in 1977, when Jones was in law school at the University of Alabama, he read about Baxley and his prosecution of Chambliss, and took a week off to attend the trial.

In 2001, as he prepared to go to trial himself, this time against Thomas Blanton, Jones was deeply worried about the outcome. He knew his case was mostly circumstantial, much as the case against Chambliss had been, and it was hard to be certain what a jury would do. But he had discovered a couple of bone-chilling tapes hidden deep in the files of the FBI—surveillance audios made by the agency, in which Blanton had made reference to constructing a bomb, and had laughed about the bombing of the Birmingham church. The tapes were at the heart of an emotional case, and in a "trial of atonement," as one scholar put it, they were enough for the jury. On May 1, 2001, Blanton was convicted and sentenced, at the age of sixty-one, to spend the rest of his life in prison.

Bill Baxley was happy when he learned of the outcome, but "livid" also with the FBI. The agency had never told him of the tapes, despite all the years he had "requested, demanded and begged," seeking the evidence he needed in the case. In the intervening years, Blanton, Herman Cash, and Bobby Frank Cherry had been free to live their unrepentant lives. Cash had died in 1994, having never been prosecuted for the crime, and "for more than two decades," Baxley wrote in an article for the *New York Times,* "Mr. Blanton and Mr. Cherry evaded indictment and prosecution because the FBI held back these recordings."

The agency insisted it was not deliberate, but for many of the veterans of the civil rights movement, who had learned the details of J. Edgar Hoover's opposition to the cause—his buggings and wiretaps of Martin Luther King, his frenzied conviction that King was a communist—the agency's bland and dismissive denials had the ring of a lie. Whatever the truth, the pursuit of justice didn't end until 2002, when Bobby Frank Cherry was convicted of the crime. He was convicted primarily on the basis of his boasts, repeated many times to his family and his friends, that he had been the one who had actually carried the bomb, concealing it carefully against the wall of the church.

For the families of the victims, there wasn't any sense of closure or elation as the tired, gaunt, and bewildered former Klansman was led away in handcuffs to spend the rest of his life in a prison. "Closure is just a word," said Alpha Robertson, whose daughter, Carole, was one of those killed. "I have often wondered why they associate that word with this affair."

But Fred Shuttlesworth, the old warhorse, said there was value in the verdict, even after the passage of so many years. "Thank God," he said, when the trial finally ended. "Today, you can say Birmingham is rising out of the dust."

There were those who said it had already risen. Claude Wesley, whose daughter, Cynthia, was another of the victims, told a reporter in 1977 that Birmingham was different from the way it had been. "The '60s emancipated Birmingham," he said. "Birmingham is now a good town. It wanted to be a good town then, but it was in the grip of the wrong political hands. But I think everybody knew the South couldn't stay the way it was. Change was going to come, and white people make me feel they are just as proud as we are to get rid of this burden."

As Wesley looked around, the signs of the change seemed to be everywhere. David Vann, one of the city's white liberals who had opposed Bull Connor in 1963, was now the mayor, and he would soon be succeeded by Richard Arrington, the first black mayor of Alabama's largest city. Chris McNair was in the state legislature, and within a few weeks of Wesley's interview, a predominantly white jury would convict Robert Chambliss. Only a few years earlier, all these things would have been inconceivable.

But if Birmingham was different, there were other communities where the story was more troubling. Mobile, for example, known for its moderation in the 1950s, was becoming polarized by the 1970s. One of the first public signs of the city's regression came in 1967 when the home of John LeFlore was bombed. Since the 1920s LeFlore had waged his personal war on segregation, patient, relentless, though he seldom seemed angry. He worked most nights on an old typewriter that he kept in the dining room, writing letters or complaints, pounding away until two or three in the morning. On the night of June 28, he finished a little early, sometime around one, and started for bed. There was a window behind the chair where he sat, and that was where the dynamite exploded, turning the side of his house into rubble. LeFlore was in his bedroom, and suffered a cut over his left eye, but nothing more. His wife, Teah, the rock of the family, was shaken, but unhurt.

Mobile mayor Arthur Outlaw immediately posted a reward for information leading to the capture of the bombers, and as the police began to investigate the crime, there were reports of a black man running from the scene. Nobody could say if he had planted the bomb, but everybody knew in the summer of 1967 that it was not beyond the realm of possibility. By the late 1960s LeFlore and Mobile's other civil rights veterans, including R. W. Gilliard, the tough-minded leader of the NAACP, were the objects of scorn by a new group of militants.

In June 1966 a group of maybe fifteen people met at the home of David Jacobs, an articulate, light-skinned Mobile native, a schoolteacher by trade, who was increasingly influenced by the Black Power movement. There was always a subtlety about Jacobs's views. As far as the people who knew him could tell, he had no animosity toward white people, and in 1966, when he helped to start a new organization, the Neighborhood Organized Workers (NOW), its emblem was a black hand clasping a white one. But Jacobs and others who were drawn to the group were impatient with the leadership of LeFlore and his white ally, Joseph Langan, a city commissioner who was widely regarded as one of the leading white liberals in the state.

Ever since the 1940s LeFlore and Langan had worked together on a variety of causes—securing equal pay for black teachers, ending segregation on the Mobile buses, trying to get black people registered to vote. In the 1940s Langan had persuaded Gov. Jim Folsom to appoint a like-minded man, E. J. Gonzalez, to the Mobile Board of Election Registrars, and by 1963, two years before the voting rights movement came to Alabama, there were eleven thousand blacks on the rolls in Mobile.

Despite those gains, as the 1960s drew to a close Mobile's government was still all-white; a third of the city's housing was substandard; and poverty in parts of the community was so extreme that blacks were living on the garbage at the dump. Jacobs and his successor as president of NOW, Noble Beasley, a nightclub owner, were convinced that Langan and LeFlore were to blame. The two racial moderates had managed to achieve just enough through the years to create a pervasive illusion of progress and to prevent the development of a mass movement in the city.

By 1968 NOW was holding mass meetings every week, spirited gatherings attended by two to three hundred people, where the rhetoric was militant but rarely antiwhite. There were whites, in fact, who came to every meeting, particularly the priests and nuns from the Most Pure Heart of Mary, a Catholic mission in the Mobile ghetto. Noble Beasley, a massive man of more than three hundred pounds, had a reputation for violence that struck fear in the hearts of the Mobile establishment, but he could be an affable person in private—solicitous, even, toward whites who were sympathetic to the cause.

In his public pronouncements, however, he was sounding more and more like a revolutionary. On many occasions, he borrowed directly from Stokely Carmichael, a man he admired, promising to use "any means necessary" to bring about change, and to "turn Mobile upside down until black folks finally get some justice."

By 1969 firebombings were common on the streets of Mobile; there were ninety-six in that year alone, and many of the targets were white-owned businesses accused of discrimination in hiring. Despite persistent rumors in the city, NOW denied responsibility for the bombings, including the attack on John LeFlore, and even many people who came to the meetings could never be sure if they were part of a nonviolent movement of the masses or the respectable cover for revolutionary violence. Whatever the truth, it was clear that NOW had amassed a large following, giving voice to an anger that was there all along, and in the process, it had stripped the veneer of Mobile's civility.

In 1969, under the leadership of Beasley, NOW decided to break the power of LeFlore. The opportunity came in the city elections, when Joe Langan was running for reelection. His opponent was Joe Bailey, a conservative Democrat who, among other things, ran ads with pictures of Langan and LeFlore, and a caption that read: "Will you let this pair run your city for another four years?"

To LeFlore the choice could not have been clearer, but NOW urged blacks to stay away from the polls, partly as a repudiation of LeFlore and partly to deliver a message to Langan that he had delivered too little too late. With a reduced turnout, Joe Bailey won—a deliberate race-baiter who owed his victory to the Black Power movement. Such was the state of things in Mobile.

As the city was moving toward the end of the decade, a new white militancy was on the rise also, a more open expression of racial animosity than the community had seen since the 1940s. An organization called STAND (Stand Together and Never Divide) was battling a new plan for school desegregation, and at some of the campuses in Mobile County, PTA meetings began to sound like Klan rallies. In the town of Tanner Williams, the assignment of two black teachers to the school prompted a protest rally with signs that read: GET RID OF THE NIGGERS, and at another meeting at a local high school, a group of angry whites, some of them armed, threatened a Mobile reporter whose beat was civil rights.

As the mood of the city grew uglier, there were no white voices any longer to oppose it, and with the black community divided, Mobile was entering a decade of hate—a racial backlash compounded by economic hard times. Late in his term, President Johnson announced the closing of Brookley Air Force Base, a cornerstone of the Mobile economy, and the cloud that hovered over the city's frame of mind lasted well into the 1980s. Part of the drama played out in the schools, where racial fighting forced high schools to close, and school board meetings offered frightening proof that attitudes were getting harder by the day.

At one of those meetings in 1969, a white segregationist addressed the board, defending white teachers in the Mobile schools who called their black students "niggers," occasionally as a noun of direct address. When the segregationist had finished, the school board chairman told him politely, "Mr. Westbrook, we feel like you are our conscience, and we hope you will continue to prod us." About the same time, a historian at the University of South Alabama offered a critique of a textbook used in the schools, which depicted slaves singing happily for their masters and showing "bright rows of white teeth." The same board chairman dismissed him curtly, and in the public outcry that followed the critique, some people wondered if the professor was a Communist.

It was a way of thinking that had once been familiar, and if it was beginning to recede in many other places, in the city of Mobile it was getting worse. There was a glimmer of progress in 1972, when a black attorney named A. J. Cooper was elected mayor of Prichard, a working-class community adjacent to Mobile. Cooper, a supporter of the civil rights movement, joined Tuskegee mayor Johnny Ford in the growing ranks of black elected officials. But in Mobile itself, the city government remained all white, and some people were determined to keep it that way.

There was a public outcry in 1975 when a group of blacks led by civil rights activist Wiley Bolden challenged the at-large form of local government—three commissioners elected citywide—as being discriminatory against blacks. The case made its way to the docket of U.S. district judge Virgil Pittman, a smallish, balding man with dark-rimmed glasses, whose judicial sensibilities were similar to those of Judge Frank Johnson. In his ruling of October 21, 1976, Judge Pittman took note of Mobile's racial polarization and ordered a new mayor-council form of city government, with nine council members elected from districts. Only then, said the judge, could blacks be assured of a place at the table in a city where their interests were trampled roughshod.

"The sad history of lynch mobs, racial discrimination and violence raises specters and fears of legal and social injustice in the minds of blacks," Pittman wrote, and he said it was time for that history to end.

The Mobile newspapers denounced his ruling, and a white citizens' group, the Constitutional Crisis Committee, bought a half-page ad with a banner headline, "Impeach! Appeal! Arrest!" Among other things, the CCC drew up a grassroots petition for Pittman's impeachment, and Mobile mayor Lambert Mims promised to sign it at the next regular meeting of the city commission.

Despite the denunciations of the judge, events in the city would soon make it clear that his view of history was not overstated. Two episodes stood out from the rest. On March 28, 1976, Mobile police were called to a downtown fast-food restaurant where two black men were acting suspiciously. Police arrested one of the men, but the other, twenty-seven-year-old Glenn Diamond, ran from the restaurant and hid in the crawl space under a house. Eight police officers found him there, handcuffed him, and tied a hangman's noose around his neck. They looped the rope across the limb of a tree and threatened to lynch him unless he confessed to his part in an earlier armed robbery.

There was a cry of revulsion, led by the NAACP, and a spirited defense of the police, led by the Klan, and eight police officers were suspended from their jobs. But the episode, outrageous as it was, paled in comparison to the one that followed. The case of Glenn Diamond was only a mock lynching. The real thing happened in 1981.

Michael Donald, who was only nineteen, was on his way to the store when a group of Klansmen kidnapped him at random. They cut his throat and hung his mutilated body from a tree—a ritualized murder reminiscent of those that were a commonplace occurrence a half century earlier. Eventually, four Klansmen were convicted of the crime, and the Southern Poverty Law Center, based in Montgomery, filed suit against the Klan on behalf of Beulah Mae Donald, the grief-stricken mother of the teenage victim. In 1987 the center won a judgment of $7 million, bankrupting the United Klans of America, the umbrella alliance of Klan organizations that had beaten the freedom riders, bombed the Sixteenth Street Baptist Church, and murdered Viola Liuzzo outside of Selma.

In the time of atonement for the murder of Michael Donald, the city of Mobile managed to pull itself back from the abyss. In 1985, in a settlement of the lawsuit that had languished in a tangled mass of appeals, Mobile adopted a new form of government—a mayor-council system with a formula for district representation that virtually assured an interracial government. By the end of the century, its reputation for racial moderation was restored. But there were still a few who remembered those earlier years when Mobile had stood as a symbol of the backlash—that ugly counterforce set free, ironically, by the civil rights movement.

Fortunately, there were other communities in the state—Birmingham, Huntsville, little hamlets in the Black Belt—where the measures of progress were concrete and undeniable. Whatever the difficulties that remained, as Alabama moved toward a period of calm, the evidence overall seemed to be overwhelming. Nothing would ever be the same as it had been.

Epilogue

WHAT, IN THE END, DID IT all mean, this heroic moment in the history of the country? Amid all the symbols of backlash and progress, what were the incontrovertible accomplishments?

For many of the people caught up in those times, the answers to both those questions were subtle. Stokely Carmichael, in his book *Black Power*, wrote of the existential revolution, the redefinition of what it meant to be alive, when black people refused to accept segregation or the right of white people to keep them from voting. As Martin Luther King often put it in his speeches, this was a period of psychological triumph, when black citizens decided to straighten their backs—"and a man can't ride your back unless it's bent."

On that critical level, especially in places like the Alabama Black Belt, the movement lasted longer than many of its chroniclers and commentators acknowledged. Long after the nation had tired of the story and the demonstrations ceased to make national headlines, the black citizens of

Alabama—and those in other places in the South—continued to fight every day for their freedom. Gradually, they discovered that they were not alone, for there were white people, too, who shared in the Negro's sense of liberation.

In Lowndes County, Alabama, the white-haired probate judge Harrell Hammonds told a reporter in the 1970s that he now felt freer to be who he was. Hammonds had always been a wealthy man, the owner of some twenty thousand acres of land, where he raised his cattle and cotton through the years, and became an aristocratic politician. Some black people said he was a paternalist, less prejudiced perhaps than some of his neighbors, but a craggy-faced pillar of the segregated order. But Hammonds was also a racial moderate, who argued that blacks and whites should be treated equally in a court of law and later supported black representation on the board of education.

Because of those stands, mild as they may have appeared on the surface, Hammonds paid a price. In the racially charged atmosphere of Lowndes County, there were threats on his life, and his cattle were poisoned, and there was a mysterious fire one day at his home. But the 1970s brought a measure of relief, and he thought it was something that many people shared. "Even in the bad times," he said, "there were people who wanted to do what was right, but they were afraid or they didn't know where to start. I think most people will tell you the changes had to come. They were long overdue."

Hammonds was not alone in feeling that way. With the eventual demise of the segregated order and the creation of a fledgling interracial democracy, there was also a change in public attitudes. Among blacks and whites, there was a new and pervasive assumption of equality. It was not always acted upon or honored, but it was now the norm and not the radical exception—a contagious idea in every corner of society.

In Escambia County on the Florida line, there was a community of Creek Indians, tiny and impoverished, the last remaining band in the Alabama forests of what had once been a powerful Indian confederacy. Inspired in part by the civil rights movement, the Creeks reasserted their identity in the 1960s, laying claim to the land that had been taken from them and demanding to be recognized as a tribe. They had lived in a hovel of rundown houses, working as loggers, sharecroppers, or migrants—whatever they could find to do with their hands. Twenty years later the changes were stunning—new houses, paved roads, a feeling of Indian identity and pride—and as one of them told an Alabama reporter, if they had any doubts about whether they could make it, all they had to do was look at the blacks.

For John Lewis, everywhere he turned in the American South, and certainly in his own home state of Alabama, he thought he saw "a greater sense of hope" than he sometimes found in other parts of the country, a widespread belief that things could really change. People in the region had come so far, partly because they had so far to come. Lewis himself was part of that final generation of Negro citizens who were born to an expectation of fear—a fear of violence without any cause, of catastrophic retribution at the hands of whites for even the most minor and unintended offense. They didn't have to live that way anymore, and in Lewis's mind it was not a change to be taken lightly.

But he thought he saw a change in white people too. One day in 1979 George Wallace asked to see him in Montgomery, and it became the first of several conversations in which the governor of Alabama asked to be forgiven. "It was," said Lewis, "almost like someone confessing to a priest." C. T. Vivian had the same experience, and the former voting rights activist, like John Lewis, thought the governor's confessions came from his heart. Wallace, by then, was partly paralyzed and often in pain—the victim of a bullet from a would-be assassin during his presidential run in 1972. Lewis and Vivian believed it had changed him, made him more empathetic to the suffering in the world.

Not everybody accepted that view. There were reporters who had covered Wallace through the years who thought he was merely auditioning for heaven, making his peace with almighty God or at the very least with the tens of thousands of black voters in his state. But in a way, it didn't matter if the cynics were right, for that was also a measure of the change. Wallace had built his career on fear, teaching his followers to think in code, ennobling their insecurities and prejudice, and creating an ideology of rage. But in the latter stages of his life, he found no grist for his ambition there, and that, too, said something about the state of the world.

That, at least, was the view of John Lewis, who would soon become a politician of national standing himself. In 1986 he was elected to Congress from a district in Atlanta, and he became in the course of the next decade one of the most respected members of the House. He was still a champion of the country's underdogs, but he seemed to go about his business with hope, an optimism rooted in his memories of the movement.

Both as a writer and a son of the South, I'm inclined to share John Lewis's perspective. I remember my interview with John Patterson, a far less emotional encounter for sure than those that Lewis had with George Wallace. Nevertheless, it was a moment that I won't soon forget—the former governor, who had become a distinguished Alabama judge, sitting ramrod straight at his desk in Montgomery, speaking with dignity and unexpected candor about the most painful moment in his political career. He was eighty years old, but still full of vigor, chatting pleasantly at the start of our talk about the cattle farm in Tallapoosa County that he still worked himself.

He could have spent his whole life as a gentleman farmer, doing law on the side, or maybe it might have been the other way around. But politics beckoned with the death of his father, and almost immediately the preeminent issue of his day was segregation. I asked him how it felt years later, knowing his own progressive instincts, to have found himself on the wrong side of history.

"We were victims of circumstances," he said. "Only history can judge."

Yes, I said, but that's not what I asked. We already know about the judgments of history. But what do you think? What sort of regrets, if any, do you feel when you stare at yourself in the mirror every morning?

Patterson, as I already understood clearly, was one of those proud and dignified men who are not much given to public hand-wringing. But the question seemed to strike him as a fair one to ask, and he began to talk about the things he could have done. After his election in 1958, he could have worked to create a color-blind democracy, "bringing blacks into the political process." But his ambition had turned him away from that chance, and it was, he said, "one of my big regrets."

I thought there was a genuine sadness in his voice—not only for that personal blemish on his record but for the crippling, inescapable realities of history, for a time that never should have been the way it was.

I left his office on that warm summer day and headed toward Selma, driving west through the rolling hills of Lowndes County. I remembered an earlier visit to that place, an afternoon in 1966 when I was coming home from college and stopped for gas in the town of Fort Deposit. I guess I knew it was a stronghold of the Klan, but I wasn't really thinking about it at the time as I pulled in beside a small general store.

As I remembered it later, after I pumped the gas and went in to pay, there was a young black girl, maybe twelve years old, waiting at the counter. She presented a candy bar to the clerk, a gruff and red-faced man who scowled down at her and demanded her money. Timidly, she laid a quarter next to the candy, matching precisely the price on the wrapper, but the clerk quite clearly was not satisfied.

"What the hell is this?" he demanded.

"It's a quarter, suh," the little girl answered.

"What about the tax?" the white man hissed. "Are you too ignorant to know, too stupid to know, that you have to pay taxes in the state of Alabama?"

By the end of the sentence, he was beginning to shout, and the little girl trembled in bewilderment and fright. The other customers in the store, all of them white, went about their business, as if the transaction at the counter were routine, and maybe it was, for it was part of the casual cruelty of the times—the browbeating of a child for the sake of a penny that she owed in taxes. I had lived in Alabama long enough to know that the situation was not only silly but dangerous. If I chose to intervene— and there really didn't seem to be any way around it—I would have to do it carefully. So I smiled at the clerk, and looked him in the eyes, and laid a penny on the counter beside the little girl's candy.

Now the people in the store paid attention. Every sound dried up, the muffled conversation, the shuffle of the feet, as they contemplated the intervention of a stranger—as basic and unspectacular as it was, the defense of a Negro against the provocations of a white man. As a few of the men began to move in closer, I smiled once again at the red-faced clerk and told him simply, "No use gettin' upset about a penny."

He seemed surprised by the Alabama accent, and in his moment of brief hesitation, I handed the candy bar to the girl and told her gently that her family was waiting for her outside.

With that, it was over—a little bit of residual grumbling perhaps, as I paid for the gas and headed back to the car, contemplating, on a level more personal than I had felt it before, the fundamental flaw in the southern way of life.

Thirty-five years later, of course, it was different. Everywhere I went in the rural counties of central Alabama, once the fiercest battlegrounds of resistance, there was an unblemished courtesy in the casual encounters between black and white. As basic as it sounds, for those old enough to remember how it was, that is not a small piece of change.

And yet that is only one side of the story. All across the country in the beginning years of the twenty-first century, there were people black and white who were far less sanguine, who found themselves caught in a nagging ambivalence, even a feeling of disappointment, about all the things that hadn't really changed. For the veterans of the civil rights movement especially, their hopes at the start had been so high, the promise of the movement so noble and vast. But a generation later, there were still the old patterns of poverty and prejudice, which numbed and crippled people's lives every day.

Cynthia Wilson certainly thought that was true. In February 2002 she was living in Montgomery in a public housing project, Apartment 634 in Cleveland Courts, a sprawling expanse of red brick buildings constructed sometime in the 1940s. Her own apartment was a cornerstone of history—the dwelling place of Rosa Parks on that December day in 1955 when she boarded a bus and was arrested for failing to give up her seat.

Cynthia Wilson, who came of age in the 1960s, had told the story of Rosa Parks to her son, Deon, a seventh-grader in 2002, and she was happy to learn that her apartment building in Cleveland Courts had been named to the National Register of Historic Places. But on a gray and chilly February day, when a reporter came by to ask her about it, she wanted to talk more about the present than history. In a memorial more fitting than a marker on the wall, Wilson herself was a modern-day activist—head of the residents' association at Cleveland Courts, a woman who had given her time to the fray, raising the issues that mattered in the lives of her neighbors.

One of those, ironically, was poor bus service in an area where most people don't own cars.

"If you want to make her a hero," Wilson said of Rosa Parks, "get us some decent public transportation. The bus boycott took place. There are no buses. We shouldn't have to feel so trapped."

In the testimony of people like Wilson, the picture emerges of a never-ending struggle, a society that never quite seems to get it right. "In the twenty-first century," says Fred Shuttlesworth, "we're still dropping nineteenth-century baggage." Part of the problem, Shuttlesworth argues, is the same old gulf of misunderstanding, a difference in perception between black and white, which could have been eased by a little more resolve from the leaders in the movement. After Selma, he said, he tried to get Martin Luther King to understand that the next great push needed to be in the schools—a commitment to desegregation nationwide so the next generation would come to understand, "We are one human family under the fatherhood of God."

But the push on a massive scale never happened, and over time the courts turned away from the issue, and the coming generations, Shuttlesworth said, will have to find other paths to racial understanding.

"But all in God's own time," he concluded.

In 1998 Shuttlesworth was one of the keynote speakers at a Birmingham conference of civil rights leaders, some of them veterans of the movement in the '60s, others who barely remembered those times. They came in search of a new agenda for reform, and in the areas of education, health care, housing, and employment, the group saw a wide variety of problems, most of them with racial overtones. But after three days of spirited discussion, they were forced to concede: "Adopting a new regional strategy eluded us."

For Charles Hamilton, a political scientist from Columbia University, none of this is surprising. It is in the nature of history and political change that the story never ends, and there are times when the issues are clearer than others. Hamilton, who wrote *Black Power* with Stokely Carmichael, concluded in a new edition of the book that the gains from the civil rights movement were undeniable.

"Black people are able to vote," he wrote, "in places where this privilege was previously denied." As a result, blacks by the thousands had been elected to office, including one southern governor and many members of Congress, and in the great upsurge that began with the movement, there were corporate and professional opportunities opening up that African Americans could only have dreamed of before. And yet, said Hamilton, everywhere in the country there were the worsening problems of bad housing, poor health, and violent crime, and there were black children falling through the cracks in the schools.

In the closing years of the twentieth century, as urban poverty became intertwined with a culture of criminality and drugs, those same maladies were seeping from the cities to the rural countryside in the South. "Problems like drugs are everywhere," said William Branch, the civil rights leader in Greene County, Alabama.

On a late spring morning in 2001, Charles Hamilton settled back with a visitor at his home and talked about these things—the complicated, bittersweet legacy of the movement. He was a handsome, dark-skinned man, recently retired from his post at Columbia, but still active in his studies, preparing for a summer of research in South Africa. The shelves in his den were filled with his books, and over near the wall was a precious artifact—a small wooden podium taken from a church outside of Tuskegee, where Booker T. Washington had often made his speeches. To his visitor it was an unexpected possession, for here was Hamilton, a Black Power advocate, paying homage to the apostle of incremental freedom.

But for Hamilton it was part of a larger understanding—that the struggle for justice goes back into time, and it is the duty and opportunity of each generation to seek perspective, not perfection, from the people in the trenches. Hamilton himself spent a little time there—a scholar-participant who taught at Tuskegee and went to Lowndes County for the Black Panther elections. He experienced the tension of it firsthand, squaring off verbally with a white poll worker who hated the invasion of people like himself. "We have a right to be here," Hamilton insisted, and as the confrontation became more heated, Stokely Carmichael stepped in to pull him away.

"Doctor, Doctor," he said with a smile, sensing that this was not Hamilton's turf, "we better get you out of here."

From the visceral reality of his personal experience, and from his scholar's understanding of the broad view of history, Hamilton came to his assessment of the civil rights era. In a sense, he thought, it came down to this: The war for human freedom, which had its roots in the past, would continue its ebb and flow for generations. But important battles were won in the movement, and there was no reason not to celebrate the triumphs.

Whatever the difficulties that remained, there was a heroism at the heart of the story. It was not a time, he said, that should ever be forgotten.

Notes and Acknowledgments

IN A SENSE, I'VE BEEN WRITING this book for most of my life. I came of age during the civil rights era in Alabama, and the issue became the primary political and moral reference point for many of the people of my generation. I began my career covering civil rights for the *Mobile Press Register*, moved from there to the *Race Relations Reporter* magazine, and then covered the landmark school busing case in Charlotte, North Carolina, for the once-distinguished newspaper in that city, the *Charlotte Observer*. I brought all that to bear on the task of writing and researching this book, but honesty compels me to acknowledge that this work is composed primarily of the knowledge and understanding of other people. I read through much of the literature on the subject, primarily those works listed in the bibliography that follows; I made use of primary sources including diaries, letters, and newspaper and magazine articles written at the time; and I did numerous interviews with people who lived the civil rights story.

This book, like the movement it covers, is not merely the story of Martin Luther King and the other great leaders of the era, or even the people of legend such as Rosa Parks. They are a part of the story, but the civil rights movement consisted of thousands of ordinary people caught up bravely in extraordinary times, and I have tried to focus on those people as well. There are many others who could have been included, should have been included, but in the end the roster of heroes is simply too full. There will be other books, and there should be. In the meantime, this book is one attempt to bring the story alive, to give it a face, and it represents a synthesis of knowledge, information, and perspective gleaned from interviews conducted over a two-year period, interwoven with primary and secondary sources.

The notes that follow are intended as an acknowledgment of my debt and gratitude, and as a description of the way the book was put together—of why I have written it the way I have. In the end, I take responsibility for the final product, including the flaws, but whatever strengths the narrative contains would have been impossible without the people and sources listed below.

NOTES

Prologue

I first wrote the story of the arrest of Martin Luther King for a family memoir *Lessons from the Big House*. William Faulkner's quote about the human heart in conflict with itself is taken from Faulkner's acceptance speech for the Nobel Prize for Literature, delivered December 10, 1950. The speech appears in its entirety (as does Dr. King's "I Have a Dream" speech) in *The Craft of Prose* edited by Robert H. Woodward and H. Wendell Smith. Fred Shuttlesworth's quote about Birmingham reaching an accord with its conscience appears in many places, including the biography of Shuttlesworth *A Fire You Can't Put Out* written by Andrew M. Manis (p. 387).

C. Eric Lincoln's powerful anecdote about his attack at the hands of an Alabama white man appears in my book *Southern Voices* (pp. 202–3), and in Lincoln's memoir *Coming through the Fire* (p. 22). His memories of his

Alabama childhood are taken from his memoir and from numerous conversations that he and I had starting sometime early in the 1970s.

The statistics on lynchings in the South and in Alabama were based on those in Joel Williamson's *A Rage for Order* and Charles W. Eagles's *Outside Agitator.* The specific lynching in Lowndes County was described in Eagles (p. 102). The story of the Alabama Constitution of 1901, which provided the legal underpinnings for white supremacy, is told with great clarity in Harvey H. Jackson's essay, "White Supremacy Triumphant, Democracy Undone," which appears in *A Century of Controversy.* The Democratic Party's conclusion that blacks were "incapable of self-government" appears on p. 21, as does the quote from the *Wilcox Progressive.* The cautionary note from former governor William Oates that the "disfranchisement of the whole Negro race would be unjust and unwise" appears on p. 22, as does the *Mobile Register's* assessment of convention president John B. Knox. The quotes from Knox appear on p. 23.

John Egerton offers a compelling portrait of Aubrey Williams, one of Alabama's leading white liberals in the 1930s, in his book *Speak Now against the Day.* Taylor Branch profiles Vernon Johns, Martin Luther King's predecessor at the Dexter Avenue Baptist Church, in his book *Parting the Waters.* The quote from Johns's nationally heralded sermon appears on p. 10 of that book. Johns's personal protest against bus segregation in Montgomery—a harbinger of things to come—appears on p. 14.

Chapter 1

The account of the Montgomery bus boycott was based, in part, on the telling of the story by other writers, including the following: Juan Williams in *Eyes on the Prize;* Taylor Branch in *Parting the Waters;* David Garrow in *Bearing the Cross;* Ralph David Abernathy in his memoir *And the Walls Came Tumbling Down;* David Goldfield in *Black, White, and Southern;* Fred Gray in *Bus Ride to Justice;* Stephen B. Oates in *Let the Trumpet Sound;* Robert Graetz in *A White Preacher's Memoir,* and J. Mills Thornton in his lengthy article "Challenge and Response in the Montgomery Bus Boycott of 1955–56," which appeared in the *Alabama Review.* Thornton's splendid book *Dividing Lines,* which I highly recommend, was not published until after I finished this book.

Occasionally I use the word "Negro" instead of "African American" or "black." Usually the word is in quoted material, but I sometimes use it to give a feeling for the times—when it was, in fact, the polite southern expression for African Americans.

I interviewed a number of people who lived through the Montgomery story or knew the leading characters well. Thanks especially to Thomas Gray, a board member of the Montgomery Improvement Association; Robert and Jeannie Graetz, two of the leading white supporters of the boycott; John Porter, an assistant minister to Dr. Martin Luther King Jr. at Dexter Avenue Baptist Church; Doris Crenshaw, a young friend and protégée of Rosa Parks, who went on to take her own strong and courageous stands for civil rights; three of Alabama's finest reporters, Ray Jenkins, Wayne Greenhaw, and Bob Ingram, who shared their insights into the character and personality of some of the boycott's leaders; and, some years before I began the actual writing of this book, Martin Luther King Sr.

There are slight discrepancies in many of these accounts, but none that are major, and the synthesis contained in these chapters is my own. The description of the first mass meeting at Holt Street Baptist Church is based primarily on the memory of Robert Graetz. The visual descriptions are supplemented by photographs at the Civil Rights Museum in Memphis, Tennessee, and by my own visit to Holt Street Baptist, which at the time of this writing was sadly and tragically in need of repair. The quote, "That audience was on fire . . . on fire for freedom," comes from reporter Joe Azbell of the *Montgomery Advertiser,* who wrote important, early stories about the boycott. The quote appears in extended form in Juan Williams's *Eyes on the Prize* (p. 74). The story of Martin Luther King's self-doubts before his first address at Holt Street Baptist is told in several places, most vividly in Stephen B. Oates's *Let the Trumpet Sound.*

The story of the arrest of Rosa Parks is taken from the accounts of historians Taylor Branch, David Goldfield, Juan Williams, and David Garrow. The quote from the bus driver James Blake differs slightly in the various accounts. The precise wording here is taken from the account by Branch (p. 128). There are a number of stories about Rosa Parks's work with African American young people in Montgomery. The version here is taken primarily from an interview with Doris Crenshaw, a member of the NAACP Youth Council when Mrs. Parks served as the group's adviser. The story of the Highlander Folk School, which Mrs. Parks visited at a critically important moment in her life, is taken from descriptions in David Goldfield's *Black, White, and Southern* and John Egerton's award-winning book *Speak Now against the Day,* as well as my own visits to the school some years ago. The quote from Myles Horton about getting blacks and whites to eat together is taken from Goldfield (p. 96).

The quote from Rosa Parks when the bus driver threatened to have her arrested is taken from Williams, *Eyes on the Prize* (p. 66). Ray Jenkins's description of E. D. Nixon—"He had the bearing of an African prince"— comes from an interview I did with Jenkins, as does the story of their public handshake. The story of the arrest of Claudette Colvin nearly nine months prior to the arrest of Rosa Parks is told in detail by Taylor Branch. The description of the character of Clifford and Virginia Durr is based primarily on the recollection of reporter Wayne Greenhaw, offered in an interview with me. The quote from Rosa Parks agreeing to cooperate with E. D. Nixon's plans to make a test case out of her arrest comes from *Eyes on the Prize* (p. 67).

The story of Jo Ann Robinson's role in the boycott is taken from her book *The Montgomery Bus Boycott and the Women Who Started It* and from David Garrow's *Bearing the Cross.* The quote from Mrs. Robinson about her own ordeal on a Montgomery bus was taken from Garrow (p. 14). The text of her flyer calling for a boycott is contained in Juan Williams's *Eyes on the Prize* (p. 68).

The descriptions of Ralph Abernathy are taken from his memoir, from my own extensive encounters with him, and from interviews with people who knew him, including Andrew Young and the Reverend Thomas Gilmore, a civil rights leader in Greene County, Alabama. It was Gilmore who said, "He was tough as iron." The account of Robert Graetz's decision to support the boycott is taken from an interview with Graetz. The chronology of events on December 5, 1955, the first day of the boycott, is a composite of accounts by Taylor Branch, David Garrow, and J. Mills Thornton. The story of the hiring of Martin Luther King by Dexter Avenue Baptist is taken from an interview with Deacon R. D. Nesbitt. The story is also told by Taylor Branch and David Garrow. John Porter's recollections of King and his character came in an interview with me. Civil rights leader Diane Nash had similar recollections of Dr. King and the humility and calm at the heart of his character. King's quote, "A man can't ride your back unless it's bent," came from the film *Eyes on the Prize*.

Dr. King's landmark speech on December 5 at Holt Street Baptist has been quoted in many places, perhaps most extensively by Taylor Branch.

Chapter 2

The summary of the desegregation protest in Clarendon County, S.C., is based in part on the superb book *Simple Justice* by Richard Kluger. The quote "If they had only given us a bus" was offered by Clarendon County civil rights leader Billie S. Fleming in an interview with me. The story of the original demands of the bus boycott is based on a number of sources, including David Garrow and Ralph Abernathy. The account of the civil rights movement in Mobile, where a seating arrangement on the buses served as a potential model for Montgomery, is based, in part, on interviews with Walker LeFlore and Janet LeFlore, the son and daughter-in-law of civil rights stalwart John LeFlore. I also interviewed Joseph Langan on several occasions and relied on written accounts in the Ph.D. dissertation "The National Association for the Advancement of Colored People in Alabama, 1913–1952" by Dorothy A. Autrey, and the book *Mobile: The Life and Times of a Great Southern City* by Michael Thomason and Melton McLaurin.

The story of the killing of army private Henry Williams on a Mobile bus came from accounts in the *Mobile Register* in August 1942, from Autrey's dissertation, and from Allen Cronenberg's essay "Mobile and World War II, 1940–1945." For the account of the race riots at the Alabama Dry Dock and Shipbuilding Company, I relied on the extensive coverage by the *Mobile Register* in May 1943, and on the account by Dorothy Autrey.

The story of John LeFlore's scuffle on a Mobile streetcar has been told by a number of sources, including Thomason and McLaurin, and in the documentary film *A Quiet Revolution* produced by the Mobile County Public Schools. The details in this account were provided by Janet LeFlore in an interview with me. This, she said, was the way her father-in-law told the story to her.

The story of Joseph Langan's role in the struggle is based primarily on interviews I did with him, starting February 23, 2001. These were supplemented by Bill Sellers's profile in the *Mobile Register,* May 16, 1990, and Roy Hoffman's profile of Langan, which appeared in his book *Back Home*.

There are a number of accounts of the frustrating negotiations between the Montgomery Improvement Association and city officials of Montgomery. I relied primarily on those of David Garrow, Taylor Branch, and Mills Thornton. The quotes by bus company attorney Jack Crenshaw were taken from Thornton (pp. 202–3).

The story of the arrest of Bob Graetz was taken from an interview with Graetz and from Tom Johnson's story in the *Montgomery Advertiser*, January 10, 1956. The story of the arrest of Martin Luther King—and the religious experience that followed it—was taken from accounts by David Garrow and Taylor Branch. The statistics on the growth of the White Citizens Council and the descriptions of its purpose were taken primarily from Thornton and from Juan Williams's *Eyes on the Prize*. The account of the bombing of King's house, including the defiant quote from C. T. Smiley, came primarily from Taylor Branch (pp. 165–66). The quotes from Dr. King came from David Garrow (pp. 60–61).

Thomas Gray's account of his own understanding of the character of King and his commitment to nonviolence came from my interview with Gray. Martin Luther King Sr.'s reminiscence is taken from a story I did for the *Charlotte Observer*, March 19, 1979. His observation that "it's better to be a live dog than a dead lion" was taken from Taylor Branch (p. 167).

Chapter 3

It was Taylor Branch who called the filing of the lawsuit demanding desegregation of the buses "the social equivalent of atomic warfare" (p. 158). Dr. King's quote about compromise was taken from Mills Thornton (p. 220). The story of the lawsuit was taken from Fred Gray's *Bus Ride to Justice*, Frank Sikora's *The Judge*, and Jack Bass's *Unlikely Heroes*. Additional insight into Judge Frank Johnson came from Hal Crowther's profile "The Last Southern Hero" in his book *Cathedrals of Kudzu*. Judge Richard Rives is profiled eloquently by Bass. The dramatic story of the trial comes primarily from Sikora and from transcripts of the case, *Browder vs. Gayle*.

The account of the desegregation of Spring Hill College came from

Charles S. Padgett's article "Without Hysteria or Unnecessary Disturbance." The story of the failed first attempt to desegregate the University of Alabama was taken from the superb account in *The Schoolhouse Door: Segregation's Last Stand at the University of Alabama* by E. Culpepper Clark. In that struggle the black students received steady counsel from the NAACP's Ruby Hurley, a minor character in many published accounts, but a woman who was a tireless advocate for civil rights across the South.

The story of Rosa Parks's second visit to the Highlander Folk School, this time in the company of Bob and Jeannie Graetz, was taken from a series of interviews with Graetz. In those interviews, and in his book *A White Preacher's Memoir* Graetz also told of the bombing of his house.

Chapter 4

The quotes from Martin Luther King at the victory celebration at Holt Street Baptist come from Frank Sikora's *The Judge* (p. 44). (A slightly different quote was used by Garrow.) The exchange between a Montgomery bus driver and King was taken from *Unlikely Heroes* (p. 76). Dr. King's assessment of the meaning of the bus boycott is clear in his book *Stride Toward Freedom*.

The story of Fred Shuttlesworth's meeting with King and the bombing of Shuttlesworth's home in Birmingham was taken from an interview I did with Shuttlesworth. A good chronology of Shuttlesworth's extraordinary life is available in Manis's biography *A Fire You Can't Put Out*. The story of the experiences of Shuttlesworth's secretary, Lola Hendricks, on the Birmingham buses came from a series of interviews with Mrs. Hendricks.

The account of retributions against Aurelia Browder came from Sikora. Reprisals against Judge Richard Rives were detailed by Jack Bass. The story of the bombing of Ralph Abernathy's house came primarily from Abernathy's memoir *And the Walls Came Tumbling Down* (pp. 180–81) The account of the second bombing of Bob Graetz's house came from an interview with Graetz.

The story of John Patterson's rise to political power came from a lengthy interview that I did with Patterson, supplemented by accounts in *Alabama Governors*, Taylor Branch's *Parting the Waters*, and Robert J. Norrell's *Reaping the Whirlwind: The Civil Rights Movement in Tuskegee*. I relied primarily on Norrell for the account of events in Tuskegee, along with Bernard Taper's *Gomillion vs. Lightfoot*. Charles Hamilton, formerly a sociologist at Tuskegee and later coauthor of the book *Black Power*, talked about the character of Charles Gomillion in an interview with me. So did journalist Ray Jenkins. All quotes from Gomillion appeared in *Reaping the Whirlwind*.

The quote from civil rights lawyer J. L. Chestnut about the courtroom demeanor of Judge George Wallace was taken from the documentary film *George Wallace: Settin' the Woods on Fire* produced and directed by Daniel McCabe and Paul Stekler and written by Steve Fayer, McCabe, and Stekler. Wallace's campaign commercial in 1958 also appeared in that film, and so did John Patterson's quote about segregation: "Once you let the bar down, it's all over."

Chapter 5

The story of Bruce Boynton is based on an interview with Boynton and on the U.S. Supreme Court's decision in *Bruce Boynton vs. Commonwealth of Virginia*. The story of Robert Smalls is taken from *Black Men of the Sea* by Michael Cohn and Michael Platzer; from Okon Edet Uya's *From Slavery to Public Service: Robert Smalls, 1839–1915;* and from a research paper on Smalls by Tracy Gaillard. The quote from Robert Smalls comes from an essay by Smalls titled "Election Methods in the South," transcribed by Carolyn Sims of the Department of History at Furman University, appearing in the *North American Review* 151 (pp. 593–600).

The story of John Lewis and his early involvement in the civil rights movement comes from an interview with Lewis (March 2001), from Lewis's autobiography *Walking with the Wind* written with Michael D'Orso, and from David Halberstam's *The Children*. Lewis's quote about raising chickens was taken from a story I wrote for the *Charlotte Observer* in 1988, reprinted in the book *Southern Voices: Profiles and Other Stories* published in 1991. His account of protesting segregation in the Pike County Library comes from *Walking with the Wind*. The description of the personality and character of Lewis's mentor in Nashville, Kelly Miller Smith, comes from *Walking with the Wind, The Children,* and Will Campbell's civil rights memoir *Forty Acres and a Goat*. Campbell's recollections of Kelly Smith's fears and faith regarding his first-grade daughter's desegregation of schools comes from an interview with Campbell (January 2002).

Bernard Lafayette's memories of American Baptist Theological Seminary, which became a cradle of the civil rights movement, and those of C. T. Vivian are taken from a series of interviews with Lafayette and Vivian in 2001. The story of James Lawson is told most eloquently in David Halberstam's *The Children* and Taylor Branch's *Parting the Waters*. John Lewis's quote about the redemptive power of suffering is taken from *Walking with the Wind* (p. 77). Bernard Lafayette's account of his own wrestling with the concept of nonviolence was taken from an interview with Lafayette. The story of the sit-in at Alabama State College and the quote from the college's president, H. Councill Trenholm, are taken from *Parting the Waters* (pp. 280–82). The account of the sit-ins in Tuskegee is based on an interview with Charles Hamilton (May 2001) and from *Reaping the Whirlwind: The Civil Rights Movement in Tuskegee* by Robert Norrell.

The description of the first sit-in in Nashville is taken from *Walking with the Wind*. The story of John Lewis's defiance of the advice of his more moderate elders has been told in *The Children*, *Parting the Waters*, *Walking with the Wind*, and *Forty Acres and a Goat*. I also relied on an interview with Will Campbell.

Chapter 6

Bernard Lafayette's memories of the fear inherent in the civil rights movement and of the taunts of the white toughs at a sit-in near the Vanderbilt campus come from an interview with Lafayette. The story of the private Freedom Ride by Lafayette and John Lewis is taken from an interview with Lafayette and from *The Children*. The story of the refusal of Bernard Lafayette's parents to allow him to go on the Freedom Rides comes from an interview with Lafayette, and with his father, Bernard Lafayette Sr. The story is also told in *The Children*. The account of the "last supper" before the Freedom Rides comes from *Walking with the Wind* and from an interview with John Lewis. The exchange between Lewis and the young thug in Rock Hill, S.C., is recounted in *Walking with the Wind*. Martin Luther King's warning to the freedom riders was recounted in *The Children*.

Governor John Patterson's thoughts about the freedom riders and the

Kennedys came from a lengthy interview with Patterson (July 2001). The account of the role of undercover agent E. L. Cowling in saving the lives of the freedom riders in Anniston is based on the interview with Patterson and on Fred Powledge's invaluable collection of interviews in his book *Free at Last? The Civil Rights Movement and the People Who Made It.* Additional information about the attack on the freedom riders in Anniston and later in Birmingham comes from *Parting the Waters* and *The Children.* Former television reporter Howard K. Smith offered his eyewitness recollections of the attack in Birmingham in his memoir *Events Leading Up To My Death.*

The great civil rights leader Fred Shuttlesworth offered his reflections on the Birmingham attacks and the mission to rescue the freedom riders in Anniston in an interview that I did with him (March 15, 2001). The story of his role is also contained in Manis's book *A Fire You Can't Put Out.* The story of the men who actually went on the rescue mission—and their act of bravery during an attempted bombing of Shuttlesworth's church—comes from Manis's book, and from interviews with Shuttlesworth, Colonel Stone Johnson, who was one of the rescuers, and from Lola Hendricks, Shuttlesworth's secretary who remembered her fears when her husband, Joe, was sent on the mission. The quote from Mrs. Hendricks was taken from a series of interviews in 2001.

John Seigenthaler, former assistant to Atty. Gen. Robert Kennedy, offered his reflections on a meeting between Kennedy and Martin Luther King, both in *The Children* and an interview with me (July 2001). His memory of the quotes from Dr. King came from my interview. The quote about his negotiations with Delta Airlines, trying to get the freedom riders out of Birmingham, is taken from that same interview, as is his account of conversations with Diane Nash, trying to talk her out of resuming the rides. The story of Nash's earlier confrontation with the mayor of Nashville comes from *The Children.* Her quote in a conversation with Seigenthaler comes from my interview with Seigenthaler, substantiated in its essence during an interview with Nash (September 2001).

Chapter 7

The account of the resumption of the Freedom Rides was taken in part from an interview with Nash and in part from a talk she made at the

University of Alabama in Huntsville on September 13, 2001. I also relied on accounts in interviews with John Lewis, Bernard Lafayette, Fred Shuttlesworth, and John Seigenthaler and on written accounts in *The Children, Walking with the Wind,* and *Parting the Waters.* The account of Bernard Lafayette's solitary reflections leading up to the rides was taken from *The Children* and from an interview with Lafayette.

The story of the arrest of the first group of freedom riders and their late-night encounter with Bull Connor was taken from *The Children* and *Walking with the Wind* and from an interview with Lewis. The physical description of Connor and his defiant quote on the issue of integration were taken from the biography *Bull Connor* by William Nunnelley. The quote from the policeman who initiated the arrest of the freedom riders at the Birmingham city limits—"Y'all have got to be Freedom Riders"— comes from John Lewis's account in *Walking with the Wind* (p. 147). Additional information about the arrest comes from *Parting the Waters* and *The Children.*

The reflections on the importance of music to the movement begins with Ralph Abernathy's recollection in his memoir *And the Walls Came Tumbling Down* about the hymns at the Holt Street Baptist Church on the first night of the Montgomery bus boycott. Robert Graetz, in an interview in 2001, also offered his memories of the importance of music that night. The work of folksinger Guy Carawan in teaching freedom songs to young people in the movement was described in *The Children* and also in interviews I did with Bernard Lafayette and with folksinger Si Kahn, a friend and colleague of Carawan.

The story of Bull Connor kidnapping the freedom riders from jail and leaving them in the middle of the night near the Tennessee-Alabama border was based on interviews with John Lewis, John Seigenthaler, and Diane Nash, and on a brief conversation with activist Leo Lillard, who came to the rescue of his friends. The story is also well told in *The Children, Walking with the Wind, Parting the Waters,* and *Free at Last?* The quotes from Seigenthaler came from the Seigenthaler interview. The quotes from freedom rider Katherine Burks and Bull Connor come from David Halberstam's account in *The Children* (p. 295). (Ms. Burks's name is spelled differently in the separate accounts of John Lewis, Halberstam, and Taylor Branch. I have used the most common spelling, which is the one offered by Lewis.) The exchange between John Lewis and the elderly couple who provided the freedom riders with a safe haven in Ardmore, Alabama, was based on Lewis's accounts in *Walking with the Wind* and in interviews with me.

Bernard Lafayette's memories of the standoff at the Birmingham bus station, just before the freedom riders left for Montgomery, was based on interviews with Lafayette. Governor John Patterson's quote, "You can't guarantee the safety of a fool," was taken from the documentary film *Eyes on the Prize*. The story of the tense negotiations between Patterson and Seigenthaler was based primarily on interviews that I did with both men (their memories of the conversation were surprisingly compatible), substantiated by accounts in *The Children, Parting the Waters,* and *Free at Last?* Fred Powledge, author of *Free at Last?,* did one of the most extensive interviews with Floyd Mann, who played such a pivotal role in the story. John Patterson's reference to "the niggers" in his negotiations with Seigenthaler is based on Taylor Branch's account in *Parting the Waters* (p. 441). The quotes in the exchange between Seigenthaler and Patterson were taken from the Seigenthaler interview. So were Floyd Mann's quote and Seigenthaler's assessment of the relationship between Mann and Patterson.

John Patterson's memory of negotiations between state officials and Police Commissioner L. B. Sullivan of Montgomery was offered in my interview with Patterson. The quote from the bus driver who refused at first to drive the freedom riders is found in several places. The version here is a composite from *Walking with the Wind* and *Parting the Waters*. The account of the attack on the freedom riders at the Montgomery station was pieced together from the interviews with John Lewis, Diane Nash, and Bernard Lafayette, and the versions of the story in *Free at Last? Parting the Waters,* and *The Children,* and from the documentary film *Eyes on the Prize*. The story of the attack on John Seigenthaler was taken primarily from my interview with Seigenthaler. The story of Floyd Mann's heroism is based on the account in *The Children* and on the interview with Mann done by Fred Powledge in *Free at Last?*

White activist Bob Zellner's personal postmortem on the bus station attacks was based on my interviews with Zellner in March 2001.

Chapter 8

The account of the emotional conversation between Robert Kennedy and

John Seigenthaler when Seigenthaler was hospitalized in Montgomery is taken from my interview with Seigenthaler. Jim Zwerg's quote—"We will continue the Freedom Ride. We are willing to accept death . . . "—comes from the film *Eyes on the Prize*. Freedom rider William Barbee's quote was recounted by Bernard Lafayette in his interviews with me.

Doris Crenshaw's memory of attempting to rescue the freedom riders when she was still a teenager was offered in an interview with me. (Crenshaw was an important young activist in Montgomery, who also participated in the sit-ins there.) The remarkable story of the siege at Ralph Abernathy's church is based on the accounts in *Parting the Waters, A Fire You Can't Put Out,* and *The Children,* and on interviews with Fred Shuttlesworth, John Lewis, Bernard Lafayette, and John Patterson. Fred Shuttlesworth, in his interview with me, described his own role in detail. His quote about his own "divine insanity" and his memory of what he said as he bulldozed his way through the mob at the church were taken from that interview. Will Campbell's personal reflections on Shuttlesworth's faith, courage, and ego were taken from interviews I did with Campbell in the fall of 2001 and the winter of 2002. The story of Shuttlesworth's arrest in Birmingham and the anecdote about accidentally shaving off his mustache were taken from his interview with me, confirmed by the account in *A Fire You Can't Put Out.* The quotes were taken from the interview.

In this section, I refer to CORE's national director, James Farmer, as the man who initiated the Freedom Rides. There were others who also played important roles. Taylor Branch reports that the idea was first offered by CORE staff member Gordon Carey, and another young CORE staffer, Thomas Gaither, went on a scouting expedition to Alabama before the rides, correctly predicting trouble in Anniston. According to some accounts, it was Gaither who actually conceived of the rides.

The description of the freedom riders posing as members of the choir during the siege at Abernathy's church was taken from my interviews with Bernard Lafayette. The description of Solomon Seay presiding bravely in the pulpit during a time of mounting tension outside was based on *Parting the Waters.* So was the description of Martin Luther King's decision to venture outside—supplemented by my interview with Bernard Lafayette and the account in *A Fire You Can't Put Out.* Fred Shuttlesworth's pulpit indictment of Gov. John Patterson is shown in the film *Eyes on the Prize* and quoted in *A Fire You Can't Put Out*.

John Patterson's decision to declare martial law is a matter of public record. His reflections on the process of making that decision and his ruminations about his own guilt with regard to the issue of race were offered in his interview with me. The quote from Tom Posey, one of Patterson's men on the scene, came from that same interview. The startling anecdote about the state trooper urinating in the coffee he was delivering to the church came from an interview with Bob Ingram, one of Alabama's legendary reporters. The description of the sleeping arrangements in the church came from Taylor Branch's *Parting the Waters*. And Bernard Lafayette's memories of the old woman who took him home with her and stood guard while he slept came from my interviews with Lafayette.

The awkward confrontation between Diane Nash and Martin Luther King about King's participation in the Freedom Ride came from an interview with Nash and from the written accounts of Halberstam and Taylor Branch. The quotes from King and Wyatt Tee Walker come from Branch (p. 467). The reactions of Bernard Lafayette and John Lewis came from interviews I did with those men.

C. T. Vivian's description of the ride from Montgomery to Mississippi—and his reflections on the central role of Alabama in the movement—came in an interview with me (2001). The story of the ambition of George Wallace and his teenage proclamation that he would one day be governor came from Dan T. Carter's excellent biography of Wallace *The Politics of Rage*. The description of Wallace's father as "something of a ne'er-do-well" was offered by Carter in the documentary film *George Wallace*. Seymore Trammell's memory of George Wallace's vow never to be "outniggered" again came from the same documentary. The remark was first reported by journalist Marshall Frady in his searing biography *Wallace*. Journalist Ray Jenkins's description of Wallace's "Faustian bargain" was also offered in the documentary film *George Wallace* and in an interview with me.

The account of Wallace's proclamation of defiance toward the U.S. Commission on Civil Rights came from *The Politics of Rage* and *Reaping the Whirlwind*. The powerful testimony of Macon County farmer Hosea Guice was recounted in *Reaping the Whirlwind*. The story of Wallace's late-night visit to U.S. district judge Frank Johnson was told in Frank Sikora's biography *The Judge*, as was Johnson's reaction to Wallace's blatant distortion of the record. Wallace's quote about "integrating, scalawagging, carpet-bagging liars" comes from the film *George Wallace*. The story of Wallace's speechwriter Asa Carter is taken from *The Politics of Rage* and from Wayne Greenhaw's typescript "Asa Carter: The Man with Two Identities." The story of the random castration of the innocent black man Edward Judge Aaron was told in *A Fire You Can't Put Out* (pp. 147–48).

John Patterson recalled his reaction to Wallace's inaugural address— "segregation now, segregation tomorrow, segregation forever"—in an interview with me.

Chapter 9

The account of the Birmingham movement is based on interviews with many of the participants, including Fred Shuttlesworth, John Porter, John Cross, Lola Hendricks, James Armstrong, Colonel Stone Johnson, Freeman Hrabowski, John Hulett, Odessa Woolfolk, Horace Huntley, Bernard Lafayette, Barbara Cross, Carolyn Maul, Murphy Archibald, U. W. Clemon, and others. In addition, I relied on contemporary accounts in the *New York Times* and the written accounts in Taylor Branch's *Parting the Waters;* Diane McWhorter's *Carry Me Home;* S. Jonathan Bass's *Blessed Are the Peacemakers;* Glenn Eskew's *But for Birmingham;* Andrew Manis's *A Fire You Can't Put Out;* John Egerton's *Speak Now Against the Day* and *A Mind To Stay Here;* David Garrow's *Bearing the Cross;* Howell Raines's *My Soul Is Rested;* E. Culpepper Clark's *The Schoolhouse Door;* Robin D. G. Kelley's *Hammer and Hoe;* and the Birmingham Historical Society's *A Walk To Freedom.*

The description of Birmingham in the 1930s is taken primarily from *Hammer and Hoe, Carry Me Home,* and *Speak Now against the Day.* The account of poor people's dissatisfaction with the Red Cross comes primarily from *Hammer and Hoe.* Colonel Stone Johnson's story about a black woman's abuse at the hands of relief officials came from an interview I did with Colonel Johnson. The description of the protest in 1933 in which several thousand poor people vowed to "stop the insults of the Red Cross" is taken from *Hammer and Hoe* (p. 33). The story of coal company owner

Charles DeBardeleben and his personal army is taken from *Carry Me Home* (p. 52). The profile of Joseph Gelders, the bookish labor organizer, is a composite of the descriptions in *Carry Me Home* and *Speak Now Against the Day*. The description of the gathering of Alabama progressives in Birmingham in 1938, including the quotes from Virginia Durr and Frank Porter Graham, comes from *Speak Now Against the Day* (pp. 185–97).

Fred Shuttlesworth's description of his early days in Birmingham was taken from an interview that I did with him in Cincinnati on March 15, 2001. The account of the banning of the NAACP in 1956 is taken from *A Fire You Can't Put Out* (p. 193). Shuttlesworth's quote is taken from his interview with me, as is the story of the warning by attorney Arthur Shores. The account of the founding of the Alabama Christian Movement for Human Rights is taken primarily from that interview as well, but the quote from Shuttlesworth, "If anybody is arrested, it'll be me" is taken from *A Fire You Can't Put Out* (p. 98). The reaction of Birmingham barber James Armstrong, who became one of Shuttlesworth's most ardent supporters, is taken from a series of interviews I did with Armstrong at his home in Birmingham, both in person and by telephone, beginning in May 2001. The quote from Shuttlesworth on the importance of school integration came from his interview with me. The story of Shuttlesworth's beating as he attempted to enroll his children in school and the castration of the black man Edward Judge Aaron are taken from *A Fire You Can't Put Out* (pp. 148–52). So was Shuttlesworth's heroic admonition against violence (p. 156).

The story of the frustrating civil rights struggle in Albany, Georgia, had been told in a number of places. I relied primarily on the account in Juan Williams's *Eyes on the Prize*. Shuttlesworth's thoughts on why Birmingham would be different have also been written about many times. I relied on the account in his interview with me. The description of Shuttlesworth's personality comes from a number of sources, including *Carry Me Home, A Fire You Can't Put Out, Parting the Waters,* and *But for Birmingham*. His secretary Lola Hendricks offered her unique perspective in an interview with me, as did the Reverend John Porter. Both interviews were done in Birmingham in November 2000. Shuttlesworth described his occasional impatience with Martin Luther King in his interview with me.

The account of the attempt by business leader Sidney Smyer and attorney David Vann to overthrow Bull Connor is taken primarily from the versions in *Carry Me Home,* supplemented by those in *But for Birmingham* and *Parting the Waters.* The account of Shuttlesworth's meeting with the white leaders is taken from my interview with Shuttlesworth and from *Carry Me Home* (p. 291) and *A Fire You Can't Put Out* (p. 324). Shuttlesworth's quote varies slightly in each telling. I relied on Shuttlesworth's memory of what he said.

The assault on Dr. King by a member of the American Nazi party has been told in numerous places, including *Parting the Waters* and *Bearing the Cross.* I also relied on the eyewitness memories of Lola Hendricks. The quote from Mrs. Hendricks comes from her interview with me.

Chapter 10

The account of the planning of Project C, which later became known as the Birmingham movement, is based primarily on Taylor Branch's *Parting the Waters.* That critically important meeting, which took place in Savannah, involved not only King, Shuttlesworth, and Wyatt Walker, those mentioned in the text of chapter 10, but eight other important King advisers: Joseph Lowery, Dorothy Cotton, Ralph Abernathy, Andrew Young, James Lawson, Stanley Levison, Jack O'Dell, and Clarence Jones.

The descriptions of Miles College, its president Lucius Pitts, and student leaders Frank Dukes and U. W. Clemon are taken primarily from John Egerton's *A Mind to Stay Here,* supplemented by accounts in Diane McWhorter's *Carry Me Home* and an interview I did with Clemon in 1970. The account of Shuttlesworth's exchange with Bull Connor regarding the judgments of history is taken from my interview with Shuttlesworth. The enmity between Connor and Shuttlesworth has been described in most of the accounts of the Birmingham movement.

The memories of Murph Archibald, a white student at Birmingham Southern who was one of a handful who lent their support to the black students at Miles, was taken from a series of conversations that I had with Archibald, who is now an attorney in Charlotte, N.C., and a longtime friend.

The account of Wyatt Walker's preparations for the Birmingham demonstrations comes in part from *Parting the Waters* and in part from my interviews with Lola Hendricks, who worked with Walker on many of the details. Mrs. Hendricks's protective thoughts about Martin Luther King and her observations of his approachability and informality—and his love of soul food at the Fraternal Restaurant—were offered in those same interviews. The descriptions of the first demonstrations beginning on April 3 are a synthesis of accounts in a variety of sources, chiefly *Parting the Waters, Carry Me Home, But for Birmingham, Bearing the Cross,* and *A Fire You Can't Put Out.*

The summary of *To Kill a Mockingbird* and the reflections on the influence of the book are based primarily on my own reading of it and the reactions I saw in Alabama when the book came out. The similarities between Atticus Finch and Judge James Edwin Horton, who presided over the first trial of the Scottsboro boys, are essentially my own interpretation, but it is a matter of record that Harper Lee was aware of the Scottsboro case as she was growing up in Monroeville. A good account of that case was provided by Dan T. Carter in a paper titled "'Let Justice Be Done': Public Passion and Judicial Courage in Modern Alabama," presented at the Ray Rushton Distinguished Lecturer Series at the Cumberland School of Law, April 24, 1998. Carter's piece makes clear why the death sentences (later overturned) of all but the youngest of the defendants in the case struck terror into the hearts of black Alabamians.

The account of the Palm Sunday march of 1963 is based primarily on my interviews with John Porter, as are his thoughts on Martin King's brother, A. D. King, and the anecdote about Reverend Porter's father. The account of the Good Friday arrest of Martin Luther King, Ralph Abernathy, and Fred Shuttlesworth is a synthesis of those in *Parting the Waters, Carry Me Home, But for Birmingham,* and *A Fire You Can't Put Out,* along with my interviews with Shuttlesworth and my personal memories of King's arrest, which I witnessed as a teenager in Birmingham. King's poignant plea to Abernathy to go to jail with him—"I am asking you to go with me"—is taken from *Parting the Waters* (p. 729). In Abernathy's autobiography, *And the Walls Came Tumbling Down,* he gives a different account of his exchange with King. "Ralph," he remembers King saying, "Sunday is Easter and you're the only preacher at West Hunter Church. If anything happens to me, Daddy will be there to lead the congregation on the highest day in Christendom. But your people won't have anybody. So you go back to Atlanta." "Martin," Abernathy replied, "if you're going to march, then I'm going to march too. Don't worry. West Hunter will be all right."

Whatever the precise exchange, there is no doubt that King wanted Abernathy with him on that occasion. Andrew Young's confirmation of that fact and his thoughts on the relationship between King and Abernathy were offered in an interview that I did with Young in 1971, researching a profile on Abernathy that appeared in the *Race Relations Reporter* magazine. The description of the demeanor of King, Shuttlesworth, and Abernathy as they marched is based in part on the photograph from the Birmingham Public Library Archives, which appeared in *Carry Me Home*. The quote about King's bearing at the time of his arrest—"a stoicism that seemed to shade into sadness"—is taken from my own family memoir *Lessons from the Big House*.

The most extensive account of King's time behind bars and his famous "Letter from a Birmingham Jail" appears in the book *Blessed Are the Peacemakers* by S. Jonathan Bass, which tells the story of the white ministers whose letter of criticism prompted King's reply. As a good historian, Bass works hard to demythologize the story, demonstrating conclusively that a document smuggled from the jail in pieces was reworked and polished by King and his staff, even after King's release from the jail. Under the leadership of Wyatt Walker, the letter became a part of the publicity machine, equal parts contrivance and an eloquent outpouring of King's honest views. In constructing this account of the letter, I have relied primarily on the accounts of Bass and Taylor Branch in *Parting the Waters*. The quote from the letter itself is taken from one of the many versions of it still in print. John Porter's account of the strategy session after King's release is taken from an article I did for *New West* magazine (which also appeared in the *Charlotte Observer* and the *Louisville Courier–Journal Sunday Magazine*) in 1977.

The story of James Bevel and the children's marches is synthesized from the accounts in *Parting the Waters*, *But for Birmingham*, *Carry Me Home*, and David Halberstam's *The Children*. The phrase, "Jewish beanie," describing the yarmulke that Bevel usually wore, is taken from Taylor Branch (p. 753), as is the idea for comparing Bevel to Vernon Johns, King's predecessor at Dexter Avenue Baptist Church. The quote from R. D. Nesbitt, a deacon at the Dexter Avenue, about the combative nature of Johns is taken from a March 2001 interview I did with Nesbitt in

Montgomery. The account of King's agony about the children's marches and his indecisive retreat to his hotel room before the march of May 2 is taken from *Bearing the Cross* (p. 248) and *But for Birmingham* (p. 264).

The civil rights observer who said the Birmingham fire hoses were rolling young demonstrators along "like a pebble at high tide" was Will Campbell, a white Southern Baptist sympathizer with the movement who offered that metaphor in a series of conversations with me. The anguished quote from black businessman A. G. Gaston when he first saw the fire hoses being used appears in several places, including *Parting the Waters* (p. 759).

Chapter 11

The story of Freeman Hrabowski who went from being a child protester in Birmingham to the presidency of the University of Maryland at Baltimore comes from an interview I did with Hrabowski in August 2001. He also told his story in Spike Lee's documentary film *Four Little Girls* and in a paper he wrote in September 1996, which he shared with me at the time of our interview. The paper was titled "The Role of Youth in the Civil Rights Movement: Reflections on Birmingham." Another account of Hrabowski's involvement appeared in *Baltimore* magazine, July 1993. The movement lore about the black German shepherd who seemed to be the meanest of all the police dogs was offered by Bernard Lafayette in a series of interviews with me and in a presentation he made to members of Congress who had come to Birmingham in March 2001 as part of a commemoration of the civil rights movement. In the film footage that appears in *Eyes on the Prize,* among other places, one of the dogs in the foreground is, in fact, solid black.

The story of King and Abernathy reassuring the parents whose children are being held outdoors at the State Fairgrounds is taken from *Parting the Waters*. Abernathy's quote appears on p. 773. The account of the watershed children's demonstration on May 7, 1963, is taken from those in *Parting the Waters, But for Birmingham, Carry Me Home,* and *A Fire You Can't Put Out.* King's quote, "the nonviolent movement's coming of age," appears in the documentary *Eyes on the Prize.* Shuttlesworth's quote, "Martin, this is it!" appears in *A Fire You Can't Put Out* (p. 377). The account of Shuttlesworth being blasted by a Birmingham fire hose is taken from the same book, including his quote, "Let's go. I'm ready to march" (p. 378). I also relied on the version of the story told by Taylor Branch and on Will Campbell's eyewitness account, which he offered in interviews with me. Bull Connor's callous quote in response appears in several places, including *But for Birmingham* and *A Fire You Can't Put Out*. I used the version from *A Fire* (p. 379).

The story of negotiations to bring about an end to the demonstrations is synthesized from the accounts in *Parting the Waters, A Fire You Can't Put Out*, and *But for Birmingham*. Shuttlesworth's quote about "scalding the hog" comes from *A Fire* (p. 383). There is a particularly pointed analysis in *But for Birmingham* about the divergent interests of King and his staff, who were playing to a national audience, and Shuttlesworth and the local leaders in Birmingham, who wanted concrete change for their city.

The quote from Klan wizard Robert Shelton denouncing the compromise reached between the movement and Birmingham's white business leaders is found in *Parting the Waters* (p. 793). The quote from another Klan leader calling for "stiff-backed men" is found on that same page, and in Diane McWhorter's book on p. 426. Taylor Branch offers a powerful account of the bombing of the home of A. D. King. The exasperated quote from Birmingham police chief Jamie Moore in his exchange with Al Lingo comes from p. 796 of *Parting the Waters,* as does Lingo's reply. The description of Lingo as a "a tough, pot-bellied, bug-eyed archetype of southern law enforcement" comes from historian E. Culpepper Clark in his book *The Schoolhouse Door* (p. 192). The assessment of Lingo's character and lack of law enforcement experience comes primarily from Clark and from Dan T. Carter in his book *The Politics of Rage.*

The story of the civil rights uprising in Gadsden is based on the accounts of three participants, Joseph Faulkner, J. D. Cammeron, and the Reverend L. A. Warren. The quote from Atty. Gen. Richmond Flowers comes from a motion he filed in Alabama circuit court. All other quotes were provided by the three participants in interviews with me beginning in August 2001.

Chapter 12

This account of George Wallace's stand in the schoolhouse door is based primarily on Dan Carter's *The Politics of Rage* and Culpepper Clark's *The Schoolhouse Door*, supplemented by the documentary film *George Wallace* and by Taylor Branch's *Parting the Waters*, David Halberstam's *The Children*, Howell Raines's *My Soul Is Rested*, and Arthur Schlesinger's *A Thousand Days*. I also benefited from a remarkable interview with Bob Ingram, former capitol correspondent for the *Montgomery Advertiser* and one of history's most astute observers of George Wallace, and Robert Inman, a former Alabama journalist turned novelist, who offered his insights into the reporting style of Bob Ingram. I also interviewed Bernard Lafayette about the Klan attacks following Wallace's stand and a speech to the nation by President Kennedy.

George Wallace's quote when he pledged to stand in the schoolhouse door is taken from Clark (p. 154). The paragraphs on Wallace, Bear Bryant, and the psyche of Alabama are essentially my own observations from having lived and grown up in the state. Culpepper Clark also writes eloquently on the symbolism of the University of Alabama. The story of George LeMaistre, the businessman who spoke out against Wallace, is taken primarily from the account in Dan Carter's *The Politics of Rage*. The Calvin Coolidge quote to describe LeMaistre's speaking style is found on p. 130, as are the quotes from LeMaistre himself and Wallace's astonishing observation that "law and order is a communist term."

The description of black student Vivian Malone is based primarily on Clark's account and on interviews with the family of John LeFlore, who knew and admired her as she was growing up in Mobile. I also relied on Howell Raines's interview with Malone in his book *My Soul Is Rested*. The account of the state of Alabama's unsuccessful attempts to dig up dirt on Malone, including the quote from investigator Ben Allen, is also taken from Raines (pp. 360–64). Malone's response to the investigation was offered in a letter to Thurgood Marshall, February 21, 1961. The letter is part of the papers of John LeFlore. The descriptions of James Hood and Dave McGlathery are taken primarily from Clark. The quote from Judge Lynne's injunction against George Wallace is also taken from Clark (p. 203). The story of Robert Kennedy's visit with Wallace and his frightening reception at the hands of Alabama State Troopers is told by both Carter and Clark.

The description of Jeff Bennett, the tough and courageous administrator at the University of Alabama, is based primarily on Clark. Bennett's report to Robert Kennedy that Wallace seemed nervous appears on p. 217. Clark also details the important role of university trustee Winton Blount in keeping open the lines of communication. The account of the Kennedy administration's preparations is synthesized from those in Clark, Carter, and Arthur Schlesinger's *A Thousand Days.* The quote from Wallace adviser John Kohn assuring the governor that he had divine blessing appears in slightly longer form on p. 223 of *The Schoolhouse Door.*

Bob Ingram's recollections of the standoff at the door came from my interviews with him. I also relied on Clark's descriptions (pp. 225–31). The quotes from Katzenbach and Wallace are taken from Clark (p. 226) and Carter (p. 149). The quote from Gen. Henry Graham asking Wallace to step aside is taken from Clark (p. 230). Bob Ingram's view that the whole episode was a charade and his account of his revealing conversations about it with Wallace came from Ingram's interviews with me.

The quotes from President Kennedy's foreign policy address at American University are taken from Schlesinger (pp. 901–2). The quotes from Kennedy's heartfelt civil rights address come from Schlesinger (p. 965) and Carter (p. 153). Martin Luther King's telegram in support of the speech, complete with errors in typing, is quoted by Taylor Branch (p. 824).

One of the most vivid descriptions of the murder of Medgar Evers is offered by Carter (p. 153). I relied on that account and Branch's (p. 825). The story of the attack on Bernard Lafayette comes from interviews I did with Lafayette, beginning in March 2001, and from David Halberstam's *The Children.*

Chapter 13

There have been many accounts of the meeting between President Kennedy and the civil rights leadership, June 22, 1963. I relied on those in *A Thousand Days* (Arthur Schlesinger was a participant in the meeting), John Lewis's memoir *Walking with the Wind,* and Taylor Branch's *Parting the Waters.* The A. Philip Randolph quote appears in all three versions, most fully in Schlesinger's.

The description of the background of Bayard Rustin and his brilliant organization of the March on Washington are taken primarily from Branch (see pp. 169–70 and pp. 872–79) and also from the memoir of

John Lewis. The story of Fred Shuttlesworth's last-minute inclusion as a speaker and the quote from his remarks are taken from *A Fire You Can't Put Out* (p. 401). The account of the tense negotiations surrounding John Lewis's speech is taken from those in Lewis's memoir *Parting the Waters,* in David Halberstam's *The Children,* and in my own interviews with Lewis. The quotes from the original draft of the speech come from *Walking with the Wind* (pp. 219, 221). The quotes from Martin Luther King and A. Philip Randolph seeking to persuade Lewis to tone down the speech appear on pp. 225–26 of the same memoir. The excerpts from the speech he delivered are taken from a longer quotation on p. 228.

The entire text of Martin Luther King's "I Have a Dream" speech appears in the book *The Craft of Prose* edited by Robert H. Woodward and H. Wendell Smith. I selected quotes from that text. King's spontaneous decision to use the "I Have a Dream" sequence is described in David Garrow's *Bearing the Cross* (p. 283). John Kennedy's response, "He's damn good," was recounted in *Parting the Waters* (p. 883). And Shuttlesworth's assessment of the speech is excerpted from a quote that appears on p. 401 of *A Fire You Can't Put Out.*

The story of the civil rights movement in Anniston was taken from an interview with Phillips Noble, one of the white leaders in the city, who has written a book on the struggle titled *Beyond the Burning Bus.* The story of the movement in Huntsville is taken primarily from interviews with Sonnie Hereford III, supplemented by the documentary film *A Civil Rights Journey* coproduced by Hereford and Wayman Burke. The quote from Huntsville's police chief Chris Spurlock about Wallace being "a sick man" appears in *The Politics of Rage* (p. 170). The story of Wallace's opposition to school desegregation in Tuskegee and the white leaders there who resisted the governor is told in the book *Reaping the Whirlwind* by Robert J. Norrell (pp. 128–43).

The account of the desegregation struggle in Birmingham that eventually led to the bombing of the Sixteenth Street Baptist Church is based primarily on interviews I did with James Armstrong, the lead plaintiff in the case, and Fred Shuttlesworth. The recollections of educator John K. Wright about standing guard duty at his house when he was a boy of thirteen were taken from an interview I did with Wright in the fall of 2000. The account of the bombing of Arthur Shores's house was taken from those in *The Politics of Rage* and the contemporary accounts in the *New*

York Times, including a page 1 story by Claude Sitton on September 5, 1963. The precise time of the bombing was taken from Sitton's story. (Other accounts differ by a few minutes.) The description of the National States Rights Party headquarters is based on a *New York Times* story by Fred Powledge, September 6, and the quotes from Wallace defending the violence of the National States Rights Party and calling for "a few first-class funerals" appeared in a September 6 article by John Herbers. Bob Ingram's analysis of that quote came in an interview with me.

The description of the student taunting of Dwight and Floyd Armstrong as they entered Graymont Elementary School—"adult obscenities in the soft treble voices of little boys"—comes from a story by Lillian Foscue in the *Birmingham Post-Herald,* September 11, 1963. The quote also appears in Diane McWhorter's *Carry Me Home* (p. 506).

James Armstrong's account of his concern about the safety of his children and his horror at the news of the Birmingham church bombing came from his interviews with me. The image of Martin Luther King's depression at hearing the news is based on an interview I did with his daughter Yolanda King in 1977 for an article that appeared initially in *New West* magazine. That article is also included in my book *Southern Voices: Profiles and Other Stories.* The interview, for me, was one of the most memorable that I ever did. Yolanda King, a remarkably articulate woman, was eight years old at the time of the bombing, but the memories of her father's anguish remained vivid to her years after the event.

Chapter 14

There are powerful accounts of the Birmingham church bombing in a number of the books on the civil rights movement—*Parting the Waters, Carry Me Home,* and many more. Spike Lee did a fine documentary film on the subject, often praised for its accuracy, and the church-bombing segment of *Eyes on the Prize,* perhaps the greatest civil rights documentary series of all time, is particularly moving. But in telling the story here, I have relied primarily on interviews I did with a number of the people associated with the church, starting with Sixteenth Street's minister, John Cross. I met him initially in 1977, which was the first time he told me the story of finding Denise McNair's patent leather shoe (see *Southern Voices* [p. 54]). I talked to Reverend Cross again on November 29, 2000, this time in the company of his daughter Barbara Cross. All the quotes from the awful day of the bombing are based on those interviews, except for the quote from M. W. Pippin, "I'd like to blow the whole town up." That anguished cry appears in *Carry Me Home* (p. 526) and was confirmed by Maxine McNair, Denise McNair's mother, in an interview with me on March 29, 2003. There was one point of confusion, however. In *Carry Me Home* the quote was attributed to F. L. Pippin, who was misidentified as Denise's grandfather but who was, in fact, Denise's great-uncle, M. W.'s brother. F. L. Pippin was also there and, according to Mrs. McNair, carried Denise's shoe in his hand as he wept at the horror of what had just happened. Not surprisingly, the subject is deeply painful even now, and I am grateful to Mrs. McNair and her daughter Lisa McNair for their patience and generosity in sorting through it with me. Thanks also to Reverend Cross. I am grateful to him for his time.

The account of the civil unrest in Birmingham that followed the bombing is based primarily on those in *Carry Me Home; Parting the Waters; Pillars of Fire* also by Taylor Branch; *The Politics of Rage;* and *A Fire You Can't Put Out.* Kennedy emissary Burke Marshall's discomfort going into a black neighborhood on the night of the rioting is recounted in a number of places, including *Pillars of Fire,* but is described most vividly in *A Fire You Can't Put Out.* Civil rights attorney Oscar Adams's derisive quote about Marshall appears on p. 404 of that book. Mayor Albert Boutwell's "all of us are victims" quote appears on p. 534 of *Carry Me Home.* Accounts of the poignant speech by Charles Morgan appear in numerous places. The quotes are taken from the account in *The Politics of Rage* (p. 181). The quote from Atty. Gen. Richmond Flowers appears on the following page of the same book. The quote from Carole Robertson's mother refusing to allow her daughter's funeral to become a movement event appears on p. 892 of *Parting the Waters.*

In his interview with me, John Cross described how he and Fred Shuttlesworth preached the eulogy at Carole's funeral. Also in an interview with me, John Porter described the funeral of the other three girls. His quote about seeing the bodies of the children at the hospital came from that same interview. The quote from King's eulogy is the same one I used in the book *Southern Voices* (p. 54), and the story of my encounter with Claude Wesley, father of Cynthia Wesley—a meeting that occurred in the summer of 1977—appears on pp. 57–58 of that same book.

Klansman Robert Chambliss's boast that after his next attack blacks in Birmingham would "beg us to let them segregate" appears on p. 175 of *The Politics of Rage*. Strong descriptions of Chambliss and his faction of the Klan appear in *Carry Me Home* and Frank Sikora's *Until Justice Rolls Down*. The story of the shrapnel bomb detonated by the Klan appears on p. 189 of *The Politics of Rage*. Wallace's disingenuous boast that state investigators had "beaten the Kennedy crowd to the punch" when they arrested Chambliss and another Klansman appears on p. 189 of that same book.

A good account of the rage of Diane Nash and James Bevel after the church bombing and their plan for massive protests in response appears in David Halberstam's *The Children*. I relied primarily, however, on my own conversations with Nash, starting in September 2001. Fred Shuttlesworth's initial rejection of the plan is recounted in *A Fire You Can't Put Out* (pp. 405–6). Nash's quote about King's rejection of the plan also came from her interview with me.

Chapter 15

The account of Fred Shuttlesworth's visit to the White House following the bombing of the Birmingham church is taken from *A Fire You Can't Put Out* by Andrew Manis (p. 407) and from my own interviews with Shuttlesworth. The first quote from Shuttlesworth ("four innocent little girls") is taken from Manis (p. 407), as is the quote from Kennedy. The depth of Shuttlesworth's admiration for Kennedy was made clear in his interview with me.

The story of Martin Luther King's impact on the 1960 presidential election and Kennedy's response to King's jailing in Georgia is taken primarily from the accounts in *A Thousand Days* by Arthur Schlesinger (pp. 73–74) and *Parting the Waters* by Taylor Branch (pp. 356–74). Branch in particular, as he so often does, offers an intricate account of that event. King's quote about the death of President Kennedy comes from *Parting the Waters* (p. 922). The story of John Lewis's response to the murder of the president and his suggestion of a vigil at Arlington Cemetery is taken from David Halberstam's *The Children* (pp. 469–70) and from Lewis's memoir *Walking with the Wind* (pp. 245–47). Excerpts from the minutes of a SNCC discussion about Kennedy's death appear in Danny Lyon's

Memories of the Southern Civil Rights Movement (pp. 119–23). They reveal a mixture of genuine grief about Kennedy's death and chilly ambivalence about his civil rights record.

The quote from Fred Shuttlesworth about Kennedy and his legacy are taken from Shuttlesworth's interview with me. The story of whites cheering in Tuskegee, Alabama, when they heard the news of Kennedy's assassination is taken from *Reaping the Whirlwind* by Robert J. Norrell (p. 155), and the story of George Wallace's adviser John Kohn dancing in the streets is taken from my interview with Montgomery journalist Bob Ingram, who covered the careers of Wallace and Kohn. Wallace's quotes come from *The Politics of Rage* by Dan T. Carter (p. 199).

In *Parting the Waters* Taylor Branch writes about the role of Vice President Johnson in the Kennedy administration, particularly with regard to its civil rights policies. The article by Louis Lomax, the black southern journalist who saw Johnson's potential as president, appeared in the March 10, 1964, issue of *Look* magazine under the headline "A Negro View: Johnson Can Free the South."

John Kennedy's quote "But for Birmingham" appears in *A Fire You Can't Put Out*. Historian Glenn Eskew used that quote as the title for his excellent book on Birmingham but attributed the words to Shuttlesworth not Kennedy. The story of Shuttlesworth leading a test of the Civil Rights Act of 1964 appears in *A Fire You Can't Put Out* (p. 416). The account of Sheriff Jim Clark using a cattle prod on July 4, 1964, to personally repudiate the Civil Rights Act is told in *Pillar of Fire* by Taylor Branch (p. 391). Clark used the prod on Silas Norman of SNCC, when Norman tried to place an order at the Thirsty Boy Drive-In in Selma.

Movement foot soldier J. D. Cammeron's memories of the change in atmosphere in Gadsden following the passage of the Civil Rights Act were offered by Cammeron in his interview with me.

Also in interviews with me, Montgomery reporter Bob Ingram described George Wallace's appearance on *Meet the Press* shortly before his stand in the schoolhouse door, including the Greek band playing "Dixie" on the flight to New York. The description of Wallace's air of command ("The tremble left his hands and the quaver left his voice") came from Associated Press correspondent Jules Loh and was quoted in *The Politics of Rage* (p. 136). Wallace's quote when the show was over, "All they wanted to know about was niggers," appears in both *The Politics of Rage* (p. 138) and *The Schoolhouse Door* by Culpepper Clark (p. 200). Both books offer detailed descriptions of the show. I also relied on Bob Ingram's memories.

The description of George Wallace's visit to Harvard and his verbal sparring match with Bob Zellner is taken from Zellner's account, which he offered in an interview with me, and from *The Politics of Rage* (pp. 197–98). The *Tacoma Tribune*'s assessment of Wallace is quoted on p. 200 of *The Politics of Rage*. Wallace's quote about the Civil Rights Act ("a nefarious piece of legislation") is taken from a speech I heard him give at Vanderbilt University in March 1965. The account of Wallace's showing in the 1964 presidential primaries is taken mostly from *The Politics of Rage* (pp. 202–16) and from the documentary film *George Wallace*. His quote, "I have tried to speak the truth, nothing more," appears on p. 205 of *The Politics of Rage*.

The quote from Martin Luther King's Nobel Prize address is taken from Taylor Branch's *Pillars of Fire* (p. 541).

Chapter 16

The account of James Bevel and Diane Nash trying to lure Dr. King into Selma is taken from a speech Nash gave at the University of Alabama in Huntsville on September 13, 2001, and from an interview I did with Nash shortly afterward. The story of Sam and Amelia Boynton is taken primarily from my interviews with Mrs. Boynton and with others who knew her, including Bernard Lafayette, JoAnne Bland, F. D. Reese, and Mrs. Boynton's son Bruce. I also relied on Mrs. Boynton's memoir *Bridge Across Jordan*. Her description of a white attacker as looking like "the very Devil himself" is taken from my interview (November 10, 2000).

Bernard Lafayette's assessment of Jim Clark and how he could be manipulated by the movement is taken from a series of interviews I did with Lafayette, beginning in February 2001. Lafayette's description of the memorial service for Sam Boynton was also offered in those same interviews. In 1977 I interviewed the Reverend L. L. Anderson, who has since died, about the Selma movement, and he also described that meeting at the church and the opposition he faced from his deacons. The story is also told in *Pillar of Fire* (pp. 82–84).

Annie Cooper offered a vivid and detailed account of her involvement in the Selma movement in an interview with me on September 28, 2000. Her story is also told in *Pillar of Fire* (p. 566). The quote from Judge James Hare's injunction against any civil rights activity in Selma is taken from *Pillar of Fire* (p. 553). The story of "the courageous eight" and their decision to defy the injunction and invite Martin Luther King into Selma is taken from interviews I did with F. D. Reese, Amelia Boynton, and JoAnne Bland. I listed several of the "eight" in the text of this book. The entire list comes from F. D. Reese: James Gildersleeve, Ernest Doyle, Marie Foster, Amelia Boynton, Ulysses Blackmon, the Reverend J. D. Hunter, Henry Shannon, and Reese. Nearly forty years later, these are still, within the black community of Selma, arguably the most honored people in its history.

The description of John Lewis's ruminations as he prepared for Martin Luther King's first mass meeting in Selma comes from interviews I did with Lewis in March 2001 and from Lewis's autobiography, *Walking with the Wind*. The distinction in the attitudes of Dallas County sheriff Jim Clark and Selma police chief Wilson Baker comes largely from Lewis, though others who lived and worked in Selma, including C. T. Vivian, had the same impression. In *Pillar of Fire* Taylor Branch quotes Baker as saying Clark was "out of control" (p. 562). The quote from King at the January 2, 1965, mass meeting appears in David Garrow's *Bearing the Cross* (p. 372). The description of the January 18 march led by King and Lewis comes from *Bearing the Cross* and *Walking with the Wind*, as well as Lewis's recollections in an interview with me. The description of the attack on Martin Luther King comes primarily from Lewis's memoir, as does the description of the arrest and rough treatment of Amelia Boynton by Sheriff Jim Clark. Mrs. Boynton talked about it also in her interview with me. The description of the confrontation between Wilson Baker and Clark comes from *Walking with the Wind* (p. 322).

In our interview in May 2001 F. D. Reese gave a detailed account of the teachers' march; Mrs. Boynton talked about it also. Film footage appears in *Eyes on the Prize* and the story is told in *Pillar of Fire* (p. 564). The quotes attributed to Reese and A. J. Durgan come from the interview with Reese. The description of the arrest and beating of Annie Cooper, following her legendary scuffle with Jim Clark, is based primarily on Mrs.

Cooper's account in an interview with me and on the January 26, 1965, *New York Times* story by John Herbers. The quote from the Reverend L. L. Anderson comes from *Pillar of Fire* (p. 566).

The account of Malcolm X's visit to Selma is taken from those in *Pillar of Fire* (pp. 578–79) and *Walking with the Wind* (p. 324). Malcolm's quote comes from *Walking with the Wind*. The story of the confrontation between Sheriff Clark and C. T. Vivian is taken in part from my interviews with Vivian and in part from the spellbinding footage in *Eyes on the Prize*.

Chapter 17

The account of the spread of the voting rights movement from Selma to the surrounding countryside is told in many places, including *Pillar of Fire* and *Walking with the Wind*. I relied on those accounts, as well as the recollections of C. T. Vivian, which he shared in interviews with me. The story of the attack on the peaceful demonstrators is taken primarily from John Herbers's dispatch in the *New York Times* (February 19, 1965). The shooting of Jimmy Lee Jackson, perhaps the most important martyr in the history of the movement, is described in vivid detail in *Pillar of Fire* (p. 593) and *Walking with the Wind* (p. 328). It is one of the inexcusable ironies of history that Jackson, whose death led directly to the Montgomery march, is less familiar to casual students of the period than, say, Viola Liuzzo or James Reeb, who were also killed at about the same time. The story of James Bevel coming downstairs in the middle of the night from his motel room in Selma and describing his "vision" for a march to Montgomery was recounted by Annie Cooper in her interview with me. Mrs. Cooper was working as the motel's night clerk.

My description of Martin Luther King's reaction to the assassination of Malcolm X and King's response to the brief meeting between the two men is taken primarily from *Bearing the Cross.* (pp. 319, 392–94). C. Eric Lincoln's thoughts on Malcolm X were offered in numerous interviews and conversations with me, beginning early in the 1970s and continuing nearly until Lincoln's death in the year 2000. The quote from King to his valued colleague Joseph Lowery ("Come on and walk with me, Joe") is taken from *Bearing the Cross* (p. 394). John Lewis also writes about the death threats against King.

In *Walking with the Wind* John Lewis writes about the debate within SNCC regarding the validity of the march (pp. 330–31). The story of the bravery of Cager Lee, Jimmy Lee Jackson's grandfather, is told in David Halberstam's *The Children* (pp. 503–4). The story of the coin flip to see who would lead the first attempted march to Montgomery is told by Lewis in *Walking with the Wind* and was told to me by SNCC organizer Bob Mants. Mants also was in the front ranks of the march. The quote from the Reverend L. L. Anderson ("We weren't equipped for a march of that distance") appears in my book *Race, Rock, and Religion* (p. 22) and was taken from an interview I did with Reverend Anderson back in 1977.

The account of the banter between John Lewis and Hosea Williams when they first caught sight of the line of state troopers blocking their path is taken from *Walking with the Wind,* as are Lewis's memories of the original standoff. I also relied on David Garrow's account in *Bearing the Cross* and on the eyewitness account of *New York Times* reporter Roy Reed as it appeared in his page 1 story, May 8, 1965. Amelia Boynton's memories of the attack were recounted in her interview with me, including her poignant quote, "I just couldn't imagine." The quote from Jim Clark, "Let the buzzards eat them," is also taken from the interview with Mrs. Boynton. It is what somebody told her they heard Clark say, but despite the secondhand nature of the quote, I have used it here because it is consistent with the sheriff's character, as it was revealed in numerous confrontations over time.

JoAnne Bland offered her childhood recollections of the attack at the bridge in an interview with me on September 28, 2000. It remains for me one of the most memorable interviews I did for this project. James Perkins, Selma's first black mayor, described himself as a "seasoned protester" at the age of twelve in a conversation we had in early March 2001. Annie Cooper's memories of the attack were also offered in her interview with me, including her quotes ("they were like savages" and "the only way you could tell they were alive was by the quivering of their skin").

The chilling moment-by-moment log of the attack maintained by SNCC can be found in the organization's archives at the Martin Luther King Center in Atlanta and is excerpted in detail in Danny Lyon's powerful book *Memories of the Southern Civil Rights Movement* (pp. 168–70). Bob Mants first called my attention to the log, which was based largely on the eyewitness reports of Lafayette Surney.

David Garrow describes Wilson Baker's intervention to stop the attack (*Bearing the Cross,* p. 399), as does John Lewis (*Walking with the Wind,* p. 342). Baker's advance fears of a bloodbath are recounted by Garrow (p. 397). (Garrow is also the author of the prize-winning book *Protest at Selma: Martin Luther King Jr. and the Voting Rights Act of 1965.*)

The quote from Mayor Joe T. Smitherman ("I did not understand how big it was") appears in Juan Williams's book *Eyes on the Prize* (p. 272). Bob Ingram's account of George Wallace's reaction came in Ingram's interviews with me. The strategy considerations by Wallace and his staff in advance of the march are recounted in *The Politics of Rage* (pp. 246–47) The transcript of Al Lingo's testimony before Judge Frank Johnson is excerpted in *The Politics of Rage* (p. 247). A more extended account of the exchange between Lingo and the judge and civil rights lawyer Fred Gray, including Lingo's hedgings, appears in Frank Sikora's *The Judge* (pp. 217–18).

The ironic story of George Wallace greeting an old black friend at a rally of segregationists in Birmingham appears in Diane McWhorter's *Carry Me Home* (p. 503).

Chapter 18

The rage of the victims at the Edmund Pettus Bridge was recounted by Andrew Young in the film *Eyes on the Prize* and by F. D. Reese in an interview with me. Reese's quote about the salvation of nonviolence came from that interview.

The story of the white Alabamians who marched in Selma on the day before Bloody Sunday is told by John Lewis in *Walking with the Wind* (pp. 330–31). Theoda Smith's story about the nun who saved the life of her daughter appears in my book *Race, Rock, and Religion* (p. 22), and is based on an interview I did with Mrs. Smith in 1977.

The intense debate over strategy between Martin Luther King and the leaders of SNCC is recounted in *Walking with the Wind* (pp. 346–48), and the counterpressure from Lyndon Johnson's representative LeRoy Collins is described in *Bearing the Cross* (pp. 401–4). The SNCC records from Bloody Sunday confirm the times of the SNCC delegation's heading for Selma (Lyon, *Memories,* p. 168). King's quote from his conversation with LeRoy Collins ("I cannot agree to do anything") is taken from

Bearing the Cross (p. 402). The troopers' odd gesture during the "turn-around" march on March 9— stepping back to open the highway to the marchers just as King was beginning his retreat—is recounted in *Walking with the Wind* (p. 348) and *Bearing the Cross* (p. 404). James Forman's denunciation of King's "trickery" was recounted by Lewis in an interview with me. His own mind-set at the time is described in *Walking with the Wind* and confirmed in that same interview. His quote ("George Wallace and segregation are the enemy") appears on p. 349 of his memoir. (His position was reiterated by SNCC's Ivanhoe Donaldson, who said tensions between King and SNCC were a "family" matter within the movement.)

The description of Walker's Cafe, the soul food restaurant where James Reeb had his last meal, comes from John Lewis, both in his book and in his interviews with me; the memories of the Silver Moon come from F. D. Reese in his interview with me.

The descriptions of the SNCC demonstrations in Montgomery come from interviews I did with Gwen Patton and Bob Mants, and from the account in Robert J. Norrell's *Reaping the Whirlwind* (pp. 172–73). Gwen Patton's memories of reading *Invisible Man* were offered in a conversation we had on May 14, 2001, as was her quote about Charles Gomillion. Bob Mants was the activist who used the phrase "the great pee-in" in one of the many conversations he had with me, beginning in the summer of 2001.

In the film *Eyes on the Prize* C. T. Vivian recounts the reaction of Martin Luther King to Lyndon Johnson's civil rights speech, and his memories are corroborated by John Lewis in *Walking with the Wind*. The speech itself has been quoted in many places. The excerpts I chose were similar to those in Lewis's book (p. 353) and *The Politics of Rage* (p. 255). Mayor Joe Smitherman's reaction to the speech and his quote about it ("a dagger in your heart") are taken from Juan Williams's book *Eyes on the Prize* (p. 278). I also asked about the speech in an interview with Smitherman in 1977.

SNCC photographer Danny Lyon's reaction to Johnson's speech was offered in *Memories of the Southern Civil Rights Movement* (p. 175). The quote from James Forman appears in Lewis's memoir (p. 354).

The description of the violent confrontation in Montgomery on March 16, 1965, was taken primarily from accounts in the *New York Times,* particularly a page 1 story by Roy Reed that appeared on March 17.

On March 18 *Times* reporter Ben Franklin wrote about Judge Frank Johnson's ruling granting King and his followers the right to march to Montgomery. The quotes from the ruling come from Franklin's article and from *The Politics of Rage* (p. 255).

The angry quote from James Forman about the table of democracy appears in several places (*Reaping the Whirlwind, Bearing the Cross,* and *Walking with the Wind*). I used the version in *Walking with the Wind* (p. 354).

James Armstrong's emotions at the beginning of the triumphant Selma to Montgomery march were described in an interview with me in July 2002. Rabbi Abraham Heschel's resemblance to God in the eyes of some of the marchers comes from John Lewis (p. 357). The description of the landscape along the march route comes from Lewis, Armstrong, and F. D. Reese in interviews with me. The story of Rosa Steele, the Lowndes County widow who offered her farm as a campsite, comes primarily from my interviews with Bob Mants, who knew Mrs. Steele and admired her deeply.

Sonnie Hereford recalled his role as one of the doctors on the march during an interview with me in July 2002. Also in an interview, F. D. Reese described his pride on behalf of his hometown of Selma as the marchers finally arrived in Montgomery. Amelia Boynton remembered carrying the petition for George Wallace. In one of our interviews, Bob Ingram, who was with George Wallace, described the governor's reaction to the size of the crowd ("My God, it looks like an army"). The governor's reaction is also recounted in the documentary film *George Wallace.* King's powerful speech has been quoted in many places, though the printed page doesn't do it justice. Parts of it are seen in *Eyes on the Prize.*

Annie Cooper, one of the most eloquent of the movement's foot soldiers, described her reaction to the speech in an interview with me.

Chapter 19

The story of prosecutor Arthur Gamble's grim discovery of the murder of Viola Liuzzo was told by his wife, Roberta Gamble, in an interview with me. The basic outline of the crime comes from the *Time* magazine account, April 2, 1965.

Bernard Lafayette told the story of his encounter with Mrs. Liuzzo in an interview with me. The story of Gary Thomas Rowe, the violence-prone FBI informer, has been told in many places, including Diane McWhorter's *Carry Me Home* and in contemporary newspaper accounts of the trial. The quotes from President Johnson's speech come from *Time*, as does the response from George Wallace and the odd anecdote about the Alabama legislature's charges of "much fornication" among the marchers and John Lewis's response.

The descriptions of Arthur Gamble come from his brother-in-law Tom Peacock, a North Carolina writer, and from Marie Peacock, Tom's wife. Roberta Gamble described her own feelings about the civil rights movement in the interview with me, as well as her memories of the Liuzzo trial. The quote from Imperial Wizard Robert Shelton comes from an Associated Press dispatch in the May 4, 1965, *Montgomery Advertiser*. I read Jimmy Breslin's dispatches in the *New York Herald Tribune* during the week of the trial, and the summary of them is mine. Tom Wolfe's description of Breslin is taken from Wolfe's book *The New Journalism* (p. 13). Young Leroy Moton's account of Mrs. Liuzzo singing "We Shall Overcome" at the moment just before her death is taken from his testimony at the trial as reported in the May 5 *Birmingham Post-Herald*, along with Moton's cross-examination at the hands of Klan attorney Matt Murphy. The description of Murphy is based on a photograph in the May 7 *New York Times* and on the memory of Roberta Gamble. A photograph of presiding judge Werth Thagard appeared in the May 3 *Birmingham News*.

Gary Thomas Rowe's testimony was reported in the May 5 *Birmingham Post-Herald*, including his quote of the murderer of James Reeb. Roberta Gamble related the anecdote about the son of a Klansman speculating on the fate of Rowe. The jury summations of Matt Murphy and Arthur Gamble appeared in the May 7 *New York Times*. The story of the hung jury is taken from the May 8 *Montgomery Advertiser* and the reflections of Roberta Gamble. Arthur Gamble's one break from his silence regarding the case and its implications occurred in a conversation with me.

Lyndon Johnson's quote about the power of the ballot appears in John Lewis's *Walking with the Wind* (p. 361). The story of the protests in Tuskegee is taken from Robert Norell's *Reaping the Whirlwind* (pp. 174–79), from an interview with Gwen Patton, and from the book *Black*

Power by Stokely Carmichael (who later changed his name to Kwame Ture) and Charles V. Hamilton. The figures on the new voting strength of blacks come from *Black Power* (p. 136), as do the quotes from Paul Puryear (p. 124) and Stokely Carmichael (p. 144).

The general description of Stokely Carmichael is based on conversations with a number of people who knew him, including Charles Hamilton, Bob Mants, John Hulett, Thomas Gilmore, and Francis Walter, and on my own encounter with Carmichael at Vanderbilt University in 1967. The best account of the life of Jonathan Daniels is contained in Charles Eagles's fine book *Outside Agitator*. The anecdotes about his relationships with the black children of Selma come from the book *Selma, Lord, Selma* (p. 131), from *Outside Agitator* (p. 77), and from my own interviews with JoAnne Bland. The account of the arrest and killing of Daniels is taken primarily from *Outside Agitator* (chap. 6); from Marshall Frady's account in *Newsweek,* which also appears in his book *Southerners* (pp. 138–56); and from my interviews with Francis Walter and John Hulett. The account of Stokely Carmichael at Daniels's funeral comes from *Outside Agitator* (p. 184).

Chapter 20

Bob Mants's memories of his growing up—from the murder of Emmett Till to the stories of his great-aunt Molly—were recounted in a series of interviews with me, beginning in 2001. So were his recollections of his initial contacts with the elders in Lowndes County. Of all the SNCC workers, Mants and Stokely Carmichael had the greatest impact on the county, but Mants is careful to give credit to others, including Willie Vaughn and Judy Richardson who were also among the SNCC pioneers in what was arguably the toughest county in Alabama.

The story of the sharecroppers' strikes in 1935 is based on the book *Hammer and Hoe* by Robin D. G. Kelley (pp. 165–66) and on an interview I did with Charles Smith, who was one of the participants. The quote from Lemon Johnson appears in *Hammer and Hoe,* as does his picture (p. 45). The account of the shooting of union organizer Willie Witcher is based primarily on the eyewitness memories of Charles Smith and differs slightly from the version in *Hammer and Hoe.*

The account of John Hulett's background, including his time in

Birmingham, is based on his numerous interviews with me, which began in 2001. The same is true of his recollections of the earliest voting rights meetings and the first attempts of black people to register, as well as his assessment of the character of Probate Judge Harrell Hammonds. The story of the early voting rights struggle also appears in *Outside Agitator* (pp. 120–21), including the quote from voting registrar Carl Golson.

Mants was emphatic in giving credit to local leaders, whose strength and wisdom were partly attributable, he thought, to the perspective that several of them gained from living outside the county at various times in their lives—John Hulett in Birmingham, Charles Smith in Mobile, and Robert Strickland and Lillian McGill in Montgomery. The ideas of Mants and Hulett on the subject of armed self-defense were offered in their interviews with me. The anecdote about Stokely Carmichael talking with columnist James Reston was told by Charles Hamilton in an interview with me, and the story of Carmichael dropping his gun in Selma was told to me by John Hulett. Mants's quote about Carmichael also came in an interview with me. Francis Walter's assessment of Carmichael was taken primarily from Walter's civil rights diary, a copy of which he shared with me, and from interviews with Walter. John Hulett offered his quote about the Black Panther emblem in several of our interviews.

The story of the elections of 1966 is taken primarily from the book *Black Power*, including the quote from the Black Panther billboard (p. 98), and from the memories of Hulett, Mants, Hamilton, Walter, and Charles Smith. Mants's quote about the proper role of an organizer ("a termite and not a woodpecker") came from his interviews with me. John Hulett recalled the visit of Huey Newton to Lowndes County, and the description of the Black Panther Party in California is based on the film *Eyes on the Prize*. The election results in 1966 were recounted in *Black Power* and in the Ph.D. dissertation "Carry It On" by Susan Ashmore. The description of black poll worker Andrew Jones as a man who "didn't raise no sand" was offered by John Hulett in an interview with me. Hulett's quote "we won't give up" appears in *Black Power* (p. 115).

The story of the evolving relationship between John Hulett and the killer of Jonathan Daniels was told by Hulett in our series of interviews. The quote from journalist Marshall Frady describing the trial of the killer, Tom Coleman, comes from *Southerners* (pp. 145–46), as do the quotes from the witnesses in the trial (p. 147). Charles Hamilton's assessment of the absence of revenge in the motivations of many black leaders in Alabama was offered in conversations with me. The interview with farmer Earvin Hinson and his quotes about the importance of having a black sheriff appeared originally in an article I did for *New West* magazine in 1977 and also appear in my book *Race, Rock, and Religion* (pp. 25–26).

Interestingly, in that initial interview Hinson offered two different versions of his quote about justice in Lowndes County. He first said, "It's better than it has been, but it ain't justice," and that is the way I quoted him in the magazine article. But a few minutes later in the same interview, he reversed the emphasis, saying, "No, it ain't justice, still a long way from it. But it's better than it has been." That is the version I used this time. Having thought about it now for more than twenty-five years, I believe that emphasis fits best with the overall thrust of the interview. Either way, it was an eloquent insight.

Chapter 21

Francis Walter's stories of the evolution of his own racial understandings were offered in a series of interviews with me. His memories of his early years in Selma were recounted in those same interviews and confirmed in the pages of his civil rights diary, which he shared with me, and in the pages of a newsletter he published at the time. The story of the black woman in Gees Bend, Alabama, who overcame her fear of white people came from Walter, as did the description of the Witherspoons. He also wrote about these grassroots leaders in his civil rights diary.

Susan Ashmore describes the Agricultural Stabilization and Conservation Service elections in her carefully researched dissertation "Carry It On" (pp. 280–86), as does Charles Eagles in *Outside Agitator.* The story of the courage of civil rights supporters living in tents after being evicted from their homes was told by Bob Mants. The account of the support given to the Lowndes County struggle by Black Belt expatriates living in Detroit was offered by Mants and supported by John Hulett. Francis Walter offered the account of similar evictions in Wilcox County.

The story of Lewis Black and his grassroots credit union in Hale County is taken from Ashmore's "Carry It On" (pp. 261–65). The story of the fight for federal antipoverty funding in Dallas County is taken from Ashmore and from interviews with Francis Walter. The quote from Selma mayor Joe Smitherman was offered in an interview with me in 1977 and appears in *Race, Rock, and Religion* (p. 23). In that same interview Smitherman made the connection between his channeling of federal money into black neighborhoods in Selma and his own ability to win black votes. The story of the struggle for adult education funding in Lowndes and Wilcox Counties is based on the account in Ashmore's dissertation and on interviews with Francis Walter. The quotes from George Wallace, including his vicious attack on Lowndes County leader Robert Strickland, come from Ashmore (pp. 340–41). Ashmore also gives a good account of Strickland's life, including his early troubles with the law (pp. 275–76).

The story of SWAFCA is based primarily on Ashmore and the original reporting done by the *Southern Courier,* a fine newspaper published in Alabama in the 1960s. The quote from Selma mayor Joe Smitherman castigating SWAFCA supporter Shirley Mesher appears on p. 386 of "Carry It On." The quotes from SWAFCA leaders Ezra Cunningham and Joe Johnson appear on pp. 402 and 405, respectively.

The concluding quote from Francis Walter about "the great upsurge" that went with the movement came in his interviews with me.

Chapter 22

Thomas Gilmore, the first black sheriff of Greene County, told the story of his life and his participation in the movement in two lengthy interviews with me in January and February 2001. William McKinley Branch, the first black probate judge in Alabama since Reconstruction, told his story in an interview on April 11, 2001. It was Branch who quoted the white sheriff, Bill Lee, as saying "a cotton patch nigger" would never take his job. The quote is consistent with those in Marshall Frady's story in *Newsweek,* May 16, 1966, and in his book *Southerners* (pp. 157–66). Frady's quote from Lee that I used in this chapter appears on p. 159 of *Southerners.* The story of Lee cursing William Branch—and then asking forgiveness—was told by Branch. Thomas Gilmore's reflections on the fears and uncertainty of the county's new black voters were offered in his interview with me. His quote from a conversation with Frady appears on p. 160 of *Southerners.* His quote about young people having "somebody they can look up to" appears on p. 331 of Ashmore.

Gilmore told me the story of his encounter with Martin Luther King in the spring of 1968. The date of King's visit to Alabama and his itinerary were confirmed in David Garrow's biography *Bearing the Cross* (p. 606). The film *Eyes on the Prize* offers a powerful account of King's priorities and frame of mind in the last days of his life, and King's quote about the "bombs of Vietnam" is taken from that film. Gilmore also remembered King's concern about the country's string of "long, hot summers"—the urban rioting beginning in Harlem in 1964, continuing in Watts in 1965, and spreading to a hundred cities by 1967. For an understanding of the undertow of despair in this part of King's life, I also relied on interviews I did with Ralph Abernathy in the 1970s and on Abernathy's autobiography, *And the Walls Came Tumbling Down*. The anecdote about King in a pillow fight only minutes before his death was offered by Andrew Young in the film *Eyes on the Prize*.

The story of the National Democratic Party of Alabama was taken from Susan Ashmore's "Carry It On" and from an interview with Jack Drake, one of the white supporters of the party. Gilmore and John Hulett also praised the effectiveness of the NDPA in their interviews with me. In those same interviews, Gilmore also talked about the intricacies of being a sheriff without a gun.

Chapter 23

The first sentence in this chapter—the simple assertion that the civil rights movement began to lose momentum in the 1970s—will be controversial in the eyes of many historians. Indeed, it has become something of a truism in academic circles that the movement lost momentum after 1965, if not earlier. And that is accurate if you measure its power by national headlines and television footage, rather than the intensity of the struggle being waged. But it is an incontrovertible fact that black Alabamians, along with their counterparts in many other places, continued to fight for their freedom every day, long after much of the country had lost interest. To assert otherwise, I believe, is to dishonor the memory of what really happened.

The story of Robert Kennedy's visit to the University of Alabama is based on the account in *RFK: Collected Speeches;* the quote from his speech appears on pp. 334–35. I also saw Kennedy that same day when he came to Vanderbilt University, and I developed a personal sense of the intensity of his appeal. The quotes from George Wallace's contrasting speech appear on p. 313 of Dan T. Carter's *The Politics of Rage.* John Lewis's quote about Robert Kennedy appears on p. 215 of *Walking with the Wind.* When Kennedy was killed and Mobile songwriter Dick Holler wrote his tribute anthem, "Abraham, Martin, and John," I wrote about Holler for the *Mobile Register.*

The story of the desegregation lawsuit against the University of Alabama's football team is taken from a special report, *The Black Athlete—1970,* published by the Race Relations Information Center and coauthored by Bernard Garnett and me. The quotes from U. W. Clemon, the black attorney in the case, were taken from an obituary for Coach Paul "Bear" Bryant that I wrote for the *Charlotte Observer* on January 27, 1983.

The story of the solution of the Birmingham church bombing case is based partly on Diane McWhorter's *Carry Me Home,* but primarily on Frank Sikora's book *Until Justice Rolls Down,* easily the clearest and most concise account of the case. The quotes from convicted church bomber Robert Chambliss appear on pp. 93–95; those from Elizabeth Cobbs, on p. 111; and the conversation between Bill Baxley and Chris McNair, on p. 112.

The accounts of the later prosecutions of Thomas Blanton and Bobby Frank Cherry are based primarily on those that appeared in the *New York Times.* The idea of these being "atonement trials" was voiced by Jack Davis, a professor at the University of Alabama at Birmingham in the May 12, 2002, edition of the *Times* in a story written by Rick Bragg. Prosecutor Doug Jones's worries about the strength of his case were reported in the May 5, 2001, *Times,* and former Alabama attorney general Bill Baxley offered his pointed criticisms of the FBI in a May 3, 2001, op-ed piece. Alpha Robertson's quote, "Closure is just a word," appeared in the May 12, 2002, article by Rick Bragg. Fred Shuttlesworth's quote about Birmingham "rising out of the dust" appeared May 23, 2002.

Claude Wesley's quote about the changes in Birmingham appear in my book *Race, Rock, and Religion* (p. 20). I covered the bombing of John LeFlore's house in June 1967 for the *Mobile Press Register.* This account of the crime is based on that article—which appeared on June 28 and accompanied a graphic photograph of the damage—and on interviews with LeFlore's son, Walker LeFlore, and daughter-in-law, Janet LeFlore.

The story of the Neighborhood Organized Workers (NOW), Mobile's militant civil rights organization, is based in part on an article by Nahfiza Ahmed titled "The Neighborhood Organization Workers of Mobile, Alabama." In 1968–69 I covered NOW extensively for the *Mobile Press Register* and wrote about the group in an article in the spring 1971 issue of the journal *Katallagete.* The descriptions of NOW's original president, David Jacobs, and his successor, Noble Beasley, are based on my coverage of them. The account of the organizational meeting of NOW appears in Ahmed's article (pp. 27–28). Noble Beasley's threat to "turn Mobile upside down" appears in *Katallagete* (p. 30). Ahmed quotes NOW leaders as threatening to "burn Mobile down" (p. 29).

The total number of firebombings in Mobile—ninety-six in the year 1969—was taken from Ahmed (p. 34). The account of Joe Langan's defeat at the hands of NOW is taken from Ahmed, from Keith Nicholls's essay "Politics and Civil Rights in Post–World War II Mobile," and from my own interviews with Langan. Despite the ironic results of the 1969 election, Ahmed gives NOW credit for concrete successes, including the hiring of blacks in Mobile stores. Both as a reporter at the time and as a commentator looking back later, I thought NOW's primary importance was providing an outlet for the legitimate anger of the masses of black people, something they had not had in Mobile.

The story of the radical segregationist group STAND is taken from *Katallagete,* as are the anecdotes about the segregationist attitudes of the Mobile school board. The *Mobile Register* on September 13, 1972, reported the election of A. J. Cooper as the first black mayor of the city of Prichard. The story of the lawsuit challenging Mobile's all-white city government and the quotes from U.S. district judge Virgil Pittman are taken from Nicholls, as is the story of the mock lynching carried out by Mobile police. The story of the real lynching of Michael Donald was taken from Nicholls and from the Web site for the Southern Poverty Law Center, whose lawsuit on behalf of the mother of the victim bankrupted the United Klans of America (http://www.splcenter.org/centerinfo/ci-index.html).

Epilogue

Lowndes County probate judge Harrell Hammonds's quotes appear in my book *Race, Rock, and Religion* (p. 25). I wrote about the resurgence of the Creek Indians in the book *As Long as the Waters Flow* (pp. 36–52). John Lewis's quote about "a greater sense of hope" was offered in an interview with me, as was his story of the confessions of George Wallace. C. T. Vivian also talked with me about Wallace. Modern-day activist Cynthia Wilson's quotes appear in Roy Hoffman's superb article in the February 10, 2002, *Mobile Register.* Fred Shuttlesworth's quotes came from interviews with me. Charles Hamilton's quote about blacks now being able to vote appears in his afterword in the 1992 edition of *Black Power* (p. 206). William Branch's quote about drugs in rural Alabama was offered in an interview with me. Also in a conversation with me, Charles Hamilton told the story of Stokely Carmichael pulling him away from a confrontation in Lowndes County and offered his basic summation of the movement: The war for freedom may last for generations, but important battles have been won along the way, and there is no reason not to celebrate the victories.

ACKNOWLEDGMENTS

Additional thanks are owed to the people and institutions without whose support this book would not have come together. Auburn University offered both financial and intellectual support, especially through its Center for the Arts and Humanities, and I am grateful to David Wilson, Allen Cronenberg, Jay Lamar, David Carter, and Jeff Jakeman for their wisdom and guidance—and to Melanie Welch and Steve Murray for their help with research. My daughter Tracy Gaillard also performed ably in the role of research assistant, particularly with regard to research on the Internet. Thanks also to my wife, Nancy Gaillard, for her support of this project and all her love and support through the years.

My writing colleagues Amy Rogers, Charisse Coleman, and Ashley Warlick read the pieces of the manuscript as I wrote it, as did my wife, Nancy, and all of them offered important suggestions and expressions of support. Thanks also to John Egerton and David Carter for their willingness to critique the completed manuscript and to Anne R. Gibbons for her sensitive and careful job of editing. Alabama is blessed with several fine museums that help keep the civil rights story alive, including the Birmingham Civil Rights Institute, the Rosa Parks Museum in Montgomery, and the National Voting Rights Museum in Selma. There are superb civil rights archives at Trenholm State College. My thanks to Odessa Woolfolk, JoAnne Bland, Gwen Patton, and others who helped introduce me to these resources.

I am grateful to all the participants in the movement who made time for interviews, but I am especially indebted to Bob Mants, Francis Walter, Bernard Lafayette, Thomas Gilmore, C. T. Vivian, and Will Campbell who made themselves available not only as sources of specific information but also as sounding boards for the shape of the project. Fred Shuttlesworth was also especially generous with his time, as were several of the movement's foot soldiers: Robert Graetz, Sonnie Hereford, James Armstrong, and John Hulett. Thanks also to Ray Jenkins and Murphy Archibald for sharing portions of their personal libraries, and to Roberta Gamble for making available her extensive collection of newspaper clippings and other material.

I hope this project, in the final analysis, is worthy of the support it has been given.

Bibliography

Abernathy, Ralph David. *And the Walls Came Tumbling Down: An Autobiography.* Harper and Row, 1989.

Ahmed, Nahfiza. "The Neighborhood Organization Workers of Mobile, Alabama: Black Power Politics and Local Civil Rights Activism in the Deep South, 1968–1971." *Southern Historian* 20 (spring 1999): 25–40.

Alabama Bureau of Tourism and Travel. *Alabama's Black Heritage.* 5th ed. Alabama Bureau of Tourism and Travel, 2001.

Ashmore, Harry S. *Civil Rights and Wrongs.* Pantheon, 1994.

Ashmore, Susan Youngblood. "Carry It On: The War on Poverty and the Civil Rights Movement in Alabama, 1964–1970." Ph.D. diss., Auburn University, 1999.

Autrey, Dorothy. "The National Association for the Advancement of Colored People in Alabama, 1913–1952." Ph.D. diss., University of Notre Dame, 1985.

Bass, Jack. *Unlikely Heroes.* Simon and Schuster, 1981.

Bass, S. Jonathan. *Blessed Are the Peacemakers: Martin Luther King Jr., Eight White*

Religious Leaders, and the "Letter from Birmingham Jail." Louisiana State University Press, 2001.

Branch, Taylor. *Parting the Waters: America in the King Years, 1954–1963.* Simon and Schuster, 1988.

———. *Pillar of Fire: America in the King Years, 1963–1965.* Simon and Schuster, Touchstone Books, 1998.

Campbell, Will D. *Forty Acres and a Goat.* Peachtree Publishers, 1986.

Carmichael, Stokely [Kwame Ture], and Charles V. Hamilton. *Black Power: The Politics of Liberation.* Random House, Vintage Books, 1992.

Carter, Dan T. *The Politics of Rage: George Wallace, the Origins of the New Conservatism, and the Transformation of American Politics.* Louisiana State University Press, 1996.

Chestnut, J. L., Jr., and Julia Cass. *Black in Selma: The Uncommon Life of J. L. Chestnut Jr.* Farrar, Straus and Giroux, 1990.

Clark, E. Culpepper. *The Schoolhouse Door: Segregation's Last Stand at the University of Alabama.* Oxford University Press, 1993.

Cohn, Michael, and Michael K. H. Platzer. *Black Men of the Sea.* Dodd Mead, 1978.

Cronenberg, Allen. "Mobile and World War II, 1940–1945." In *Mobile: The New History of Alabama's First City,* ed. Michael V. R. Thomason, 209–46. University of Alabama Press, 2001.

Crowther, Hal. *Cathedrals of Kudzu: A Personal Landscape of the South.* Louisiana State University Press, 2000.

Daniel, Pete. *Lost Revolutions: The South in the 1950s.* University of North Carolina Press for the Smithsonian Institution, 2000.

Eagles, Charles W. *Outside Agitator: Jon Daniels and the Civil Rights Movement in Alabama.* University of Alabama Press, 2000.

Egerton, John. *A Mind to Stay Here: Profiles from the South.* Macmillan, 1970.

———. *Speak Now against the Day: The Generation before the Civil Rights Movement in the South.* Alfred A. Knopf, 1994.

Ellison, Ralph. *Invisible Man.* 2d ed. Random House, Vintage Books, 1995.

Eskew, Glenn T. *But for Birmingham: The Local and National Movements in the Civil Rights Struggle.* University of North Carolina Press, 1997.

Eyes on the Prize: America's Civil Rights Years. Vols. 1, 3, and 5. PBS Home Video. Blackside, 1986–87.

Four Little Girls. An HBO Documentary Film in association with 40 Acres and a Mule Filmworks. Directed by Spike Lee. HBO Documentary, 1997.

Frady, Marshall. *Jesse: The Life and Pilgrimage of Jesse Jackson.* Random House, 1996.

———. *Southerners: A Journalist's Odyssey.* New American Library, 1980.

Gaillard, Frye. *As Long as the Waters Flow: Native Americans in the South and East.* John F. Blair, 1998.

———. *Lessons from the Big House: One Family's Passage through the History of the South.* Down Home Press, 1994.

———. "Mobile." *Katallagete* 3, no. 3 (spring 1971): 25–32.

———. *Race, Rock, and Religion: Profiles from a Southern Journalist.* East Woods Press, 1982.

———. *Southern Voices: Profiles and Other Stories.* Down Home Press, 1991.

Garnett, Bernard E., and Frye Gaillard. *The Black Athlete—1970.* Race Relations Information Center and Belfast University Press, 1970.

Garrow, David J. *Bearing the Cross: Martin Luther King Jr. and the Southern Christian Leadership Conference.* William Morrow, 1986.

———. *Protest at Selma: Martin Luther King Jr. and the Voting Rights Act of 1965.* Yale University Press, 1978.

George Wallace: Settin' the Woods on Fire. Big House and Midnight Films Production for *The American Experience.* WGBH Boston, 2000.

Goldfield, David R. *Black, White, and Southern: Race Relations and Southern Culture 1940 to the Present.* Louisiana State University Press, 1990.

Graetz, Robert S. *A White Preacher's Memoir: The Montgomery Bus Boycott.* Black Belt Press, 1998.

Gray, Fred D. *Bus Ride to Justice: Changing the System by the System: The Life and Works of Fred D. Gray.* Black Belt Press, 1995.

Gray, Fred. D., W. S. Leventhal, F. Sikora, and J. M. Thornton III. *The Children Coming On: A Retrospective of the Montgomery Bus Boycott.* Black Belt Press, 1998.

Guthman, Edwin O., and C. Richard Allen, eds. *RFK: Collected Speeches.* Viking, 1993.

Halberstam, David. *The Children.* Random House, 1998.

Hemphill, Paul. *The Ballad of Little River: A Tale of Race and Restless Youth in the Rural South.* Simon and Schuster, Free Press, 2000.

———. *Leaving Birmingham: Notes of a Native Son.* Viking, Penguin Books, 1993.

Hoffman, Roy. *Back Home: Journeys through Mobile.* University of Alabama Press, 2001.

Jackson, Harvey H., III. "White Supremacy Triumphant, Democracy Undone." In *A Century of Controversy: Constitutional Reform in Alabama,* ed. Bailey Thomson, 17–33. University of Alabama Press, 2002.

Kelley, Robin D. G. *Hammer and Hoe: Alabama Communists during the Great Depression.* University of North Carolina Press, 1990.

Kennedy, Caroline, ed. *Profiles in Courage for Our Time.* John F. Kennedy Library Foundation, 2002.

King, Martin Luther, Jr. *Stride toward Freedom.* Ballantine, 1961.

Kluger, Richard. *Simple Justice: The History of Brown v. Board of Education and Black America's Struggle for Equality.* Alfred A. Knopf, 1976.

Lewis, John, with Michael D'Orso. *Walking with the Wind: A Memoir of the Movement.* Harcourt, Brace, 1998.

Lincoln, C. Eric. *Coming through the Fire: Surviving Race and Place in America.* Duke University Press, 1996.

————. *Race, Religion, and the Continuing American Dilemma.* Hill and Wang, 1984.

Lomax, Louis. "A Negro View: Can Johnson Free the South?" *Look,* March 10, 1964.

Lyon, Danny. *Memories of the Southern Civil Rights Movement.* University of North Carolina Press, 1992.

Manis, Andrew M. *A Fire You Can't Put Out: The Civil Rights Life of Birmingham's Reverend Fred Shuttlesworth.* University of Alabama Press, 1999.

McLaurin, Melton A., and Michael V. R. Thomason. *Mobile: The Life and Times of a Great Southern City.* Windsor Publications, 1981.

McWhorter, Diane. *Carry Me Home: Birmingham, Alabama: The Climactic Battle of the Civil Rights Revolution.* Simon and Schuster, Touchstone, 2001.

Newfield, Jack. *A Prophetic Minority.* Signet Books, New American Library, 1966.

Nicholls, Keith. "Politics and Civil Rights in Post–World War II Mobile." In *Mobile: The New History of Alabama's First City,* ed. Michael V. R. Thomason, 247–76. University of Alabama Press, 2001.

Noble, J. Phillips. *Beyond the Burning Bus.* NewSouth Books, 2003.

Norrell, Robert J. *Reaping the Whirlwind: The Civil Rights Movement in Tuskegee.* University of North Carolina Press, 1985.

Nunnelley, William A. *Bull Connor.* University of Alabama Press, 1991.

Oates, Stephen B. *Let the Trumpet Sound: The Life of Martin Luther King Jr.* Harper and Row, 1982.

Padgett, Charles S. "Without Hysteria or Unnecessary Disturbance: Desegregation at Spring Hill College, Mobile, Alabama, 1948–1954." *History of Education Quarterly* 41 (summer 2001): 167–88.

Powledge, Fred. *Free at Last? The Civil Rights Movement and the People Who Made It.* HarperPerennial, 1991.

Raines, Howell. *My Soul Is Rested.* Bantam Books, 1978.

Robinson, Amelia Platts Boynton. *Bridge across Jordan.* Schiller Institute, 1991.

Robinson, Jo Ann Gibson. *The Montgomery Bus Boycott and the Women Who Started It.* University of Tennessee Press, 1987.

Rogers, William Warren, R. D. Ward, L. R. Atkins, and Wayne Flynt. *Alabama: The History of a Deep South State.* University of Alabama Press, 1994.

Rosengarten, Theodore. *All God's Dangers: The Life of Nate Shaw.* Alfred A. Knopf, 1974.

Schlesinger, Arthur M., Jr. *A Thousand Days: John F. Kennedy in the White House.* Houghton Mifflin, 1965.

Sherrill, Robert. *Gothic Politics in the Deep South: Stars of the New Confederacy.* Ballantine, 1968.

Sikora, Frank. *The Judge: The Life and Opinions of Alabama's Frank M. Johnson Jr.* Black Belt Press, 1992.

———. *Until Justice Rolls Down: The Birmingham Church Bombing Case.* University of Alabama Press, 1991.

Smalls, Robert. "Election Methods in the South." Transcribed by Carolyn Sims. *North American Review* 151: 593–600.

Smith, Howard K. *Events Leading Up to My Death: The Life of a Twentieth-Century Reporter.* St. Martin's Press, 1996.

Taper, Bernard. *Gomillion versus Lightfoot: Apartheid in Alabama.* McGraw-Hill, 1962.

Terkel, Studs. *Race: How Blacks and Whites Think and Feel about the American Obsession.* Doubleday, Anchor Books, 1992.

Thomason, Michael V. R., ed. *Mobile: The New History of Alabama's First City.* University of Alabama Press, 2001.

Thomson, Bailey, ed. *A Century of Controversy: Constitutional Reform in Alabama.* University of Alabama Press, 2002.

Thornton, J. Mills. "Challenge and Response in the Montgomery Bus Boycott of 1955–56." *Alabama Review* 33 (July 1980): 163–235.

———. *Dividing Lines: Municipal Politics and the Struggle for Civil Rights in Montgomery, Birmingham, and Selma.* University of Alabama Press, 2002.

Uya, Okon Edet. *From Slavery to Public Service: Robert Smalls, 1839–1915.* Oxford University Press, 1971.

Webb, Samuel L., and Margaret E. Armbrester, eds. *Alabama Governors.* University of Alabama Press, 2001.

Webb, Sheyann, and Rachel West Nelson, with Frank Sikora. *Selma, Lord, Selma.* University of Alabama Press, 1997.

White, Marjorie L. *A Walk to Freedom: The Reverend Fred Shuttlesworth and the Alabama Christian Movement for Human Rights, 1954–1964.* Birmingham Historical Society, 1998.

Williams, Juan. *Eyes on the Prize: America's Civil Rights Years, 1954–1965.* Penguin Books, 1987.

Williamson, Joel. *A Rage for Order: Black/White Relations in the American South since Emancipation.* Oxford University Press, 1986.

Wolfe, Tom. *The New Journalism.* Harper and Row, 1973.

Woodward, Robert H., and H. Wendell Smith. *The Craft of Prose.* 4th ed. Wadsworth Publishing, 1977.

Index